VOLUME·TWO

DEMOCRACY

IN DEVELOPING COUNTRIES

AFRICA

Also Available:

Volume 1, Persistence, Failure, and Renewal

Volume 3, Asia

Volume 4, Latin America

VOLUME • TWO

DEMOCRACY
IN DEVELOPING COUNTRIES

AFRICA

Edited by
Larry Diamond
Juan J. Linz
Seymour Martin Lipset

Lynne Rienner Publishers •
Boulder, Colorado

Adamantine Press Limited •
London, England

Published in the United States of America in 1988 by
Lynne Rienner Publishers, Inc.
948 North Street, Boulder, Colorado 80302

Published in the United Kingdom by Adamantine Press Limited,
3 Henrietta Street, Covent Garden, London WC2E 8LU

Library of Congress Cataloging-in-Publication Data

Democracy in developing countries.

Bibliography: p.
Includes index.
Contents: — v. 2. Africa.
1. Developing countries—Politics and government.
2. Democracy. I. Diamond, Larry Jay. II. Linz, Juan J.
(Juan José), 1926– . III. Lipset, Seymour Martin.
D883.D45 1988 320.9173′4 87-23457
ISBN 1-55587-039-2 (v. 2)
ISBN 1-55587-040-6 (pbk. : v. 2)

British Library Cataloguing in Publication Data

A CIP record for this book is available from the British Library.
ISBN 0-7449-0006-9
ISBN 0-7449-0007-7 (pbk.)

Printed and bound in the United States of America

The paper used in this publication meets the
requirements of the American National Standard
for Permanence of Paper for Printed Library
Materials Z39.48-1984.

• Contents •

• Tables and Figures •

• Preface •

This comparative study of democracy in developing countries—encompassing this and three other volumes—was undertaken at a time of tremendous democratic ferment in the developing world. The movement toward democracy that witnessed, in the mid-1970s, the toppling of Western Europe's last three dictatorships, in Greece, Portugal, and Spain, then moved on through Latin America. In the ensuing decade, most Latin American military dictatorships collapsed or withdrew, defying predictions of a longer reign for the "bureaucratic-authoritarian" regimes. Democratic progress was apparent in East Asia as well, in the Philippines, Korea, and even to some extent Taiwan. In the old British South Asian raj, both the more authoritarian states of Pakistan and Bangladesh and the democratic ones, India and Sri Lanka, were facing recurrent tensions and conflicts that could lead to a restoration or revitalization of democracy, or to deeper crisis.

Among the states of Africa, which found it difficult to establish new nationhood and democratic regimes, there have also been signs of democratic emergence or renewal. Uganda, for example, is struggling to put an end to decades of anarchy, tyranny, and civil strife, in order to fulfill its hopes for democracy and human rights. Despite intense repression, the black and coloured peoples of South Africa continue their struggle for a nonracial democracy through an increasingly powerful trade union movement. In Nigeria and Ghana, debate proceeds under military regimes over the constitutional structure for new attempts at democratic government.

These and similar dramas in Asia, Africa, and Latin America form the backdrop for renewed political and intellectual concern with the conditions for democratic government. To be sure, there is no guarantee that the recent and continuing democratic progress will not be reversed. If the past is any guide, many of the new democratic and semidemocratic regimes are likely to fail. Indeed, a number appear to be perched precariously on the precipice of new breakdowns into one-party or military rule or even chaos.

But the 1980s have seen an unprecedented growth of international concern for human rights—including (prominently) the rights to choose democratically the government under which one lives and to express and organize around one's political principles and views. As torture, disappearances, and other grave human rights violations have become more widespread, but also more systematically exposed and denounced around the world, there has developed a renewed and deeper appreciation for the democratic institutions that, with all their procedural messiness and sluggishness, nevertheless protect the integrity of the person and the freedoms of conscience and expression. The growth of democratic norms throughout the world is strikingly evident in the degree to which authoritarian regimes find it necessary to wrap themselves in the rhetoric and constitutional trappings of democracy, or at least to state as their goal the eventual establishment of democracy.

The great competing ideologies of the twentieth century have largely been discredited. Fascism was destroyed as a vital force in World War II. The appeals of Marxism-Leninism have declined with the harsh repressiveness, glaring economic failures, and loss of revolutionary idealism of the existing communist regimes. More limited quasi-socialist or mass mobilizational models—the Mexican, the Yugoslav, the Nasserite—have also lost their aura. Military regimes almost universally lack ideological justification, and legitimacy beyond a temporary intrusion to correct political and social problems. With the important but still indeterminate exception of the Islamic fundamentalist state—for that large portion of the world from Indonesia to West Africa where Islam is a major or dominant religion—democracy is the only model of government with any broad ideological legitimacy and appeal in the world today.

• STUDIES OF THE CONDITIONS FOR DEMOCRACY: A BRIEF INTELLECTUAL HISTORY •

An important element of this new global *zeitgeist* is the renewed proliferation of intellectual concern with the conditions of the democratic order. Beginning perhaps with the four-volume work on *The Breakdown of Democratic Regimes* in Europe and Latin America, edited by Juan Linz and Alfred Stepan,[1] one can trace a growing efflorscence of academic literature on transitions to and from democracy, and the sources of democratic persistence and failure. Studies have focused on varying themes, such as the means for accommodating ethnic or other sectional cleavages within a democratic framework,[2] the role of political institutions and political violence,[3] and the place of competitive elections in the development of democracy.[4] This outpouring of intellectual interest has recently produced a new four-volume study of transitions to democracy,[5] the most prominent in a rich new harvest of literature on the subject. On the more theoretical level of the definition of democracy and the debate surrounding its concepts, relationships, and forms, a stream of stimulating new work is appearing, of which the recent two-volume contribution of Giovanni Sartori should be considered an essential reference.[6]

Of course, intellectual concern with the social requisites, correlates, or conditions for democracy and other types of political systems has a long tradition, dating back at least to the classical Greek thinkers. Aristotle argued that democracy is more likely to occur where the middle strata are large, oligarchy and tyranny where the population is overwhelmingly poor. The Renaissance political theorist, Machiavelli, also placed an emphasis on class distribution in specifying the sources of political systems. The subsequent writings of Hobbes, Locke, and Montesquieu heavily influenced the founding fathers of the American democratic experience in their emphasis on the restraint of state powers through the institutionalization of checks and balances. Turning to the young American republic for clues to the development of democracy, the rule of law, and personal freedom, Alexis de Tocqueville emphasized in his writings the impact of voluntary associations as mediating institutions and contervailing forces to the central government; the division of powers in a federal system; and the relative socioeconomic equality that fostered political participation. In different ways, the role of the middle class in fostering liberty and democracy was also emphasized by the laissez-faire disciples of Adam Smith and by the Marxists.

However, while democracy slowly took root in much of northern Europe, as well as in North America and Australasia, attempts in Southern, Central, and Eastern Europe and in Latin America were generally less successful. These abortive democratic openings unleashed levels of political and social moblization that alarmed established interests such as the aristocracy, the landed elite, the church, and the military. As these groups, often allied with a weaker bourgeoisie, formed reactionary coalitions, the prospects for democracy dimmed. These various trends culminated during the 1920s and 1930s with the establishment of communist dictatorship in the Soviet Union, fascism in Germany and Italy, a host of other rightist dictatorships throughout Europe, and populist autocracies in Argentina, Brazil, and Mexico.

The pessimism about democracy and free institutions occasioned by the events of this period was inverted by the victory of the Allied powers in World War II. Democracy was imposed on Germany, Italy, and Japan, and surprisingly took hold and endured. Beginning with India in 1947, a host of new nations in Asia, Africa, and the Middle East that had been colonies of the Western democracies were granted independence under constitutions and following election procedures modeled on those of their former colonial rulers. The wave of excitement and optimism about the prospects for democracy and rapid development in these newly independent nations spawned a new generation of scholarly thinking and research.

More extensively than ever before, theory and empirical research in political development examined the world outside the West. Employing a multidimensional, functionalist framework, *The Politics of the Developing Areas* (1960) was (to quote its coeditor, Gabriel Almond) "the first effort to compare the political systems of the 'developing' areas, and to compare them systematically according to a common set of categories."[7] There followed a wealth of case studies of emerging political systems in the new nations, as well as comparative studies. Almond and Verba's *The Civic Culture* was the first scholarly attempt to apply the methods of modern survey analysis to the comparative analysis of political systems, in this case the relationship between democracy and political attitudes and values in five nations (four of them Western, but also including Mexico).[8] With increasing statistical sophistication, a new style of social science analysis examined quantitatively the relationship between democracy and socioeconomic modernization, or political development more broadly, across nations throughout the developed and developing worlds.[9] Some scholars, such as Samuel Huntington, focused a more skeptical eye on the sources of political disorder and breakdown in the new nations.[10] Also in this period came the ambitious and controversial sociological-historical effort of Barrington Moore to account for the emergence of democracy, authoritarianism, and totalitarianism in the world.[11]

Probably the most ambitious and important project of the decade was the work of the Committee on Comparative Politics of the Social Science Research Council (SSRC), which produced a series of nine volumes (mostly during the 1960s) on the relationship between political development and such social and political subsystems as bureaucracy, education, parties, and political culture. Much of this work was synthesized and distilled theoretically in *Crises and Sequences of Political Development,* which argued that patterns of political development, including the chances for stable democracy, could be explained by the way in which countries encountered and dealt with five characteristic problems of state- and nation-building.[12] The publication that same year (1971) of Robert Dahl's classic study, *Polyarchy,* can be seen as the crowning work on democracy of the political development decade.[13] To this day, it remains one of the most important treatments of the historical, social, economic, cultural, and political factors that foster or obstruct the development of stable democracy, and it has much influenced our own work. Although centered on the European historical experience, the work of Stein Rokkan has also been extremely fruitful for our understanding of the conditions under which states and party systems emerged and the variety of coalitions involved.[14]

The study of democracy was to sag through most of the 1970s. By 1970, critiques of pluralist political development studies as ethnocentric and even reflective of U.S. imperialism were in full cry. Although these criticisms were often based on a superficial and ideologically biased reading of these works,[15] they nevertheless pushed the study of comparative political systems into the background. The fields of comparative politics, political development, and international political sociology became dominated by issues relating to economic dependence and by theories of international dependency—often carrying with them the Marxist assumption that political systems were mere superstructures and "bourgeois democracies" largely illusory and epiphenomenal. To the extent they dealt with the political system explicitly, theories of dependency maintained that political exclusion and repression of popular mobilization were inevitable concomitants of dependent economic development and peripheral status in the world division of labor.[16] Cynicism about political democracy in the developing countries was reflected and deepened by a new cycle of democratic breakdowns in Latin America into particularly harsh, "bureaucratic-authoritarian" dictatorships. This development was interpreted as a consequence of the inherent strains and pressures of economic dependence at a particular, middle stage of development.[17] But the collapse of these and other dictatorships around the world—beginning with the transitions to democracy in southern Europe in the mid-1970s—along with the revalorization of political democracy as an end in itself (partly in response to the extraordinary brutality of many recent authoritarian experiences), has now refocused the attention of the scholarly world on the conditions for liberal democracy.

• THE PROJECT ON DEMOCRACY IN DEVELOPING COUNTRIES •

The growth of political and intellectual interest in democracy in developing countries provided a propitious climate for the study we wanted to launch. Despite the rich profusion of literature, it seemed to us that there remained huge gaps in our understanding of the factors that fostered or obstructed the emergence, instauration, and consolidation of democratic government around the world. All of the existing studies were limited in important ways: to a particular period of time; to particular regions (usually Europe or Latin America); to particular moments or segments of the historical record (such as crises and breakdowns, or transitions); or to a limited range of theoretical variables. While understanding that any one study would inevitably be bound more or less by such limits, we undertook to design a comparative historical analysis that would, nevertheless, reach wider and further than had any previous one.

The resulting four-volume work is, we believe, somewhat unique in several respects. In geographical scope, it is the first study of democracy to compare systematically the historical experiences of individual countries throughout Asia, Africa, and Latin America. In the "developing" world, only the Middle East (for reasons we will later explain) is excluded. In sheer size, it may be the largest comparative study of national political systems to date, with chapters on twenty six different countries. Significantly, these chapters are not the loose collection of varied papers and themes one sometimes encounters. Each was written specifically for this project, in response to a common set of guidelines, definitions, and theoretical concerns. Also we as editors took a broadly inclusive approach theoretically. Rather than pursuing some new, elegant, "parsimonious" model, we deliberately eschewed monocausal and reductionist interpretations in favor of an exhaustive examination of all the historical, cultural, social, economic, political, and international factors that might affect the chances for stable democracy; how they interact; and the conditions that might mediate their salience or their effects.

The contributions to this work are also distinctive in that they deal with the entire history of a country's experience with democracy. This includes the whole range of phenomena: establishment, breakdown, reequilibration, and consolidation of democratic government; periods of democratic persistence, crisis, authoritarianism, and renewal; and all of the ambivalences and oscillations in between. In the process, we consider each country's early cultural traditions, analyze (where relevant) the colonial experience, consider all of its postindependence history, but give special emphasis to post-World War II developments. Whereas most other works cut horizontally through the history of countries to focus on limited time spans and particular processes (usually ignoring the phenomena of democratic consolidation and stability),[18] our study cuts vertically through historical phases in order to explain the overall path of a country's political development.

While it can be enormously fertile, this historical approach is not without certain methodological problems. In particular, it runs the risk of attributing contemporary political patterns to antecedents far removed in time, without clearly demonstrating that those factors (or characteristics resulting from them) are operating at a later time and account for the failure or success of democracy. The past, to be relevant, must in one way or another be present at the time the realities we want to explain happen. We feel, however, that within the constraints of space, the authors of the case studies have generally avoided accounting for events at time t^{20} by reference to factors that appear only at time t^{1} or t^{5}, although sometimes the link with t^{19} might have been made more explicit.

The result is an eclectic, but also very rich, analysis of the opportunities and obstacles for democracy in the developing world today. Indeed, it is the very richness of our study that presents to us, as perhaps it will to many of our readers, the greatest frustration. As our colleague Robert Dahl remarked at a recent scholarly meeting where our work was discussed, a key problem with the previous generation of work on democracy was the paucity of comparative evidence in relation to the abundance of theorizing; on the other hand, the current generation of work, including this comparative study, appears destined to suffer from an abundance of evidence for which there will be a relative dearth of theory. Readers of Volume 1 in this set will find no shortage of theoretical arguments and lessons drawn from this study. But we concede that these are not integrated into a single, all-encompassing theory, and that it will be some time (if ever) before the field produces one.

We began our study by inviting distinguished comparativists and country specialists to write case studies of individual countries' experiences with democratic and authoritarian government. Each of our authors was given the same broad set of guidelines, flexible enough to permit them to do justice to the uniqueness of the society and its history, but structured enough so that each case study would share a common conceptual orientation, analytical purpose, and framework for organizing the material.

The first section of each chapter was to review the country's political history, describing the major experiences with democratic and nondemocratic government, including the structure, nature, and characteristic conflicts and tensions of each regime. The second section would explain the fate of each regime (especially each democratic one), why it persisted or failed or evolved as it did, and why successive ones emerged as and when they did. Alternatively, authors were given the option of combining these tasks of historical review and analysis, which many did. In a third (or second) section, the author was asked to offer a summary theoretical judgment of the factors that have been most important in determining the country's overall degree of success or failure with democratic government—to abstract across the various regimes and events the most consistently significant and salient factors from among the broad inventory of variables in our project outline (and any others we might have neglected). Finally, each author was asked to consider the future prospects for democratic government in the country, along with any policy implications he or she might wish to derive. In addition, each author was asked to assess (somewhere in the chapter) the country's overall experience with democratic government, using our six-point scale (of ideal types ranging from stable and consolidated democratic rule to the failure or absence of democracy.[19]

The task we gave those who wrote our case studies was an imposing one. What made it even forbidding—and sometimes (especially for countries with long and variegated political histories) nearly impossible—was the space constraint we were forced to impose as a result of the economic realities of contemporary book publishing. Thus, each author was compelled to be selective and often painfully brief, both in the treatment of important historical developments and in the analysis of theoretical variables. Although we have sought to make our case studies readily accessible to readers with little or no prior knowledge of the country—in part to encourage the wide reading across regions we feel is essential—we could not avoid giving many key problems and events little or no attention. Our readers are thus cautioned that the case studies provide no more than capsulized surveys of a country's experience, which will, we hope, inspire wider study from among the many other sources they cite.

The theoretical framework for the study grew out of an extensive review of the previous literature, one which appears in Volume 1. The ten theoretical dimensions in this framework covered the gamut of factors that various theoretical and empirical works have associated with democracy: political culture; regime legitimacy and effectiveness; historical development (in particular the colonial experience); class structure and the degree of inequality; national structure (ethnic, racial, regional, and religious cleavage); state structure, centralization, and strength (including the state's role in the economy, the roles of autonomous voluntary associations and the press, federalism, and the role of the armed forces); political and constitutional structure (parties, electoral systems, the judiciary); political leadership; development performance; and international factors.

These broad dimensions encompassed dozens of specific variables and questions, from which we derived forty nine tentative propositions about the likelihood of stable democratic government. Obviously, it would have been foolish to pretend that our study could have "tested" these propositions. In spite of having twenty six countries, we still had the problem of "too many variables, too few cases" to enable us to reach any definitive conclusions about the effects of these variables. But we did believe that the evidence and conclusions from twenty six carefully selected cases, if structured systematically, could shed much light on how these variables affected the democratic prospect, and how these effects might vary with other conditions.

• CONCEPTS, DEFINITIONS, AND CLASSIFICATIONS •

Depending on the individual, ideology, paradigm, culture, or context, the term "democracy" may mean many different things. In fact, it is reflective of the political climate of our time that the word is used to signify the desirable end-state of so many social, economic, and political pursuits, or else to self-designate and thus presumably legitimate so many existing structures. Hence, it is imperative that we be as precise as possible about exactly what it is we are studying.

We use the term "democracy" in this study to signify a political system, separate and apart from the economic and social system to which it is joined. Indeed, a distinctive aspect of our approach is to insist that issues of so-called economic and social democracy be separated from the question of governmental structure. Otherwise, the definitional criteria of democracy will be broadened and the empirical reality narrowed to a degree that may make study of the phenomena very difficult. In addition, unless the economic and social dimensions are kept conceptually distinct from the political, there is no way to analyze how variation on the political dimension is related to variation on the others. But most of all, as we will argue shortly, we distinguish the concept of political democracy out of a clear and frankly expressed conviction that it is worth valuing—and hence worth studying—as an end in itself.

In this study, then, democracy—or what Robert Dahl terms "polyarchy"—denotes a system of government that meets three essential conditions: meaningful and extensive *competition* among individuals and organized groups (especially political parties) for all effective positions of government power, at regular intervals and excluding the use of force; a highly inclusive level of *political participation* in the selection of leaders and policies, at least through regular and fair elections, such that no major (adult) social group is excluded; and a level of *civil and political liberties*—freedom of expression, freedom of the press, freedom to form and join organizations—sufficient to ensure the integrity of political competition and participation.[20]

While this definition is, in itself, relatively straightforward, it presents a number of problems in application. For one, countries that broadly satisfy these criteria nevertheless do so to different degrees. (In fact, none do so perfectly, which is why Dahl prefers to call them polyarchies). The factors that explain this variation at the democratic end of the spectrum in degrees of popular control and freedom is an important intellectual problem. But it is different from the one that concerns us in these four volumes, and so it is one we have had largely to bypass. This study seeks to determine why countries do or do not evolve, consolidate, maintain, lose, and reestablish more or less democratic systems of government.

Even this limited focus leaves us with conceptual problems. The boundary between democratic and nondemocratic is sometimes a blurred and imperfect one, and beyond it lies a much broader range of variation in political systems. We readily concede the difficulties of classification this variation has repeatedly caused us. Even if we look only at the political, legal, and constitutional structure, several of our cases appear to lie somewhere on the boundary between democratic and something less than democratic. The ambiguity is further complicated by the constraints on free political activity, organization, and expression that may often in practice make the system much less democratic than it appears on paper. In all cases, we have tried to pay serious attention to actual practice in assessing and classifying regimes. But, still, this has left us to make difficult and in some ways arbitrary judgements. For countries such as Turkey, Sri Lanka, Malaysia, Colombia, and Zimbabwe, the decision as to whether these may today be considered full democracies is replete with nuance and ambiguity.

We have alleviated the problem somewhat by recognizing various grades of distinction among less-than-democratic systems. While isolated violations of civil liberties or modest and occasional vote-rigging should not disqualify a country from broad classification as a democracy, there is a need to categorize separately those countries that allow greater political competition and freedom than would be found in a true authoritarian regime but less than could justifiably be termed democratic. Hence, we classify as *semidemocratic* those countries where the effective power of elected officials is so limited, or political party competition is so restricted, or the freedom and fairness of elections so compromised that electoral outcomes, while competitive, still deviate significantly from popular preferences; and/or where civil and political liberties are so limited that some political orientations and interests are unable to organize and express themselves. In different ways and to different degrees, Senegal, Zimbabwe, Malaysia, and Thailand fit in this category. Still more restrictive is a *hegemonic party system,* like that of Mexico, in which opposition parties are legal but denied—through pervasive electoral malpractices and frequent state coercion—any real chance to compete for power. Descending further on the scale of classification, *authoritarian* regimes permit even less pluralism, typically banning political parties (or all but the ruling one) and most forms of political organization and competition, while being more repressive than liberal in their level of civil and political freedom. Paying close attention to actual behavior, one may distinguish a subset of authoritarian regimes that we call *pseudodemocracies,* in that the existence of formally democratic political institutions, such as multiparty electoral competition, masks (often, in part, to legitimate) the reality of authoritarian domination. While this regime type overlaps in some ways with the hegemonic regime, it is less institutionalized and typically more personalized, coercive, and unstable. Nevertheless, we prefer not to ignore the democratic facade, because, as we argue in Volume 1, its coexistence with an authoritarian reality may generate distinctive problems for a transition to democracy.

Democratic trappings aside, authoritarian regimes vary widely in the degree to which they permit independent and critical political expression and organization. By the level of what the regime allows, one can distinguish between what O'Donnell and Schmitter call "dictablandas," or liberalized autocracies, and "dictaduras," harsher dictatorships that allow much less space for individual and group action.[21] By the level of what groups in the society recurrently demand (which may or may not overlap with the above), one can distinguish, as we do in Volume 1, between authoritarian situations with strong democratic pressures and those with weak democratic pressures. In selecting cases for this study, our bias was toward the former. Finally, of course, are the *totalitarian* regimes, which not only repress all forms of autonomous social and political organization, denying completely even the most elementary political and civil liberties, but also demand an active commitment by the citizens to the regime.[22] Because our concern in this study was primarily with democracy, these regimes (mainly now the communist ones, although not all of them are totalitarian) were excluded from our analysis.

The "dependent variable" of our study was concerned not only with democracy, but also stability—the persistence and durability of democratic and other regimes over time, particularly through periods of unusually intense conflict, crisis, and strain. A *stable* regime is one that is deeply institutionalized and consolidated, making it likely therefore to enjoy a high level of popular legitimacy. (As we argue in Volume 1, the relationship between stability and legitimacy is an intimate one.) *Partially stable* regimes are neither fully secure nor in imminent danger of collapse. Their institutions have perhaps acquired some measure of depth, flexibility, and value, but not enough to ensure the regime safe passage through severe challenges. *Unstable* regimes are, by definition, highly vulnerable to breakdown or overthrow in periods of acute uncertainty and stress. New regimes, including those that have recently restored democratic government, tend to fall in this category.

• THE SELECTION OF COUNTRIES •

One of the limitations, as well as one of the values, of our enterprise is the great heterogeneity of the twenty six countries included. The value is that the country studies provide us with insights into the whole range of factors relevant to our study, rather than limiting us to those variables for which there are data for all countries of the world (as with the social and economic statistics of the United Nations and the World Bank) or those factors shared by a relatively homogeneous set of countries. The major disadvantage, however, is that—unless we turn to studies and data not included in our volumes—the lack of statistical representativeness (which is, anyhow, dubious in dealing with states) precludes a statistical approach to testing hypotheses. In fact, our introductory volume contains a substantial quantitative analysis, based on data for over eighty countries, of the relationship between socioeconomic development and democracy, a relationship found to be basically positive.[23] Still, for the most part, we believe that the study of twenty six carefully chosen countries, by scholars familiar with each of them, and guided more or less by the concepts and issues suggested, provides us with a better understanding of the complex problems involved.

The criteria for the selection of countries were complex and, although not ad hoc, do not entirely satisfy our plans and ambitions for the well-known reasons encountered in any such large-scale comparative project. The foremost, perhaps debatable, decision was to exclude Western Europe, the North American democracies, Australia, New Zealand, and the most advanced non-Western industrial democracy, Japan—although their historical experiences are analyzed separately in Volume 1. Essentially, these are the OECD countries, members of the Paris-based Organization for Economic Cooperation and Development.[24] All of these countries have been stable democracies since World War II, if not earlier, with the exceptions of Greece, Portugal, and Spain, which joined the club in the mid-1970s and have been stable democracies for over ten years. The southern European experience, however, enters into our thinking and will occasionally be mentioned (if for no other reason than that it is an area of scholarly interest of one of the editors). All in this first group of countries excluded from our study are advanced industrial, capitalist democracies with higher per capita gross national products than the most developed of the countries we included. (The one exception is Portugal, whose per capita GNP is lower than a few of our developing countries, including Argentina and South Korea).

Another basic decision was not to include any communist countries. One of their distinctive characteristics is that, in those with a more or less democratic past (some in Eastern Europe), the absence of democracy is explained more by the power politics of Soviet hegemony than by any internal historical, social, economic, political, or cultural factors (although these might have been important before 1945). Another crucial distinction is that there is little prospect among them of a transition to democracy, but only of liberalization of communist rule. Outside of Eastern Europe, communist countries have little or no past democratic experience, and the present communist rule excludes, for the forseeable future, any real debate about political democracy in the sense defined by us.

Less justifiable, perhaps, is the exclusion of most of the Islamic world from Morocco to Iran, in particular the Arab world. In part, this stemmed from the limits of our resources, which were stretched thin by the scope of the project.

But it was a decision made also in response to theoretical priorities. With the exception perhaps of Egypt, Lebanon, and certainly Turkey (which appears in our Asia volume), the Islamic countries of the Middle East and North Africa generally lack much previous democratic experience, and most appear to have little prospect of transition even to semidemocracy. However, our study does not completely ignore the Islamic world. In addition to the "secularized" Islamic polity of Turkey, we include Pakistan, which shared, until partition, the history of British India and has tried democracy; Malaysia, a multiethnic, multireligious, but predominantly Muslim polity with significant democratic institutions; Senegal, an African Muslim country whose recently evolved semidemocracy is coming under growing challenge from Islamic fundamentalist thinking; and the farthest outpost of Islam, Indonesia, with its syncretic cultural traditions. These five Islamic countries, with their heterogeneity, clearly are not a sample of the world's Islamic polities and, therefore, will not enable us to explore in sufficient depth the complex relationship between Islamic religion and society and democracy.

Otherwise, our twenty six countries are quite representative of the heterogeneous world of those loosely called "Third World" or "developing" countries. These terms are largely misleading, and we want clearly to disassociate ourselves from assuming that such a category is scientifically useful in cross-national comparisons. Certainly, it seems ridiculous to put Argentina or Uruguay or South Korea in the same classification of countries as Ghana, Papua New Guinea, or even India, in terms of economic development, social structure or cultural traditions, and prospects of socioeconomic development. Nevertheless, all twenty six countries included in this study are less developed economically and less stable politically than the established, industrialized democracies of Europe, North America, Australasia, and Japan. And all share the same pressure from within to "develop" economically and socially, to build stable political institutions, and—as we argue in Volume 1—to become democracies, whatever the probabilities of their success in doing so. In this sense, all of these countries may be considered "less developed," or as we most often term them, for lack of a better common label, "developing."

Some readers might feel that all the countries in our study share one characteristic: that they have capitalist economic systems (although some have tried various socialist experiments), but such a characterization again becomes in its vagueness almost meaningless. To what extent can a dynamic, industrial, export-oriented capitalist economy like South Korea be covered by the same term as Uganda, whose population lives largely from subsistence agriculture, with a small native entrepreneurial class based heavily in the informal sector; or as other African countries in which business class formation entails more the access to and abuse of power to attain wealth than it does productive economic activities (which are subject to interference by the state if not extortion by the rulers)? Certainly the term "capitalist economy" covers too much to be meaningful sociologically when it is used simultaneously to describe advanced, industrial, market-oriented economies; state-dominated economies in which much of private enterprise is relegated to the informal sector; and largely subsistence, peasant, agricultural societies with isolated (and often foreign-owned) capitalist enclaves.

For the sake of argument, we might agree that all our countries have nonsocialist economic systems, which, therefore, allows us to ask questions about how "capitalism" in its very different forms may be related to democracy. We start from two obvious facts. First, all democracies (in our sense) are to some degree capitalist. Some are capitalist welfare states, with extensive public sectors and state regulation of the economy; some are capitalist with social democratic governments and more or less mixed economies. But, in all of the world's political democracies, prices, production and distribution of goods are determined mainly by competition in the market, rather than by the state, and there is significant private ownership of the means of production. Second, there are many capitalist countries with nondemocratic governments. But interestingly, among this latter group, those most advanced in their capitalist development (size of market sector of their economy, autonomy of their entrepreneurial class) are also those that have been most exposed to pressures for democracy, leading, in many cases, to the emergence or return of democratic government. This is despite the forceful arguments of some theories that postulated that the authoritarian regimes they suffered were more congruent or functional for their continued capitalist development. In addition, it is not clear how much certain types of nonsocialist authoritarianisms—particularly sultanism[25]—are compatible with the effective functioning of a capitalist economy.

Certainly, our effort can make a contribution to the continuing debate about the relationship between capitalism and democracy, and the even more lively one on the relationship between dependent, peripheral capitalism and democracy. This we seek to do in our theoretical reflections in Volume 1. In doing so, we emphasize that our study did not begin with any *a priori* assumption equating democracy with capitalism. To reiterate an earlier theme, democracy as a system of government must be kept conceptually distinct from capitalism as a system of production and exchange, and socialism as a system of allocation of resources and income. The fact that (to date) one does not find democracy in the absence of some form of capitalism is for us a matter of great theoretical import, but we do not assume that this empirical association must hold inevitably into the future. In our theoretical volume, we suggest why state socialism (which some would insist is only state or statist capitalism) has been so difficult to reconcile with political democracy, and ponder what alternatives to capitalism might potentially be compatible with democracy.

Culturally, our effort includes the Christian societies of Latin America, India with its mosaic of traditions (including the distinctive Hindu culture), five largely Islamic societies, two Buddhist countries, one a mixture of Buddhism, Confucianism, and Christianity, and several African countries that have experienced what Mazrui calls the "triple heritage" of Christianity, Islam, and traditional African religion and culture. Unfortunately, the limited treatment in our country studies does not enable us to deal adequately with the complex issues of the relation between democracy and religious and cultural traditions, although we are unable to ignore them.

One of the most complex and intractable problems in our world is the tension between the model of ethnically, linguistically, and culturally homogeneous societies that satisfy the ideal of the nation-state and the multiethnic, multilingual societies that face the difficult task of nation- or state-building in the absence of the integration and identification we normally associate with the idea of the nation-state. Certainly, even in Europe, before the massive and forced transfers (if not destruction) of populations, most states did not satisfy that ideal, but outside of Europe and Latin America, even fewer do. In our study, only a few Latin American countries—Costa Rica, Venezuela, Argentina, Uruguay, Chile, perhaps Colombia—seem to satisfy that model. Others, like Brazil, the Dominican Republic, Mexico, and above all Peru, include not only descendants of the *conquistadores* and European immigrants, but also substantial populations (intermixed to varying degrees with the above) of Indians and descendants of black slaves. To the list of the relatively homogeneous countries could be added South Korea, Turkey (with some significant minorities), and Botswana (which still has major subtribal divisions). Our remaining cases confront us with the problem of democracy in ethnically and culturally divided societies, some of them, like Sri Lanka, with populations linked culturally with another, neighboring country.

One experience that almost all of the countries in our study share is a previous history of domination by an outside imperial power. Only Turkey and Thailand have been continuously independent countries, and only in the latter do we find a continuity with a premodern traditional monarchy. Our study, therefore, does not cover a sufficient number of countries to deal with the question: does continuous legitimacy of rule by an indigenous state facilitate both modernization and ultimately democratization, by contrast with the historical trauma of conquest and colonial domination?

For those who have raised the question of the relation between size and democracy,[26] our study includes the largest (most populous) democracy, India, and some of the smallest. In each part of the world it includes the largest country and at least some significant smaller ones: Brazil and Costa Rica, Nigeria and Botswana, India and Sri Lanka. Since the major countries—with their political influence and their capacity to serve as models—occupy a special position in their respective areas, where some speak of subimperialisms, we feel our selection on this account is well justified.

In addition to trying, as much as possible, to maximize variation in our independent variables, we have also sought a richly varied pool of cases with regard to our dependent variable, stable democracy. Save for the deliberate exclusion of countries with no prior democratic or semidemocratic experience, or no prospect of a democratic opening, our study encompasses virtually every type of democratic experience in the developing world. Some of our countries are now democratic, some are semidemocratic, some are authoritarian, and one is a hegemonic regime. Some of the democracies have been relatively stable for some time (such as Costa Rica and, so far at least, Botswana and Papua New Guinea); some have persisted in the face of recurrent crises and lapses (India, and now less democratically, Sri Lanka); and some have been renewed after traumatic and, in some cases, repeated breakdowns (e.g., Brazil, Uruguay, and Argentina). Some countries have experienced recurrent cycles of democratic attempts and military interventions, from which Turkey has managed to emerge with a generally longer and more successful democratic experience than Thailand, Ghana, or Nigeria. We have countries in varying stages of transition to democracy at this writing, from the recently completed but still fragile (the Philippines), to the partial or continuing and still undetermined (South Korea, Uganda, Pakistan), to the prospective (Nigeria), to the obstructed (Chile).[27] And, still, we have at least one case (Indonesia) of a failed democracy that seems to have been consolidating a distinctive form of authoritarian rule.

The sheer number of our case studies compelled us to break them up for publication into several volumes. This presented another editorial dilemma. We have opted for the established mode of division into regional volumes, as this follows the dominant organizational logic of scholarship, instruction, and intellectual discourse in the field. But we hasten to underscore our feeling that this is not the most intellectually fruitful or satisfying way of treating such material. It would perhaps have made more sense to group the cases by the characteristic types of regimes and problems they have experienced. But any method of division inevitably breaks the unity of our twenty six cases and disperses the multitude of different comparisons that spring from them. We know of no solution to this problem other than to invite our readers to read widely across the three regional volumes, and to work back and forth between the theory in our introductory volume and the evidence in our cases, as we ourselves have attempted to do over the past three years.

• THE NORMATIVE QUESTION: WHY STUDY DEMOCRACY? •

Finally, we cannot close this introduction to our work without confronting the question (or critical challenge) that is often put to us: Why study political democracy at all? Some critics suggest it is the wrong problem to be studying. They ask: Are there not more pressing issues of survival and justice facing developing societies? Does the limited question of the form of government not conceal more than it reveals? Others contend our choice of topic betrays a value bias for democracy that is misplaced. They ask (or assert): If in some societies democracy in our (liberal) sense has to work against so many odds, as our research unveils, is it worth striving for and encouraging an opposition that purports to establish it, or are there alternatives to democracy that should be considered and whose stability should be supported?

We wish to state quite clearly here our bias for democracy as a system of government. For any democrat, these questions carry serious implications. The former suggest that economic and social rights should be considered more important than civil and political liberties. The latter implies granting to some forms or cases of authoritarian rule the right to use coercive measures, in the name of some higher good, to suppress an opposition that claims to fight for democracy. For ourselves, neither of these normative suppositions is tenable.

If there were many nondemocratic governments (now and in the past) committed to serving collective goals, rather than the interests of the rulers, and ready to respect human rights (to refrain from torture and indiscriminate violence, to offer due process and fair trial in applying laws which, even if antiliberal, are known in advance, to maintain humane conditions of imprisonment, etc.), we might find these questions more difficult to answer. However, nondemocratic regimes satisfying these two requirements are few, and even those that begin with a strong commitment to the collectivity and sensitivity to human rights often become increasingly narrow, autocratic, and repressive (although these trends, too, are subject to reversal).

We emphasize the service of collective goals to exclude those authoritarian systems in which the rulers blatantly serve their own material interests and those of their family, friends, cronies, and clients; and to exclude as well those systems serving a narrowly defined oligarchy, stratum, or a particular ethnic or racial group (which might even be the majority). But even excluding such transparent cases (the majority, unfortunately), who is to define those collective goals, if we disqualify the majority of citizens from doing so? Inevitably, it means a self-appointed minority—a vanguard party, a charismatic leader and his followers, a bureaucracy, army officers, or perhaps intellectuals or "experts" working with them. But why should their definition of societal goals be better than that of any other group with a different concept of the collective good? Only if we were totally certain that one ideological (or religious) concept is the expression of historical reason—true and necessary—would we be forced to accept such an authoritarian alternative as better than democracy. To do so, as we know, justifies any sacrifices and ultimately terrible costs in freedom and human lives. The option between ultimate value choices would inevitably be resolved by force. Thus, democracy—with its relativism and tolerance (so disturbing to those certain of the truth), and its "faith" in the reasonableness and intelligence of the common men and women, including those uneducated and those with "false consciousness" (a concept that assumes others know better their real interests), deciding freely (and with a chance to change their minds every four or five years) and without the use of force—seems still a better option.

Of course, even committed democrats know that the empirical world, and so the normative issue, is full of variation and ambiguity. But this should not lead to intellectual and political confusion. A few authoritarian regimes that manifest commitment to collective goals and human rights might have redeeming qualities, particularly if they are stable and do not require excessive force to stay in power. But that does not make them democracies. Their supporters should be free to argue the positive aspects of their rule, without ignoring or denying the negative ones, but they should not attempt to claim that they are democracies. Not all nondemocracies are totally bad. Nor are all democracies, and especially unstable democracies, good for the people. But, certainly, nondemocracies are not likely to achieve those social and moral goals that require democratic institutions and freedoms. Therefore, from the point of view of a democrat, they will always be undesirable. Moreover, should they turn out to betray the ideals and hopes of their founders (as they have done so repeatedly), there is no easy way to oust them from power by peaceful means. Indeed, the almost law-like inevitability of the abuse and corruption of authoritarian power throughout history constitutes, we believe, one of the most compelling justifications for the institutionalized checks and accountability of a democracy.

For all these reasons, we (along with an increasing proportion of the world's population) value political democracy as an end in itself—without assuming that it is any guarantee of other important values. And we believe that a better understanding of the conditions for it is a worthwhile intellectual endeavor, which does not require us to deny the positive accomplishments of some nondemocratic regimes and the many flaws of democratic governments and societies.

Larry Diamond
Juan J. Linz
Seymour Martin Lipset

• NOTES •

1. Juan J. Linz and Alfred Stepan, eds., *The Breakdown of Democratic Regimes* (Baltimore: Johns Hopkins University Press, 1978).

2. Arend Lijphart, *Democracy in Plural Societies: A Comparative Exploration* (New Haven: Yale University Press, 1977); Donald L. Horowitz, *Ethnic Groups in Conflict* (Berkeley: University of California Press, 1985).

3. G. Bingham Powell, *Contemporary Democracies: Participation, Stability and Violence* (Cambridge: Harvard University Press, 1982).

4. Myron Weiner and Ergun Ozbudun, eds., *Competitive Elections in Developing Countries* (Washington: American Enterprise Institute, 1987).

5. Guillermo O'Donnell, Philippe C. Schmitter, and Laurence Whitehead, eds., *Transitions from Authoritarian Rule* (Baltimore: Johns Hopkins University Press, 1986).

6. Giovanni Sartori, *The Theory of Democracy Revisited* (Chatham, N.J.: Chatham House Publishers, 1987).

7. Gabriel A. Almond and James S. Coleman, eds., *The Politics of the Developing Areas* (Princeton: Princeton University Press, 1960), p. 3.

8. Gabriel A. Almond and Sidney Verba, *The Civic Culture* (Princeton: Princeton University Press, 1963).

9. Notable early works here were Daniel Lerner, *The Passing of Traditional Society* (Glencoe, Ill.: The Free Press, 1958); Seymour Martin Lipset, "Some Social Requisites of Democracy," *American Political Science Review* 53 (1959): pp. 69–105, and *Political Man* (New York: Doubleday & Co., 1960), pp. 27–63; and Karl W. Deutsch, "Social Mobilization and Democracy," *American Political Science Review* 55 (1961): pp. 493–514.

10. Samuel P. Huntington, *Political Order in Changing Societies* (New Haven: Yale University Press, 1968).

11. Barrington Moore, Jr., *Social Origins of Dictatorship and Democracy* (Cambridge: Harvard University Press, 1966).

12. Leonard Binder, James S. Coleman, Joseph La Palombara, Lucian Pye, Sidney Verba, and Myron Weiner, *Crises and Sequences in Political Development* (Princeton: Princeton University Press, 1971). The work of this committee, and the evolution of political development studies from the 1960s to the present, is surveyed in a sweeping and erudite review by Gabriel Almond, "The Development of Political Development," in Myron Weiner and Samuel P. Huntington, eds., *Understanding Political Development* (Boston: Little, Brown and Co., 1987), pp. 437–490.

13. Robert A. Dahl, *Polyarchy: Participation and Opposition* (New Haven: Yale University Press, 1971).

14. See, for example, Stein Rokkan, *Citizens, Elections, Parties: Approaches to the Comparative Study of the Processes of Development* (Oslo: Universitetsforlaget, 1970).

15. Almond, "The Development of Political Development," pp. 444–450.

16. Peter Evans, *Dependent Development* (Princeton: Princeton University Press, 1979), pp. 25–54.

17. Guillermo O'Donnell, *Modernization and Bureaucratic-Authoritarianism: Studies in South American Politics* (Berkeley: Institute of International Studies, University of California, 1973); see, also, David Collier, ed., *The New Authoritarianism in Latin America* (Princeton: Princeton University Press, 1979).

18. This neglect is, to some extent, overcome in Arend Lijphart's creative and enterprising study, *Democracies: Patterns of Majoritarian and Consensus Government in Twenty-One Countries* (New Haven: Yale University Press, 1984). However, the focus is mainly on political structure, and the comparison is limited to the continuous and stable democracies of the advanced, industrial countries.

19. Specifically, the points on this scale were: (1) *High success*—stable and uninterrupted democratic rule, with democracy now deeply institutionalized and stable; (2) *Progressive success*—the consolidation of relatively stable democracy after one or more breakdowns or serious interruptions; (3) *Mixed success—democratic and unstable* (e.g., democracy has returned following a period of breakdown and authoritarian rule, but has not yet been consolidated); (4) *Mixed success—partial or semidemocracy*; (5) *Failure but promise*—democratic rule has broken down, but there are considerable pressures and prospects for its return; (6) *Failure or absence*—democracy has never functioned for any significant period of time and there is little prospect that it will in the coming years.

20. Dahl, *Polyarchy*, pp. 3–20; Joseph Schumpeter, *Capitalism, Socialism and Democracy* (New York: Harper and Row, 1942); Lipset, *Political Man*, p. 27; Juan Linz, *The Breakdown of Democratic Regimes: Crisis, Breakdown and Reequilibration* (Baltimore: Johns Hopkins University Press, 1978), p. 5.

21. Guillermo O'Donnell and Philippe C. Schmitter, *Transitions from Authoritarian Rule: Tentative Conclusions about Uncertain Democracies* (Baltimore: Johns Hopkins University Press, 1986).

22. The distinction between authoritarian and totalitarian regimes has a long intellectual history predating its fashionable (and in some ways confusing) use by Jeanne Kirkpatrick in "Dictatorships and Double Standards," *Commentary* 68 (1979): pp. 34–45. See Juan J. Linz, "Totalitarian and Authoritarian Regimes," in *Handbook of Political Science*, Fred I. Greenstein and Nelson W. Polsby, eds, (Reading, Mass.: Addison-Wesley, 1975), vol. 3, pp. 175–411.

23. For a review of the literature on the subject from 1960 to 1980, see the expanded and updated edition of Lipset's *Political Man* (Baltimore: Johns Hopkins University Press, 1981), pp. 469–476.

24. In point of fact, the twenty-four-member organization also includes Turkey, but its per capita GNP ($1,160 in 1984) clearly places it among the middle ranks of developing countries (at about the level of Costa Rica or Colombia, for example).

25. Linz, "Totalitarianism and Authoritarianism," pp. 259–263.

26. Robert A. Dahl and Edward Tufte, *Size and Democracy* (Stanford: Stanford University Press, 1973).

27. One of the most important countries in the world now struggling (against increasingly forbidding odds, it appears) to develop a full democracy—South Africa—we reluctantly excluded

from our study not only because it has lacked any previous experience with democracy (beyond its limited functioning among the minority white population), but because the context of pervasive, institutionalized racial domination generates a number of quite distinctive obstacles and complexities. Although we feel our theoretical framework has much to contribute to the study of the conditions and prospects for democracy in South Africa, the unique character of that problem may make it more suitable for exploration through monographic studies, of which there is a proliferating literature. See, for example, Arend Lijphart, *Power-Sharing in South Africa* (Berkeley: Institute of International Studies, University of California, 1985), and Heribert Adam and Kogila Moodley, *South Africa Without Apartheid: Dismantling Racial Domination* (Berkeley: University of California Press, 1986).

• Acknowledgments •

This comparative study of democracy and the conference held in December 1985 to discuss the first drafts of the case studies were made possible by a generous grant from the National Endowment for Democracy. The endowment is a private, nonprofit organization that seeks to encourage and strengthen democratic institutions around the world through nongovernmental efforts. Since its creation in 1983, N.E.D. has been an extremely creative and effective institution. The editors and authors gratefully acknowledge the support of the endowment and, in particular, its president, Carl Gershman, and director of program, Marc F. Plattner.

The Hoover Institution, with which Diamond and Lipset are affiliated, also contributed in many substantial ways to the project during its more than three years of organization, writing, and production. We wish to thank especially the director of the Hoover Institution, W. Glenn Campbell, and the principal associate director, John F. Cogan.

A number of people assisted us in preparing manuscripts and arranging the 1985 conference. We thank in particular Janet Shaw of the Hoover Institution for her editing, typing, and administrative support; Lisa Fuentes, now at UCLA, who was our research and administrative assistant during 1985–1986; and Katherine Teghtsoonian, now at the University of Seattle, who produced the proceedings of our conference.

MELILLA
CEUTA
Tunis
Algiers
TUNISIA
Rabat
MOROCCO
Benghazi
Tripoli
Cairo
El-Ayoun
ALGERIA
LIBYA
EGYPT
WESTERN SAHARA
CAPE VERDE IS.
Praia
MAURITANIA
Nouakchott
MALI
NIGER
CHAD
Khartoum
SUDAN
SENEGAL
Dakar
THE GAMBIA
Banjul
Bamako
Niamey
BURKINA FASO
Ouagadougou
Ndjamena
DJIBOUTI
Djibouti
GUINEA-BISSAU
Bissau
GUINEA
Conakry
BENIN
Porto Novo
ETHIOPIA
Freetown
SIERRA LEONE
IVORY COAST
Abidjan
NIGERIA
Addis Ababa
Monrovia
LIBERIA
GHANA
Accra
Lagos
TOGO
Lome
CENTRAL AFRICAN REPUBLIC
Bangui
CAMEROON
Yaounde
SOMALIA
Mogadishu
EQUATORIAL GUINEA
Malabo
UGANDA
Kampala
KENYA
Nairobi
SAO TOME E PRINCIPE
Libreville
GABON
RWANDA
Kigali
ZAIRE
CONGO
Brazzaville
Kinshasa
BURUNDI
Bujumbura
TANZANIA
ZANZIBAR
Dar es Salaam
Luanda
SEYCHELLES IS.
Victoria
ANGOLA
Lilongwe
MALAWI
Moroni
COMORO IS.
ZAMBIA
Lusaka
Harare
MOZAMBIQUE
Antananarivo
ZIMBABWE
NAMIBIA
MAURITIUS
Port Louis
MADAGASCAR
REUNION
BOTSWANA
Windhoek
Gaborone
Pretoria
Maputo
SWAZILAND
Mbabane
SOUTH AFRICA
LESOTHO
Maseru

AFRICA

• CHAPTER ONE •

Introduction: Roots of Failure, Seeds of Hope

LARRY DIAMOND

Since Ghana led the way to independence three decades ago, Africa's experience with liberal democracy has not been a happy one. In a relatively short period of time, virtually all of the formally democratic systems left behind by the departing colonial rulers gave way to authoritarian regimes of one kind or another. In most cases, the demise of constitutional democracy began with the movement to one-party and, typically, one-man rule. In some countries, such as Senegal and the Ivory Coast, this followed from the electoral supremacy of the ruling party and the high degree of elite cohesiveness before independence, although the consolidation of authoritarian rule was not achieved without repression. In others, primarily former British colonies such as Kenya, Zambia, Ghana, and Uganda, one-party regimes (*de jure* or *de facto*) were established only several years after independence, but with extensive coercion and personalization of power. In the case of Nigeria, the persistence of a multiparty regime for five years after independence masked the consolidation of single-party rule in each of its the three regions and increasingly severe constraints on liberty and electoral competition. There and elsewhere (as in Sierra Leone and Zaire), growing instability surrounding electoral competition paved the way for military intervention, which also swept away the more fragile one-party regimes. By the early 1970s, virtually all of the independent regimes in sub-Saharan Africa were either military or one-party.[1]

However, this was and is not the whole story. Multiparty democracy has endured in three African countries, Botswana, Gambia, and Mauritius (all of them small in population and former British colonies). It has persisted, as well, to a considerable degree in independent Zimbabwe, albeit for a much shorter period of time and under considerably greater strain. A few African one-party states have begun to move away from the concentration and personalization of power, although it is not yet clear whether this will produce a democratic political system as we have defined it in this book (see our preface). This evolution has, so far, proceeded the furthest in Senegal, which has opened electoral competition to a wide range of opposition parties while tolerating considerable pluralism and dissent. Some African countries—including (in this study)

Nigeria, Ghana, and Uganda—have overthrown or forced the withdrawal of authoritarian regimes and launched new democratic experiments. Most of these, too, have failed, and yet the search for a viable democratic order continues.[2]

Our task here is severalfold. We must, of course, explain why democratic government has so far failed to develop and endure in most of sub-Saharan Africa. We do not pretend that the salient cases presented here—Nigeria, Ghana, Senegal, and Uganda—are representative of the full range of African states and experiences, but they may be particularly instructive. The French and, still more so, the British colonies were thought to have the better prospects for democracy after independence, and Senegal in particular represented the peak of democratic hopes and intentions among France's African colonies, as did Nigeria and Ghana among Britain's.

Second, we must try to understand what accounts for the few democratic exceptions in Africa. For this purpose, Botswana represents a significant and illuminating case. Third, there is the issue of what may explain or foster the liberalization, and, perhaps eventually, the full democratization of one-party authoritarian regimes. Having gone the furthest, Senegal may have the most to teach us. Fourth, we need to identify the factors that undermine authoritarian regimes in African countries and thus enable the quest for democracy to continue there.

Finally, as we should not yield to cynical despair over past democratic failures in Africa, so we should not blithely assume that the few current democratic or democratizing regimes are secure. As each of the case studies does, we will conclude this introduction with a view to the future, seeking to identify the threats to democratic persistence and progress and the changes that might strengthen the democratic prospect.

• THE SYMPTOMS OF FAILURE •

Two types of developments, distinct but not mutually exclusive, have signaled the failure of democratic systems in Africa following independence. In a great many countries, especially the former French colonies, the new rulers and ruling parties eliminated political competition, more or less quickly, and established one-party regimes. Where political support was too divided or political leadership insufficiently willful and authoritarian to permit the construction of single-party hegemony, political competition typically tore the polity apart in spasms of deadlock and crisis, ethnic polarization, partisan violence, state repression, and electoral fraud.

In Ghana, Senegal, and Uganda, it was the elected independence leaders who eliminated democracy through various measures that amounted to executive coups. After three years of political insecurity, authoritarian overreaction, and abuse of power, Ghana's "coup" was carried out through the ballot box in the form of a national referendum in 1960, establishing a highly centralized presidential system. Simultaneously, Kwame Nkrumah was overwhelmingly elected to the new executive position, from which he was able quickly to consolidate a repressive, one-party, and highly personalized dominion.

Significantly, the transition from political pluralism to authoritarianism was also marked and consolidated in Senegal and Uganda by constitutional change from a parliamentary to a presidential system, with extreme concentration of power in the presidency and marked diminution of legislative authority. In the years following independence in 1960, executive power in Senegal was increasingly strengthened, centralized, and personalized, with civil liberties constrained, until constitutional change in 1963 formalized the transition to an authoritarian presidential system. In the subsequent three years, all remaining opposition parties were either outlawed or induced to merge into Léopold Senghor's ruling Union progressiste sénégalais (UPS). However, the transition to one-party rule in Senegal was somewhat distinct in that it "never went so far as to set up an arbitrary or absolute dictatorship."[3]

In Uganda, the decay of democracy could be traced initially to the defection of opposition members of Parliament (MPs) to Prime Minister Milton Obote's ruling Uganda Peoples' Congress (UPC). This enabled him to dissolve his alliance with the party of the pivotal, proud, and economically well-off kingdom of Buganda (in southern Uganda), whose king was the country's presidential head of state. As tension between Obote's government and the semiautonomous kingdom deepened, and Obote's political position deteriorated, he executed an authoritarian coup by arresting his critics, suspending the constitution, deposing the president, and assuming full state powers early in 1966. Shortly thereafter, he introduced a new constitution terminating the special constitutional protections for Buganda (and the three other southern kingdoms) and establishing a centralized presidential system. One month later, in May, he dispatched the army to crush Buganda's resistance. In the following three years, political opposition withered under escalating repression, and, in December 1969, Obote formally declared a one-party state with a socialist program.

Underlying each of these three executive coups was a sense of political insecurity. We have already mentioned the opposition Obote faced from the powerful Buganda kingdom. As Omari Kokole and Ali Mazrui explain, this was just one dimension of the fragility of Obote's political base as an Ugandan northerner who relied on an ethnic base with less than a fifth of the population and governed within a strange federal-unitary system, with weak central control and powerful fissiparous tendencies. Facing rising criticism and heavy opposition even from within his own party, Obote struck to save himself politically.

Although not so immediately threatened, Nkrumah's political base was also insecure. Composed of poorer and more marginal ethnic and social groups, his Convention People's Party had a weak resource base and thin support among the civil service and traditional authorities. "It consequently overreacted to opposition activities" and ethnic unrest, Naomi Chazan maintains, and abused government power and resources to augment its party machinery. But these abuses of the Westminster system did not solve Nkrumah's political problems, and, by 1960, he was faced with the choice of respecting democratic practices or expanding and monopolizing state control in order to meet the inflated expectations of his supporters. "The impulse for control . . . won over the principle of competition."[4]

Despite its preindependence electoral dominance, Senghor's UPS also faced difficult challenges after independence. These included: the failure of the short-lived Federation of Mali in 1960; bitter internal political conflict within the ruling party, splitting the UPS and the National Assembly between President Senghor and his prime minister; a revolt by students and trade unions in the years 1968–1969; and the increasing alienation of the rural population, whose return on peanut cultivation was poor and declining. These political and social tensions, Christian Coulon argues, "pressed toward a hardening and a centralization of power" in the early years of the regime.[5]

Although an authoritarian outcome is by no means yet determined in Zimbabwe, and democratic institutions remain considerably more intact six years after independence than they have in the typical African country, some of these same political insecurities and authoritarian responses have been apparent in Zimbabwe. The government of Prime Minister Robert Mugabe, Masipula Sithole writes, "faced cruel dangers right from its inception. ZANU (PF) came to power in an atmosphere of fear, uncertainty, and mutual suspicion between blacks and whites, as well as among various black factions themselves."[6] Indeed, by far the most serious challenge to the regime has been the armed insurgency of the minority black faction, the Ndebele, and their party, ZAPU, which refused to accept the secondary political status accorded it in the elections. It was to respond to this violent challenge to its authority that the Mugabe government resorted to repressive and, at times, brutal measures in Matebeleland, while preserving many of the coercive instruments and emergency measures of the former Rhodesian state. There remains a signficant commitment to democracy in Zimbabwe, but Sithole warns that repression can be "habit-forming," and the longer the state of emergency continues in Matebeleland, the greater the danger that democratic values will be supplanted by a culture of authoritarianism and violence.

Should democratic breakdown come in Zimbabwe, its mode would figure to be an executive coup, featuring the declaration of the one-party state that ZANU (PF) has long envisioned. But the situation in Zimbabwe also reflects the political violence, repression, instability, and the severe ethnic polarization that have typically paved the way for military overthrow of multiparty regimes in Africa. In these circumstances, elections have become "a focus for unbridgeable political rivalries," and often the blatant rigging or disputed conduct of elections has robbed electoral outcomes and, by extension, the democratic system of legitimacy.[7] This has been the formula for democratic failure in Nigeria. In both the First and Second Republics, the struggle for power was a desperate, zero-sum affair, in which parties and candidates were willing to go to any lengths of demagogy, tribalism, chicanery, violence, and fraud in order to triumph. Although the Second Republic was far less ethnically polarized than the First, its crucial first test of electoral renewal was no more peaceful and legitimate, and its politicians were even more blatantly corrupt.

All of these were symptoms of a democratic system that was, in reality, not functioning democratically. This, in turn, destroyed its legitimacy and provoked the military to intervene. Although they never were allowed to reach the crucial test of electoral renewal, both Ghana's Second and Third Republics were victimized by poor democratic performance (especially ineptitude and intolerance in dealing with opposition and dissent), as well as corruption. By comparison, Zimbabwe's ruling party has at least managed to limit corruption and administer relatively free and fair elections. This has helped to preserve the regime's legitimacy and, hence, its immunity to military coups.

Even more so has democratic rectitude been a prominent feature of the regime in Botswana, where free and fair elections have repeatedly been held and open dissent has been tolerated in a relatively liberal spirit. But the Botswana Democratic Party (BDP) government in Botswana has not yet faced the kinds of daunting challenges and acute political insecurity that have many other new regimes in Africa. Hence, as John Holm suggests, it is not clear which way the ruling elite will turn if they become confronted with a truly serious challenge to their political dominance.

As we have suggested, the repression and elimination of political opposition and dissent, the desecration of the rules of democratic competition, and the consequent exhaustion of political legitimacy are only symptoms or manifestations of democratic failure. It remains to be explained why independence leaders embraced authoritarian solutions, and why political competition has been so riddled with antidemocratic behavior. We now turn to this task of explanation, with the help of the theoretical variables we have employed in this comparative study.

• EXPLAINING DEMOCRATIC FAILURE AND PROGRESS •

The near universal failure of democracy in the new states of postcolonial Africa must be seen in the light of the immense challenges with which they were immediately confronted. We have seen that the new regimes felt politically insecure for a variety of reasons. But this was only one dimension of a more general weakness of state authority, which was aggravated by a number of other imposing "historical and structural handicaps" (to quote Chazan). Prominent among these were deep ethnic divisions, a very shallow sense of nationhood, thinly established political institutions with little depth of experience, lack of indigenous managerial and technical talent, extreme economic dependence, and revolutionary popular expectations generated by the independence struggle. The new state structures were generally lacking in the power, resources, legitimacy, and societal support to meet these challenges. This fragility impelled them in an antidemocratic direction. To quote Ali Mazrui, as Chazan does to illuminate the case of Ghana, "the African state is sometimes excessively authoritarian to disguise the fact that it is inadequately authoritative."[8]

Many of these problems had their origins in colonial conquest and rule.

The Colonial Legacy

The colonial experience was far from uniform, and it is important to assess how variations in colonial rule may have contributed to variations in democratic performance and prospects in Africa. Throughout Africa, however, colonial rule did share certain common features. To begin with, the European powers carved up the map of Africa without regard for the integrity of existing cultural groups and state systems. "There was little quest for cultural congruence between the unit of the state and the national unit or even for cultural similarities among the different units being ruled by the same colonial government."[9] Hence, some large ethnic groups were split between colonial states, while others with little in common, save in some instances a history of warfare and enmity, were drawn together into the new state boundaries.

Beyond the fragility of nationhood and powerful fissiparous tendencies to which this ethnic fragmentation gave rise, many of the indigenous democratic practices in Africa were negated. These varied from the constitutional limits on monarchical authority of Nigeria's Yoruba and Senegal's Wolof to the decentralized, egalitarian, and individualistic values of the Igbo of Nigeria, the Kikuyu of Kenya, and the peoples of northern Uganda. But, as Kokole and Mazrui note, in the tensions of political interaction and conflict with other ethnic groups, the traditional cultural liberalism of the more democratic groups "sometimes stiffens into a kind of defensive intolerance."[10] Even the limited constitutional traditions of many African chiefdoms and kingdoms could not become established at the level of the modern state precisely because this would have meant that "the political traditions of one ethnic group would have to be accepted by all, which was very unlikely."[11] (In addition, where the colonial administration instituted "indirect rule," it mainly took hold in the more centralized and authoritarian traditional kingdoms, like the emirates of Northern Nigeria, rather than in the more democratic traditional polities).

Nor was the period of colonial rule sufficiently long and deep (and concerted in intention) to have the extent of cultural impact in developing democratic values that it did, for example, in India or Jamaica. In fact, the effort to impose the political institutions of the metropole, through constitutions that "scarcely acknowledged [African] cultural traditions and indigenous political predispositions," was bound to be deeply troubled.[12] Because the new constitutions were generally seen as "alien in spirit and design," their constituency was a thin and fragile one.[13]

Despite important variations, all of "the colonial empires had set an example of authoritarian government. Even the more liberal systems such as those developed by the British in West Africa had allowed only limited popular participation in government, and this itself was confined to a small elite."[14] In fact, it was not until very late in the colonial experience—in the final decade or two for the British and French colonies, at the last minute for the Belgian (if that), and not at all for the Portuguese—that Africans began to be prepared for taking over the legislative, executive, and bureaucratic organs of the colonial state. Even then, as Michael Crowder notes, this preparation was often very superficial.[15] For most of the sixty or so years of colonial rule, "colonial governors enjoyed very wide powers without brakes from below," as well as the symbolic trappings of supreme and exalted status.[16]

To this model of authoritarian power and privilege must be added the colonial precedent of state violence and repression. To quote Crowder again, "The colonial state was conceived in violence rather than by negotiation," and "it was maintained by the free use of it." Resistance and protest were forcibly, and often bloodily, repressed, although the colonial military machine was quite small by present standards. "It must be remembered too that the colonial rulers set the example of dealing with . . . opponents by jailing or exiling them, as not a few of those who eventually inherited power knew from personal experience."[17] As Sithole argues for Zimbabwe, the intolerant and antidemocratic character of postindependence politics must be traced, in part, to the repressiveness and lack of democratic preparation during colonial and settler rule.

The colonial legacy was not only authoritarian, but also statist. To be sure, the colonial bureaucracy was much smaller and the mission of the colonial state was much more limited than those of the successor states after independence.[18] However, the colonial powers imposed extensive state controls over internal and external trade in their African colonies, and, in the later stages of colonization, this intervention broadened and deepened.[19] Perhaps most significant was the establishment of state monopoly control over agricultural cash exports through various statutory marketing boards. Private investment in agriculture was thus discouraged in most places, and the state gained direct control over the greatest source of cash income in the colony. Rather than supporting agricultural development and farm income, marketing board funds became a primary source of state revenue and the leading factor in its expansion during the commodities booms of the 1950s.[20] The colonial state also established its exclusive control over the mining of minerals and the development of infrastructure. It discouraged the development of an indigenous capitalist class by favoring the metropole's industrial exports and foreign firms, and, as Chazan notes in the case of Ghana, by curtailing individual access to the land. Both for its resonance with socialist and developmentalist ideologies and for its obvious utility in consolidating power and accumulating personal wealth, this legacy of statism was eagerly seized upon and rapidly enlarged by the emergent African political class after independence. This mushrooming state ownership and economic control, and the consequent emergence of the state as the primary basis of dominant class formation,[21] was to have profound consequences for the nature of political competition after independence.

At the same time, the new African states were left at independence in conditions of more or less acute economic dependence. This is not the place to revisit or revise the debate over whether European colonialism "underdeveloped Africa," or whether dependence retards or distorts economic growth. What must be appreciated for our purposes, however, is the tremendous sense of economic vulnerability that African leaders felt for their new countries. In many cases, this intensified or, at the very least, served to justify the concentration of power as a means of asserting control. At a more objective level, it also made the economies highly vulnerable to swings in international commodity markets, complicating the challenge of economic development.

Finally, one may trace the underdevelopment of indigenous administration in part to colonial administrative practice, "which restricted and even widely prevented the involvement of Africans in higher, nonclerical levels of administration."[22] When Africanization of the bureaucracy was undertaken, it began "too late to enable Africans to fill most senior government posts at the time of independence."[23] This, too, weakened the authority and effectiveness of the new African states. It also encouraged them to embark on "rapid and wholesale Africanization" after independence, which deflated rather than enhanced government capability and, in the absence of developed traditions and mechanisms of probity and responsibility, fostered the growth of corruption.[24]

Notwithstanding these many general features, there were also important distinctions in the nature of colonial rule, and these have differentially affected the democratic prospect in Africa. It is not by coincidence that the African countries with the most democratic experience or, at least, continuing pressure for democracy are former French and especially former British colonies. The British and French, in contrast to the Belgian and Portuguese colonial authorities, "created their own forms of representative institutions, endowed with sufficient power to make their control a great political prize."[25] In particular, "British Africans, more than black people in any other part of colonial Africa, obtained some experience in the exercise of executive power," and power was transferred from London to local African governments by a constitutional machinery.[26] In Nigeria, vigorous electoral competition and regional self-rule developed during the final decade of colonial rule, during which new constitutions emerged not only through negotiations with indigenous elites, but also through extensive popular involvement.

French colonies had less experience with self-government, and French rule was heavily paternalistic; but educated French Africans were given a voice in the French Chamber of Deputies and a stake in local government. It is interesting to note that the French colony in which the African elite was given the earliest and most significant role in political life—Senegal—is today the most democratic of France's former African colonies. From the mid-nineteenth century, the Senegalese elite acquired the habit of political debate and skills of political mobilization, organization, and management. Despite its restricted scope, this tradition of political competition "made it very difficult to impose restrictions on a people who, for more than a century, had been used to political battles." Thus, it discouraged the construction of a much more monolithic authoritarianism.[27]

The French and, again, especially the British also allowed more scope for the development of an independent press and associational life during the period of nationalist agitation. Further, in contrast to Portuguese colonial rule, exposure of the emergent African elite to British and French culture (especially through higher education during the late colonial period), diffused democratic values and aspirations to some extent. Again, in Francophone Africa this effect was most striking (and significant for democratic development) in Senegal; elsewhere it was limited.

One irony of the comparative colonial legacy is that the empire that did the most to advance the political construction of democratic states also generated some of the most debilitating challenges to democratic consolidation. Ali Mazrui has argued that, whereas the French, with their cultural arrogance and centralizing traditions, did more to lay a foundation of common nationhood, the British policy of indirect rule advanced the cause of state formation at the expense of nation-building.[28] Our case studies of Uganda and Nigeria demonstrate, as Mazrui argues, that the preservation by the British of strong indigenous kingdoms (in particular, the *kabaka*ship of Buganda and the Muslim emirates of Northern Nigeria) contributed to the tensions that erupted in democratic breakdown and civil strife in those two countries in the last half of the 1960s.[29] Indirect rule also reinforced ethnic divisions in Ghana.

This was only one element of a British imperial policy that was heavily devoted to encouraging ethnic and regional, as opposed to national, consciousness. This was perhaps most graphically demonstrated in Nigeria, where the North and South were ruled as two separate protectorates, and then three regions, which the British insisted on preserving through independence despite the clear propensity of the system to ethnic hegemony and polarization, and the well-reasoned and impassioned appeals for more states. In Uganda, as in Nigeria, the tension and lack of integration between a far more economically and educationally advanced south and a politically or militarily advanced north would constitute the most destructive element of Britain's colonial legacy. If this explosive contradiction was partly the result of uneven penetration of diverse forces of modernization, it was also a consequence of deliberate colonial policy.

One final salient variable in colonial rule was the nature of decolonization. Where the transition to self-government did not require extensive mass mobilization and, especially, an armed struggle of national liberation, the new state was spared a potentially potent source of antidemocratic pressure. In this sense, five of our six cases stand in sharp contrast to the experiences in Algeria, Angola, Guinea-Bissau, and Mozambique. Coulon maintains, for example, that the absence of a mass-mobilizing or revolutionary struggle for independence in Senegal limited violence as a method of political expression and permitted the development of a more moderate and democratic style of political leadership and behavior. In contrast, the "commandist nature of mobilization and politicization under clandestine circumstances gave rise to the politics of intimidation and fear," and to the prominence of antidemocratic (Marxist-Leninist) ideological persuasions in postliberation Zimbabwe.[30]

And yet, even where nationalist movements won independence through much more limited and mild-mannered mobilization, the process of stirring up popular sentiment for independence disposed nationalist leaders to make extravagant promises of a social and economic transformation once freedom had been obtained from colonial rule. The resulting "semi-Messianic expectations . . . created a political mortgage for the future, a liability that the new leaders would often find difficult to discharge."[31]

On balance, one is tempted to conclude that—whatever their intentions—even the British and French colonial regimes did more to defeat democracy than to develop it. Certainly this would seem to be true in the short run, given the lack of political and administrative preparation and the acute handicaps of political structure, ethnic divisiveness, and economic dependence that weighed so heavily at independence. But it is important to keep in mind the new elements of political pluralism—parties, trade unions, organized interest groups, newspapers—that emerged under French and British colonial rule and the attachment to liberal and democratic values that was, at least to some degree, introduced to or strengthened among a portion of the elite by cultural contact. In many African countries (including the ones in this study), these legacies have survived initial and even repeated democratic trials or failures. It is also a useful restraint on the tendency to attribute too much—bad and good—to the colonial legacy to observe that the country in our study with the most minimal colonial impact and the least experience with electoral politics prior to independence—Botswana—has been the only one to sustain a democratic system through two decades of independence.

Ethnicity

Although ethnic pluralism and cleavage is a central fact of political life in Africa, the systems of ethnic heterogeneity vary widely in their demographic balances and in the way they articulate with political structures. These variations have important implications for democratic politics. One important distinction is between what Donald Horowitz terms "centralized"—as opposed to "dispersed"—ethnic systems. In the former, "a few groups are so large that their interactions are a constant theme of politics at the center," whereas the latter disperse conflict to many different points because of the multiplicity of small groups. Hence, "the structure of dispersed ethnic systems abets interethnic cooperation, while the structure of centralized ethnic systems impedes it."[32]

The three cases in this study in which ethnic conflict has presented the steepest challenge to political stability (democratic or otherwise) also have the most centralized ethnic systems. However, the Nigerian case demonstrates that the demographic balance is only part of the picture and, hence, that the centralization of ethnicity is not immutable. When the federal system encapsulated the three largest ethnic groups (Hausa-Fulani, Yoruba, and Igbo—about 60 percent of the population) in three regions, it reified the political importance of these groups while denying Nigeria's numerous ethnic minorities any significant political leverage. But when the system was restructured into first twelve and then nineteen states, splitting up the three major groups and creating numerous ethnic minority states, subethnic cleavage was activated and a much more fluid and decentralized pattern of ethnic cleavage developed.

In something of a reverse sense, the enormous fractionalization of ethnic groups in Uganda—with the largest group constituting less then a fifth of the population and several important ones accounting for only a few percent—has nevertheless been polarized into a highly centralized alignment because of the historical factors that have pitted south against north and Bantu against non-Bantu groups. Although it is true that this centralization has also followed from the sharp cultural and linguistic differences between northern and southern tribes, Uganda has never had a federal system sufficiently thorough and complex to activate the dispersed character of its ethnic tapestry.

In Zimbabwe, ethnicity is highly centralized in that the Shona and Ndebele constitute, between them, almost the entire population. As in Uganda, the two groups have markedly different cultural traditions, with the Ndebele minority (like the Bantu kingdoms of Uganda) having had much more highly centralized polities and stratified societies. The historic tension between these two groups produced a seemingly inevitable struggle for dominance, which split the nationalist movement and postindependence politics. But within each of these two groups, and especially the much more numerous Shona, are subethnic divisions that could potentially disperse ethnic conflict under different political structures. Indeed, subethnic cleavages produced a pattern of shifting alliances during most of the nationalist struggle, and this historic fluidity still "augurs well for pluralistic democracy in Zimbabwe."[33]

Even though ethnicity has been a continual source of political tension in Ghana, it has not consistently polarized the polity as it has in Nigeria, Uganda, or Zimbabwe because of the more decentralized demographic and cultural profile. Although the Akan linguistic group comprises over 40 percent of the population, it is subdivided into many significant groups, and none of the several other groups has more than a sixth of the population. As in all of the other multiparty systems in our study (and throughout Africa), party organization and electoral support throughout Ghana's three republics have been significantly correlated with ethnicity, and party mobilization in democratic regimes has highlighted ethnic differences, especially during elections. The latter factor, in particular, has accentuated the vulnerability of democratic regimes, but has not been a leading cause of their crises or demise.

Demographic balance and political structure are not the only factors that determine the character of ethnic political interaction. In Senegal and Botswana, two other factors have mitigated the partially centralized ethnic balance. First, each country has had some overarching element of cultural unity. In Senegal, Islam (as the religion of 90 percent of the Senegalese people) has played this integrating role, "uniting people of different ethnic origins around common experiences and common symbols" and inspiring "new feelings of belonging to a national and even an international community."[34] In Botswana, this unity flows from the similarity in language and cultural traditions of the Tswana tribes. Second, the dominant group in each country has struck an accommodating stance toward other groups, rather than seeking to impose political hegemony. In Senegal, Wolof is only one of six official languages (in addition to French). In Botswana, the ruling party can forge a parliamentary majority almost exclusively with the monolithic support it receives from the largest subethnic group (the Bamangwato, 35 percent plus) and one other, but has instead chosen to treat all groups alike, even leaning over backward to provide government services and resources to less politically friendly groups. Further, as we will see below, Botswana's decentralized political structure ensures some considerable autonomy for its eight subethnic groups of the Tswana people.

Because ethnicity is such a fluid and malleable phenomenon, it would be mistaken to conclude that the mere presence of deep ethnic divisions has doomed African countries to democratic failure. To be sure, these divisions have presented a stiff challenge to democratic regimes; the greater the cultural differences, socioeconomic imbalances, historic rivalries, and centralization of demographic structure, the stiffer the challenge has been. Political leadership and structure, however, have shown significant scope either to magnify and inflame these divisions or to soften and crosscut them. In this sense, ethnicity is best viewed as an intervening or contributing variable, albeit often a pivotal one, in explaining democratic outcomes in Africa.

Moreover, we should not lose sight of the positive benefit that derives from ethnic heterogeneity. Ethnic cleavage also represents a basis of social pluralism and political competitiveness. In Zimbabwe, Sithole finds that "continued Ndebele support for Nkomo's ZAPU has slowed down ZANU's speed toward countrywide hegemony and the one-party state."[35] In Nigeria, the depth and complexity of ethnic divisions have made the country exceedingly difficult to manage by authoritarian means, since ethnic stability requires a greater decentralization, distribution, rotation, and representation of power than authoritarian regimes have provided. In general, where ethnic groups have been mobilized for group political consciousness and expectations of political autonomy and representation, these expectations and demands have retained remarkable resilience as a force for political pluralism.

Political Culture

Another obvious source of democratic decay has been the lack of commitment to democratic principles and procedural norms. Where democracy has failed, the abuse of power and failure to play by the rules of the game have been prominent and even pervasive features of political life. It is a short and easy, and not wholly inappropriate, step to extrapolate from this behavior that political beliefs and values have been anti- or at least ademocratic. As a leading historian of Africa has recently argued, most nationalist leaders accepted and participated in democratic elections during decolonization as a means to an end, a vehicle or condition for independence. "It is clear that for all but a few leaders—Seretse Khama of Botswana and Dauda Jawara of The Gambia being the notable exceptions—the commitment to liberal democracy was a transitory one."[36]

Without question, this view illuminates the gradual destruction of democracy from above in Ghana, Uganda, Nigeria, and Senegal after independence and the contemporary pressures in this direction in Zimbawe. It also informs the antidemocratic behavior of political opposition as well—a matter that is frequently neglected in academic analyses. Sithole traces Zimbabwe's postindependence political travails in large part to ZAPU's refusal to accept its electoral defeat. The arms caches, military maneuvers, and defections from the national army of ZAPU's guerilla army after independence signaled to the ruling party that ZAPU could not be trusted, that it was preparing to seize by force the power it could not win democratically. These "illegitimate and disloyal opposition tactics" have fueled the authoritarian reaction and demands for a one-party state within the ruling party and the government.[37] But the previously noted features of Zimbabwe's history—the repressiveness and racism of the white minority regime, the violent and conspiratorial nature of the liberation struggle, and the resulting prominence of Marxism-Leninism in ideological discourse—have helped to produce the current tendencies toward intolerance, distrust, extremism, and violence in the political culture.

However, democratic values have not been uniformly or completely lacking at either the elite or mass levels. This complexity cautions against culturally deterministic explanations of democratic failure. It compels us to search for other, structural factors behind the political violence, intolerance and abuse of power. It further requires a careful examination of how variations in the form and extent of democratic values have affected the different experiences with democracy.

At the opposite end of our spectrum of regimes, one may link Botswana's relative democratic successs to the greater commitment to democratic values of its leadership (with the qualification that it has yet to be truly tested). The fact that the Senegalese regime never went as far in an authoritarian direction, and has been the first to travel so far back toward democracy, can be traced in part to the liberal, pluralistic, and pragmatic impulses in the complex personality of Léopold Senghor and to the value system of the Senegalese elite more generally.

This same liberal and pragmatic spirit, along with the military stalemate in the civil war, has tempered Prime Minister Robert Mugabe's pursuit of his ambition for a socialist one- party state, constraining it within the boundaries of the Lancaster House constitution (to which all parties agreed) and of respect for the integrity of electoral and judicial institutions. Similarly in Uganda, Yoweri Museveni's willingness to compromise his leftist ideology in order to build a broad democratic coalition bespeaks a pragmatic and liberal value orientation that gives some hope for the democratic prospect in that troubled land.

Popular beliefs and cultural traditions have also played a significant role. While the largely illiterate and uneducated populations of the new African countries may have had little understanding and appreciation for the democratic structures that were imposed on them, their indigenous cultural traditions served in many instances to limit or undermine authoritarianism. One cannot but be struck by what Naomi Chazan refers to as the resilience of the democratic ethos in Ghana in the face of virtually continuous abuse and corruption by political elites, civilian and military. "A deeply ingrained indigenous culture of consultation, autonomy, participation, and supervision of authority . . . has enabled Ghanaians to combat the uncertainties of state domination and the tyranny of its leaders. Lawyers, students, unions, and traders have also evolved a liberal culture of resistance to interference in their affairs."[38] In Nigeria as well, democratic values of freedom and public accountability have become entrenched in a richly articulated associational life, and have merged with ancient cultural traditions (in the South and middle North) to confront state repression and to pressure for adherence or return to constitutional, democratic government.

In Senegal, a "mixed" political culture corresponds to the semidemocratic character of the regime. Traditional political cultures were "a combination of rather authoritarian values and beliefs, compensated for by a propensity for debate, political game-playing" and constitutional limits on monarchical authority.[39] The liberal influence of Western culture further presses in a democratic direction, but this is counterbalanced and threatened by the lack of support for democracy among the alienated lower classes and the growing interest in authoritarian Islamic doctrines among a segment of the elite. Exposure to English and Western institutions has bred a strong attachment to democratic values among Uganda's southern ethnic groups (especially the Baganda), despite their far more hierarchical and authoritarian cultural legacies than the northern groups. With their traditional concern for the rule of law, this new attachment (in part perhaps a reaction to the depths of tyranny and anarchy) may be seen as a hopeful sign.

If the lack of articulation between modern democratic systems and ancient cultural traditions may help to explain the general failure of independence constitutions in Africa, the unusual degree of continuity between past and present in Botswana may help us to understand its atypical success. The ruling party has built on the tradition of the *kgotla,* a communal assembly to consult public opinion and mobilize public support, in seeking local approval for development policies before any implementation. It has also used the traditional chiefs, who retain popular esteem, to legitimate the new political structures and solicit community support. Although traditional political structures were highly authoritarian in many respects, the emphases in Tswana traditional culture on moderation, nonviolence, and obedience to the law, along with public discussion and community consensus, have clearly facilitated the development and persistence of democratic government.

Performance and Legitimacy

We have seen that democratically elected governments in Africa have generally performed quite poorly in respecting democratic norms and procedures. This has been both an element of democratic decay and a source of delegitimation. But equally important in the loss of legitimacy has been the poor, often disastrous, economic performance of democratic regimes.

Ghana may be seen as the archetypal instance of a progressive squandering of economic promise. In addition to the formidable structural handicaps we have noted, the Gold Coast also had some significant advantages when it attained its independence in 1957, and it

> was widely recognized as Britain's model colonial possession on the continent. It had more schools and health services per capita and a better road system than any other British territory in Africa. It also boasted a robust, non-plantation, peasant economy, a prosperous middle class, a distinguished history of higher education, an able administrative elite, and a widespread respect for representative institutions.[40]

But Nkrumah failed to bring the prosperity and development progress he had promised. As his government pursued an increasingly socialist and statist path, production and consumption declined precipitously, indebtedness grew, and public discontent intensified. This record of economic mismanagement placed a heavy burden on Nkrumah's successors. Furthermore, successive regimes, democratic and military, continued to mismanage, distort, and plunder the economy. In just two years of the Second Republic, Kofi Busia's government accumulated a debt equaling Nkrumah's. The timid, ineffective policies of the Third Republic only intensified the problems of agricultural decline, inflation, corruption, and foreign indebtedness. These performance failures have cumulated over time, Chazan argues, not only to undermine particular regimes, but to induce a detachment of society from the state and a withdrawal into the parallel economy. A similar legacy of economic mismanagement has left a ravaged, depleted, indebted economy, a crippled and decaying infrastructure, a weakened state, and a flourishing parallel economy in Uganda, where economic reconstruction now constitutes one of the primary challenges to democratic development.

The squandering of economic promise has been even more spectacular in the case of Nigeria, which was given the bounty of billions of dollars annually in oil revenues. But successive governments failed to use this to construct a productive base outside of oil, and the Second Republic exceeded all previous records for corruption, greed, waste, and ineptitude. Pervasive mismanagement at every level of government drained the economy of resources and prevented any kind of measured adjustment to the decline in oil revenue. Along with the staggering corruption, the familiar signs of performance failure—steep declines in agricultural and industrial production, skyrocketing prices and mounting shortages of basic consumer goods, collapse of government services, and swelling foreign debt—thoroughly alienated the people from their second democratic experiment, as they did less spectacularly from the first.

Although the Senegalese regime has so far managed to survive despite its two decades of economic stagnation, mounting indebtedness, and extensive corruption, there are growing signs that these failures are eroding the support base of the regime and, crucially, the capacity of the Muslim brotherhoods and marabouts to play the mediating role between state and society that has so far contained disaffection.

These failures of economic development are clearly indicated in Table 1.1. Particularly striking here are the low or negative rates of per capita economic growth, the high rates of inflation, the stagnation or decline of agricultural production, and the slow pace of educational expansion in Ghana, Uganda, and Senegal.

The data also highlight the relative economic success of Botswana and Zimbabwe, which has contributed to their greater democratic success. "In a decade and half, Botswana has moved from being one of the poorest countries in Africa to one of the richest," with per capita GNP increasing from $100 to over $900.[41] Although Botswana has had the benefit of mineral deposits, the keys to this growth have been moderate, prudent policies and effective, honest management. Botswana has been one of the few African countries to give priority to the development of agriculture and infrastructure. Heavy and well-distributed investments have also been made in social services, education, health, and housing, while administrative expenditures and political and bureaucratic corruption have been contained. Parastatals are generally self-sufficient and even profitable. Part of the reason for this effective management is that Botswana has also been one of the few African countries not to engage in the wholesale Africanization of administration. Hence, it still remains extraordinarily dependent on expatriate personnel and foreign investment. This element of vulnerability notwithstanding, the remarkable success and reasonable spread of economic development in Botswana since independence has been a major pillar of legitimacy for the democratic regime. Similarly in Zimbabwe, the impressive strides in health, education, literacy, and agriculture since 1980 and the Mugabe government's pragmatism in working with white technical and business personnel to maintain economic growth have been an important foundation of legitimacy for that regime.

Table 1.1 Selected Development Indicators, 1965–1984

	Nigeria		Ghana		Senegal		Uganda		Zimbabwe		Botswana	
	1965	1984	1965	1984	1965	1984	1965	1984	1965	1984	1965	1984
Population in millions		96		12		6		15		8		1
Population growth rate 1973–1984		2.8		2.6		2.8		3.2		3.2		4.4
Projected rate 1980–2000		3.4		3.5		2.9		3.3		3.4		3.4
GNP per capita in U.S. dollars		730		350		380		230		760		960
Average annual growth rate, GNP per capita in percent, 1965–1984		2.8		−1.9		−0.5		2.9		1.5		8.4
Average annual rate of inflation												
1965–1973		10.3		8.1		3.0		5.6		1.1		4.4
1973–1984		13.0		52.2		9.0		64.5		11.4		9.8
Average annual growth rate of agricultural production												
1965–1973		2.8		4.5		0.2		3.6		—		6.4
1973–1984		−0.5		0.2		−0.2		−0.7		1.1		−4.0
Percent of labor force in agriculture (1965 & 1980)	72	68	61	56	83	81	91	86	79	53	89	70
Life expectancy at birth												
Male	40	48	45	51	40	45	43	49	46	55	46	55
Female	43	51	49	55	42	48	47	53	49	59	49	61
Infant mortality rate per 1,000 births	179	110	123	95	172	138	122	110	104	77	108	72
Percent enrolled in primary school (1983)[a]	32	98	69	79	40	53	67	57	110	131	65	96
Percent enrolled in secondary school (1983)	5	—	13	38	7	12	4	8	6	39	3	21
Percent in cities	15	30	26	39	27	35	6	7	14	27	4	20

Source: World Bank, *World Development Report 1986* (New York: Oxford University Press, 1986).
[a] The percentages may exceed 100 because of enrollment of students outside the standard age group.

Political Leadership

Our evidence on performance, both political and economic, repeatedly calls attention to the importance of political leadership. The values and skills of political leaders have figured prominently in the destruction or nurturance of democracy. Nkrumah's corrupt, authoritarian, megalomaniacal leadership launched Ghana on a path of political and economic decay from which it has yet to recover, three decades later. Busia was ineffective in building political institutions, mobilizing democratic participation, and managing dissent and opposition with democratic grace. The Third Republic's Limann was feeble and inept. The general verdict on Ghana's democratic leaders is valid as well for Nigeria's, Uganda's and those of most of Africa's failed democracies. They have "displayed an intolerance of criticism and a distaste for true consultation and compromise."[42] They have been unwilling or unable to learn from past political mistakes. They have organized, incited, or, at a minimum, condoned political violence. When they have not been personally corrupt, they have been (like Tafawa Balewa of Nigeria's First Republic and Shehu Shagari of the Second) too weak to discipline and limit the venal tendencies in their party and government machineries.

We have seen that the more consistently democratic countries in our study have also had the benefit of more able and democratically committed leaders. Senghor's relative liberalism and moderation, and his concern for Senegal's international image, led him to initiate democratic reforms in 1974 and then to set a precedent in Africa by voluntarily departing from the presidency in 1981. The fact that his successor, Abdou Diouf, has shared these liberal instincts has been crucial to the further political opening since then. Robert Mugabe has resisted pressure from within his ruling party to exceed constitutional limits and immediately declare a one-party state in Zimbabwe. He made a considerable effort to foster harmony with his opponents after taking power in 1980. Although this conciliatory posture stiffened after the discovery of opposition arms caches in 1982, he has continued to accommodate the white economic elite in pragmatic fashion and to discourage political corruption. Botswana's two leaders since independence, Seretse Khama and Quett Masire, have been moderate, pragmatic, tolerant, competent, and uncorrupt, and these qualities also characterize the ruling political elite more generally.

Political Institutions and Structures

The weakness of political institutions has been a defining feature of Africa's failed democratic experiments. On the output side, state structures were sorely lacking in resources, authority, penetration, and indigenous capacity at independence. Their subsequent atrophy under pressure of relentless abuse and then societal withdrawal in Ghana, Uganda, and elsewhere has placed their elementary capacity to govern—and so to govern democratically—in grave doubt.

On the input side, political parties have generally been fragile, shallow, and weak. As a result, democratic systems have not struck deep popular roots. Here again, Ghana is a first and archetypal instance of the centralization and narrowing of the circle of power, beginning with Nkrumah. But Nkrumah did have a populist streak, while the more committed democrats of the middle class have been too removed from the people and still too inclined to curtail channels of participation. Ruling coalitions have been narrow in all three democratic attempts, purposely excluding major groups, and hence "party structures have not been able to mature and institutionalize themselves."[43]

Virtually everywhere in Africa, the formal political arena has remained narrow, even when it has not been narrowed as a deliberate authoritarian strategy. After two decades, Botswana's ruling party, the Botswana Democratic Party (BDP), is still basically a collection of local notables rather than a mass-based party. The political elite is highly paternalistic, fearing that the bulk of the population, which is not formally educated, cannot be trusted with democratic rights and responsibilities. Hence, parliamentary eligibility remains restricted to those who can speak and read English. And, outside the cities, the popular commitment to liberal democracy appears superficial.

Similarly in Senegal, the ruling UPS was and is essentially a composition of clientele networks that compete at all levels for party and, therefore, state control. More imminently than in Botswana, this institutional shallowness constitutes a growing challenge to the viability of democratic or semidemocratic government. As "social forces, expectations, and grievances have been unable to find a means of expression in the structures and organizations that Senegalese democracy has made available to them," the gap between civil and political society has widened, and the people have begun to channel their demands through other institutions and processes.[44] As Chazan has noted, the growth of these nonformal participatory modes and structures has been one of the most vibrant and striking political developments in postindependence Africa, with promising democratic implications (which we will soon explore).[45] But, as Senegal's recent experience shows, nonformal participation can be violent and extremist as well as peaceful and democratic, and the exclusion and detachment of the bulk of the people from the formal political arena cannot augur well for the maturation of democracy. Unless reversed, it becomes a formula for regime delegitimation, political crisis, and decay.

Even when parties have elicited greater popular involvement, they have tended to reflect ethnic and regional particularities too closely to provide a fresh, crosscutting basis for political conflict. This has been the characteristic problem of Nigerian politics, but it was beginning to change in the Second Republic as a result of the nineteen-state structure and various electoral provisions requiring broad ethnic representation in parties as a condition of registration. Still, the party system of Nigeria's Second Republic was victimized by a lack of time, in advance of the full onset of electoral competition, to develop fresh leaderships, new and coherent identities, and broad constituencies. As a result, the new parties were weak and extraordinarily volatile, and politics were greatly destabilized by the chaos of their divisions, defections, expulsions, and permutations. The greater ethnic breadth of elite representation and internal cohesion of the ruling parties in Botswana and Senegal has contributed to regime stability.

Our earlier mention of the Nigerian case highlighted the importance of political structures in decentralizing and managing ethnic cleavage. Even short of a fully federal system, decentralization of power and autonomy for local governments can do much to preclude or reduce ethnic and regional polarization. In Botswana, the system of local authority—featuring directly elected councils for the nine districts and four towns—is described by Holm as "the centerpiece of Botswana democracy." It gives each tribe some sense of autonomy over its own affairs while also affording communities some responsibility and control over issues of local development. By contrast, the excessive centralization of power has contributed to ethnic tension and political alienation in Zimbabwe and in Senegal, where a violent separatist movement has grown in the Casamance region.

Botswana also stands out in having effective structures to control corruption, such as an independent audit under the supervision of the National Assembly. Most African countries have lacked structures with adequate autonomy and strength to check not only corruption, but other abuses of power as well. The courts have helped to preserve rights of political opposition and dissent in Botswana and Zimbabwe, and, at times, in Nigeria and Ghana; but in most countries, they have lacked the autonomy, resources, and effective authority necessary to safeguard liberty. Electoral institutions have been heavily penetrated by partisan and corrupt pressures in most African democratic experiments, with Nigeria and Uganda being prime examples.

State and Society

Democratic government in Africa has been victimized by political violence and intolerance, intense ethnic conflict, poor economic performance, and extensive corruption. But, contrary to some interpretations, these are not inherent and immutable features of the African political scene. They do not spring from deep roots in African culture, nor are they predestined by the low level of economic development, as Botswana's experience affirms. Neither is it useful to view them simply as the product of a rotten, selfish class or generation of African politicians. These problems have been generated by a web of factors in the social and political structure, at the hub of which we find the characteristic relationship between state and society.

The typical African state may be described as "swollen" in that it is at once both too large and too weak. It owns or controls the vast share of wealth outside the subsistence economy, in mining, agriculture, and even industry and services. It has become the primary source of wage employment and the primary source of money expenditures. Its regulation of the formal economy is pervasive. Although this statism began under colonial rule, it has grown relentlessly since independence.[46] And yet we have seen that the African state is also weak, not only vis-à-vis external actors, but even as regards its own society. It is poorly, sometimes barely, institutionalized and authoritative. It can command and expend vast resources, but it cannot get things done. As Chazan has said of Ghana's civil service, it is "overestablished, but underbureaucratized."[47] Of our six cases, the only signficant departures from this pattern are the one continuing democracy, Botswana, and the one embattled democracy, Zimbabwe, which is becoming more endangered as it also becomes more statist.

The swollen nature of the African state has had diffuse and profound consequences for democracy. In particular, by making the state the primary arena of class formation and state control the primary means for the accumulation of personal wealth, it has put too much at stake in the competition for power. This sweeping economic premium on power (not only for individuals, but also for communities) has heavily motivated the drive toward the monopolization of power by a single party and narrow elite in countries such as Ghana, Uganda, and Senegal. It has also been—with especially striking clarity in Nigeria—the core factor underlying the brutality, intolerance, and zero-sum nature of political conflict. Moreover, Chazan notes, as political participation in competitive elections increases, so do the destabilizing effects of this statism.

Related to this, the swollen state has also been a major cause of the devastating growth of political corruption in Africa. In countries as diverse as Ghana, Morocco, and Zambia, corruption has grown in incidence and scale with the growth of state corporations, marketing boards, trade controls, and so forth. As John Waterbury has put it, "the scope for corrupt patronage has expanded with the state itself."[48] As corruption has flourished and political institutions have failed to develop, government and politics have become absorbed in patron-client relations to the point where state office is awarded primarily as an entitlement to accumulate personal wealth.[49] Moreover, when such a "prebendal" system, in the Weberian sense, is wedded to a structure of political party competition and mass political participation, it must expand to accommodate a much wider network of clients, especially at the bottom levels of the system.[50] But, outside these networks, this corruption has undermined democratic legitimacy as it has enervated economic development and fostered glaring inequalities.

State expansion has also stimulated ethnic conflict in two senses. First, it is widely recognized that the growth and concentration of resources in the state has increased the salience of state control for ethnic groups as much as for individuals and, hence, has produced a zero-sum ethnic struggle for political power.[51] This was a central feature of political decay in Nigeria's First Republic, as it has been throughout Uganda's experience. And it, too, tends to be aggravated in the context of formal political competition and mass political mobilization.[52] Second, with the whole process of class formation and consolidation at stake for the political class, politicians have been prone to manipulate ethnic attachments and fears as a means both for mobilizing electoral support and for diverting attention from their own corrupt accumulation and abuse of power.[53]

Finally, statism has been a major factor in the economic failures of democratic (and authoritarian) regimes. In part, this is because of the deflation of capacity that has accompanied the rapid inflation of bureaucratic employment and funding after independence.[54] In part, too, it is because of the heavy drag on economic development imposed by oversized, overowning, and overregulating states.[55] During the 1970s, public expenditures in Africa grew almost three times as fast as private consumption, and African states devoted about twice as high a percentage of their total expenditures to wages and salaries as did the nations of any other region (save Latin America, which they exceeded by half).[56] In Senegal, state administration accounts for almost half of all national wage employees and more than half of the national budget.[57] Such massive overhead costs have preempted much of the investment that was needed in physical and human capital. Overregulation took its toll by discouraging production (especially in agriculture, where producer prices were deliberately depressed as a means of extracting wealth from the peasantry) and overvaluing local currencies, which discouraged exports and induced a squandering of foreign exchange on artificially cheap consumer imports. The rapid growth of state-owned corporations crowded out private enterprise and further strained state finances, as these parastatals—with their overemployment and weak discipline—typically required steady subsidies to make up for continuous operating losses.[58] Added to this were the multiple costs of statist corruption: the massive draining of public resources into private accounts; the outflow of much of this capital to foreign banks; the diversion of entrepreneurial energies from productive activity; and the weakening of administrative competence.[59]

To say that the state has become the primary vehicle of dominant class formation in Africa is also to underscore the absence of an indigenous, productive bourgeoisie (beyond petty trade). The bourgeoisie that has developed in most African states has been bureaucratic or political, nonproductive, and even parasitic. This has not only had all of the developmental and political consequences we have just reviewed, it has also meant the absence of that class that pressed for the expansion of democratic rights and limitation of state power during the early development of democracy in the industrialized West.

The relationship between such a state-centered class structure and democratic instability and decay is further suggested by the cases of Botswana and Zimbabwe. In Botswana, the fact that the BDP leadership consists predominantly of owners of large cattle herds, who thus have a significant source of income outside of politics, may help to account for the relative tolerance, civility, and integrity of political life there.[60] Similarly in Zimbabwe, although many ruling party officials have accumulated wealth in office, much of the country's wealthy elite is firmly implanted in the private sector, which has more status in the eyes of the upwardly mobile. Sithole sees the continuing growth of a black middle class, independent of the state, as a positive factor in Zimbabwe's struggle for democracy. With recent economic reforms, it could become one in Nigeria as well.

Civil Society

Despite the lengthening shadow of the state over economic and social life in Africa, a rich and vibrant associational life has developed in many African countries independent of the state, and this pluralism in civil society has been one of the most significant forces for democracy. In Nigeria and Ghana in particular, it has repeatedly resisted and frustrated efforts to perpetuate authoritarian rule. The articulation and mobilization of opposition by intellectuals, chiefs, professionals, trade unions, and religious groups were instrumental in bringing down Kwame Nkrumah's dictatorship. Similar mobilization by organized (particularly urban) interest groups undermined Ignatius Acheampong's military regime in the mid-1970s, culminating in a massive nationwide strike in July 1977, organized by the Association of Recognized Professional Bodies. More recently the Bar Association has refused to sanction the extrajudicial procedures of Jerry Rawlings's public tribunals, and has led popular resistance to his assault on the judiciary. The bar played a similar role in opposing General Buhari's excesses in Nigeria after the 1983 coup. During both military interregnums in Nigeria, a whole host of organized interest groups—students, trade unions, journalists, and various business and professional associations—have spearheaded opposition to authoritarian measures and pressured for a return to democracy. Their efforts have been significantly buttressed by a vigorous press, the largest, most sophisticated, and pluralistic in black Africa.

In Senegal and Uganda, the increasing pluralism and autonomy of associational life have strengthened the democratic prospect. These trends were fostered by political liberalization, which opened up not just the party system, but also the trade union movement in Senegal, and—despite Obote's fraudulent election and authoritarian instincts—brought the return of opposition parties, newspapers, and interest groups to Uganda after the overthrow of Idi Amin's tyranny. This greater pluralism made possible the successful mobilization against Obote that has created a chance for genuine democracy in Uganda. Beyond the state's control over most of the media, considerable organizational pluralism exists in Zimbabwe, but it is somewhat shadowed by a corporatist streak in the goverment's approach to organized labor. The more rudimentary state of interest group development in Botswana may suggest an element of democratic fragility, and it is consistent with the paternalistic character of democracy there. Trade unions are closely regulated, and the press is largely controlled by or in sympathy with the government. However, there are signs that the independence and pluralism of these groups may be increasing in some respects.[61]

The Military

Surprisingly, given its central role in the political arena for much of the post-independence period, the structure and character of the military cannot be identified as a primary independent cause of democratic failure in Africa. As I have argued in the case of Nigeria, the military has intervened to overthrow democratic regimes only when they have lost legitimacy because of poor performance economically and politically. In this sense, most such coups have been "reconstitutive" in that the officers have acted "out of a sense of social duty . . . with limited goals, intending merely to purify a contaminated political system, rather than to rule indefinitely."[62] While it would be hard to characterize Idi Amin's coup in these terms, it fits the first coups in Nigeria and Ghana, and in many other African countries such as Sudan, Zaire, and Sierra Leone.

The problem is that once the military intervenes in politics, its role conception begins to change. It becomes politicized, as it sees itself as the guarantor of political stability and national integrity or acquires an irresistible taste for the fruits of power. Hence, with each coup, the threshold of military intervention is lowered and new coups become more likely. This was part of the cause of the Second Republic's downfall in Ghana in January 1972, when the military intervened "in advance of a popular demand for Busia's ouster, to advance its own narrow interests."[63] Moreover, as motives for intervention become more narrow and personalistic, military rule tends to become more corrupt and oppressive, leaving (as in Ghana and Uganda) a legacy of structural decay from which it may take many years to recover.

In other words, once the genie of military politicization is unloosed, it is very hard to put it back in the bottle. As Kokole and Mazrui argue, this is one of the primary challenges that confronts the future of democracy in Uganda: how to reassert civilian control over the military. Their proposals, such as giving the military some civilian role in development, may be controversial, but no one will dispute that the task is urgent and that it cannot be accomplished without the construction of strong political institutions that can both generate countervailing power to the military and preclude the political deterioration that invites military attention.

The External Environment

Finally, our cases call attention to the possible role of the regional and international environment in encouraging, or more frequently undermining, democracy. We have seen that Senghor's sensitivity to Senegal's image abroad moderated his authoritarian moves and later added to pressure for a democratic opening. Senegal's pursuit of full membership in the (democratic) International Socialist Movement and its need to appeal to Western aid donors have also exerted pressure for democratic evolution. There is likewise a strong compatibility, and probably some causal association, between the persistence of liberal democracy in Botswana and its heavy reliance on Western investment, aid, and expertise. In addition to its aforementioned dependence on expatriate technical and professional personnnel, Botswana is the world's fourth largest recipient (per capita) of official development assistance and the largest in Sub-Saharan Africa, even though it is also one of Africa's wealthiest countries.[64]

Of course, economic dependence can have negative consequences for democracy too. The tremendous sense of economic weakness and vulnerability at independence fed the drive for concentration of power. Dependence on one or a few primary commodities (e.g., peanuts in Senegal, cocoa in Ghana, oil in Nigeria) has been a key element of the economic instability that has weakened democracy. When massive foreign assistance is forthcoming for an authoritarian regime—as it was for the Muslim Idi Amin from the Arab oil states (among others)—it can prop up a dictatorship that might otherwise crumble.

By far the most serious contemporary external danger to democracy is the military insecurity of escalating regional conflict, especially in Southern Africa. While democracy in Zimbabwe benefited in its first few years from relatively benign treatment by its neighbors and superpowers, this has begun to change. Recently, Zimbabwe has been buffeted by increasing commando raids from South Africa, a withdrawal of economic assistance by the Reagan administration, and an escalating war in Mozambique, which increasingly involves Zimbabwean forces. To the extent these rising pressures force Zimbabwe onto a war footing, they could also, Sithole suggests, push it further in an authoritarian direction. Even more ominously, Botswana, which had no military in its first decade of independence, has had to create and build up one in response to the violent conflict that has spilled over into its territory from first Rhodesia and now South Africa. As the military and police increase their fighting capacity to protect Botswana's sovereignty against aggression, they also increase their political influence. The envelopment of Botswana in a regional war could so threaten the country's integrity and strain its politics as to invite the suppression of basic freedoms or even a military coup.

• SEEDS OF HOPE •

The collective picture presented by the six case studies in this book is, in many respects, a discouraging one. These countries, like their African neighbors, were poorly prepared for democratic self-government by their colonial rulers. In general, they have been burdened with heavy stuctural handicaps and poorly served by their political leaders and elites. In some cases, the legacies of misrule, both democratic and authoritarian, are so colossal one wonders how they will ever be surmounted.

Yet, if the situation is a discouraging one, it is not without real hope. For one thing, authoritarian regimes have been no more (and often less) effective than democratic ones, and the people of Nigeria, Ghana, and Uganda have explicitly and repeatedly rejected authoritarianism as a premise of government. Even when dictatorship has lingered with a heavy hand for long periods of time, as in Sudan, opposition movements have managed to survive and, in many cases, the democratic spirit has strengthened.[65] If democracy has failed to become institutionalized in Africa, so has authoritarianism. In this sense, the playing field is still even.

Second, as state structures and formal political institutions have decayed, civil society has witnessed a promising and, in some countries, prodigious efflorescence of nonformal participation.[66] Where repression has not been so thorough and brutal as to eliminate all space for independent organization, African peoples have joined together in a breathtaking variety of voluntary associations. These have taken the form of both ascriptive associations (e.g., ethnic and local improvement associations) and functional interest groups (professional, economic, youth, student, women, and so on). As they proliferate and mature, such groups spin a web of social pluralism that makes the consolidation of authoritarian domination increasingly difficult. Although they are not explicitly political, they constitute a significant and often potent constituency for responsive and accountable government. While they are not inevitably democratic in their purposes or organization, quite often they are, providing "small-scale settings for meaningful political participation," constitutional means for the transfer and rotation of power, consultative processes of decision-making, and "innovative means of information collection and communication."[67] In short, the expansion of nonformal participation in autonomous, voluntary associations has become a major means for the limitation of state power and the creation from below of an informed, efficacious, vigilant citizenry. Where it has progressed the furthest, in Ghana and Nigeria, it has become (in different and distinctive ways) the cutting edge of the effort to build a viable democratic order.

Related to the above has been the emergence of new, productive economic activity and a more authentic and autonomous bourgeoisie in the informal economy. This has several hopeful implications for democracy. Economically, it embodies a real expansion of entrepreneurship and production, and the resurgence of the profit motive and individual initiative outside the stifling control of an overregulating state. Socially, it has opened a new path of class formation outside the state[68] and, more generally, new and wider avenues of upward social mobility for the disadvantaged. Politically, the growth of nonformal modes of economic exchange and production joins with the growth of voluntary associations to provide "alternative loci of power, authority, and legitimacy," hastening the evolution away from authoritarianism and statism toward a more meaningful democracy.[69] Of course, the growth of the black market has negative implications as well. In particular, as Kokole and Mazrui note, its illicit nature undermines respect for the law. The need to accommodate these new, spontaneous forms of production and exchange within the law is one compelling reason why the thicket of state controls must be heavily pruned.

In fact, the increasing movement away from statist economic policies and structures is among the most significant boosts to the democratic prospect in Africa. Along with many other African countries, Ghana, Nigeria, Senegal, and Uganda have all been moving in recent years to reduce controls over trade, increase agricultural producer prices, devalue currencies to realistic exchange rates, and reduce or limit the number of public employees and corporations. Although these structural adjustment programs have typically been adopted under heavy pressure from the IMF and the international banking community, they also reflect the growing conviction of African leaders and policy-makers that statism must be rolled back and market mechanisms and incentives expanded if their economies are ever to be revived. Should these policies bear fruit, as they have begun to do in Ghana and Nigeria, they will not only rekindle economic growth, but will loosen the connection between state control and class formation. Both of these trends would bode well for democracy.

Policy Directions

The continuation and deepening of economic liberalization is an important element in the construction of a viable democratic order in Africa. But, as Coulon notes, the new momentum toward limiting the state must not only foster an independent entrepreneurial class, it must also incorporate the bulk of the population—especially the long-neglected rural population—in the process of economic development and growth. This means redirecting infrastructural investment and services to the countryside (which will also slow the swelling of overburdened cities). It also means an emphasis on peasant producers and, hence, smaller-scale and intermediate technology in national development plans and international aid projects. Unless the people are incorporated in the development process, their alienation from the state will intensify and the possibility of any kind of stable authority will diminish.

Decentralization is needed in political life as well. It is not coincidental that the country in our study with the most elaborate provisions for local government, Botswana, has also been the most democratic and the least victimized by ethnic political conflict. Political autonomy and policy participation for each locality and ethnic group has been crucial to the regime's legitimacy. In fact, Holm argues for giving more policy independence to the local councils. It appears that the reconstruction of democracy in Nigeria will put new and unprecedented emphasis on local government, deepening a federal system that, as we noted, has made great strides in managing and diffusing ethnic conflict.

But, elsewhere among our cases, and in Africa more generally, the centralization of power is a major obstacle to democracy. In Senegal, where the French Jacobin tradition has left the regions void of any power and autonomy, it has fed the specific alienation of the Casamance region, where separatist violence has been increasing, and the general detachment of society from the state (as in Ghana). Both these problems argue strongly for giving local communities control over their own affairs through their own elected assemblies and administrations. In Zimbabwe, where local government is elected but district administrators and provincial governors are appointed from the center, Sithole appeals for more local autonomy and control. Popular election of governors would enable minority groups like the Ndebele to control their own provincial government. Direct election of mayors, as well as governors, could enhance the perceived power, status, and attractiveness of these positions and, so, further relieve "the present fixation with politics at the national level."[70]

Institutional means are also needed for checking and balancing executive power. This requires more power and autonomy for each of the other two branches of government, the legislature and the judiciary. Given the tendency for presidential authority to run rampant over legislatures and judiciaries, it may also recommend a closer look at the parliamentary form of government as a possible means for limiting the concentration of power and also compelling the formation of broader political coalitions.[71] However, these traditional means for distributing power are unlikely to be sufficient in Africa, where the premium on power is so great and the constraints on powerholders are so weak. Hence, new types of institutional arrangements may be necessary to ensure public accountability and to insulate crucial procedural institutions (e.g., electoral administration and the judiciary) from partisan abuse. One possible arrangement, a nonpartisan national oversight body, is outlined in my chapter on Nigeria. While this may not be the answer for all countries, it highlights the need for African countries to innovate in designing political institutions that fit their special circumstances and rich cultural traditions.

Such institutional innovation is equally necessary for the management of ethnic conflict. In addition to federalism and administrative decentralization, electoral laws can be used to encourage cross- and transethnic forms of political mobilization. Nigeria's banning of ethnic parties and symbols, plus its requirements for ethnic breadth in party organization, represent a useful model. Its new innovation of a mandatory two-party system may go even further, so long as the system does not, in practice, decompose on north-south lines, but at the price of some loss of political pluralism. Milton Obote's proposal for members of parliament to represent several constituencies in different parts of the country is another approach through constitutional engineering, which, Kokole and Mazrui suggest, might also foster the more gradual erosion of ethnic divisions through cross-ethnic marriages. A third model, with potentially wide applicability in Africa, is the West German one. It retains the local representation and control provided by the territorial district method of election, but provides for half of the parliamentary seats to be filled by proportional representation from national party lists. This would make the legislature more of a national institution and further pressure parties to craft transethnic appeals.

Finally, without exhausting the list of possible and useful changes, one may note the need for civic education to develop a more tolerant political culture, a deeper commitment to and understanding of democratic institutions, and a more mutually trustful political climate. In addition to the schools, such an effort at political socialization could make use of and reinforce the growing pluralism of associational life.

This brief review has focused intentionally on the policies of the African countries themselves. If nothing else, the colonial experience surely urges caution in exporting particular constitutional forms. This is emphatically not to say that democracy cannot work in Africa. Democracy is not the unique property of the West, and African history encompasses a wealth of democratic traditions and forms. But, if democracy is to work in Africa, it must respond innovatively to each country's distinctive cultural traditions, political problems, and social forces.

Neither do we mean to suggest that the established democracies have no role to play in the development of democracy in Africa. There is an urgent need for economic assistance to help African countries rebuild their infrastructures, improve their physical quality of life, invigorate their private sectors, and increase their technical and managerial capacities. Even though prosperity is not a prerequisite for democracy, sustained and broad-based development will enchance the democratic prospect. In addition, external assistance (both private and official) can help to foster the economic and social pluralism that has become perhaps the most powerful source of democratic energy, initiative, and pressure in Africa. By enhancing the organizational resources and human capabilities of these multifold associations, the West can assist the search for democracy in Africa at the grassroots without imposing political formulas or demands. External assistance (even through the simple medium of advertising income) may also enable struggling publications to establish themselves financially and, thus, embellish the generally limited pluralism of the African press.

These and other forms of assistance can help to promote democracy in Africa. So can diplomatic initiatives and pressures to bring a democratic solution to the conflict in South Africa, before a widening civil and regional war engulfs the democratic aspirations and potential of its neighbors. But the future of democracy in Africa lies primarily in the hands of Africans themselves. And, increasingly, it will be shaped not just by the elite, but by the people themselves. Unheralded and even unnoticed as it has been to date, the growth of democratic organization and participation at the popular level may offer the greatest hope for the democratic prospect in Africa.

• NOTES •

1. For an analysis of the patterns of this postindependence political change, see, in particular, Ruth Berins Collier, *Regimes in Tropical Africa: Changing Forms of Supremacy, 1945–75* (Berkeley: University of California Press, 1982), chap. 4.

2. For recent reviews of the status of democracy in Africa and the challenges to it, see Richard L. Sklar, "Democracy in Africa," Presidential Address to the Twenty-fifth Annual Meeting of the African Studies Association, 5 November, 1982, *African Studies Review* 26 (September–

December 1983); Robert H. Jackson and Carl G. Rosberg, "Democracy in Tropical Africa: Democracy Versus Autocracy in African Politics," *Journal of International Affairs* 38, no. 2 (Winter 1985); and Larry Diamond, "Sub-Saharan Africa," in Robert Wesson, ed., *Democracy: A Worldwide Survey* (New York: Praeger, 1987).

3. Christian Coulon, "Senegal: The Development and Fragility of Semi-Democracy," in this volume, p. 149.

4. Naomi Chazan, "Ghana: Problems of Governance and the Emergence of Civil Society," in this volume, p. 98.

5. Coulon, "Senegal," p. 152.

6. Masipula Sithole, "Zimbabwe: In Search of a Stable Democracy," in this volume, p. 240.

7. Collier, *Regimes in Tropical Africa*, p. 110.

8. Ali Mazrui, "Political Engineering in Africa," *International Social Science Journal* 25, no. 2 (1983): p. 293.

9. Ali Mazrui, "Francophone Nations and English-Speaking States: Imperial Ethnicity and African Political Formations," in Donald Rothchild and Victor A. Olorunsola, *State Versus Ethnic Claims: African Policy Dilemmas* (Boulder, Colo.: Westview Press, 1983).

10. Omari Kokole and Ali Mazrui, "Uganda," p. 00.

11. Robert H. Jackson and Carl G. Rosberg, "Democracy in Tropical Africa: Democracy Versus Autocracy in African Politics," *Journal of International Affairs* 38, no. 2 (Winter 1985): p. 296.

12. Chazan, "Ghana," p. 122.

13. Robert H. Jackson and Carl G. Rosberg, *Personal Rule in Black Africa: Prince, Autocrat, Prophet, Tyrant* (Berkeley: University of California Press, 1982), p. 22.

14. L. H. Gann and Peter Duignan, *Burden of Empire: An Appraisal of Western Colonialism in Africa South of the Sahara* (Stanford: Hoover Institution Press, 1967), p. 331.

15. Michael Crowder, "Whose Dream Was It Anyway? Twenty-Five Years of African Independence," *African Affairs* 86, no. 342 (January 1987): pp. 14–15.

16. Ibid., p. 15.

17. Ibid., pp. 11–13.

18. Peter Duignan, "Introduction," in Peter Duignan and Robert H. Jackson, eds., *Politics and Government in African States, 1960–85* (London: Croom Helm, and Stanford: Hoover Institution, 1986), pp. 18–19.

19. Gann and Guignan, *Burden of Empire*, pp. 253–272.

20. Robert H. Bates, *Markets and States in Tropical Africa* (Berkeley: University of California Press, 1981), pp. 12–13.

21. Richard L. Sklar, "The Nature of Class Domination in Africa," *Journal of Modern African Studies* 17, no. 4 (1979): p. 536.

22. Robert H. Jackson, "Conclusion," in Duignan and Jackson, *Politics and Government in African States*, p. 411.

23. Duignan, "Introduction," p. 11.

24. Jackson, "Conclusion," p. 411.

25. Gann and Duignan, *Burden of Empire*, p. 320.

26. Ibid., p. 321.

27. Coulon, "Senegal," p. 146.

28. Mazrui, "Francophone Nations and English-Speaking States."

29. Ibid., p. 28.

30. Sithole, "Zimbabwe," p. 248.

31. Gann and Duignan, *Burden of Empire*, p. 332.

32. Donald L. Horowitz, *Ethnic Groups in Conflict*, (Berkeley: University of California Press, 1985), p. 39.

33. Sithole, "Zimbabwe," p. 238.

34. Coulon, "Senegal," p. 164.

35. Sithole, "Zimbabwe," p. 243.

36. Crowder, "Whose Dream Was It Anyway?" p. 20.

37. Sithole, "Zimbabwe," p. 252.

38. Chazan, "Ghana," p. 121.

39. Coulon, "Senegal," p. 159.

40. A. H. M. Kirk-Greene, "West Africa: Nigeria and Ghana," in Duignan and Jackson, *Politics and Government in African States*, p. 30.

41. John D. Holm, "Botswana: A Paternalistic Democracy," in this volume, p. 197.

42. Chazan, "Ghana," p. 130.

43. Ibid.

44. Coulon, "Senegal," p. 156.

45. Naomi Chazan, "The New Politics of Participation in Tropical Africa," *Comparative Politics* 14, no. 2 (January 1982).

46. Duignan, "Introduction," p. 19; Jackson, "Conclusion," pp. 413–414; David Abernethy, "Bureaucratic Growth and Economic Decline in Sub-Saharan Africa," (Paper presented to the Twenty-Sixth Annual Meeting of the African Studies Association, Boston: December 1983).

47. Chazan, "Ghana," p. 129.

48. John Waterbury, "Endemic and Planned Corruption in a Monarchical Regime," *World Politics* 25, no. 4 (1973): p. 538. See also, for example, Victor T. Le Vine, *Political Corruption: The Ghana Case* (Stanford: Hoover Institution Press, 1975), pp. 17–18; Morris Sfetzel, "Political Graft and the Spoils System in Zambia—the State as a Resource in Itself," *Review of African Political Economy* 24 (May–August 1982); and, for a synthesis of the evidence and more comprehensive analysis, Larry Diamond, "The Political Economy of Corruption in Nigeria," (Paper presented to the Twenty-Seventh Annual Meeting of the African Studies Association, Los Angeles: 1984).

49. Richard Joseph, "Class, State and Prebendal Politics in Nigeria," *Journal of Commonwealth and Comparative Politics* 21, no. 3 (1983). See also in the same journal issue, Nelson Kasfir, "Introduction: Relating State to Class in Africa," and Thomas Callaghy, "External Actors and the Relative Autonomy of the Political Aristocracy in Zaire." This journal issue has also been published under the title *State and Class in Africa*, Nelson Kasfir, ed. (London: Frank Cass, 1983.)

50. Joseph, "Class, State and Prebendal Politics," p. 33; and Donal O'Brien, *Saints and Politicians* (Cambridge: Cambridge University Press, 1975).

51. On this point, see for example, Robert Jackson, "Conclusion," p. 414.

52. Robert Melson and Howard Wolpe, "Modernization and the Politics of Communalism: A Theoretical Perspectivde," in Melson and Wolpe, *Nigeria: Modernization and the Politics of Communalism* (East Lansing: Michigan State University Press, 1971), pp. 19–21; and Larry Diamond, "Class, Ethnicity and the Democratic State: Nigeria, 1950–66," *Comparative Studies in Society and History* 25, no. 3 (1983): pp. 486–489.

53. Richard L. Sklar, "Political Science and National Integration—A Radical Approach," *Journal of Modern African Studies* 5, no. 1 (1967): p. 6.

54. Jackson, "Conclusion," p. 410.

55. Duignan, "Introduction," p. 18.

56. David Abernethy, "Bureaucratic Growth and Economic Decline in Sub-Saharan Africa," pp. 8, 14.

57. Coulon, "Senegal," p. 162.

58. Jackson, "Conclusion," p. 413. On parastatal expansion, see Abernethy, "Bureaucratic Growth and Economic Decline," pp. 12–13.

59. Diamond, "The Political Economy of Corruption," pp. 29–34.

60. However, the greatly disproportionate share of the country's wealth commanded by this small cattle-owning elite, along with the disproportionate benefits they derive from government programs, indicate a degree of inequality that could some day become a political problem. See L. H. Gann and Peter Duignan, "Namibia, Botswana, Lesotho and Swaziland," in Duignan and Jackson, *Politics and Government in African States*, p. 365.

61. U. S. Department of State, *Country Reports on Human Rights Practices for 1986* (Washington, D. C.: U. S. Government Printing Office, 1987), p. 20.

62. Donald L. Horowitz, *Coup Theories and Officers' Motives: Sri Lanka in Comparative Perspective* (Princeton: Princeton University Press 1980), p. 201.

63. Chazan, "Ghana," p. 106.

64. World Bank, *World Development Report 1986* (New York: Oxford University Press, 1986), p. 220.

65. Colin Legum, "Democracy in Africa: Hopes and Trends," in Dov Ronen, ed., *Democracy and Pluralism in Africa* (Boulder, Colo.: Lynne Rienner Publishers, Inc., 1986), pp. 186–187.

66. On this and subsequent points in this paragraph, the reader is again referred to Naomi

Chazan's seminal analysis, "The New Politics of Participation in Tropical Africa."

67. Ibid., pp. 174–176.

68. On this development and its origins and ambiguities, see, in particular, Nelson Kasfir, "State, Magendo and Class Formation in Uganda," *The Journal of Commonwealth and Comparative Politics* 23, no. 3 (1983).

69. Chazan, "Ghana," p. 121.

70. Sithole, "Zimbabwe," p. 253.

71. Juan Linz, *Democracy: Presidential or Parliamentary. Does It Make a Difference?* (Paper presented to the Workshop on "Political Parties in the Southern Cone," Wilson Center, Washington, D. C.: 1984). In cases like Nigeria, however, where presidentialism is part of an institutional strategy for crosscutting ethnic divisions, the case for a presidential system would be stronger.

• CHAPTER TWO •

Nigeria: Pluralism, Statism, and the Struggle for Democracy

LARRY DIAMOND

The Nigerian experience with democracy has been paradoxical and even schizophrenic. Twice the country has undertaken to govern itself under liberal democratic constitutions, following carefully staged transitions. Both these efforts were ruined by antidemocratic behavior and then ended by popular military coups. And yet, Nigeria has never been content with authoritarian rule, and no military regime that has not committed itself to a transition to democracy has been able to survive. Through their country's turbulent quarter-century of independence—which has encompassed eight governments, five successful military coups, a civil war, and a dizzying economic boom followed by a crushing depression—Nigerians have maintained a profound commitment to personal freedom and political participation. Amidst the continual drama of political crisis and economic disarray has been the quiet but steady growth of the social infrastructure of democracy—a free press, a rapidly expanding educational system, a sophisticated legal system, and a diverse array of autonomous social, cultural, and economic organizations. Moreover, although the ethnic complexity of the country has generated intense and sometimes catastrophic political conflict, it also represents an irrepressible social pluralism that cannot be effectively managed by authoritarian means. But over these promising currents of pluralism falls the growing shadow of a swelling state, feeding political corruption and instability. In the struggle between pluralism and statism the search for a viable system of democratic government continues.

• HISTORICAL REVIEW •

Developments Before Independence

Nigeria has an enormous diversity of ethnic groups, as indicated by the presence of some 248 distinct languages.[1] Many of these linguistic groups are tiny and politically insignificant. But three comprise collectively two-thirds of the population: the Hausa-Fulani (two peoples who are typically grouped together

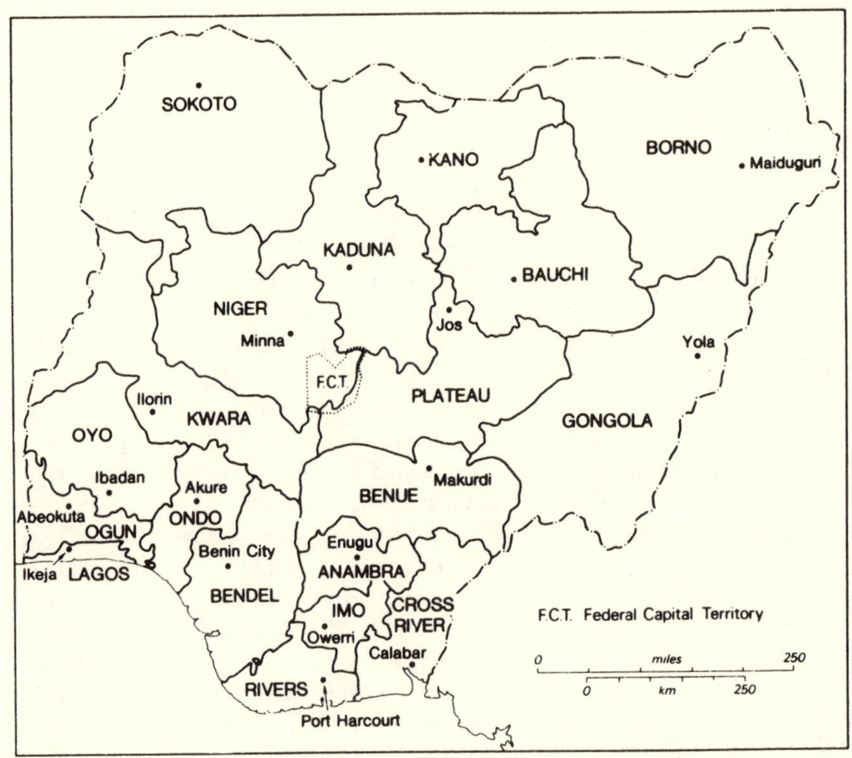
SOKOTO
KANO
BORNO
Maiduguri
KADUNA
BAUCHI
NIGER
Minna
Jos
Yola
F.C.T.
PLATEAU
Ilorin
KWARA
GONGOLA
OYO
Ibadan
Akure
Makurdi
Abeokuta
BENUE
OGUN
ONDO
Enugu
Benin City
ANAMBRA
Ikeja
LAGOS
BENDEL
IMO
CROSS RIVER
Owerri
Calabar
RIVERS
Port Harcourt
F.C.T. Federal Capital Territory
0 miles 250
0 km 250

NIGERIA

because of their substantial cultural and political integration), the Yoruba, and the Igbo (see Table 2.1). In this respect, Nigeria has what Horowitz would term a relatively "centralized" ethnic structure, which presents a greater challenge to ethnic harmony.[2]

Although there were significant democratic traditions among the more decentralized and acephalous of Nigeria's ethnic groups (such as the Igbo and Tiv), and mechanisms for limiting power in the constitutional monarchies of the Yoruba, the history of democratic government in Nigeria must begin with the history of the nation itself, which was the creation of British colonial rule. For half a century—from the time that separate protectorates were declared for Northern and Southern Nigeria in 1900 to the Constitutional Conference of 1950—Nigeria was ruled in essentially authoritarian fashion by the colonial power. But that fashion was not uniform across the country. Even after the formal amalgamation of the two protectorates in 1914, the British continued to rule Nigeria, in effect, as two countries. In the North, a native authority system was constructed to rule indirectly through the centralized and steeply hierarchical structures of traditional authority in the Muslim emirates. In the South, where power was more dispersed and there was more accountability of rulers to ruled, indirect rule worked poorly and even broke down in places. At the same time, Western (European) education and religion were permitted to spread rapidly in the South but heavily restricted in the Muslim North, creating enormous disparities in economic and technological development. In addition, political

Table 2.1 Distributions of Nigerian Ethnic Groups, 1952–1953 and 1963

Group		Percent of Population[a] 1952–1953	1963
Hausa	18.2	28.1	29.5
Fulani	9.9		
Kanuri		4.2	4.1
Tiv		2.5	2.5
Nupe		1.1	1.2
Yoruba		16.6	20.3
Edo		1.5	1.7
Igbo		17.9	16.6
Ibibio-Efik		2.7	3.6
Ijaw		1.1	2.0
Total: Hausa-Fulani, Yoruba, and Igbo		62.6	66.4

Source: Etienne Van de Walle, "Who's Who and Where in Nigeria," *Africa Report* 15, no. 1 (1970).
[a] The census has been a subject of continuing scholarly debate and political conflict in Nigeria for three decades, and hence no set of figures can be accepted as precise. Because the 1963 census was ensnarled in intense controversy, the 1952–1953 figures, compiled by the more neutral colonial administration in a less politically charged atmosphere, may represent more accurately the demographic balance of peoples.

participation was permitted earlier in the South. From 1923 until 1947, only Southern Nigerians were allowed to elect members of the Legislative Council (advisory to the British governor).[3]

The separate character of development in Nigeria, and the political tensions to which it gave rise, were rooted in the regional structure created by the British. In 1939, Nigeria was divided into four administrative units: the colony of Lagos, and the Western, Eastern, and Northern Provinces. The power of these provinces grew, and in 1951 they were designated "regions," becoming constituent units in a quasi-federal system. The boundaries of these regions coincided with and reified the primary ethnic division in the country: the Igbo were the dominant group in the East, the Yoruba in the West, and the Hausa-Fulani in the North. But each region also contained significant minorities of other ethnic groups that feared and resented the domination of these "big tribes." Despite the intense lobbying for separate states by ethnic minority groups throughout the decade, and the profound concerns of Southerners about a system in which one region, the North, was more populous than all the others combined, the British were unalterably committed to this regional structure, and "after 1948 every effort was made to encourage 'regional thinking.'"[4]

The decisive first step toward self-rule and popular participation came in 1948, with several reforms in response to rising nationalist agitation. Africani-

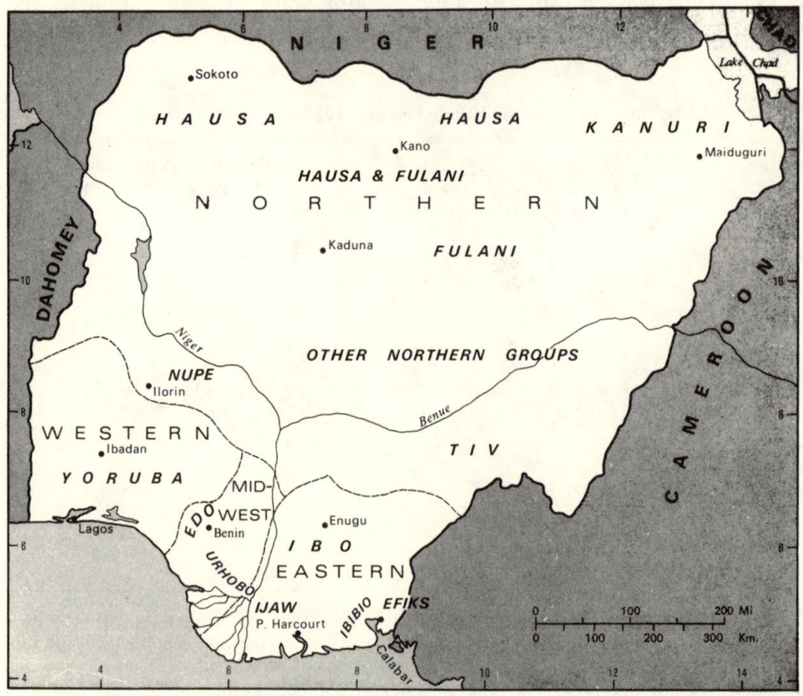

Figure 2.1 Nigeria: Ethnic Groups and Four Regions
From Crawford Young, *The Politics of Pluralism,* University of Wisconsin Press.

zation of the senior civil service was accelerated. The native authority system was democratized, and scrapped altogether in the East, in favor of a hierarchy of elected councils. Primary and secondary education were rapidly expanded and colonial efforts were extended to higher education.[5] Most important, a process of constitutional revision was launched that entailed extensive and unprecedented popular participation.

Out of this two-year process came the 1951 constitution, which launched the first period of full-scale electoral politics in Nigeria.[6] This provided for regional assemblies elected indirectly through a system of electoral colleges and a central legislature (half from the North) elected by the regional assemblies. No provision was yet made at either level for elected executives.[7]

The 1951 constitution made the regions the more important locus of political life. Through the end of colonial rule and the life of the First Republic, the growing regional emphasis was to tilt the national political balance decisively in favor of conservative forces, as the British had no doubt intended. Growing regional autonomy protected the position of the aristocratic Northern ruling class from the challenge and infiltration of better educated and more cosmopolitan Southern elites and from any interference by the central government.[8] Moreover, the Northern Region's absolute population majority in the country made it likely that its dominant class would also be the dominant political force in Nigeria. But inherent in this strange federal structure was an explosive contradiction between the political power of the North and the socioeconomic power of the South, which generated deep insecurity and recurrent conflict.[9]

The regional system made control of regional government the *sine qua non* for both traditional and rising elements of the emergent political class.[10] This put an enormous premium on the 1951 regional elections. Given the coincidence of regional with ethnic group boundaries, it was virtually inevitable that these first elections would see the organization of political parties along ethnic and regional lines. Hence, although the leading nationalist organization, the National Council of Nigeria and the Cameroons (NCNC), had sought with some success to reach out beyond its Igbo core to construct a multiethnic, national base, it was able to win only the election in the Eastern Region. In the West and North, power was captured by openly regionalist political parties formed by ethnic elites for the express purpose of winning regional power against the challenge of the Igbo-led and better organized NCNC.[11] In the West, the formation of the Yoruba-dominated Action Group (AG) followed years of intense competition between Yoruba and Igbo elites.[12] In the North, the transformation of the Northern Peoples' Congress (NPC) from a sagging cultural organization into a modern political party was in defense of both class and ethnic interests.[13]

The aggressive mobilization of Southern parties and groups stirred a "political awakening" among a new generation of Northern elites whose exposure to Western education had bred reformist inclinations and who had become alarmed to discover their region's massive and pervasive disadvantage in every aspect of modernization.[14] The social dominance of the traditional ruling class of the Northern emirates (the *sarakuna*) was threatened by political competition not only from militant and culturally alien Southerners, determined to dismantle the "feudalistic" structures of the emirates, but also from radical young Northern commoners (*talakawa*) similarly pledged to sweeping reform. Stunned by victories of the radical party, the Northern Elements Progressive Union (NEPU), in the early stages of the 1951 Northern elections, the "awakened" Northern elites revitalized the NPC just in time to win a sweeping victory in the final stage of voting.[15]

The 1951 victories of the NPC, the AG, and the NCNC in their home regions established a close identity between region, party, and ethnicity that was to heighten over the course of the 1950s. The constitution of 1954 not only created a genuinely federal system, but gave enormous autonomy and control over resources to each of the three regions. As the regions became the primary centers of power and wealth in Nigeria, the struggle between their ruling parties for socioeconomic resources came to dominate Nigerian politics. This struggle was manifested in repeated political conflicts over such issues as the timing of self-government, revenue allocation, and the NPC's effort to purge southerners from the Northern bureaucracy and economy. But most of all, it was evinced in electoral competition.

Political competition during colonial rule peaked in the federal elections of 1959. By then, Nigeria had conducted three regional elections in the East, two each in the North and West, and one in the federation as a whole. The subsequent regional elections had tightened the grip of the ruling parties, but in the 1954 federal elections, the NCNC won not only in the East, but also (narrowly) in the West, joining the NPC in a coalition of expedience at the center. When the office of federal prime minister was created in 1957, NPC President Sir Ahmadu Bello chose (revealingly) to remain the premier of the North, and the party's vice-president, Abubakar Tafawa Balewa, became prime minister. He then constructed a coalition cabinet embracing all three major parties. But this grand coalition would last only until the 1959 elections, which would produce the first fully elected national government and the one that would lead the country to independence the following year.

As with previous campaigns of the decade, the 1959 campaign was characterized by blatant appeals to ethnic prejudice and vituperative rhetoric, which completely drowned out the substance of party programs and proposals. Also, violence and repression marred the democratic character of the campaign. Repression was most prevalent in the North, where the NPC regularly used its control of traditional systems of justice and administration to obstruct, harass, and punish opposition candidates and their supporters. This repression reached new levels in 1959. Perhaps because electoral outcomes were not so much secured through institutional means of repression in the South, the campaigns were much more violent there. From the inception of electoral competition in 1951, parties fielded bands of thugs to disrupt, intimidate,. and attack the opposition, and injuries in the hundreds were not uncommon. In the high stakes of the 1959 election, such violence spread to the North as well, frequently victimizing Southern and NEPU campaigners.[16]

Despite the significant antidemocratic currents in the 1959 election, the "steel frame" of colonial administration maintained some semblance of political order and electoral integrity, and the keen anticipation of independence produced a postelection spirit of accommodation. Although battered by the extraordinary bitterness of the campaign, the tacit preelection alliance between the NPC and the NCNC matured into a coalition government led by the former, which was only a few seats short of an absolute majority in Parliament. The alliance was facilitated not only by the NCNC's desire to bridge the North-South divide on the eve of independence, but also by both parties' resentment of the AG's aggressive efforts to mobilize ethnic minority groups in their regions.

The First Republic

Nigeria thus achieved independence on 1 October 1960 with a functioning parliamentary system. Legislative power was vested in an elected Parliament, especially in the powerful lower chamber, the House of Representatives, which was responsible for the laws and finances of the federation. Executive power was vested in a cabinet, headed by a prime minister, who was to be appointed by the governor-general (and, after 1 October 1963, when Nigeria became a republic, by the president) upon demonstrating majority support in the House. Judicial power was vested in an independent court system, including a Federal Supreme Court with power to decide cases involving the constitutions and laws of the federation and the regions.[17]

Constitutionally, the system was democratic. Power was distributed between three branches of government. Regular parliamentary elections were required at least every five years. The primary restriction on adult suffrage and eligibility for elective office was in the North, where these political rights were restricted to males. Otherwise, political and civil liberties were formally guaranteed in the constitution's detailed chapter on fundamental rights.

There were also other democratic features of the political landscape. A number of political parties competed for power. Their contestation was increasingly flawed, but still it existed. And although plagued by zealous partisanship, inexperience, irresponsibility, and economic and political pressure from the parties and governments that owned most of the newspapers,[18] the Nigerian press was a significant source of political pluralism and critical inquiry. In fact, some outside observers saw it as "the most potent institution supporting democratic freedom in Nigeria."[19]

In other dimensions, however, Nigeria fell much wider of the democratic mark. Loopholes in the constitution facilitated abuse. Each provision on human rights excepted laws that were "reasonably justifiable in a democratic society" in the interest of national defense, public order, etc. These exceptions could be widened much further during a state of emergency, which could be declared by a simple majority vote of each house of Parliament. In addition, the constitution enabled Parliament (by a two-thirds vote of each house) to take over the law-making functions of a regional government. In a system where parliamentary opposition was regionally based, this created enormous potential for intimidation.

More troubling was the actual performance of political actors. In all three regions, regional powers were used increasingly to harass and repress political opposition. In the North, "the freedoms normally regarded as essential if a two-party system is to work simply [did] not exist."[20] Genuine political competition was becoming constricted to the federal arena, as one-party states emerged in each region. In the regional elections of 1960 and 1961, each ruling party significantly consolidated its dominance, leaving the opposition shattered and demoralized.

Beyond escalating the insecurity in the federal system, the regional elections exposed again the shallow commitment of political elites to democratic norms of tolerance and fair play. These antidemocratic currents make it difficult to classify Nigeria at independence as a democracy. It was a quasi-democracy struggling to establish fully democratic government.

The assault on the edifice of democracy continued relentlessly over the five and a quarter years of the First Republic. During these years, the political system was buffeted by a succession of five major crises that heightened ethnic and regional polarization, intensified political violence and intolerance, and heavily eroded the popular legitimacy of the regime.

The first crisis began as an internal conflict within the ruling party of the Western Region, pitting the AG national leader, Chief Obafemi Awolowo, who resigned as premier in 1959 to lead the party's federal campaign, against his successor as premier, Chief S. L. Akintola. The conflict was partially personal and factional, but also heavily ideological. Long committed to a moderate socialist program, Chief Awolowo moved, after the AG's sweeping 1959 defeat, to a much more radical stance, vowing to replace the regional system with a structure of multiple states and to forge a political alliance against the NPC. A transformation of the regional system threatened not only to unravel the social and political dominance of the Northern ruling class, but also to weaken the political classes of the Eastern and Western Regions, since smaller regions would mean smaller bases of patronage for the ruling parties and very likely different ruling parties in some of the new regions. Regionalism thus coincided with the conservatism of the Akintola faction while Awolowo's antiregionalism was the logical spearhead of his radical challenge to the status quo.[21]

In a federal system with only three regions, no serious political conflict could long remain contained within a single region. When the Awolowo faction succeeded in deposing Chief Akintola as premier, the NPC/NCNC Federal Coalition took action. Seizing upon internal disorder in the Western Region House, it declared an emergency and prevented the Awolowo faction from taking power. After six months of heavily biased emergency rule, Chief Akintola was reinstated as premier at the helm of a new party. By the time the full effects of federal emergency rule had been felt, a fourth region (the Mid-Western) had been created out of the Western Region, Chief Awolowo and his close associates had been convicted of treason and sentenced to prison, and the AG had been destroyed as a national political force. The crisis not only alienated a large segment of Nigerian youth and intelligentsia who had been attracted to Awolowo's radical egalitarian appeals, but it also left the Yoruba feeling victimized as a people.[22]

The second crisis partially overlapped the first. By 1962, Nigerians were being mobilized intensively for the national census. With the distribution of power and resources between the regions hanging on its outcome, the census became the object of heated political competition. Controversy flared when the initial results revealed much larger population increases in the South—sufficient to end the North's population majority—and demographic tests showed some of the Eastern Region's figures to have been "grossly inflated." When the North then claimed to have discovered eight million people more in a "verification check" (thus preserving its population majority), the ensuing crisis forced Prime Minister Tafawa Balewa to cancel the census and order a new one for later in 1963. But now that the census had been blatantly established as an instrument of ethnic and regional competition, mass political mobilization was even more intense and mutual suspicion even more profound. The result was an even greater fiasco—an "altogether incredible" national increase of 83 percent in ten years and a continued Northern population majority.[23] Despite bitter rejection by the Eastern Region's NCNC government, the NPC used its parliamentary power to win official acceptance of the figures.

The census crisis not only heightened the salience of ethnicity and region in politics, but it also marked the beginning of fiercely polarized competition between the NPC and the NCNC, who were both looking toward the critical federal election due before the end of 1964. With the decimation of the Action Group, the political system was realigning around a bipolar struggle: as progressive elements of the NCNC and AG began to unite, Chief Akintola's party moved closer to the NPC. But before these sectional tensions could cumulate in the electoral struggle, a third crisis erupted.

Late in 1963, wage laborers in Nigeria began to focus their indignation over declining real income and gross economic inequality into militant demands for government attention and higher pay. For the next year, the severely fractured trade union movement united in a concerted challenge to the country's political class. Following months of government arrogance and procrastination, the unions launched a devastating general strike in June of 1964, which brought the economic life of the nation to a standstill for thirteen days. In addition to the overwhelming support of Nigerian workers, both organized and unorganized, the strike also drew widespread popular support, especially in the cities.[24] This came in response to the larger political issues in the strike: the enormous disparities in the official wage structure and the glaring corruption and extravagant consumption of the nation's political elite. The strike also drew some support from progressive AG and NCNC politicians, but it was really an expression of disgust with the entire political class. Although the government was finally compelled to make significant concessions, the effect of the strike was to further weaken the regime's legitimacy and to expose the weakness of its authority.[25]

By the time the strike was over, the two leading parties were busy organizing contending alliances for the 1964 federal election. The NCNC first formed an alliance with the Action Group, which was joined on 1 September by NEPU and the minority party of the Christian lower North in the United Progressive Grand Alliance (UPGA). Meanwhile, the NPC drew in Chief Akintola's party and various minor Southern parties to form the Nigerian National Alliance (NNA). These alliances—dominated by the Igbos of the East and the Hausa-Fulani of the North—reduced national politics to a bipolar struggle along the great cumulative divide of ethnicity, region, and party, reinforced by the ideological cleavage between progressive, antiregionalist forces (in UPGA) and conservative, regionalist forces (in the NNA).

With the entire distribution of national power and resources at stake, electoral conflict became more abrasively tribalistic and more violent than ever before. The class consciousness of the June general strike was drowned in an emotional resurgence of ethnic attachments,[26] and the democratic character of the 1964 election was obliterated by organized political thuggery and official obstruction and repression of opposition campaigns.[27] This led UPGA to boycott the election, provoking a tense showdown between the NPC prime minister and the NCNC president of Nigeria in which, for several days, the specter of secession and possible civil war loomed large. Wishing to avoid mass bloodshed, and unable to win military and police support, President Nnamdi Azikiwe finally yielded, and the NPC returned to the federal government more powerful than ever, with the NCNC obtaining a reduced role in a new and even more superficial coalition government. For the third consecutive time, the NPC had triumphed totally in a decisive confrontation with a Southern party.

This pattern prevailed through the final crisis of the First Republic, the October 1965 Western Region election, which pitted Chief Akintola's ruling party and the Action Group in a "do-or-die" struggle for control of the West. Hated for its corruption, extravagance, neglect, and collaboration with the "oppressor" of the Yoruba people, the Akintola regime was compelled to employ massive coercion as a substitute for legitimate authority. Still, it had to resort to wholesale electoral fraud to salvage a claim to reelection. With the announcement of this preposterous result, the Western Region erupted into popular rebellion. The wave of violence and destruction made the region effectively ungovernable. This only further accelerated the process of political decay, which had been advanced earlier in the year by a spate of scandals involving federal government corruption and by a growing consciousness of the degree to which official corruption swollen salaries, waste, and recurrent political crises were squandering the nation's resources. These developments combined to rob the regime of what little legitimacy it still retained, especially among the educated "counter-elite" in the intelligentsia, the civil service, and the military.

Military Rule, 1966–1975

On 15 January 1966, a group of young army majors and captains overthrew the First Republic, assassinating the prime minister, the premiers of the Western and Northern Regions, and a number of high-ranking military officers. Although an ethnic motive has been deduced from their predominantly Igbo composition and the fact that leading Igbo politicians were spared, the coupmakers struck primarily "to end a corrupt and discredited despotism that could only be removed by violence."[28] Their disgust with the First Republic was shared by a broad cross-section of the population, which welcomed the coup in an effusive outpouring of joy and relief. However, the young coupmakers failed fully to execute their plans, and governmental power was wrested from them by one of their intended victims, Major General J. T. U. Aguiyi Ironsi, General Officer Commanding of the Nigerian army, who—like most of the plotters—was Igbo.

Initially, General Ironsi struck swiftly against corruption and graft, detaining a number of former political office holders. He also promised an early return to civilian rule, appointing panels to draft a new constitution and to study problems of the judiciary and economy. But in administering the country, Ironsi tended to confirm mounting fears and suspicions (especially in the North) that the coup had been designed to impose Igbo hegemony on the country.

As concern grew over Igbo bias in his military promotions and choice of political advisers, Ironsi blundered disastrously on 24 May 1966. "Without waiting for the report of his constitutional study group or submitting their report to the promised constituent assembly," he announced a new constitution abolishing the federal system and unifying the regional and federal public services.[29] For Northerners, who had long feared that their educational disadvantage could open the way for Southern domination of their civil service (and the entire state system), this was anathema. Within days, hundreds of Igbos were killed in riots in Northern towns. Although Ironsi backed away somewhat from his original plan, Northern alarm and bitterness persisted, culminating in a bloody countercoup by Northern officers in July, which killed Ironsi and many other Igbo officers and soldiers. Out of the chaos and uncertainty, the army chief of staff, Lieutenant Colonel Yakubu Gowon, a Northern Christian from a minority ethnic group, emerged as a compromise choice for head of state.

At first, Gowon also spoke in terms of an early return to civilian rule. After reinstating the old regional system, he organized meetings of regional opinion leaders to prepare the groundwork for a constitutional conference. There support gathered for a stronger central government and creation of more states. But Gowon could not bridge the years of enmity and suspicion, nor heal the wounds of two bloody coups. With the Eastern Region's governor and military commander, Colonel Chukwuemeka Ojukwu, refusing to recognize Gowon's authority, and with Eastern Region delegates insisting on extensive regional autonomy, the deliberations stalled, and were abruptly ended in early October 1966 by a new wave of Igbo massacres in the North. Subsequently, more than a million Igbos poured back into the Eastern Region while Ojukwu ordered all non-Easterners to leave.

The soldiers proved even less adept than the politicians at managing the country's explosive divisions. Amid rising secessionist pressure in the East, efforts to negotiate some kind of compromise, confederal arrangement failed. With centrifugal pressures also growing in the West and Mid-West, the Northern emirs finally agreed to the creation of additional states as the only hope for preserving the federation. On 27 May 1967, Gowon announced the division of the country into twelve states (six in the North, and three each in the East and West). This at once broke the monolithic power of the North and granted the longstanding aspirations of ethnic minorities, who along with the Yoruba, found their commitment to the federation renewed. But the alienation of the Igbo was now irreparable. Three days later, Ojukwu announced the secession of the Eastern Region as the Republic of Biafra, and in early July the Nigerian civil war began.

Short of total defeat in war, there is probably no greater trauma for a nation than civil war. For the East in particular, which suffered immense destruction and hundreds of thousands of military and civilian fatalities, the thirty-month war was a horrific experience. Nevertheless, Nigeria emerged from the experience with a hopeful future, owing in part to General Gowon's magnanimous policy of reconciliation with the defeated East, and in part to the development of oil production, which, by the end of the war in January 1970, was beginning to generate substantial revenue. With the specter of national disintegration now definitively laid to rest and a more effective federal system in place, attention turned to two overriding national problems: postwar reconstruction of the economy and society, and political reconstruction of civilian democratic government.

The war period had seen the imposition of stern authoritarian measures, including strict controls on trade unions, a ban on strikes, and a crackdown on movements for new states. Although these "had all been accepted as part of the necessary restrictions on a nation at war,"[30] democratic aspirations remained strong. Some continuity with civilian rule was maintained by the presence in the wartime government of prominent civilians, led by the previously jailed Chief Obafemi Awolowo.

With the end of the war, Nigerians eagerly awaited the announcement of a program for transition to civilian rule. Not until ten months later, on 1 October 1970, was it announced. The military was to remain in power for another six years while it pursued a nine-point program of reconstruction. The armed forces were to be reorganized, the economy rebuilt and revived, corruption eradicated, a new census conducted, a new constitution drafted, and the thorny questions of additional states and revenue allocation settled. Following this, genuinely national political parties would be organized and elections conducted. Although many Nigerians, not least the former politicians, were stunned and disappointed by the length of the transition, the setting of a definite date for return to civilian rule met with popular favor.

As oil production reached two million barrels a day in 1973 and oil prices quadrupled during 1973 and 1974, Nigeria entered a breathtaking economic boom. Ironically, this was when the popular consensus behind Gowon's rule began to unravel. Once more, the census generated a damaging political crisis, as it produced not only an incredible total count but bitterly disputed state results. With the North preserving its population majority by an even larger margin than in 1963, the census drowned in charges of fraud and ethnic domination, and the results were never formally adopted.

Alarmed by the resurgence of ethnic conflict, realizing that little progress had been made on most of the points of his transition program, and pressured by an increasingly venal circle of military officers who sought to extend their control over the juicy resources of power, Gowon shocked the nation on 1 October 1974 by announcing an indefinite postponement of the return to civilian rule.[31]

At the time of his announcement, General Gowon committed himself to new reforms: a new constitution, new states, new military governors, and new federal commissioners. But no progress was forthcoming on any of these fronts in the subsequent ten months. Popular disillusionment sharply intensified as the twelve state governors became ever more entrenched, and arrogant and brazen in their corruption, while venality and mismanagement exacted a mounting toll on the national economy as well. The inept handling of the Udoji Commission's proposals for large wage increases for government workers brought a steep rise in inflation that actually reduced the purchasing power of urban workers. Strikes crippled banking and health services. Shortages of essential commodities occurred. The ports became hopelessly jammed with ships waiting to offload fantastic amounts of cement inexplicably ordered by the government. And in yet another scandal, severe shortages of gasoline mysteriously developed, forcing dawn-to-dusk queues. General Gowon became increasingly remote not only from public opinion and protest, but from military officers outside his narrow ruling circle, who worried increasingly that the corruption and mismanagement of his regime were dragging the entire armed forces into disrepute.[32]

The Transition to the Second Republic

On 29 July 1975 (nine years to the day he assumed power), General Gowon was overthrown in a bloodless coup while attending an OAU summit. The coup was engineered by reform-minded senior officers determined to clear out the rot in the government and bureaucracy and return the country to civilian rule. The new head of state, Brigadier Murtala Muhammed, moved swiftly and boldly to achieve these goals. To great popular acclaim, he removed the twelve state governors within hours of taking power. Over the following weeks, more than 10,000 civil servants at every level of government were dismissed for abuse of office or unproductivity. Following this, the army itself was purged, and plans drawn up to reduce its size from 250,000 to 100,000. Commissions were appointed to investigate several major scandals and the assets of public officers, to study and make recommendations on the creation of new states, and to explore the possibility of moving the federal capital from impossibly congested Lagos.

Most significant of all, Murtala Muhammed responded forthrightly to the mounting pressures for a transition to democracy. Through the previous decade of military rule, democratic aspirations had remained alive. These were sustained in part by the vigor of the Nigerian press, which, despite repressive decrees and continuous threats, harassment and arrests, managed to preserve its freedom and integrity to a considerable degree.[33] "In the absence of a democratically elected Parliament, newspapers found themselves playing the role of a deliberative assembly, reflecting the feelings of the people [about] . . . government policies and actions. . . ."[34] Risking imprisonment, journalists and editors had taken the lead in exposing and denouncing corruption; in demanding the release of political detainees, the lifting of press restraints, and the restoration of other liberties; and in criticizing government policies and performance.[35] Through repeated strikes, boycotts, declarations, demonstrations, and other means of mass mobilization, university students also played a crucial role in demanding accountability, responsiveness, and basic freedoms from the Gowon government.[36]

On 1 October 1975, General Murtala announced a precise deadline and detailed timetable for the restoration of civilian, democratic government. In five stages over a period of four years, a new constitutional and political foundation was to be carefully laid. First, the issue of new states would be resolved and a Constitutional Drafting Committee would be given twelve months to produce a draft constitution. Second, local government would be reorganized and new local governments elected, to be followed by the election of a Constituent Assembly to review and amend the draft constitution. Stage three would lift the ban on political parties by October 1978. Stage four would elect state legislatures and stage five a federal government, in time to transfer power to "a democratically elected government of the people" by 1 October 1979.[37]

Despite the tragic assassination of Murtala Muhammed in a failed coup attempt on 13 February 1976—when he was riding the crest of an unprecedented wave of national popularity—and despite a bitter debate within the Constituent Assembly over whether to establish an Islamic *Sharia* court of appeal at the federal level—which threatened explosive religious and regional polarization until it was resolved by compromise and skillful mediation[38]—Murtala's timetable was implemented faithfully and skillfully by his successor, General Olusegun Obasanjo.

Several aspects of the transition process appeared to augur well for the future of democracy in Nigeria. The volatile issue of new states, which had been the focus of intense ethnic and subethnic political mobilization, was tackled early and decisively with the creation of seven more states in April 1976 (implementing one of Murtala Muhammed's final policy announcements). In addition to creating several new ethnic minority states, the major Yoruba state was broken in three and the major Igbo state was split in two. The new nineteen-state system—containing four predominantly Hausa-Fulani states, four Yoruba, two Igbo, and nine ethnic minority states—seemed likely to weaken the ethnic and regional solidarities that had cursed the First Republic and to generate a more fluid and shifting pattern of alignments, with state interests representing an independent and, at least occasionally, crosscutting line of cleavage.[39]

The concern for generating crosscutting cleavages was also evident in the new constitution, which explicitly prohibited sectional parties and required broad ethnic representation in each party as a condition for recognition.[40] Constitutional provisions for an executive presidency, and requiring a presidential candidate to win at least a quarter of the vote in at least two-thirds of all the states in order to be directly elected, had a similar purpose. Together with the creation of a powerful Federal Electoral Commision (FEDECO) to certify parties and regulate campaigning, these innovations in "institutional architecture" seemed to produce a more durable political foundation.[41]

The new constitution was an elaborate and carefully crafted document. Closely modeled after the U.S. system, it provided for an elected president and vice-president (eligible for no more than two four-year terms); a bicameral National Assembly (with five senators from each state, elected by district, and 450 members of the House of Representatives, elected from federal constituencies of equivalent population); an independent judiciary, headed by a Supreme Court and State High Courts, with courts of appeal below them; and a detailed chapter on "fundamental human rights," guaranteeing not only life, liberty, and due process, but essential freedoms of expression, association, peaceful assembly, movement, and the press. In addition, contained in the constitution's Fifth Schedule was another significant innovation: an extensive Code of Conduct for Public Officers, along with a bureau and tribunal for monitoring and enforcing compliance with its provisions.

Also auspicious was the widespread popular participation in the transition process. In the six months following the presentation of the draft constitution in December 1976, the country became consumed with a free and vigorous debate on its provisions, which continued in the deliberations of the elected Constituent Assembly.[42] The thoroughness and freedom of the public debate and the national consensus behind its result suggested that "Nigeria's Second Republic was established upon a genuinely popular foundation"[43] that gave legitimacy to its political institutions.[44]

The process of transition did not give the same careful attention to the development of political party institutions, however. Not until three of the four years had passed was the ban on political parties lifted. Aspiring political parties then had only three months to apply to FEDECO for registration. In this brief period, they had to establish a national network of local and state branches, elect party officials, and conduct national conventions. After thirteen years of prohibition of political parties, this severe compression of the period for political party development had precisely the consequences the military hoped to avoid: most truly fresh political formations either fractured into more familiar forms or died stillborn. Only nineteen of some fifty emergent parties were able to file papers by the mid-December (1978) deadline, and of these only five were certified by FEDECO.[45]

These five new parties bore a strong resemblance to the parties of the First Republic, in part because of significant continuities in their leaderships and regional bases. Thus the Unity Party of Nigeria (UPN), strongest in the Yoruba states and led by Chief Obafemi Awolowo, struck many as the reincarnation of the Action Group. The National Party of Nigeria (NPN), based most powerfully in the far North and led in the presidential elections by former NPC Minister Alhaji Shehu Shagari, was widely seen as the successor to the NPC. The Nigerian Peoples Party (NPP), reduced primarily to an Igbo base after a damaging split cost it much of its Northern support,[46] and then nominating Dr. Nnamdi Azikiwe as its presidential candidate, was seen to reproduce the NCNC. And the Peoples Redemption Party (PRP), also based in the emirate North and led by Mallam Aminu Kano, seemed to reincarnate the radical NEPU, which he had led in the First Republic. Only the Great Nigerian Peoples Party (GNPP), which split from the NPP when its leader, Waziri Ibrahim, refused to step aside for Dr. Azikiwe as presidential candidate, could not be obviously linked to a major party of the First Republic.

In fact, each of these parties was broader than its supposed antecedent in the First Republic. In particular, the NPN represented the broadest ethnic base ever assembled by a Nigerian party, perhaps the first truly "national" party in the nation's history. Although party power was based on the aristocratic and modern technocratic elites of the Muslim upper North, Yoruba, Igbo and minority political and business elites played strategic roles in the party's formation, and the NPN showed signs of becoming the predominant party of an increasingly integrated and cohesive Nigerian bourgeoisie. Even after its traumatic split, the NPP continued to draw critical support from Christian areas of the "Middle Belt" (or lower North) that had never been associated with the NCNC, and the GNPP showed strength through much of the Muslim North and also in the minority areas of the southeast. While the UPN and PRP were more regionally based, they were the sharpest and least parochial in their substantive programs, seeking to build national constituencies around social democratic and socialist ideologies respectively.[47]

Nevertheless, in the brevity of the period for party development and under pressure of imminent elections, politicians tended to retreat into convenient and familiar ethnic alignments, and new political entrepreneurs were forced to look to established politicians for leadership. This not only snapped some significant crosscutting alignments—especially that represented by the original NPP—it also produced "a sad level of regional and tribal correlation in voting behaviour."[48] And it brought together politicians of such disparate ideological inclinations that their associations were bound to become sorely strained.

The Second Republic

The Second Republic was born in the elections for state and federal offices that took place in five rounds during July and August of 1979.[49] Although largely successful, their legitimacy was tarnished by charges of administrative bias and, in particular, by a serious controversy over the presidential election. Pro-NPN bias was suggested by the pattern of disqualification of candidates by FEDECO, on the grounds of nonpayment of income tax.[50] The actual conduct of the voting was also disputed. Predictably, "the various parties complained of fraud, victimization, and all kinds of electoral malpractices in places where they had not won."[51] Numerous malpractices were in fact documented, and election tribunals did order some new elections, while courageously upholding the disputed election of the PRP candidate for governor of strategic Kaduna State. On balance, the 1979 elections were relatively free and fair in their conduct.[52] Parties were free to campaign and the results in most states seemed to reflect apparent political trends. Moreover, in contrast with previous elections, the 1979 contest was impressively peaceful, due in no small measure to the active efforts of the military government to check political thuggery.

However, a truly serious challenge to the legitimacy of the 1979 elections—and of the new republic—grew out of the ambiguous result of the last round of voting for the presidency. Although the NPN candidate, Shagari, had won a plurality of the vote, the runner-up candidate, Chief Awolowo, and his UPN insisted Shagari had not satisfied the second condition for direct election because he had won 25 percent of the vote in only twelve, and hence not quite two-thirds, of the nineteen states. The ruling of the electoral commission that he was elected because he had won 25 percent in "twelve and two-thirds states" (i.e., a quarter of the vote in twelve states and two-thirds of a quarter in a thirteenth) was bitterly challenged by the UPN, but upheld by the Supreme Court. The controversy engendered lasting political enmity between the NPN and UPN that was to heavily color subsequent political developments.[53]

This tension congealed rather quickly into competing political alliances. Building upon patterns of electoral cooperation, the nine elected governors from the UPN, GNPP, and PRP began meeting late in 1979 as a kind of coordinating committee for the political opposition to the NPN. The self-styled "nine progressive governors" denounced what they alleged was repeated abuse of constitutional authority by the NPN federal government. Initially, this was countered by two alliances on the NPN side. One gave the NPP, by formal agreement, a share of executive and legislative offices in return for its legislative cooperation. The other, a *de facto* arrangement, drew into the NPN's expanding and patronage-rich political network a growing number of NPP, GNP, and PRP federal legislators (mostly senators), who were constitutionally prohibited from crossing the carpet but who gave the president reliable and often pivotal legislative support.

The NPN-NPP accord never worked as intended. Disappointed with the lack of consultations and patronage, the NPP withheld legislative support on several critical issues. By mid-1981, the accord completely collapsed, and several (but not all) NPP ministers honored their party's call to withdraw from the government. Gradually, the NPP drew closer to the opposition alliance; later in 1981, the "nine progressive governors" became twelve when they were joined by the three NPP governors. These twelve states represented the full range of Nigeria's ethnic diversity: four predominantly Yoruba, two Igbo, two Hausa, and four ethnic minority states. Meanwhile, the informal alliance became more important for the NPN, and this also cut sharply across region and ethnicity: many of the tacit collaborators with the NPN came from the two Igbo states and from elsewhere outside the party's far Northern base. These developments raised the possibility of a historic realignment in which two new political parties, one more conservative and one more progressive, would contest for power on a national basis.

Despite the increasing polarization between the ruling NPN and the UPN-led opposition, there was some cause for hope in the fact that this cleavage was far less centered on ethnicity and region than was political conflict in the First Republic. As a result of not only expanding education and communication, but also the deep inequalities and contradictions engendered by the oil boom,[54] class and ideology were coming to play a more significant role in political conflict.[55] This was particularly so in the two states carried by the PRP in 1979—Kano and Kaduna, part of the core of the old emirate system. As these states became the focus of political conflict, crosscutting cleavage became increasingly salient.

Three interrelated crises developed along this line in 1980 and 1981. The first was a deep split in the leadership of the PRP, not unlike that in the Action Group in 1962, save that the stance of moderation and national political accommodation was espoused by PRP President Aminu Kano and his aides, while it was the two elected governors of Kano and Kaduna who favored confrontation and a more radical, ideological approach. The latter faction was the larger of the two, containing most of the PRP's youth support, founding intellectals, and legislative representatives. They supported the participation of the two governors in the meetings of the nine opposition governors, while the party establishment opposed it and ordered it to cease. Out of the mutual expulsions, two opposing party structures emerged, each claiming to be the genuine PRP. In a controversial decision early in 1981, FEDECO officially recognized the Aminu Kano faction, further eroding the legitimacy of that crucial regulatory body.

Aggravating this internal division was a deepening stalemate within Kaduna State between the radical PRP governor, Alhaji Abdulkadir Balarabe Musa, and the NPN-controlled legislature. This reflected the widening class cleavage in the far North, as a new generation of radical intellectuals and professionals sought to mobilize the peasantry in a struggle to dismantle the entire structure of traditional class privilege and power, based on land and the emirate system. Even though the legislature was controlled by his political and class opponents, Balarabe Musa plunged ahead with his socialist program, abolishing exploitative local taxes, investigating land transactions, and inaugurating a mass literacy campaign. When he persisted in the face of intense legislative opposition, the NPN majority in the State Assembly, with the support of the establishment PRP, impeached him and removed him from office in June 1981. With opposition forces around the country bitterly condemning the nakedly partisan action as undemocratic and unconstitutional, the legitimacy of the Second Republic suffered. At the same time, speculation grew about a four-party alliance to wrest power from the NPN in 1983, which was further encouraged by the rupture of the NPN-NPP accord two weeks after the impeachment.

Just a few weeks later, on 10 July 1981, conflict in Kano State erupted into violence on a massive scale, burning down much of the physical infrastructure of the Kano State government and killing the political adviser of the PRP governor, Mohammed Abubakar Rimi. The immediate precipitant of the riot was an offensive letter from Governor Rimi to the Emir of Kano implying his possible removal for acts of disrespect to the state government. But the systematic character of the destruction, and considerable other evidence, indicate that the riot was organized to embarrass and intimidate the PRP administration and derail its agenda for change. Supporters of the governor and the radical PRP were convinced that the NPN and the PRP were responsible—seeking to do by violence in Kano what could not be done by impeachment, given Governor Rimi's overwhelming support in the state legislature. The massive destruction had a traumatic and deeply polarizing effect on political conflict, heightening opposition fears that the NPN and its allies were not prepared to "play by the rules." In retaliation some months later, the radical PRP impeached the deputy governor of Kano, who had backed the PRP establishment faction.

The mere fact of conflict—even recurrent and intense conflict—between the ruling NPN and the congealing opposition forces was not in itself an ominous development for democracy. Nor did the occasional heavy-handedness of the NPN federal government represent a really grave threat to democracy: despite the opposition charges of "creeping fascism," basic freedoms remained largely intact and a number of controversial government actions were reversed or enjoined in the courts.[56] What was dangerous was the aura of desperation and intolerance that infused these conflicts and the violence that often attended them. These danger signals were noted with increasing alarm by the nation's press, which repeatedly condemned "the politics of bickerings, mudslingings,

. . . lies, deceit, vindictiveness, strife and intolerance that are again creeping back into the country's political scene."[57]

Of particular concern to independent observers and opinion makers was the growing trail of violence. Even in the first two years of the Second Republic (when the 1979 elections were history but well before the 1983 election campaign had begun), casualties mounted from the repeated clashes between thugs of rival politicians, parties, and party factions. In Borno State alone, the count had run to 39 dead, 99 injured and 376 arrested by May 1981.[58] As the 1983 elections approached, violent clashes proliferated between supporters and hired bullies not only of rival parties, but also of rival candidates for party nominations, especially within the NPN and the UPN. In many states, escalating political violence brought temporary bans on public meetings and assemblies. In some communities, thuggery reached a point where people became concerned for their physical safety. Reflecting the growing public cynicism, weariness, and disgust, the press repeatedly warned of the impending danger:

> We are tired of celebrating politics as a rite of death. . . . If politics cannot inspire recognition and respect for fundamental human rights, the credibility of the captains of our ship of state is certainly at stake. . . . We can ask to be saved from politicians and their notoriously bloody style of politicking.[59]

But political violence and intolerance were not the only sources of public disillusionment. From the very beginning, concern was also manifest over the opportunistic and self-interested behavior of the politicians, as reflected in the prolonged debate over legislative salaries and perquisites that dominated the initial deliberations of the National Assembly. Cynicism was bred by the constant stream of suspensions, expulsions and defections from the various political parties, which split not only the PRP, but later the GNPP and, to a lesser extent, the NPP as well. And within states controlled by each of the five parties, state assemblies became absorbed in bitter conflicts over leadership positions or threats to impeach the governor. The tremendous instability in party structures and identities suggested a general lack of substantive commitment among the politicians, whose main motivation was the personal quest for power and wealth.

Most of all, public disillusionment was bred by the unending succession of scandals and exposés concerning corruption in government. In 1983 alone, these included the mishandling of $2.5 billion in import licenses by the minister of commerce, the alleged acceptance by legislators of large bribes from a Swiss firm, the rumored apprehension in London of a Nigerian governor trying to smuggle millions of naira into Britain, and the revelation by a federal minister that the country was losing close to a billion dollars a year in payroll fraud. The issue was dramatized in January 1983 by a shocking fire that destroyed the 37-story headquarters of the Nigerian External Telecommunications in Lagos. The fire, condemned by a leading newspaper as "a calculated act, planned and executed to cover up corruption and embezzlement in the company,"[60] symbolized the rapaciousness of the ruling elite and visibly quickened the pace of political decay. Students took to the streets in several cities, carrying signs calling for the return of the military.[61]

Such incidents and revelations only reinforced the evidence in virtually every state and community of venality, insensitivity, failed promises, and callous waste: the skeletons of unfinished hospitals and schools, the treacherous craters in ungraded roads, the abandoned bulldozers, the rusting pumps beside the undrilled boreholes. These phenomena had spread malignantly since the oil boom, but seemed to assume a wholly new and reckless momentum with the return of the politicians.

The devastating effects of corruption at all levels of government—which, by most estimates, drained billions of dollars from the Nigerian economy during the Second Republic—were compounded by the precipitous decline in oil revenue, from a peak of $24 billon in 1980 to $10 billion in 1983. As corruption and mismanagement prevented any kind of disciplined adjustment, the economy was plunged into depression and mounting international indebtedness. Imports of industrial raw materials and basic commodities were severely disrupted, forcing the retrenchment of tens of thousands of industrial workers and sending the prices of staple foods and household necessities skyrocketing. Shortages were further aggravated by hoarding and profiteering (especially of rice) by the powerful and well-connected. Sucked dry of revenue by the corruption, mismanagement, and recession, state governments became unable to pay teachers and civil servants or to purchase drugs for hospitals, and many services (including schools) were shut down by strikes. Everywhere one turned in 1983, the economy seemed on the edge of collapse. Still the politicians and contractors continued to bribe, steal, smuggle, and speculate, accumulating vast illicit fortunes and displaying them lavishly in stunning disregard for public sensitivities. By its third anniversary, disenchantment with the Second Republic was acute, overt, and remarkably broad-based.[62]

As the rot deepened, so did the popular aspiration for change. Beyond the chimera of popular rebellion (of which some leftist intellectuals dreamed and in fear of which the paramilitary wing of the police was rapidly expanded), only two possible avenues were open: to change the incumbents in power in the five weeks of national and state elections due in August and September 1983 or to displace the political system altogether and bring back the only alternative, the military. A large proportion of the Nigerian electorate had come, by 1983, to favor the latter option. My own preelection survey in Kano State, the largest and most volatile in the country, showed a majority of the state's electorate and two-thirds of the voters in Kano city to favor a military government. Probably an even larger proportion of the intelligentsia and the military had come to favor the systemic change, out of deep skepticism that reform from within was possible. Nevertheless, this group waited to see if change could come by constitutional means, viewing the elections as the last chance for the Second Republic to redeem itself.[63]

From the beginning of the process, the elections were gravely troubled. The two-week registration of voters during August 1982 ended amid widespread protests of incompetence, partisanship, and fraud. When the preliminary register of voters was displayed in March 1983, with millions of names missing, mangled, or misplaced, opposition fears heightened. These hardened into outrage and disbelief with the release (just ten days before the election) of the final register, which showed not only an absurd total of 65 million voters (certainly in excess and possibly twice the legitimate total) but the largest increases in NPN states.[64]

Even more troubling was FEDECO's refusal to register a new and powerful opposition alliance that sought recognition as the Progressive Peoples Party (PPP). Bringing together the NPP and the largest factions of the PRP and the GNPP, the PPP seemed clearly to have satisfied the constitutional requirements. In fact, with control of seven state governments (as many as the NPN), the PPP was at least the second largest and broadest political formation in the country. But FEDECO even denied the NPP's request to change its name to PPP. Such rulings (hailed by NPN officials) badly tarnished the integrity of FEDECO and of the election.[65] Although the other party factions subsequently merged into the NPP, their Northern campaign was to suffer from widespread identification of the NPP as an "Igbo" and "Christian" party—a major theme of the NPN campaign in the Muslim North. Anxiety further mounted as the election neared and FEDECO proved unable to cope with the staggering logistical preparations for five successive elections with tens of millions of voters in nineteen states.

Biased and incompetent administration was not the opposition's only concern, however. With full control of federal patronage and an extraordinarily well-financed national political machine, the NPN was a formidable national contender, even with its sorry performance in office. Probably the only hope for an opposition victory in the presidential election lay in uniting behind a common ticket. But months of negotiations between the UPN and the NPP (and their PRP and GNPP allies) under the rubric of their Progressive Parties Alliance (PPA) failed to produce agreement. Neither of the surviving political giants—Azikiwe of the NPP and Awolowo of the UPN—would step down for the other. As they divided the opposition vote, the Shagari campaign was able to brand them in the North as champions of alien ethnic and religious interests. Still, as they campaigned relentlessly against the corruption and mismanagement of the NPN administration, the two gathered new support around the country, including Northern, Muslim states they had previously failed to penetrate in their long careers.

Although it was apparent that the division of the opposition might enable President Shagari's reelection with a weak plurality, changes were widely expected at other levels. In particular, a number of massively corrupt and negligent governors figured to be booted out. Certainly no one was prepared for the scale of the NPN landslide, and even the most hardened skeptics were astonished by the degree of electoral fraud. Ballots were obtained in advance and thumbprinted en masse. Electoral officials at every level were bribed to falsify returns. Whole communities were disenfranchised. Although all the parties engaged in malpractices, those by the NPN were the most systematic and brazen. In many Northern states, NPN agents collaborated with electoral officials and police to prevent opposition party agents from observing the polling and vote counting.[66] In the absence of this crucial check (guaranteed in the electoral law), unbelievable returns were reported and announced. Not only was President Shagari reelected decisively—and by incredible margins in some states—but the following week, the NPN increased its governorships from seven to thirteen, scoring shocking upsets in several opposition states while comfortably reelecting even its most venal incumbents. Subsequently, it was to increase its standing in the National Assembly from a small plurality to two-thirds, but, by then, the credibility of the elections had been shattered and most of the electorate was no longer bothering to vote.

Despite numerous appeals, few of the results were overturned in court. All but one of the most controversial gubernatorial outcomes were upheld. In that lone case, a defeated UPN governor was found to have been reelected by more than a million votes.

As they had in 1965, the people of the Yorbua states, where the rigging had been most outrageous, exploded in a frenzy of violent protest following the gubernatorial elections. More than 100 people were killed and $100 million in property destroyed.[67] Violent protest erupted in other states as well, claiming more than thirty lives. Both Awolowo and Azikiwe charged that the election was stolen and pronounced the country "on the brink of dictatorship." A pregnant calm returned by the inauguration on 1 October, after which the reelected president took some steps to upgrade his cabinet and launch tough new austerity measures. But by then it was too little and too late.

The Second Military Interregnum

Like the first coup eighteen years before, the coup that brought the military back to power on 31 December 1983 was widely welcomed and celebrated around the country.[68] The reasons for the coup were largely apparent in the declarations of the coupmakers: to redeem the country from "the grave economic predicament and uncertainty that an inept and corrupt leadership has imposed" on the country. The new head of state, Major General Muhammadu Buhari, added to the economic indictment the rigging of the 1983 elections. Observed a former army chief of staff, "Democracy had been in jeopardy for the past four years. It died with the elections. The army only buried it."[69] If there was any hesitance at all on the part of senior officers after the election, it was surely removed by the continued rapid deterioration of the economy (which saw food prices skyrocket between September and December) and the realization that militant junior officers, from whose ranks had come several unsuccessful coup attempts over the previous four years, could not indefinitely be kept at bay.

The government of General Buhari and his second-in-command, Major General Tunde Idiagbon, moved quickly to punish corruption and eliminate waste. More than 300 top officials in the civil service, police, and customs were dismissed or retired. Hundreds of former politicians were detained—including the president, vice-president, and prominent governors, ministers, and legislators. Huge sums of cash were seized from the homes of leading politicians, and the accounts of detained and fugitive politicians were frozen. Imports and travel allowances were slashed, black market currency operations raided, and government contracts placed under review.

These initial moves were highly popular, especially with the interest groups—students, trade unions, businessmen, professionals—that had been most disgusted with the civilian regime. Newspapers and intellectuals also supported the professed intention of the new regime to restore accountability to public life. But early on, it became apparent that the Buhari regime viewed accountability only in retrospective terms, and had no more intention than the Gowon regime of allowing itself to be scrutinized and questioned. With unprecedented harshness, arrogance, and impunity, the Buhari regime turned on the constituencies that had welcomed its arrival.

Political problems crystallized in March 1984 with the announcement of several controversial decrees. Decree Number 3 provided for military tribunals to try former public officials suspected of corruption and misconduct in office. The announcement of investigations and trials was popular, but protest arose over the severity of the penalties (a minimum of twenty one years in prison) and in particular over the procedures, which placed the "onus of proving" innocence on the accused, prohibited appeal of the verdict, and closed the proceedings to the public. These provisions led the Nigerian Bar Association to boycott the trials.

In the subsequent year, Nigerians were gratified to see the conviction and sentencing of some of the country's most corrupt politicians, including former governors from a majority of the nineteen states. Acquittals of some other officeholders suggested that the tribunals were capable of fair and independent verdicts. But concern mounted over the continued detention without trial of politicians who had not been formally charged. Consternation also grew over the dearth of convictions of the most powerful kingpins of the NPN, especially those from the party's Northern power base. Given, as well, the heavily Northern composition of the Supreme Military Council, the regime came increasingly to be derided as the "military wing of the NPN."

The disenchantment was fed not only by the narrow ethnic base of the regime, but also by its increasing repressiveness and arrogance, as manifested in its assault on the press. Decree Number 4 forbade the publication or broadcast of anything that was false in any particular or that might bring government officials into ridicule or disrepute. Under this and the internal security decree (Number 2) announced in January, several prominent journalists and editors were arrested. Although journalists continued to test the regime's narrowing limits, the decrees and arrests had a chilling effect on news coverage and editorial commentary and alienated the intelligentsia.

Under Decree Number 2, which provided for the detention of any citizen deemed a security risk, the Nigerian Security Organization (NSO) was given a virtual blank check to arrest and intimidate critics of the regime. Some of Nigeria's most forceful and popular social commentators were imprisoned without trial. Others fell silent in a growing climate of fear.

Politics in the sense of articulation and representation of interests did not cease. As it had previously during military rule, mobilization continued by a panoply of assertive and clamorous interest groups. Repression became the reflexive response of the regime. Public declarations were discouraged and obstructed, meetings were forcibly dispersed, and group leaders were detained by the NSO. In addition, prominent interest groups, including the National Association of Nigerian Students and the Nigerian Medical Association were banned. Toward the end, even public discussion of the country's political future was banned.

Public disaffection was intensified by the growing economic hardships, which followed from the severe austerity measures imposed by the Buhari government. Although these brought considerable progress toward balancing Nigeria's external payments, they came at the price of deepening recession. During 1984, an estimated 50,000 civil servants were retrenched, retired, or dismissed. Tens of thousands more industrial workers also lost their jobs as factories remained desperately short of imported raw materials and spare parts. Severe shortages pushed inflation to an annual rate of 40 percent. After three years of decline in GDP by an estimated 10 percent, the 1985 budget forecast only one percent growth, cutting imports again by more than half while assigning 44 percent of foreign exchange to debt service. At the same time, credible reports spread of renewed corruption in high places, including (incredibly, given its role in the demise of the Second Republic) the allocation of import licenses.

Escalating repression not only engendered deep resentment and bitterness among a people who cherished their personal freedom, it also dangerously cut the regime off from popular sentiments and relieved it of any need to be accountable for its conduct. In trying to impose a monolithic order on Nigeria's irrepressibly pluralistic society, this narrowly based dictatorship was risking a convulsion of enormous proportions. Rumors of failed coup attempts from the junior ranks circulated anew. Perhaps most fatally for the regime, its arrogance led it to ignore critical opinion and the imperative for consensus even within its senior military ranks.

What was coming to be viewed around the country as an inevitable military coup finally happened on 27 August 1985. It was led by army chief of staff Major General Ibrahim Babangida, who became the first of Nigeria'a six military rulers to take the title of president. From its initial statements and actions and the enthusiastic popular reception it received, the Babangida coup appeared to mark a decisive rejection of the previous authoritarian trend. In his maiden address to the nation, Babangida announced an immediate review of the status of political detainees and the repeal of Decree Number 4, vowing, "We do not intend to lead a country where individuals are under the fear of expressing themselves."[70] Shortly thereafter, all journalists in detention and dozens of politicians who had not been charged or tried were released, many to heroes' welcomes. The detention centers of the NSO were exposed to public view, and a thorough probe and restructuring of the dreaded organization was undertaken. Forceful and opinionated civilians were chosen to head crucial cabinet ministries, and the ruling military council was reorganized to disperse power. Babangida also promised to present a program of political transition, beginning with the revitalization of local government.

In perhaps his most extraordinary move, the new military president opened the most sensitive and controversial policy question facing his administration—whether to take a loan from the IMF—to a vigorous public debate. Negotiations with the IMF for a $2.5 billion, three-year adjustment loan had been dragging on since well before the December 1983 coup; and upon assuming office, Babangida indicated his intention to complete an IMF agreement. On strictly economic grounds, the case for the loan seemed urgent and compelling. With foreign debt having swollen further to $22 billion and oil prices and production still sagging, the country was desperately in need of the foreign exchange that would come from the IMF loan, and from other international loans and credits that an IMF agreement would unlock. Moreover, the austerity measures attached to the loan—a steep devaluation of the currency (by more than half), trade liberalization, and substantial cuts in petroleum and other consumer subsidies—enjoyed strong support from economists in and outside the country.

But the politics of the IMF loan simply would not fly. The debate brought forth a tidal wave of popular, intellectual, and interest group opposition to the loan, not only because of the harshness of the policy measures and the diminution of national sovereignty it would imply, but also because of widespread public cynicism that such a large new infusion of cash would be managed responsibly. Babangida therefore set aside his original plans and rejected the IMF loan. Nevertheless, he proceeded to implement the IMF's harsh austerity prescriptions and to reap some of the benefit not only from the consequent economic adjustments, but also from the increased receptivity of other multilateral and private international lenders. A radical new phase of economic adjustment was thus inaugurated.

Under Babangida's ambitious and courageous program, the Nigerian economy finally began to make the adjustments long considered essential if the country is ever to build a basis for self-sustaining economic growth. Moreover, these painful changes were accepted with surprising understanding and farsightedness by the population and showed signs of improving the country's economic performance (see the last section of this chapter). But as President Babangida won support for his economic policies, his commitment to liberal and accountable government became increasingly tarnished. On the issue of accountability, the process of trying and punishing the corrupt conduct of the former politicians ground to a halt. Some of this was in a liberal, consitutional spirit: in response to recommendations of two judicial tribunals appointed in late 1985, the regime reduced the sentences of more than fifty convicted former officeholders and acquitted twelve completely. Forty-nine were banned for life from seeking public office, including the former president and vice-president when, several months later (in July 1986), they were finally released from detention. At that time, 100 other politicians were also cleared of all charges, some to the dismay of a skeptical press and public, while 800 were ordered to be tried for corruption. One year later, nothing had come of these new corruption trials, and there was growing skepticism that they would ever be held.

More disturbingly, there were growing indications of a reassertion of the repressive climate that prevailed under Buhari and Idiagbon. Many believe the principle of accountability was unjustly distorted when President Babangida, in mid-1986, banned *all* of the former politicians from future political involvement for a period of ten years.[71] Many groups also objected to the decision—rescinded under pressure from the bar and the press—to extend from three months to six the length of time a person could be detained without trial (for reasons of "state security") under Decree Number 2, which was never repealed.

Two events registered particular damage to the regime's liberal image. On 23 May 1986, police went on a rampage at Ahmadu Bello University in Zaria, killing several students (perhaps over twenty) and injuring many more. The news of this indiscriminate shooting, by police who had been summoned in response to peaceful student protests, provoked widespread popular outrage and sympathy demonstrations on other campuses, leading to further confrontation and violence.[72] The government's response over subsequent months was to quash a planned sympathy demonstration by the Nigerian Labour Congress and detain its leaders, to dissolve all student unions for the remainder of the academic year, and to reject its own commission's recommendation that police not be sent to campuses in the future with lethal weapons.

In perhaps the most shocking development to date under military rule, one of Nigeria's most talented, admired, and fearlessly independent journalists, Dele Giwa, was assassinated by a parcel bomb in October 1986. Giwa was the founding editor-in-chief of the country's leading weekly news magazine, *Newswatch,* which had become widely celebrated for its biting commentaries and aggressive investigative reporting. Just before his death, Giwa had been questioned intensely by the deputy director of the new State Security Service, who charged the liberal and nonviolent Giwa with plotting to import arms and foment a socialist revolution. These preposterous charges combined with a wealth of other circumstantial evidence to fix public suspicion on the state's security apparatus as the party responsible for Giwa's murder.[73] This suspicion was deepened by the government's refusal to launch an independent investigation and the failure of the police, nine month later, to record any progress. All of this again cast a chilling shadow over the Nigerian press. In April 1987, this shadow lengthened when the government banned *Newswatch* for six months after it published an extensive analysis of the leaked report of the political bureau Babangida had appointed to consider the country's constitutional future. The ban was strenuously condemned by the Nigerian Bar Association, the Association of Nigerian Authors, the Nigerian Union of Journalists, and numerous other groups.[74]

The continuing tension with the press and popular interest groups reflects perhaps a growing strength of the authoritarian impulse in Nigeria. It appears that a number of key military and security officials remain apprehensive about any liberalization, and particularly the mobilization by trade union, student, and other popular organizations that it might unleash. These officials would prefer to see such interest groups tightly controlled and licensed by the state through some kind of authoritarian corporatist arrangement. They share with some intellectuals and bureaucrats a deep distrust and dislike for the turmoil and divisiveness of a multiparty system. They value order and stability over freedom, and would probably wish to institutionalize some kind of "bureaucratic-authoritarian" regime along the lines of the South American regimes of the 1970s.[75]

A Summary Assessment of the Nigerian Experience

Twice in Nigeria's twenty-five years of independence, elaborate democratic constitutions have been overthrown by the military after several years of unsuccessful and unpopular operation. In this sense, democracy in Nigeria has failed. But most Nigerians are not inclined to accept this failure as inevitable or enduring. Although the disgust with politicians was still palpable four years after the demise of the Second Republic, most Nigerians, especially the educated, want their country eventually to return to some form of civilian, democratic government. Moreover, authoritarian rule has been more fundamentally unsuccessful in Nigeria, because it has been rejected not only in its actual performance, but in its moral and political logic. Somewhat lost in the drama of a quarter century of political turmoil has been the gradual emergence of an increasingly broad and sophisticated democratic infrastructure, including a vibrant and maturing press, an extensive university system, a rich array of independent business and professional associations, and a judiciary with some significant autonomy. These groups and institutions constitute a powerful constituency demanding the preservation of basic freedoms. Together with the nation's complex ethnic divisions, this growing social pluralism makes the country, in a practical sense, very difficult to govern by authoritarian means. For all these reasons, Nigeria retains considerable promise for democratic success if the structural roots of the previous failures can be identified and altered.

• ANALYSIS OF THE HISTORICAL DEVELOPMENTS •

We seek now to explain Nigeria's political development over its quarter century of independence. Specifically, why did the two attempts at democratic government fail, and why did authoritarian rule not implant itself as an alternative? We begin with the failure of the First Republic.

Why the First Republic Failed

The proximate causes of the downfall of the First Republic were manifest in the statements of the coupmakers and have been widely acknowledged by students and observers of that experience. They included first, the succession of intense political crises, the deepening polarization, the incessant political instability and strife; second, related to this, the style and tone of political behavior and conflict, the violence, repression, and failure to play by the rules of the game; and, finally, the "ten wasted years of planlessness, incompetence, inefficiency, gross abuse of office, corruption," and resulting lack of economic development.[76] These phenomena progressively destroyed the legitimacy of the republic.

It is tempting to attribute this decay and failure to an undemocratic *political culture,* lacking appreciation for "the conventions or rules on which the operation of western democratic forms depend."[77] To be sure, most Nigerian politicians manifested a weak commitment to democratic values and behavioral styles, as witnessed in the vituperation, intolerance, repression, violence, and fraud characteristic of electoral politics. But political values were far from uniformly undemocratic. Many Nigerian political leaders manifested a considerable pride in the democratic system and a sincere desire to make it work. A number of them had studied in Britain or the United States and had acquired a sophisticated intellectual and moral commitment to democracy. Moreover, the traditional political practices and values of many Nigerian peoples had significant democratic features. But values and beliefs do not wholly determine behavior. In Nigeria, democratic currents in the political culture were overrun by imperatives in the social structure. Political culture, in itself, cannot explain why political competition became a kind of warfare.

The most common conception is that the First Republic failed because of *ethnic conflict,* and, on the surface, this is indisputable. But this, again, can be a superficial and misleading explanation in itself. Certainly there were deep cultural divisions, and these were heightened by the centralized structure of ethnicity in Nigeria. But it was hardly inevitable that ethnic groups would contend in mortal political combat. This, too, must be viewed as in intervening variable, resulting from the interaction of ethnicity with social and political structures. Even the stimulus to ethnic conflict generated by the competitive pressures of modernization[78] provides only a very partial understanding of why ethnicity became so heavily politicized. Here we must make reference to three other factors: the establishment of political party competition in the absence of other crosscutting cleavages; the role of the federal structure in reifying the major, tripartite ethnic cleavage and heightening ethnic insecurity in general; and the role of the class structure in encouraging "tribalism"—the deliberate mobilization of ethnic suspicion, fear, jealousy, and hostility.

By any reckoning, the peculiar *federal structure* heavily contributed to the failure of the First Republic. Indeed, one may question the very use of the term "federal" for a system in which one region was larger and more populous—hence more powerful—than all the others combined. The additional fact that the Southern regions had huge advantages in their levels of technologial and educational development made for an "acute contradiction" prone to "political upheaval."[79] Further destabilizing was the authoritarian social structure of the Northern emirates, which the federal structure was pivotal in preserving. The polarization and bitterness of national politics owed significantly to the Northern aristocracy's determination to control the federal government at all costs not only to secure regional and ethnic interests, but also to preserve its class dominance against the mobilization of radical commoners and the winds of change whipping up from the South.[80]

Polarization was also advanced by the small number of constituent units in the federal system, enabling the tripolar structure to collapse into a bipolar struggle. That ethnic minorities lacked the security of their own regions added to the persistent tension. And with so few regions, each was compelled to exploit the internal conflicts of the others. There were simply too few regions to permit the federal system effectively to decentralize conflict and to insulate the politics of the periphery from the politics of the center.

Finally, the federal structure heavily contributed to one of the most powerful structural problems of the First Republic, the close *coincidence of major cleavages:* region, ethnicity, and party. Instead of complicating and crosscutting the centralized character of the ethnic structure, the federal structure heightened it by making the Yoruba, the Igbo, and the Hausa-Fulani, in effect, governmental as well as ethnic categories. This made the organization of political parties along this divide virtually inevitable. When every election and political conflict became a struggle for supremacy not just between parties but between ethnic groups and regions as well, everything was at stake and no one could afford to lose.

The polarizing effect of coinciding cleavages was compounded by the *cumulative pattern of conflict* it helped to produce. Until independence, some relief was provided by the shifting of alignments over time in a three-player game. But with the destruction of the Action Group in 1962-1963, conflict was reduced to a running struggle between the NPC and its Southern antagonists, with the Northern party prevailing decisively over the AG in 1962, over the NCNC in the census crisis, and over the combined forces of Southern progressives in the 1964 and 1965 elections. This pattern, constituted the maximum formula for polarization: each successive conflict involved the same cumulative line of cleavage, the same configuration of actors, and the same predictable outcome. Given that the triumphant party lacked any support in half the country, and was also feared and hated in parts of the other half, it is not surprising that it was ultimately toppled through a wholly different process.

The most basic cause of the failure of the First Republic had to do with the *structures of class and state*. Nigerian society in this era was a prime example of Richard Sklar's argument that, in the emergent states of Africa, "dominant class formation is a consequence of the exercise of power."[81] Colonial rule left in place a modern state that dwarfed all other organized elements of the economy and society. State control was firmly established over the greatest source of cash revenue in the country, cash crop agriculture, and the greatest source to be—mineral mining.[82] In addition, state monopolies were established in many other sectors, private indigenous enterprise was discouraged, and the parastatal sector was rapidly expanded.[83] In the classic sense of a class of autonomous capitalist producers, there really was no native bourgeoisie. By 1964, 54 percent of all wage earners were employed by some level of government, and most of the rest (38 percent) were employed by foreign capital.[84] Moreover, with the spread of Western education, media, and consumer goods, colonial rule fostered the rapid growth of materialist values.

In the South, material wealth became the mark of what Sklar termed the "new and rising class." Government power became the primary means for individuals to accumulate wealth and enter the rising class, and for the ruling parties to weld diverse profesional, business, and traditional elites into a new dominant class.[85] In the Northern emirates, state power became the indispensable instrument for preserving class domination by reconstituting it on a modern foundation and broadening it through the incorporation of commercial and ethnic minority elites.[86]

The brutality and intolerance of political conflict followed from the sweeping nature of the stakes in controlling state power. Political and bureaucratic offices offered not only high social status and handsome salaries and perquisites,[87] but also vast opportunities for accumulation through bribery, embezzlement, favoritism, and other types of corruption.[88] Moreover, given the scarcity of private resources and opportunities, those who did not hold state office heavily depended on those who did. Political office could deliver or block the licenses, contracts, and public loan and investment funds that could make a new enterprise or a quick fortune, as well as the scholarships, government jobs, and military commissions that could quickly lift an individual from poverty into the middle class. By the same token, the loss of political office or access threatened an abrupt plunge in socioeconomic status. Few Nigerian politicians (or their clients) had alternative careers that could offer anything like the material and status rewards of state power. At the level of the group, state power was just as indispensable to material advancement. For communities, both rural and urban, it was the source of schools, roads, clinics, pipe-borne water, electricity, factories, markets, and almost every other dimension of material progress. For cultural groups, it could be the primary threat to or the primary guarantor of their cultural integrity.

Because of this enormous premium on political power, the competition for state control became a desperate, violent, zero-sum struggle. To lose political power was to lose access to virtually everything that mattered. Hence, political actors—even those committed in principle to democracy—were willing to use any means necessary in order to acquire power. This breakdown of constitutional norms, in the context of the high premium on state control, in turn generated a high level of political anxiety—"the fear of the consequences of not being in control of the government, associated with a profound distrust of political opponents."[89] In these circumstances, it was exceedingly difficult for elite accommodation and compromise to bridge the polarization and attenuate the bitterness of political conflict because these were so deeply rooted in the relationship between state and society.

This relationship is also crucial to understanding the politicization of ethnic conflict. Although each ethnic group had a real cultural and psychological stake in its own communal identity and progress, "tribalism" was not a primordial force. Rather it was generated "by the new men of power in furtherance of their" class interests.[90] These rising and traditional class elements had to control the democratic state. To do this, they had to win elections, and in a largely illiterate, multiethnic society, with relatively scant crosscutting solidarities or national ties, no electoral strategy seemed more assured of success than the manipulation of ethnic pride, jealousy, and prejudice. As they appealed relentlessly to ethnic consciousness, the politicians inflamed group suspicion and fear to the point where ethnic mobilization assumed an explosive momentum of its own.

In two other senses as well, tribalism was significantly a product of the class structure. First, it functioned as a "mask for class privilege."[91] By focusing politics on ethnic competition for state resources and by distributing patronage to their ethnic communities, politicians diverted attention from their own class-action and precluded effective class-based mobilization against it. Second, in mobilizing mass ethnic bases, tribalism became an instrument of competition within the emerging dominant class for the limited spoils of the developing state.

The extreme dependence of class formation on a swollen state is also crucial to understanding the escalating corruption that helped to delegitimate the First Republic. Even with the princely official salaries and perquisites, the accumulation of truly sizable wealth required the illicit manipulation of political resources. Moreover, as politics became organized into hierarchical networks of patrons and clients, in the absence of effective political institutions, corruption was necessary to maintain and extend the proliferating chains of clientage.[92]

Why the Second Republic Failed

Of the two structural causes underlying the failure of the First Republic, one was understood and rectified in the subsequent period of military rule, while the other was not. By creating first twelve states in the 1967 and then nineteen in 1975, the military governments dramatically reorganized the structural imperatives toward ethnic polarization. Innovations in the 1979 constitution further encouraged the development of crosscutting political cleavages. But the problem of statism and its corollary phenomena—corruption, clientelism, and waste—only grew worse during military rule. In this failure to alter the relationship between the state and society lies the primary reason for the failure of the Second Republic.

Despite the widespread disillusionment over that second democratic failure, it is important to appreciate the significant political progress that was achieved. Although ethnicity remained the single most important basis for political identification and alignment, the identity between party and ethnicity was perceptibly weaker in the Second Republic, and was beginning to decompose in historic ways when the system unraveled in 1983.[93] In this sense, the revisions in the 1979 constitution forbidding ethnic political parties and requiring visible evidence of crosscutting support as a condition for party registration must be credited with some real success. In particular, the much more complicated federal system made a profound difference. Although the Yoruba and Igbo states tended to vote as a block in 1979, the NPN made visible inroads there in subsequent years. In the North, the Hausa-Fulani heartland became a major political battleground, with the NPN and PRP splitting control of the four key states in 1979. As had been envisioned, the ethnic minority states became the swing factor in national politics (and a powerful pressure group within the NPN), and their political alignment was the most fluid and hotly contested. And, on some issues, such as revenue allocation—where the oil states lined up against the oilless states—the nineteen-state system did generate crosscutting cleavage.

It is a matter of immense significance that the kind of ethnic and regional polarization that savaged the First Republic did not emerge in the Second Republic. There was ethnic mobilization. There were charges of "big tribe chauvinism." There was North-South tension. There were all the traditional ethnic rivalries and hostilities. In fact, ethnicity remained the most salient political clevage. But it was much more fluid and decentralized. *National* political conflict did not polarize around ethnic divisions. Rather, the experience of the Second Republic demonstrated that in a democracy, deep cultural divisions, even a centralized ethnic structure, do not inevitably produce mass ethnic conflict. Cultural complexity can be managed and centrifugal forces contained by effective political structures.

And yet, politics were not significantly less violent, vituperative, and chaotic in the Second Republic than they had been in the First Republic. This was because the relationship between the state and the class·structure had not changed. State power remained the primary locus of national wealth, the chief route of access to the resources and opportunities of class formation. If the articulation of the private sector since 1966 opened possibilities for upward mobility outside the state that had not existed in the First Republic, so the petroleum boom opened possibilities for accumulation of wealth in office that could not have been imagined then. In fact, these possibilities were so fantastic that they brought an important change in the character of economic life, what Sayre Schatz has described as a shift from "nurture capitalism" to "pirate capitalism." "For the most vigorous, capable, resourceful, well-connected and 'lucky' entrepreneurs (including politicians, civil servants, and army officers), productive economic activity . . . has faded in appeal. Access to, and manipulation of, the government-spending process has become the golden gateway to fortune."[94] In other words, power has replaced effort as the basis of social reward. Under such circumstances, "a desperate struggle to win control of state power ensues since this control means for all practical purposes being all powerful and owning everything. Politics becomes warfare, a matter of life and death."[95] From this continuing enormous premium on political power followed the familiar consequences of political chaos, intolerance, and instability: the impeachments, decampments, expulsions, thuggery, rioting, arson, and massive electoral fraud that did so much to drain the Second Republic of the considerable legitimacy with which it began.

Perhaps no less than the above, political corruption also served to delegitimate and destroy the Second Republic. The continuing expansion of the state and the paucity of private economic opportunities has steered the entrepreneurial and acquisitive spirit into all kinds of political corruption. The heavily clientelistic character of party politics has further served to increase the spread of corruption during civilian rule. But significant responsibility must also be attributed to the failure of the legal system to restrain corrupt conduct in office. Corruption in Nigeria has offered not only immense opportunities for reward, but virtually no risk of sanctions.

The makers of the 1979 constitution understood that the conduct of public officers must be carefully circumscribed, monitored, and, if necessary, punished in order to reduce corruption. That is why the constitution contained a strict code of conduct and an elaborate enforcement machinery. The code required every public officer to declare all his assets at regular intervals to the Code of Conduct Bureau, which was empowered to monitor compliance and refer charges to the Code of Conduct Tribunal. The latter, a quasi-judicial body, had the authority to impose serious penalties on offenders, including vacation of office, seizure of assets, and disqualification from public office for ten years. But neither of these bodies ever worked as intended, because the National Assembly, upon which the constitution made their activation and supervision dependent, buried the enabling legislation. Without this legislation, the bureau was unable to hire any permanent officers, or to investigate suspicions and complaints. In fact, most public officials went several years without declaring their assets. The bureau never really functioned. The tribunal never sat.

This was indicative of a fundamental flaw in the 1979 constitution. Crucial regulatory functions, on which the legitimacy of the Second Republic heavily depended, were left open to manipulation, sabotage, and abuse by the politicians. As a result, other sensitive regulatory institutions—the Federal Electoral Commission, the police, and, to some extent, even the judiciary—behaved or were perceived to behave as partisan instruments of the ruling party. The problem is unlikely to be resolved by the traditional checks and balances between the three branches of government. The integrity of the legislature and executive is so suspect, and the pressures for abuse so powerful, that some wholly new type of institutional check is necessary (see this chapter's last section).

Other factors also contributed to the demise of the Second Republic. A significant problem was the chaotic party system. The military architects of the transition to civilian rule appear to have drawn precisely the wrong lesson from the failure of the First Republic. Suspicious and mistrustful of party politics, they delayed the lifting of the ban on political parties as long as possible, after the Constitutional Drafting Committee passed on Murtala Muhammed's invitation to "feel free to recommend . . . some means by which Government can be formed without the involvement of Political Parties."[96] With so little time for new parties to develop coherent identities, broad-based constituencies, and fresh leaderships, it was highly likely that the old political divisions and leaders and anxieties would resurface in a dominant role.

The character of political leadership was also a problem. It would have been difficult even for the strongest and most heroic leaders to contain the political violence and corruption generated by the high structural premium on state power. But President Shagari never put that propositon to a test. A weak leader prone to governing by consensus, he was unable to control the venal tendencies of his party machinery and closest advisers. The meetings of his cabinet and party councils became grand bazaars where the resources of the state were put up for auction. Hence, although Shagari was not a polarizing leader, and was more inclined than most to seek some reconciliation of differences, he could not deliver effective and accountable government. Most of the elected political leaders were corrupt, and organized or at least condoned the political violence. But it is misleading to attribute these fatal excesses of the Second Republic to the failings of its political leaders. It is doubtful that a new generation of political leaders will behave differently in a Third Republic unless the relationship between state and society is altered.

Similarly, it would be simplistic to blame the failure of the Second Republic on the economic depression brought on by the collapse of the world oil market. Even in the best of circumstances, this would have sorely strained an emergent democratic system. But the economy could have adjusted to this reality—painfully, but without the degree of dislocation and consumer hardship that occurred—if governmental capacity and resources had not been so relentlessly drained by corruption. With honest and effective government that was otherwise considered legitimate, the Second Republic could probably have survived this difficult period of adjustment. On the other hand, even with continuing economic boom, it would probably have been brought down by the corruption, mismanagement, deepening inequality, and political instability.

Why Authoritarian Rule Has Not Survived

To the extent that political culture has autonomous explanatory value for Nigeria's political development, it better accounts for the failure of authoritarianism than the failure of democracy. Nigerians value personal freedom; with the expansion of education, the mass media, and political participation in the past quarter century, this commitment has heightened. Because of the relatively liberal character of British colonial rule, a vigorous press, and a vibrant associational life were able to develop with modernization, independent of state control. By the time of the first military interregnum, these autonomous interest groups and associations had established sufficiently broad constituencies and deep roots so that they could not have been eliminated without a level of violent repression that no Nigerian military regime—even that of Buhari and Idiagbon—has dared attempt. In this sense, the Nigerian case supports the classic pluralist argument that autonomous intermediate groups "provide the basis for the limitation of state power" and make society less "likely to be dominated by a centralized power apparatus."[97]

Similarly, Nigeria's volatile ethnic and religious diversity has made it difficult to institutionalize authoritarian rule. It is very difficult to manage this complex cultural cleavage by authoritarian means because of the tendency for various groups to view any regime, and particularly a nonparticipatory one, as weighted against them. When there are institutional means for rotating national leaders, changing the composition of the federal government, and electing local and state leaders and representatives, each group can develop some degree of security and retain some hope of improving its position. But in an authoritarian regime, the ethnic identity of the few top leaders assumes exaggerated importance, and the distribution of power and resources takes on an aura of permanence, which makes it much more fundamentally threatening to groups that feel excluded or inadequately included. Thus, it is under authoritarian rule that centrifugal tendencies are most likely to be unleashed. The floating of proposals for confederation during the Buhari regime by prominent Yoruba and Igbo leaders was only the most recent demonstration of this danger.

Because of these various currents of social complexity, authoritarian rule could probably only endure if it pursued some strategy of institutionalization—most likely through the mechanism of a single party—that evolved some means both for the stable division of resources and for the regular rotation of leadership positions (among not only individuals but ethnic groups), and that provided some outlet for popular participation, criticism, and debate. Independent of whether such a system could withstand Nigeria's pluralist pressures and liberal aspirations (even if it governed more effectively), it would require an effort of political institution-building perhaps no less demanding than the reconstruction of a liberal democratic system. No Nigerian military regime has yet seriously contemplated such a task.

It is revealing of the nature of the society and its political culture that every Nigerian military regime has committed itself, at least verbally, to an eventual return to civilian rule, and no regime that has seemed to betray this democratic commitment has been able to survive. Although military rule has been the norm in Nigeria—having governed for almost two-thirds of the time since independence—it continues to be viewed as an aberration or correction, a prelude to something else. When it has lingered too long or governed too harshly, the institutional reputation and integrity of the armed forces have begun to suffer serious damage, and shrewder officers have intervened to rescue them.

• THEORETICAL CONCLUSIONS •

From the preceding analysis, *the relationship between the economy and the state* and the resulting *character of class formation* constitute the most basic reason for the failure of democracy in Nigeria and the most important obstacle to its future success. In part, this supports the proposition that stable democracy is associated with an autonomous, indigenous bourgeoisie, and inversely associated with extensive state control over the economy. But the logic of this association is not simply that economic and political pluralism tend to go together or that a hegemonic state is inherently undemocratic. Even more so, it is that democracy requires moderation and restraint. It demands not only that people care about political competition, but also that they not care too much, that their emotional and tangible stake in its outcome not be so great that they cannot contemplate defeat. In Nigeria, and throughout much of Africa, the swollen state has turned politics into a zero-sum game in which everything of value is at stake in an electon, and hence candidates, communities, and parties feel compelled to win at any cost.

This is not to say that the commonly presumed bane of democracy in Africa—*ethnic conflict*—is not a crucial variable in the Nigerian case. But the difference between the experiences of the First and Second Republics highlights the importance of the *federalism* in managing deep ethnic divisions. A structure that ensures some degree of group autonomy and security while crosscutting major ethnic solidarities can do much to prevent the polarization of politics around ethnicity. A flawed federal structure or unitary system can do much to generate it. Similarly, electoral regulations and structures can either reinforce or complicate, and so gradually soften, ethnic solidarities. Moreover, if ethnic conflict does degenerate into mass violence and civil war, this tragedy can serve as a learning experience, pressing ethnic elites toward structures and styles of accommodation and intergroup cooperation. This helps to explain the concern for ethnic balancing in the structures and institutions of the Second Republic and the efforts to make it work. Thus, the Nigerian case indicates that democracy in developing countries is not incompatible with even deep and complex ethnic divisions. The effect of ethnicity on democracy is mediated by other variables.

Political culture was also found to be a significant intervening variable. The style of political behavior, the willingness to play by the rules of the democratic game, heavily affects the performance of the constitutional system and the popular perception of its legitimacy. Values, beliefs, and cultural traditions all influence behavior but their importance should not be overstated. The degree to which political actors are inclined toward tolerance, compromise, moderation, and restraint is also powerfully affected by structural inducements and constraints. Values and beliefs appear to have had greater independent influence in precluding the institutionalization of authoritarian rule in Nigeria and pressuring for renewal of democratic government.

Other features of the institutional landscape have helped sustain the commitment to democracy, even though they have not succeeded in sustaining its actual practice. The role of the *judiciary* has been somewhat positive, although not nearly as much as it could be potentially. During the Second Republic, several notable judicial decisions served to limit the power and reverse arbitrary actions of the NPN government, and so reduced the fear of opposition forces that federal power would be massively abused to undermine and eliminate them. This points to the crucial role of an independent judiciary in developing a system of mutual security between competing parties. Unfortunately, the judiciary performed much less impressively in the more urgent test of the 1983 elections, failing to overturn many patently fraudulent election outcomes. The scale of the rigging was probably too great for the judiciary to play an effective balancing role, but part of the problem lies in the degree to which the corruption and inefficiency of a statist society have infected all public institutions, including the judiciary. This infection has been made more acute by the judiciary's lack of adequate autonomy from the executive and legislative branches. The latter two control not only the appointment and number of judicial personnel, but also the funding of the judiciary. Since independence, the extreme financial dependence of the judiciary on the other two branches, and its inadequate salaries, facilities, and staff, have been important causes of its weakness and vulnerability.[98]

A maturing and pluralistic *press* has been an important democratic force in Nigeria. The press played a largely positive role during the Second Republic, both in relentlessly exposing corruption, mismanagement, and abuse of power, and in warning, forcefully and repeatedly, of the dangers of political violence, intolerance, and misconduct. Unfortunately, the politicians blithely ignored these warnings. These positive contributions were counterbalanced but not outweighed by some continuing tendency toward irresponsible sensationalism and the proclivity of some newspapers, especially those owned by state governments, to reflect and accentuate the polarization of partisan loyalties. More effectively, but at greater risk to its practictioners, the press has kept alive the commitment to democracy and has sought to establish some kind of accountability during periods of authoritarian rule. Today, Nigeria has more than twenty daily newspapers. Two of the largest are controlled by the federal government, but there are four privately owned dailies with wide readerships, and several other private newspapers compete at the state level with those owned by the state governments. Since the fall of the Second Republic, several privately owned weekly news magazines have also begun to have an important impact on an information-hungry and opinion-rich public. Increasingly, the most popular and dynamic publications are in private hands. Despite the constitutional monopoly by federal and state governments over radio and television, this enormous pluralism in the print media is one of the most favorable conditions for democracy.

Similarly, the prospects for democracy in Nigeria are strengthened by the increasing pluralism of *associational life*. Although they have not been immune from politicizing pressures, professional and other interest groups, along with more loosely organized networks of intellectuals and opinion leaders, have constituted a significant source of pressure for democratic and accountable government. During periods of authoritarian rule, many of these groups have bravely asserted their interests in the face of intimidating power and sometimes coercive repression. Prominent on this organizational landscape have been the Nigerian Bar Association, the Nigerian Medical Association, the Nigerian Labour Congress, the Nigerian Chamber of Commerce, the Academic Staff Union of Universities, the National Association of Nigerian Students, the Nigerian Union of Journalists, and women's organizations such as Women in Nigeria and the National Organization of Nigerian Women Societies. At the local level, a growing number of interest groups abounds, both as constituent units of the above and as independent entities. Most of these are independent of state control, but even those, such as the trade unions, sanctioned by it have dared to confront it on occasion.

As should be expected, the *political party system* has played a significant role in the Nigerian experience with democracy. The coincidence of party cleavage with region and ethnicity produced destructive political polarization in the First Republic, while the banning of ethnic political parties and requirements for broadly based party organizations were one of the more hopeful developments of the Second Republic. The Nigerian case strongly supports the proposition that parties should crosscut other major cleavages unless a full-blown consociational strategy is attempted.[99] It is neutral with respect to the ideal number of political parties since it has never had more than a few significant ones, and the problem with them has been not their number but their nature. Political parties have been extremely shallow, fragile, and weak. Lacking the coherence, complexity, autonomy, and adaptability that are the mark of institutionalization, they have behaved as little more than associations of expedience for the capture of power.[100] Their incessant divisions, crises, defections, and recombinations have heightened popular cynicism about the political process.

Historical developments, in particular the *colonial legacy,* have also had important effects on Nigeria's experience with democracy. This was particularly so for the First Republic, in which the inherited federal system figured so negatively. The British could also be faulted for waiting so long to begin developing a modern democratic system, as a result of which the whole process of party development and political learning was compressed into a single decade. But while the colonial legacy still weighs heavily in some senses, such as the continued state dominance over the economy, it has been overcome in others; after a quarter century of independence, the utility of attributing political failures to colonial legacies becomes increasingly dubious. Moreover, it should not be forgotten that the commitment to democracy and individual liberties has been enriched by contact with Britain and other Western nations. While it had its authoritarian and exploitative side, British colonial rule also witnessed the development of the first modern newspapers, interest groups, trade unions, and political parties in Nigeria, and this liberal side of the colonial experience may, in the long run, constitute the more important legacy.

Although the analysis here has centered on socioeconomic and political structures, individuals cannot be absolved of historical responsibility for their actions. The repeated failure of democracy in Nigeria must be attributed, in part, to the choices and behavior of *political leaders*. Nigerian political leaders have been, for the most part, lacking in integrity and commitment to the democratic system. Their behavior has tended to be highly shortsighted and self-interested. Sadly, there have been few political leaders able to rise above the pressures and temptations of the system. But analytically, this behavior cannot be divorced from social structure. As long as the premium on political power in Nigeria remains so high, it would be unrealistic—and dangerous—to expect that a generation of more committed democratic leaders will emerge.

Development performance has also affected democracy in Nigeria, as theories of democracy would predict. A primary reason why democracy has twice lost legitimacy and been overthrown is because it has not delivered the goods. Economic growth sagged during both democratic experiences, with no plan or promise of development progress. By the time of the Second Republic, the agricultural sector (which continued to employ more than half the labor force) had precipitously declined, even in real terms,[101] and economic growth had become almost entirely dependent on the isolated stimulus of oil, through government spending. It was the double misfortune of the Second Republic to have inherited such an "inert economy,"[102] along with all of the other distortions of the oil boom, and to have been the victim of falling global demand for oil in 1981. But the federal government did nothing effective to restructure the inert economy or to cushion, manage, and reverse the economic slide. Rather, governments at every level deepened the depression through massive corruption, gross mismanagement, and callous indifference and waste. To a lesser extent, these phenomena also sapped development potential in the First Republic. In both experiences, they also heightened inequality in a highly visible way, directing particular resentment at the self-aggrandizing and conspicuously extravagant "political class."

Two factors magnified the effect of these development failures on democracy in Nigeria. First, because both republics were new regimes, their legitimacy was more heavily contingent on the effectiveness of their immediate performance.[103] Second, these development performances have been especially poor relative to the high popular expectations in each instance—generated in the First Republic by the great promise of national independence and in the Second Republic by the high rate of aggregate economic growth (averaging 7.5 percent during the 1970s) and the huge infusion of cash from the oil boom. But while the oil boom made possible rapid expansion of the educational system and the middle class, it also generated numerous distortions. Beyond those already mentioned, it eroded moral values, deepened inequality, increased inflation, displaced rural labor, discouraged entrepreneurship, distorted planning, and fostered corruption and waste.[104] On balance, both for democracy and development, oil has probably been more of a curse than a blessing for Nigeria, and for other developing countries as well.[105]

It is primarily through the nexus of oil production that the *international environment* has affected democracy in Nigeria. The resulting economic dependence has made the political system extremely vulnerable to changing conditions in the global economy. But the link between economic prosperity and political stability can easily be overstated. Gowon was overthrown at the peak of the oil boom. The Second Republic would have been overthrown even if there had been no glut in the global oil market. The effect of the international environment on the democratic prospect in Nigeria is probably particularly important at the moment, when deep indebtedness and a slack oil market have tied the country's economic future—and so, indirectly, the prospect and timing of a transition back to democracy—to the decisions of the international banking and trading community. As it did during colonial rule, the international environment also had a certain cultural and political influence on the Second Republic. Increasing identification with the United States had not only the positive effect of nurturing the return to democratic rule, but also the negative effect of encouraging the adoption of a constitution modeled too closely on the U.S. system. This experience should caution the established democracies against pushing their own constitutional arrangements as a solution to the problems of democracy in the Third World.

A few of the variables in our theoretical framework have not had any particular impact on democracy in Nigeria. Unlike in Latin America, the polarization of *class cleavage* has not figured prominently in the failure of democracy in Nigeria. There are several reasons for this. First, although economic inequality has been substantial and growing more extreme, this has been crosscut and overtaken by ethnic cleavage, and the politics of tribalism and patronage have tended to distract and eclipse emergent class consciousness. Second, because land has historically been communally owned in most Nigerian (and African) villages, Nigeria has not had the grotesque inequalities in land distribution and the huge class of landless peasants that have characterized many Latin American societies. Finally, because of the low level of economic development, the urban proletariat remains limited in size and continues to have close family ties to the hinterland.

However, all of these factors are changing. The number of organized urban laborers has grown considerably since the 1960s, and despite the efforts of earlier military regimes to incorporate and contain the trade union movement, it has become increasingly militant. Rural inequality is increasing as a number of large-scale agricultural development schemes are being implemented. This not only accelerates migration to cities that cannot meet the demand for jobs, but may also be giving rise to a class of landless peasants.[106] In both the countryside and the cities, there have been signs of growing class consciousness.[107] During the Second Republic, class cleavage was beginning to appear quite strikingly in the politics of the area where stratification has historically been most steeply graded—the emirate North. Partly for this reason, political conflict was especially intense there and antidemocratic behavior especially prominent. Thus, deepening class cleavage could become a serious threat to a Third Nigerian Republic if economic development does not generate improved livelihoods and better living conditions for small peasants and urban workers.

Finally, the institutional structure and character of the *armed forces* cannot be identified as a significant factor in the failure of democracy in Nigeria. In both instances of democratic breakdown, military intervention came after civilian regimes had thoroughly discredited themselves. Personal ambitions and institutional considerations may have been contributing motives of individual coupmakers, but these did no more than facilitate an intervention that was compelled by the malfunctioning of the political system. Hence, both the January 1966 coup and the December 1983 coup—and, probably, most military coups that overthrow democratic regimes—fit within the category of what Horowitz terms "reconstitutive" coups, in that they are occasioned primarily by systemic rather than institutional, sectional, or personal factors.[108] However, there are some indications of an emergent "bureaucratic-authoritarian" mentality in the military, modeled on the more repressive regimes of recent Latin American experience, and sharing the Latin American military's sense of "institutional mission" to eliminate the internal enemies of national order and progress. In this sense, the repressiveness of the Buhari-Idiagbon regime might represent only a modest precursor of what could follow the failure of a third attempt at democratic government in Nigeria.

• POLICY IMPLICATIONS AND FUTURE PROSPECTS •

Two broad policy implications follow from the analysis above. First, although the Second Republic made impressive progress in redesigning the "institutional architecture" of democracy, further institutional innovations are needed to check the powerful tendencies in contemporary Nigeria toward the abuse of power and the desecration of the rules of democratic competition. Second, economic and social changes are needed to attack the *source* of this tendency toward political abuse. As I have argued repeatedly throughout this chapter, such changes must reduce the premium on political power. This implies, in part, a reduction in state control over the economy.

Restructuring the Political System

At the beginning of 1986, President Babangida renewed the debate over Nigeria's constitutional future by announcing a return to democratic, civilian rule in 1990 and appointing a seventeen-member Political Bureau to initiate and lead what he termed the "collective search for a new political order." This "Politburo" (as it ironically came to be known) was asked to identify the reasons for Nigeria's previous political failures, to propose a basic philosophy of government, and to gather, collate, and evaluate opinions from Nigerians around the country. In the subsequent nine months, the members of the bureau criss-crossed the country during a vigorous national debate that elicited a broad outpouring of popular and elite opinion.[109] On 27 March 1987, they submitted their report to the government.[110] This was followed on July 1 by the release of the government's white paper.[111] Together, these two documents represent a kind of blueprint for the country's constitutional future.

Among the most impressive features of the Political Bureau's report was what it did not contain. The bureau—and even more so the government—resisted the impulse to propose wholesale changes in the country's political structure. In particular, the Political Bureau rebuffed many original, provocative, and ill-conceived proposals to do away with political parties, to recast (or in effect eliminate) the federal system, and to give the military an institutionalized role in government. Yet it did not shy away from proposing significant changes.

Reflecting perhaps the strongest point of political consensus in Nigeria today, the bureau urged and the government embraced retention of a multistate federal system. Rejecting proposals to eliminate state governments, or to drastically reduce or increase their number, the bureau opted for something close to the current nineteen-state system. A majority favored creation of a few more states (from two to six) to settle long-standing ethnic and political tensions (within the existing Kaduna and Cross River States), to give the system a better ethnic balance (by creating a third Igbo state), and to bring development closer to the people (in dispersed areas of the middle North "too remote" from their current state capitals "to feel the impact of meaningful development"). A minority favored no change at all. The government accepted in principle the creation of (a few) more states.[112]

This powerful federalist sentiment reflected an appreciation of the considerable success the multistate federal system achieved during the Second Republic in breaking up the hegemony of the three largest groups, decentralizing ethnic conflict, dispersing development activity, fostering crosscutting cleavages, exposing intraethnic divisions, and generally containing the immense centrifugal pressures inherent in Nigeria's ethnic composition.[113] But, at the same time, the bureau identified an aspect of Nigerian federalism in need of strengthening.

One of the Political Bureau's most significant proposals was to deepen the federal system by enhancing the power and resources of local governments. Since the onset of the oil boom, government authority and finances have become increasingly concentrated in the central government. The changes proposed by the bureau and largely accepted by the Babangida government would reverse this trend. Viewing local government as "the basic unit for the administration and development of the country," they give Nigeria's 301 local government areas (and also the states) substantially greater responsibility over economic development activities and social services, increase local governments' share of the federation's revenue allocation pool from 10 to at least 20 percent, and allow them greater latitude to collect revenue from diverse sources.[114]

Such decentralization figures to strengthen Nigerian democracy for several reasons. First, because the locality is the level of government closest to the people in any democratic system, giving it more power and resources figures to enhance popular control. But local government is not only a vital arena of action and initiative in a federal system; it can also be a school for the development of citizen awareness and political skills. In this sense, it may help realize the bureau's goal of mobilizing and educating the citizenry at the grassroots as "the greatest deterrent to bad government such as we have had in the past."[115] Moreover, decentralizing government power and resources also means dispersing the political stakes, which could help to reduce the tremendous premium on controlling the central government in Nigeria.

Another significant institution to be retained from the Second Republic will be the presidential system of government. In fact, the government rejected even the limited changes proposed by the bureau in this regard. Once again, the president, and vice-president, and state governors will serve four-year terms, renewable once (rather than the single five-year terms proposed by the bureau). The national legislature will remain bicameral, because—in contrast to the bureau—the government recognized the value, within a federal framework, of having an upper house drawing representation equally from all states and a lower house based on population. The government also rejected the majority view of the bureau that legislative representation be based only on local government areas, which would satisfy neither of the above principles of representation.[116] The bicameral national and unicameral state legislatures will again have four-year terms, and the local government councils three-year terms.

No doubt, there are strong arguments to be made on behalf of a parliamentary system. Particularly in a polity (like Nigeria's) highly prone to polarization, a parliamentary system offers greater flexibility, more scope and pressure for compromise and coalitions, and hence less of a zero-sum game in politics.[117] However, a presidential system makes more sense for Nigeria, not only (perhaps not even) because of its presumed "merit of unity, energy and despatch," to quote the bureau,[118] but because it has become an important instrument in Nigeria's strategy of managing ethnic conflict through the fostering of crosscutting cleavage.

In the presidential system of the Second Republic, the requirements for breadth of national support forced the parties and the presidential candidates to organize and mobilize across ethnic boundaries, and made of the president, in particular, a panethnic figure whose constituency was "all of multi-ethnic Nigeria." However, as Donald Horowitz has noted, the system suffered from a damaging internal contradiction, in that the method of electing national legislators from single-member (and mostly ethnically homogeneous) territorial districts meant that the National Assembly members behaved "as delegates of their ethnic groups."[119]

This may argue for innovation in the method of electing a National Assembly to give it more of the national, panethnic character of the presidency. An electoral system based on proportional representation from national party lists would move in this direction. On the advice of the bureau, the government decided to retain the single-member-district, first-past-the-post electoral system, with its closer ties between legislators and electorates. (Indeed, it even chose to retain the very same constituencies used in the Second Republic). However, the integrative potential of proportional representation should not be dismissed.

A possible compromise might be something along the lines of the West German system, in which half of the representatives would be elected by district and half by proportional representation from national party lists. In fact, the Political Bureau took a step in this direction by proposing that women and labor each be allocated 5 percent of the legislative seats, with the candidates to "be nominated . . . by the political parties in the ratio of their relative numerical strengths in each legislature."[120] This principle of functional group representation was denied by the government. However, Nigeria could innovate by allowing political parties to take these and other groups, crosscutting ethnicity, into account in selecting lists of candidates from whom some portion (10 to 20 percent, at least) of the National Assembly would be elected by proportional representation. Such a mixed electoral system would not only give the legislative branch a more transethnic character, it would also encourage the development of more coherent and vigorous national party organizations.

It was the issue of party structure that presented the Political Bureau with one of its most vexing problems. Mistaking the instrument of political instability for the cause (as had the Murtala-Obasanjo regime), many intellectuals advanced proposals for a zero- or one-party system. And in its open meetings around the country, as well, the bureau encountered tremendous popular cynicism with party politics. Still, the bureau recognized that the political party is an indispensable instrument for the articulation, aggregation, mobilization and representation of interests in a modern democracy. Further, it perceived the dangers of authoritarianism and regimentation of opinion intrinsic to one-party systems. But the bureau apparently was not unaffected by the antiparty sentiment, and it settled on the strange hybrid of a mandatory two-party system, which was accepted by the government. Both of the parties must subscribe to the national philosophy—although this will not be the "socialism" recommended by the bureau but a set of principles so general as to be acceptable to virtually all but the most extreme and explicit antidemocrats. As in the Second Republic, each party must also "reflect the federal character" of Nigeria by being ethnically balanced in its internal structures.[121]

Mandating a two-party system presents a number of problems. Practically, it is not clear how the new National Electoral Commission (NEC) will choose if more than two political associations meet the various requirements (including demonstrated breadth of organization across states and ethnic groups). In principle, it may be seen as a diminution of democracy to limit the number of parties arbitrarily to two, even if others satisfy reasonable and objective criteria for recognition. This too could have practical consequences, weakening the commitment to democracy of excluded groups and even inducing them toward violent, antisystemic means to express their interests. It could also be seen as undemocratic to require each party to subscribe to the same basic philosophy, although again, the government's version is now so vague as to reduce, in essence, to "democracy and social justice."[122] Perhaps the greatest argument against such an arbitrary limit on the freedom of political organization and contestation is that it is unnecessary. The political system of the Second Republic was moving perceptibly toward realignment into two predominant parties. With the absence from the scene of the historic ethnic political leaders—whether through banning, retirement, or death (which took Chief Awolowo in May 1987)—a Third Republic would figure to resume this progress quickly.

Whatever the party system, however, the principal challenge of political structure in a Third Nigerian Republic will be to devise more original and far-reaching mechanisms to check, balance, and distribute power. Both of the previous attempts at democracy were sabotaged by the abuse of constituted authority and the violation of the rules of democratic competition. Crucial procedural institutions were compromised by partisan manipulation and pressure: the electoral administration, the judiciary, the police, the census, and the code of conduct machinery. Constitutional provisions for the autonomy of the executive bodies overseeing these functions have been clearly inadequate.

If the democratic process is to work in any kind of predictable and orderly fashion, and if the contending parties are thus to develop confidence in its integrity, such procedural institutions must remain above party conflict and independent of party control. The failure of conventional provisions for separation of powers points to the need in Nigeria for a new body—almost a fourth branch of government in its autonomy—that would have exclusive authority for the appointment, funding, and supervision of those executive bodies in charge of crucial procedural functions. The scope of authority for such a national council should include the Federal and State Electoral Commissions, the Code of Conduct Bureau and Tribunal, the Federal and State Judicial Service Commissions, the Police Service Commission, and the National Population Commission. New regulatory institutions, such as a network of federal and state ombudsmen and a general accounting office (designed, like the GAO of the U.S. Congress, to monitor government inefficiency and fraud) might also be included.[123]

The most difficult problem in designing such a new regulatory structure is figuring out how it can be constituted to ensure its independence from control by political parties or the executive or legislative branches. One method that has attracted some favor in Nigeria would be to give this function (and perhaps others) to the military.[124] While opposing any major institutional role for the military—because of the danger that it might politicize the military and so destabilize the country—the Political Bureau nevertheless gestured in this direction by proposing that the military nominate two of its members to serve on the election commission and that two other high-ranking officers serve on the National Population Commission. The rejection of any military involvement in the political process (even in these limited forms) represents one of the most interesting and surprising—and in the long run probably one of the wisest—of the Babangida Government's intentions for the new political system.[125] The evidence from Asia and Latin America shows quite graphically the risk of enduring and undemocratic politicization of the armed forces that comes with giving the military any institutionalized role in government.

The Political Bureau proposed that the Council of State (which includes high federal officials plus the state governors) be given increased authority over the election and judicial commissions and over judicial appointments (and, more significantly, that the judiciary be given independent control over its own recurrent expenditure).[126] However, the government rejected most of these changes. And in any case, even though this approach would have reduced direct presidential control, the involvement of politicians (who form the great bulk of the Council of State, even as the bureau proposed to alter it) in such an oversight body is precisely what must be avoided.[127]

If it is to be effective, a national oversight council must be composed of civilians not involved in or beholden to political parties. One way to do this would be to have a number of Nigeria's independent interest groups each nominate a member of the council. These groups might include the bar and medical associations, the Nigeria Labour Congress, associations of students, journalists, manufacturers, traders, women, peasants, and other groups—autonomous from both the parties and the state—that represent important collective interests.

It is beyond our scope here to review all of the important issues in constitutional design (not to mention all of the bureau's political recommendations and the government's views). But certainly one of the most crucial issues is the structure and timing of the transition to democracy. A distinguishing feature of the Political Bureau's report, and even more so of the Babangida government's response, was the concern to devise a more deliberate and gradual transition to democratic government than occurred during the previous military withdrawal. Although the Murtala-Obsanjo transition had several phases, the resurrection of competitive politics and transfer of power happened quite rapidly, in the space of less than a year. Because most of its members felt bound to President Babangida's announced target of a handover of power in 1990, the bureau actually did not allow much more time for the reconstruction of partisan political life. It proposed to begin the transition in 1987 with the creation of new states, election of local government councils, appointment of a constitution-drafting panel, and establishment of the election, population, and code of conduct commissions. This would have been followed by a census in 1988, the lifting of the ban on political parties (along with new local government elections) in 1989, and first state and then federal elections in 1990.[128]

The chief problem with this formula was that, once again, it did not allow sufficient time for political parties to develop free from the pressures of an imminent election (or series of elections) in which virtually all political power would be at stake. The clear lesson of the Second Republic is that political parties need more time to develop fresh political identities and complex, coherent organizational structures. They need time, as well, to develop between them relations of mutual tolerance and trust, which will give them the confidence that defeat will not mean political obliteration and victory will be tempered by conciliation. Such a system of "mutual security" can only grow gradually over many years and several elections, although elites can do much at the beginning to initiate it.[129] This is one reason for staggering elections, so that state and federal offices are not contested all at once. It is also an argument for phasing in elections gradually, from the bottom up, to give parties time to get accustomed to competing with one another and to internalize the rules of the democratic game, beginning at levels where the stakes are small and the risks low.

Such a strategy of phased transition of course requires extending the period of partial military rule, particularly military control over the executive branch of the federation, beyond what would the country might prefer (or even tolerate). But, during this period of phased withdrawal, the military would serve as a more effective guarantor of procedural integrity and autonomy than would any ruling party (witness the difference between the 1979 and 1983 elections). This would remove the greatest danger during the transition to stable democracy: that "when conflict erupts neither side can be entirely confident that it will be safe to tolerate the other."[130]

In his address to the nation outlining his government's transition program, President Babangida quoted from the Political Bureau to emphasize the need for "a broadly spaced transition in which democratic government can proceed with political learning, institutional adjustment and a re-orientation of political culture, at sequential levels of politics and governance beginning with local government and ending at the federal level."[131] This concern for space, deliberation, sequence and political learning led the government to pospone the final transfer of power to 1992 (as a minority of the bureau had recommended). This extended timetable gave the government the last part of 1987 and the first part of 1988 to establish the most important regulatory commissions and bodies, to inaugurate a constituent assembly, and to hold (nonpartisan) local government elections. It then allowed the remainder of 1988 for these structures to begin operating, while consolidating the task of economic adjustment and renewal. And yet, still it allowed more than three years, rather than one, from the lifting of the ban on party politics to the election of a national president. Although it entailed five elections in three years, the government's timetable introduced the crucial innovation of phasing in the electoral struggle for power at progressively higher levels, permitting the competitors after each leap into the uncertain to pause, take stock, adjust their strategies and remobilize. The final three years of this timetable were as follows:

- 2nd quarter, 1989: lifting of the ban on party politics
- 3rd quarter, 1989: recognition of two political parties
- 4th quarter, 1989: partisan local government elections
- 1st-2nd quarters, 1990: election of state legislatures and governors
- 3rd quarter, 1990: convening of state legislatures
- 4th quarter, 1990: swearing-in of state executives
- 1st-3rd quarters, 1991: census
- 4th quarter, 1991: local government elections
- 1st-2nd quarters, 1992: National Assembly elections and convening
- 3rd-4th quarters, 1992: presidential election and inauguration and final military disengagement

While much more spaced, this timetable is still quite rushed—so much so that it may defeat much of the purpose of the spacing. On the other hand, it also probably represents the best compromise realistically attainable between the needs for deliberation and phasing and the popular impatience for a return to civilian, democratic rule.

The still-hurried character of this new transition underscores the urgency of getting crucial institutions working quickly. In particular, it is crucial that the military administration begin to set some standards for democratic performance by holding itself to standards of accountability and responsibility under law. Two limited steps here would be of enormous significance as a legacy for the future. First, the military could commit itself to abide by an explicitly articulated bill of individual rights that the judiciary would have the supreme power to interpret and enforce. Second, the military must establish by example that incumbent governments can be held accountable to standards of probity. Hence, the Babangida government must, as the bureau proposed, get the Code of Conduct Bureau and Tribunal operating before it leaves office and must require that all the incumbent political officeholders comply with the code's provisions, including the declaration of assets.[132] Perhaps no single development would augur more hopefully for the future of a Third Nigerian Republic than the prior establishment of a code of conduct machinery, which would have by the inauguration of the new democratic regime sufficient independence, experience, and organizational momentum (including some convictions and sentences) to effectively deter political corruption.

Reorganizing the State-Society Relationship

Partly in response to the request for it to recommend a new "national philosophy of government" and partly, perhaps, in response to its own ideological impulses, the Political Bureau dealt extensively with economic and social questions in its report. Weighing the competing merits of capitalism, socialism, Islamic theocracy, and African communalism, the report recommended a socialist system for Nigeria. State ownership would be extended throughout the "commanding heights" of the economy, including not only public utilities and enterprises involving the nation's political integrity and security, but also all those involving heavy capital expenditures or monopoly conditions. The private sector would not be abolished, but would be limited to agriculture and small to medium-scale enterprises.[133]

This is not the place to quarrel with the bureau's condemnation of capitalism for the mass poverty, ignorance, and disease it supposedly fosters, nor with the realism of its vision of a socialist "Eldorado where human want is eliminated but freedoms are guaranteed."[134] Nor is it necessary here to point to the generally poor performance of state enterprises in Africa. Whether or not further nationalization of the economy and constriction of the private sector will bring economic and social progress and greater national autonomy, one consequence is indisputable: it will increase state control over economic and social resources. And this can only increase further the premium on getting and keeping control of the state itself. It was probably more because of its own ideological and policy orientation that the government largely rejected the bureau's socialist agenda, but, whatever the reason, democratic politics will be more viable as a result.

The statist orientation of the Political Bureau's report was apparent as well in its recommendations on the press. Fearing control of the press by wealthy individuals, it recommended that government ownership of much of the print media continue, along with the state's monopoly over radio and television. Further, it suggested "abolishing private ownership of mass media except by organisations."[135] The government, in response, was notably less wary of statism with regard to control of the press.[136]

There was a certain tension in the bureau's report over the state-society relationship. While distrusting private control of the mass media, it called for strengthening press freedoms, including "the right to receive and disseminate information and protect the source of such information."[137] Similarly, the bureau favored (and the government accepted) a more direct state role in building a new political culture through the establishment of a "national directorate of social mobilisation and political education." Yet, this will also be supplemented by greater democratic involvement of voluntary associations such as cooperative unions, women's groups, youth and student organizations, and village, ward, and clan councils.[138]

This tension is not peculiar to the "Politburo's" intellectual debates and political recommendations, nor to the government's response. It is deeply embedded in the current Nigerian situation. Pluralism is vigorously established and increasingly assertive in the country's ethnic structure, associational life, and information order. But the state elite, including influential elements of the intelligentsia, continue to push the expansion of state control. This tension between pluralism and statism may constitute the country's most pressing contradiction. Certainly it is the one with the most profound implications for the future of democracy.

It is not only for political reasons that economic statism, or its graduation into a full-blown socialism, must be questioned. There is growing understanding in the international community (by no means just among the bankers and policy makers of the First World) of the economically dysfunctional consequences of state control over the economy.

This understanding was the major impetus behind the rather daring economic adjustment program launched by the Babangida government in October 1985. Through sharp cutbacks in petroleum and other consumer subsidies, decreases in government spending and employment, a more realistic exchange rate, and elimination of import licensing and exchange controls, Babangida sought to open up the economy to competition, to reduce state interference, and to get the country to begin living within its means. These developments, it was assumed, would increase productivity and investment in "real" economic activity, foster national self-reliance, and reduce corruption and waste. The leading element of this adjustment program was an effective devaluation of the naira by about two-thirds through the creation of a "Second-Tier Foreign Exchange Market" (SFEM), which exposed the value of the naira to market forces.

Before long, these historic initiatives began to yield some impressive results. In his 1 January 1987 budget message, President Babangida reported that the SFEM had boosted government revenues and increased the competitiveness of Nigeria's agricultural exports. Industry, which had been starved of desperately needed raw materials and spare parts under import licensing, also began to rebound. For consumers, times were hard, as import prices increased dramatically, but these hardships were balanced at least somewhat by greater availability of many goods.

Most of all, perhaps, the Structural Adjustment Program began to alter economic incentives and so to direct into productive activity (especially agriculture) the entrepreneurial energy that had previously been diverted toward the huge returns and low risks of government contracts and licenses. Hence, despite the steep sacrifices exacted by an austerity program much harsher than even the IMF had asked for, Nigerians responded positively, and there appeared "a dramatic release of creative energy for internal solutions."[139]

Of course, this was only a beginning. After two years of economic adjustment, it was not clear how long austerity could remain politically viable in the face of heavy international indebtedness and slack oil prices. But the internal reforms did give the regime some significant leverage with the international banking community, enabling it to negotiate new loans and extend old ones. Although trade unions and other groups demanded higher wages and more investment in social services, Nigerians generally seemed willing to give the program a chance.

The key question for future policy is how much further reform can go in the face of entrenched interests. The government has pledged to privatize more than 100 public sector enterprises, but this is intensely opposed by political and bureaucratic elites who do not wish to relinquish the economic control of which they are assured in a statist economy. Resistance comes especially from much of the Northern establishment, which fears that wholesale privatization would deliver the economy into the hands of the much larger, richer, and better organized Southern bourgeoisie.

There are ways of organizing the privatization process to take account of these concerns. The Babangida government has pledged to give special encouragement and preference in the purchase of parastatals "to groups and institutions like trade unions, universities, youth organizations, women societies, local governments and state investment companies."[140] Certainly, regional and ethnic balance can be a consideration in the sale of government companies, even at the price of some restrictions on the competitiveness of bidding. If this gave a one-time bonanza to certain groups and inviduals who could not otherwise afford to purchase these companies, this would be better for the economy and polity than the continuing bonanza that perpetually accrues to the incumbents of state power.

If it is to succeed in the long run, privatization must not only decrease state control over the means of production, it must also increase and stimulate indigenous private ownership of productive enterprises. The Political Bureau reflected in its report the fear that privatization might open a new wedge for expansion of control by foreign capital. This is partly because of the comprador character of the bulk of the Nigerian bourgeoisie, which has preferred the quicker, easier returns of intermediary trade and relatively passive participation (including fronting as owners) in foreign-dominated enterprises. As Thomas Biersteker has argued, state fiscal policies can be designed to make ownership of shares or partnerships in these transnational enterprises less profitable for

Nigerians than new enterprises which they might be induced to initiate in needed sectors or areas with income tax credits and other incentives.[141] Food production and processing is one sector with immense potential. A strong case could also be made for permitting (if not encouraging) private ownership of broadcasting stations (at least radio, initially), not only for economic reasons, but to promote greater pluralism of ideas and information sources.

Clearly, none of this is to suggest that the state can or should withdraw from the economy altogether. Nothing like a pure reliance on markets is feasible politically, and, in any case, even a laissez-faire development strategy requires active and effective government support (e.g., provision of credit, agricultural inputs, improved transport, and other infrastructure).[142] But if there is to be any basis for self-sustaining growth and peaceful, democratic politics, there must be a transition (in Schatz's terms) from pirate capitalism to a more sophisticated and effective nurture capitalism. Nigeria must develop, for the first time, a basis of production and accumulation outside of oil and outside the state.

This will require the development of a real bourgeoisie—both grande and petite, agricultural and industrial—that will not depend on the state for its survival, and hence that will be able to view the electoral struggle with some degree of detachment. If, at the same time, real risks and penalties begin to attach to the pursuit of wealth through political corruption, the linkage between political power and class formation will have been seriously undermined, and the stakes in the struggle for power measurably reduced.

The Democratic Prospect

Nigeria stands today at a crucial and possibly decisive crossroads in its political development. It is torn between its deep commitment to personal freedom and responsible government, and its revulsion with the corruption, violence, and self-interestedness that have twice consumed promising attempts at democracy. It further suffers a deepening contradiction between the pluralism of its social and cultural life and the statism that suffocates the economy and perverts the polity. The aspiration for democracy remains sufficiently strong to make it likely that there will be a transition to a Third Republic, if not by 1992 then probably not long thereafter. However, it is unlikely that a third democratic failure would leave the country poised, despite its frustration, for another try.

The conjunction of the huge challenges of political reconstruction and economic adjustment makes this a time of unique opportunity for Nigeria. But it is also a time of great danger. The contradiction between pluralism and statism will not remain at a standoff indefinitely. If Nigeria cannot develop and maintain a democratic political system, its liberal and pluralist impulses could come under intense and possibly violent challenge from any one of several forces.

There is, as has been mentioned earlier, a growing repressive mentality in the security establishment that could, at some point of acute political polarization, exhaustion, and despair, unleash a much more brutal and zealous authoritarianism than Nigeria has ever known. There is also growing sentiment for a much more radical break with the status quo on the left, which might seek by coup or rebellion a socialism (or at least a measure of social justice) that was denied it democratically. To some extent, these two pressures feed upon one another, carrying the potential for the "Latin Americanization" of Nigerian politics. In addition, one cannot ignore the growing incidence of religious mobilization, extremism, and violence in Nigeria, which could become a growing outlet for popular frustration and cynical elite exploitation if a pluralistic democracy cannot be made to work. In a country that is roughly half Muslim and half Christian, with a bloody ethnic civil war in its past, such religious conflict must raise profound alarm.

In short, the stakes in political engineering have never been higher. Nigeria cannot afford to fail in its next attempt at democratic government. Its social pluralism, cultural values, federal system, and even perhaps the political learning from the Second Republic offer real hope for the development of democratic government. If it can reduce the economic premium on political power and institutionalize powerful, autonomous mechanisms of public accountability, the prospects for consolidating democratic government would appear to be good. But if it should fail, it might well be a generation, with much blood and bitterness behind it, before the opportunity would come again.

• NOTES •

1. James S. Coleman, *Nigeria: Background to Nationalism* (Berkeley: University of California Press, 1958), p. 15.
2. Donald L. Horowitz, *Ethnic Groups in Conflict* (Berkeley: University of California Press, 1985), p. 39.
3. Coleman, *Nigeria*, p. 50.
4. Ibid., p. 323.
5. Ibid., pp. 308–318.
6. In addition to James S. Coleman's classic work, the indispensable studies of this inaugual era of party politics in Nigeria are Richard L. Sklar, *Nigerian Political Parties: Power in an Emergent African Nation* (Princeton: Princeton University Press, 1963, and New York: NOK Publishers, 1983); and C. S. Whitaker, Jr., *The Politics of Tradition: Continuity and Change in Northern Nigeria, 1946–66* (Princeton: Princeton University Press, 1970). Other important works on this period are B. J. Dudley, *Parties and Politics in Northern Nigeria* (London: Frank Cass & Co, 1968); and K. W. J. Post, *The Nigerian Federal Election of 1959* (London: Oxford University Press, 1963). The following historical review of politics in the 1950s and the First Republic draws from Larry Diamond, "Class, Ethnicity and the Democratic State: Nigeria, 1950–66," *Comparative Studies in Society and History* 25, no. 3 (1983); and *Class, Ethnicity and Democracy in Nigeria: The Failure of the First Republic* (London: Macmillan, and Syracuse: Syracuse University Press, 1988).
7. Michael Crowder, *The Story of Nigeria* (London: Faber and Faber, 1978), p. 231.
8. Whitaker, *The Politics of Tradition*.
9. Richard L. Sklar, "Contradictions in the Nigerian Political System," *Journal of Modern African Studies* 3, no. 2, p. 209.
10. Sklar, *Nigerian Political Parties*.
11. Ibid., pp. 88–112.
12. Coleman, *Nigeria*, pp. 332–352.

13. Whitaker, *The Politics of Tradition.*

14. Coleman, *Nigeria,* pp. 353–366.

15. Whitaker, *The Politics of Tradition,* pp. 361–362.

16. Post, *The 1959 Nigerian Election,* pp. 276–292; and John P. Mackintosh, *Nigerian Government and Politics* (Evanston, Ill.: Northwestern University Press, 1966), p. 525.

17. Oluwole Idowu Odumosu, *The Nigerian Constitution: History and Development* (London: Sweet and Maxwell, 1963), pp. 193–197; and Frederick A. O. Schwarz, *Nigeria: The Tribes, the Nation or the Race—The Politics of Independence* (Cambridge, Mass.: MIT Press), pp. 196–211.

18. Ernest Adelumola Ogunade, "Freedom of the Press: Government-Press Relationships in Nigeria, 1900–1966" (Ph.D. diss., Southern Illinois University, 1981), pp. 165–218.

19. Frederick Schwarz, *Nigeria,* p. 162.

20. Mackintosh, *Nigerian Government and Politics,* p. 538.

21. Richard L. Sklar, "The Ordeal of Chief Awolowo," in Gwendolen Carter, ed., *Politics in Africa: Seven Cases* (New York: Harcourt, Brace and World, 1966), p. 156; and "Nigerian Politics in Perspective," in Robert Melson and Howard Wolpe, eds., *Nigeria: Modernization and the Politics of Communalism* (East Lansing, Mich.: Michigan State University Press, 1971), pp. 47–48.

22. K. W. J. Post and Michael Vickers, *Structure and Conflict in Nigeria* (London: Heinemann, 1973), pp. 88, 90.

23. Walter Schwarz, *Nigeria* (New York: Frederick A. Praeger, 1968), p. 158.

24. Robert Melson, "Nigerian Politics and the General Strike of 1964," in Robert I. Rotberg and Ali A. Mazrui, eds., *Protest and Power in Black Africa* (New York and London: Oxford University Press, 1970), pp. 771–774, 785.

25. A. H. M. Kirk-Greene, *Crisis and Conflict in Nigeria,* vol. 1 (London: Oxford University Press, 1971) p. 20; and Robin Cohen, *Labour and Politics in Nigeria 1945–71* (London: Heinemann, 1974), p. 168.

26. Robert Melson, "Ideology and Inconsistency: The 'Cross-pressured' Nigerian Worker," in Melson and Wolpe, *Modernization and the Politics of Communalism,* pp. 581–605.

27. Post and Vickers, *Structure and Conflict,* pp. 141–149; and Mackintosh, *Nigerian Government and Politics,* pp. 576–579.

28. N. J. Miners, *The Nigerian Army,* 1956–66 (London: Methuen and Co., 1971), p. 178.

29. Crowder, *The Story of Nigeria,* p. 269.

30. Kirk-Greene, *Crisis and Conflict in Nigeria,* p. 4.

31. Anthony Kirk-Greene, "The Making of the Second Republic," in Kirk-Greene and Douglas Rimmer, *Nigeria Since 1970: A Political and Economic Outline* (New York: Holmes and Meier, London: Hodder and Stoughton, 1981), pp. 5–7; and Crowder, *The Story of Nigeria,* pp. 278–280.

32. Kirk-Greene, "The Making of the Second Republic," pp. 7–9; Crowder, *The Story of Nigeria,* pp. 280–281; and Billy J. Dudley, *An Introduction to Nigerian Government and Politics* (Bloomington: Indiana University Press, 1982), pp. 80–82.

33. Decree Number 53, for example, made it a criminal offense to publish or report "anything which could cause public alarm or industrial unrest"; granted the police and armed forces heads the right of arbitrary detention; and suspended the writ of habeas corpus. Victor A. Olorunsola, *Soldiers and Power: The Development Performance of the Nigerian Military Regime* (Stanford: Hoover Institution Press, 1977), p. 102.

34. *West Africa,* quoted in Olorunsola, *Soldiers and Power,* p. 88.

35. Olorunsola, *Soldiers and Power,* pp. 86–101; and Lateef Kayode Jakande, "The Press and Military Rule," in Oyeleye Oyediran, ed., *Nigerian Government and Politics Under Military Rule* (London: Macmillan and New York: St. Martin's, 1979), pp. 110–123.

36. Olorunsola, *Soldiers and Power,* pp. 60–76.

37. Statement of General Murtala Muhammed, quote in Kirk-Greene, "The Making of the Second Republic," pp. 13–14.

38. David D. Laitin, "The Sharia Debate and the Origins of Nigeria's Second Republic," *Journal of Modern African Studies* 20, no. 3 (1982): pp. 411–430.

39. Jean Herskovits, "Dateline Nigeria: A Black Power," *Foreign Policy,* no. 29 (Winter 1977/78): p. 179.

40. *Constitution of the Federal Republic of Nigeria 1979* (Reprinted by New Nigerian Newspapers, Ltd., Kaduna, 1981), p. 65, sections 202–203; and Richard Joseph, "The Ethnic Trap:

Notes on the Nigerian Elections, 1978–79," *Issue* 11 (1981): p. 17.

41. C. S. Whitaker, Jr., "Second Beginnings: The New Political Framework," *Issue* 11 (1981): pp. 2–13; and Claude S. Phillips, "Nigeria's New Political Institutions, 1975–79," *Journal of Modern African Studies* 18, no. 1 (1980): pp. 1–22.

42. W. Ibekwe Ofonagoro, ed., *The Great Debate* (Lagos: Daily Times of Nigeria, 1981).

43. Richard L. Sklar, "Democracy for the Second Republic," *Issue* 11 (1981): p. 14.

44. Whitaker, "Second Beginnings," p. 7.

45. Phillips, "Nigeria's New Political Institutions," p. 15.

46. Richard Joseph, "Parties and Ideology in Nigeria," *Review of African Political Economy* 13 (May-August 1978): p. 82; and "The Ethnic Trap," p. 18.

47. Larry Diamond, "Social Change and Political Conflict in Nigeria's Second Republic," in I. William Zartman, ed., *The Political Economy of Nigeria* (New York: Praeger, 1983), pp. 35–39. For a fuller review, see Joseph, "Parties and Ideology in Nigeria."

48. Martin Dent, *West Africa,* 6 August 1979, p. 1406; see also Joseph, "The Ethnic Trap," p. 20.

49. This section draws from several of my previously published works: "Cleavage, Conflict and Anxiety in the Second Nigerian Republic," *Journal of Modern African Studies* 20, no. 4 (1982): pp. 629–668; "Social Change and Political Conflict"; "A Tarnished Victory for the NPN?" *Africa Report* 28, no. 6 (1983): pp. 18–23; "Nigeria in Search of Democracy," *Foreign Affairs* 62, no. 4 (1984): pp. 905–927; and "Nigeria: The Coup and the Future," *Africa Report* 29, no. 2 (1984): pp. 9–15.

50. The most affluent party, the NPN, suffered by far the fewest disqualifications (6 percent), while its radical and much more humble Northern challenger, the PRP, suffered the most numerous (49 percent). Moreover, the PRP and NPP presidential candidates were not finally certified to run until less than three weeks before the election, when the courts overruled FEDECO's provisional disqualification. Haroun Adamu and Alaba Ogunsanwo, *Nigeria: The Making of the Presidential System 1979 General Elections* (Kano: Triumph Publishing Company, 1983).

51. Ibid., p. 199.

52. Ibid., pp. 255–256; Walter I. Ofonagoro, *The Story of the Nigerian General Elections 1979* (Lagos: Federal Ministry of Information, 1979); and Larry Diamond, "Free and Fair? The Administration and Conduct of the 1983 Nigerian Elections" (Paper presented to the 26th Annual Meeting of the African Studies Association, Boston, 7–10 December 1983), p. 25.

53. Richard Joseph, "Democratization under Military Tutelage: Crisis and Consensus in the Nigerian 1979 Elections," *Comparative Politics* 14, no. 1 (1981): pp. 80–88; and Whitaker, "Second Beginnings," p. 13.

54. Richard Joseph, "Affluence and Underdevelopment: The Nigerian Experience," *Journal of Modern African Studies* 16, no. 2 (1978): pp. 221–239; Henry Bienen and V. P. Diejomaoh, eds., *Inequality and Development in Nigeria* (New York and London: Holmes and Meier, 1981); and Michael Watts and Paul Lubeck, "The Popular Classes and the Oil Boom: A Political Economy of Rural and Urban Poverty," in Zartman, ed., *The Political Economy of Nigeria*.

55. Diamond, "Social Change and Political Conflict."

56. Prominent government actions overturned by the courts included the president's signing into law of the 1981 Revenue Allocation Bill after it was adopted only by a Joint Senate-House Committee; the jamming of Lagos State Television by the Nigerian Television Authority; and the deportation to Chad by the Ministry of Interior of a prominent GNPP leader in Borno State.

57. *Daily Star* (Enugu), 22 July 1981.

58. *National Concord* (Lagos), 26 October 1982.

59. *Punch* (Lagos), 31 March 1983.

60. *New Nigerian* (Kaduna), 25 January 1983.

61. Diamond, "Nigeria in Search of Democracy," pp. 906–908.

62. Newspaper interviews with a wide cross-section of Nigerians revealed a profound exhaustion and disgust with the greed, corruption, opportunism, thuggery, "witch-hunting and character assassination" that had "polluted" the political system. *New Nigerian,* 3 October 1982.

63. This interpretation was later confirmed by one of the key architects of the coup that overthrew the Second Republic, Major General Ibrahim Babangida. He revealed that the army had considered staging a coup as early as July 1982, but did not want to be fixed with the blame for preventing elections, and so decided to let them proceed. With the rigging of the elections they realized that that the chance for self-correction had been lost. (*Nigeria Newsletter,* 28 January 1984, p. 12). In

addition, a confidential source in the Shagari administration informed me that the president was warned in the spring of 1983 by a group of high-ranking military officers that a coup was inevitable if basic changes in the substance and style of government were not forthcoming.

64. For an extensive analysis, see Diamond, "Free and Fair?," pp. 43–52.

65. Another controversial FEDECO decision reversed the election sequence from 1979 so that the presidential election would be held first. This maximized the chances of an NPN bandwagon through the five rounds of voting.

66. See Diamond, "A Tarnished Victory for the NPN?" and "Free and Fair?"

67. Diamond, "A Tarnished Victory for the NPN?," p. 22.

68. This section draws on several of my previous articles: "Nigeria in Search of Democracy"; "High Stakes for Babangida," *Africa Report* 30, no. 6 (1985): pp. 54–57, "Nigeria Update," *Foreign Affairs* 64, no. 2 (Winter 1985/86): pp. 326–336; and "Nigeria Between Dictatorship and Democracy," *Current History* 86 (May 1987): pp. 201–204 and 222–224.

69. Diamond, "Nigeria: The Coup and The Future," p. 13.

70. *West Africa,* 2 September 1985, pp. 1791–1793.

71. Ibid., 7 July 1986, pp. 1403–1406.

72. Ibid., 2 June 1986, pp. 1144–1146; 9 June 1986, pp. 1196–1197; and 16 June 1986, pp. 1247, 1250–1251.

73. *Newswatch* (Lagos), 3 November 1986, pp. 13–25; and 10 November 1986, pp. 15–22; *New African,* February 1987, pp. 13–15.

74. *West Africa,* 20 April 1987, pp. 748–749.

75. On bureaucratic-authoritarian regimes in Latin America, see David Collier, ed., *The New Authoritarianism in Latin America* (Princeton: Princeton University Press, 1979).

76. Lt. Col. Ojukwu, quoted in Kirk-Greene, *Crisis and Conflict in Nigeria,* p. 146.

77. Mackintosh, *Nigerian Government and Politics,* pp. 617–618.

78. Robert Melson and Howard Wolpe, "Modernization and the Politics of Communalism," in Melson and Wolpe, *Nigeria: Modernization and the Politics of Communalism.*

79. Sklar, "Contradictions in the Nigerian Political System," and "Nigerian Politics in Perspective."

80. Whitaker, *The Politics of Tradition,* p. 402.

81. Richard L. Sklar, "The Nature of Class Domination in Africa," *Journal of Modern African Studies* 17, no. 4 (1979): p. 536.

82. Robert H. Bates, *Markets and States in Tropical Africa* (Berkeley: University of California Press, 1981), pp. 12–13; Claude Ake, *Political Economy of Africa* (London: Longman, 1981), pp. 63–65; Uyi-Ekpen Ogbeide, "The Expansion of the State and Ethnic Mobilization: The Nigerian Experience" (Ph.D. diss., Vanderbilt University, 1985), pp. 37–44.

83. E. O. Akeredolu-Ale, "Private Foreign Investment and the Underdevelopment of Indigenous Enterprise in Nigeria," in Gavin Williams, ed., *Nigeria: Economy and Society* (London: Rex Collings, 1976); Sayre P. Schatz, *Nigerian Capitalism* (Berkeley: University of California Press, 1977); and David Abernethy, "Bureaucratic Growth and Economic Decline in Sub-Saharan Africa" (Paper presented to the 26th Annual Meeting of the African Studies Association, Boston: 7–10 December 1983, pp. 12–13.

84. Diamond, *Class, Ethnicity and Democracy in Nigeria, pp. 178–179.*

85. Sklar, *Nigerian Political Parties,* pp. 480–494.

86. Whitaker, *The Politics of Tradition,* pp. 313–354; Coleman, *Nigeria,* pp. 353–368; and Sklar, *Nigerian Political Parties,* pp. 134–152.

87. Richard Sklar and C. S. Whitaker, Jr., "The Federal Republic of Nigeria," in Gwendolen M. Carter, ed., *National Unity and Regionalism in Eight African States* (Ithaca, N.Y.: Cornell University Press, 1966), p. 122; and Abernethy, "Bureaucratic Growth."

88. Schatz, *Nigerian Capitalism,* pp. 190–195, 208–209, 231–232; and Larry Diamond, "The Social Foundations of Democracy: The Case of Nigeria" (Ph.D. diss., Stanford University, 1980), pp. 556–582.

89. Claude Ake, "Explaining Political Instability in New States," *Journal of Modern African Studies* 11, no. 3 (1973): p. 359.

90. Richard L. Sklar, "Political Science and National Integration—A Radical Approach," *Journal of Modern African Studies* 5, no. 1 (1967); p. 6.

91. Ibid.

92. Robert H. Jackson and Carl G. Rosberg, *Personal Rule in Black Africa: Prince, Auto-*

crat, Prophet, Tyrant (Berkeley: University of California Press, 1982); and Richard Joseph, "Class, State and Prebendal Politics in Nigeria," *Journal of Commonwealth and Comparative Politics* 21, no. 3 (1983): pp. 21–38.

93. See Diamond, "A Tarnished Victory for the NPN?"; and especially *Nigeria in Search of Democracy* (Boulder: Lynne Rienner Publishers, forthcoming), chapters 3 and 4.

94. Sayre P. Schatz, "Pirate Capitalism and the Inert Economy of Nigeria," *Journal of Modern African Studies* 22, no. 1 (1984): p. 55.

95. Claude Ake, Presidential Address to the 1981 Conference of the Nigerian Political Science Association, *West Africa,* 25 May 1981, pp. 1162–1163.

96. Murtala Muhammed, Address to the Constitution Drafting Committee, App. II, *Constitution of the Federal Republic of Nigeria 1979,* p. 123.

97. Samuel P. Huntington, "Will More Countries Become Democratic?" *Political Science Quarterly* 99, no. 2 (1984): p. 203.

98. Dan Agbese, "The Courts in the Dock," *Newswatch,* 26 May 1986, pp. 15–22.

99. Arend Lijphart, *Democracy in Plural Societies: A Comparative Exploration* (New Haven: Yale University Press, 1977).

100. Samuel P. Huntington, *Political Order in Changing Societies* (New Haven: Yale University Press, 1968), pp. 12–24.

101. World Bank, *World Development Report 1981* (New York: Oxford University Press, 1981), p. 136. Between 1960 and 1979, the contribution of agriculture to GDP fell from 63 to 22 percent.

102. Schatz, "Pirate Capitalism and the Inert Economy."

103. Seymour Martin Lipset, *Political Man* (Baltimore: Johns Hopkins University Press, 1981), pp. 64–70; Robert A. Dahl, *Polyarchy: Participation and Opposition* (New Haven: Yale University Press, 1971), pp. 129–150; Juan Linz, *The Breakdown of Democratic Regimes* (Baltimore: Johns Hopkins University Press, 1978), pp. 16–23.

104. See note 54; also Schatz, "Pirate Capitalism and the Inert Economy"; and Diamond, *Nigeria in Search of Democracy,* chap. 2.

105. Jahangir Amuzegar, "Oil Wealth: A Very Mixed Blessing," *Foreign Affairs* 60, no. 4 (1982): pp. 814–835.

106. Watts and Lubeck, "The Popular Classes and the Oil Boom," pp. 120–126.

107. A striking manifestation of this in the countryside was the violent peasant uprising at the site of the Bakalori Dam in Sokoto State in 1980. Bjorn Beckman, "Bakalori: Peasants versus State and Capital," *Nigerian Journal of Political Science* 4, nos. 1 and 2 (1985): pp. 76–104. For evidence of urban class consciousness, see Paul Lubeck, "Class Formation at the Periphery: Class Consciousness and Islamic Nationalism among Nigerian Workers," in R. L. and I. H. Simpson, eds., *Research in the Sociology of Work,* vol. 1 (Greenwich, Conn.: JAI Press, 1979).

108. Donald L. Horowitz, *Coup Theories and Officers' Motives: Sri Lanka in Comparative Perspective* (Princeton: Princeton University Press, 1980), pp. 200–209.

109. Some statistics suggest the extent of the debate and the breadth of popular involvement. "The Bureau met 149 times, visited all the 301 local government areas in the country, and received a total of 27,324 contributions, among them 14,961 memoranda, 1,723 recorded cassettes and video tapes and 3,933 newspaper articles." *Newswatch,* 13 April 1987, p. 15.

110. The publication by *Newswatch* of a detailed analysis of this report (which was later summarized but not released in full) was the cause of the government's decision to seize all available copies of the 13 April issue and ban the magazine for six months.

111. *Government's Views and Comments on the Findings and Recommendations of the Political Bureau* (Lagos: Federal Government Printer, 1987).

112. Ibid., pp. 60–62; *Newswatch,* 13 April 1987, pp 24–26.

113. Horowitz, *Ethnic Groups in Conflict,* pp. 604–613.

114. *Newswatch,* 13 April 1987, pp. 19, 26; *Government's Views,* pp. 26–29, 59–60.

115. Ibid., p. 31.

116. Government's views, pp. 22–26, 30–31.

117. Juan Linz, *The Breakdown of Democratic Regimes,* pp. 72–74, and "Democracy: Presidential or Parliamentary. Does It Make a Difference?" (Paper presented to the workshop on "Political Parties in the Southern Cone," Wilson Center, Washington D.C., 1984).

118. *Newswatch,* 13 April 1987, p. 17.

119. Horowitz, *Ethnic Groups in Conflict,* p. 638.

120. *Newswatch,* 13 April 1987, p. 18.

121. *Newswatch,* 13 April 1987, p. 20; *Government's Views,* pp. 42–43.

122. Ibid., p. 14.

123. For a fuller discussion, see Diamond, "Issues in Constitutional Design," pp. 215–221.

124. This was in fact my own initial—and I am now persuaded, mistaken—thinking. See "Nigeria in Search of Democracy," p. 913, 916–919.

125. *Government's Views,* pp. 44, 51–52, 57–58.

126. *Newswatch,* 13 April 1987, p. 19.

127. *Constitution 1979,* Third Schedule, Part I, p. 103.

128. *Newswatch,* 13 April 1987, p. 38.

129. Dahl, *Polyarchy,* pp. 10–16, 33–40.

130. Ibid., p. 38.

131. Address by Major General Ibrahim Badamasi Babangida to the Nation, "On Political Programme for the Country," 1 July 1987, p. 5.

132. *Newswatch,* 13 April 1987, p. 32.

133. Ibid., p. 16.

134. The quote is from *Newswatch* Editor-in-Chief Ray Ekpu, ibid.

135. Ibid., p. 31, *Government's Views,* pp. 72–74.

136. Ibid., p. 75.

137. Ibid., p. 73. The government viewed existing constitutional protections as adequate.

138. Ibid., pp. 70–72.

139. *West Africa,* 12 January 1987, pp. 48–9.

140. *Newswatch,* April 13, 1987, p. 33.

141. Thomas J. Biersteker, "Indigenization in Nigeria: Renationalization or Denationalization?," in Zartman, ed., *The Political Economy of Nigeria,* pp. 203–205.

142. Sayre P. Schatz, "Laissez-Faireism for Africa?," *Journal of Modern African Studies* 25, no. 1 (1987).

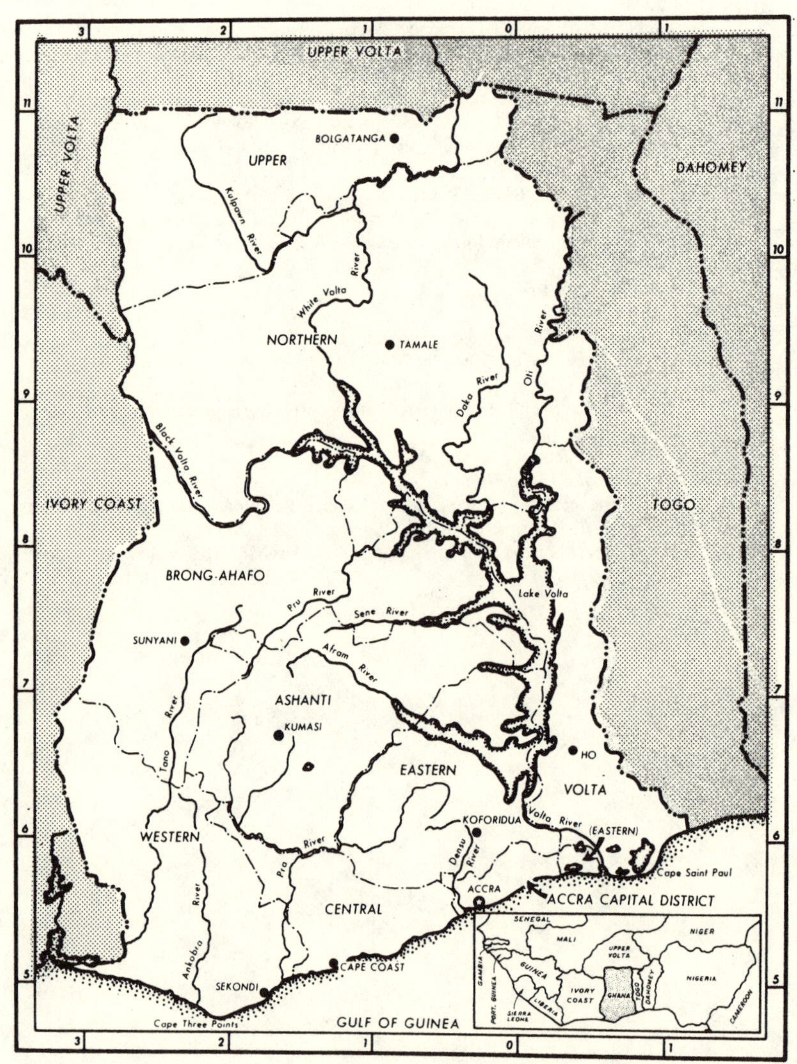

UPPER VOLTA
UPPER VOLTA
DAHOMEY
BOLGATANGA
UPPER
Kulpawn River
White Volta River
NORTHERN
TAMALE
Daka River
Oti River
Black Volta River
IVORY COAST
TOGO
BRONG-AHAFO
Pru River
Sene River
Lake Volta
SUNYANI
Afram River
ASHANTI
KUMASI
Tano River
EASTERN
HO
VOLTA
WESTERN
KOFORIDUA
Volta River
(EASTERN)
Pra River
Densu River
Cape Saint Paul
ACCRA
ACCRA CAPITAL DISTRICT
CENTRAL
Ankobra River
CAPE COAST
SEKONDI
Cape Three Points
GULF OF GUINEA
SENEGAL
MALI
UPPER VOLTA
NIGER
GAMBIA
GUINEA
PORT. GUINEA
SIERRA LEONE
LIBERIA
IVORY COAST
GHANA
TOGO
DAHOMEY
NIGERIA
CAMEROON

GHANA

• CHAPTER THREE •

Ghana: Problems of Governance and the Emergence of Civil Society

NAOMI CHAZAN

Liberal democracy has not fared well in Ghana; neither have its authoritarian alternatives. Ghana's political history in the postcolonial period is one of authoritarian rule punctuated by three brief democratic interludes (1957–1960; 1969–1972; 1979–1981). Despite the fact that Ghanaians have experienced only eight years of liberal democracy since the attainment of independence in 1957, the authoritarian form of government has been no more stable. Successive repressive regimes have succumbed to pressures for democratization. The search for democracy is a recurrent theme in Ghana's political life.

While the unstable cycle of authoritarianism and liberal democracy, of civilian and military rule, persisted during the first three decades of Ghana's history, economic and social conditions in the country steadily deteriorated. A once thriving economy was paralyzed while the initial vision of rapid development and prosperity yielded to the specter of a struggle for survival. Ghana's human resources, the bedrock of its potential, were dissipated and dispersed to other parts of Africa and the wider world. By the time Ghana had celebrated its silver jubilee in 1982, the institutions of Africa's first postcolonial state were on the verge of collapse. The cumulative effect of frequent experimentation with democratic and authoritarian rule has been to highlight issues related to the most essential task of politics: governance.

This chapter seeks to understand Ghana's problematic experiences with democratic government within the context of the repeated failures of authoritarian rule and to explain the relationship between democracy and governability in the country. Specifically, it first examines Ghana's various regimes and attempts to account for the failure of each of these efforts. It then addresses the general lack of success of authoritarian and democratic experiments and seeks to assess their implications for the cohesion of politics in the country. On this basis, it offers a theoretical analysis of the overall pattern. And finally, it explores some future prospects and policy implication.

• HISTORICAL REVIEW •

Ghanaian society, like that of most African countries, consists of various cultural groups, each with its own history, institutions, symbols, and norms of behavior. The most important linguistic constellation, namely the Akan-speaking peoples (subdivided into the Asante, Fante, Akwapim, Brong, Nzima, and other smaller groupings) inhabit the forest and major coastal areas of the country and make up 44.1 percent of the population. The Mole-Dagbani, concentrated in the north, constitute 15.9 percent; the Ewe in the east, 13.0; the Ga-Adangbe, who originated in the Accra region, 8.3; and other smaller groups spread throughout the country an additional 18.2 percent. Ethnic divisions in Ghana are accompanied by those of kinship, geography, custom, history, and administration. Households, local communities, lineages, and chieftancies are central frameworks in the daily life of Ghanaians, 73.4 percent of whom live in the rural areas.

Since special importance is attributed to group affiliation and group action, status differentials coexist with those of the cultural hierarchy. Ghana boasts a wide array of occupational groupings—including associations of lawyers, doctors, manufacturers, engineers, civil servants, and even chiefs—which thrive alongside a multiplicity of worker, farmer, and trader organizations. Students and women's groups have developed since the colonial period, together with vibrant sports clubs, "old boys'" and "old girls'" networks, literary societies, and a diversity of religious communities. One of the most outstanding characteristics of Ghana is that so many of its people have associations to pursue their interests.[1]

This intricate network of popular institutions underlines the diffuse location of social, political, and economic activity in Ghana. The interactions between these groups and central government structures have helped to define the nature of events in the country and to shape political dynamics.

Ghana has experimented with virtually every conceivable type of democratic and nondemocratic regime during its short existence. The Westminster model, introduced in 1951, gave way in 1960 to the single-party socialism of the First Republic. In 1966, Kwame Nkrumah's brand of authoritarianism was brought down by a group of moderate army officers bent on restoring administrative efficiency. The National Liberation Council (NLC), in turn, relinquished power to Kofi Busia's Western-oriented Progress Party in 1969. The experiment with liberal democracy during the Second Republic was short-lived: in 1972, Colonel Ignatius Acheampong, at the head of the National Redemption Council (later the Supreme Military Council—SMC) inaugurated a period of ill-fated military reformism. Acheampong himself was ousted by Lieutenant General Fred Akuffo in 1978. But Akuffo succumbed in 1979 to Jerry Rawlings' Armed Forces Revolutionary Council (AFRC). Participatory government was revived briefly during the Third Republic (1979-1981). On 31 December 1981, a new era of full-blown populism was ushered in as Jerry Rawlings resumed office at the head of the PNDC.

The variety of regime types in Ghana is an indication of their lack of durability: no government, whether authoritarian or democratic, has been able to survive for any significant length of time. Both the diversity of Ghanaian governments and their fragility require fuller treatment.

Nkrumah's Westminster Democracy (1957–1960)

Ghana's first democratic government was the product of the struggle for power that accompanied the final stages of decolonization. The banner of anticolonialism in the Gold Coast had long been carried by a small intellectual coastal elite that, in the postwar period, coalesced around the United Gold Coast Convention (UGCC). When Kwame Nkrumah broke away from the UGCC to form the Convention People's Party (CPP), he gave vent to the grievances of upwardly mobile social groups against the pampered professional establishment.[2] By 1951, when Britain agreed in principle to grant independence to the colony, it appeared that Nkrumah's acumen and widespread popular support would produce an early transition to independence.

The 1954 elections were called to determine the precise complexion of the government prior to the transfer of power. Organized opposition to the CPP was weak, coming almost entirely from the veteran leaders of the UGCC, then united under the banner of the Ghana Congress Party. However, because many CPP members stood for the legislature as independents, the party mustered only 55.4 percent of the vote.[3] At this juncture ethnic, regional, and religious groups, representing a medley of sectional interests, demanded attention. The National Liberation Movement, which grew out of a coalition of wealthy cocoa farmers, traditional chiefs, and Asante youngmen called for a federal constitution that would adequately reflect the cultural diversity of the country. It was joined by the Northern People's Party, the Togoland Congress, the Ga Shifimo Kpee, and the Muslim Association Party. Ethnic and cultural concerns were thus superimposed on the mass-elite divisions that had previously characterized anticolonial politics.

In the face of these demands, the British decided to hold another round of elections to determine the composition and form of the first independence government.[4] The 1956 ballot sought not only to shape future national institutions, but to do so through political competition and free choice. A mass anticolonial party, the CPP, with its urban, youthful, populist, and minority ethnic composition, was pitted against a loose rural-based constellation of elitist, entrepreneurial, traditional, and professional interests focused around the NLM. Although the contenders for office were ostensibly drawn from a small pool of businessmen, lawyers, traders, teachers, and clerks, party leaders represented differing ideological orientations and appealed to differing constituencies. The tone of the CPP was set by its populist beliefs; that of the NLM and its allies by the concerns of its middle class professionals. These two crosscutting coalitions, in fact, established the pattern of intraelite conflict that was to endure for years to come.[5]

Throughout the election campaign, the CPP championed unitary government, the weakening of traditional authority, and social reform. Its opponents rallied to the values of federalism, liberalism, tradition, localism, and social continuity. The CPP's youngmen accused the NLM and its allies of delaying independence and supporting the prolongation of colonial rule. These charges were answered by an appeal for the revitalization of traditional norms and by an outright attack against the CPP, its questionable methods, and its authoritarian tendencies. The volatility, tension, and periodic threats of violence that accompanied the campaign were indicative of the intensity of feelings about these issues.

At the local level, an additional set of specific issues was introduced into the campaign. Thus, the CPP made ethnic pleas to minorities and took advantage of chieftaincy disputes throughout the Akan areas. The other parties unabashedly highlighted where their candidates were from and what they had to offer.[6] In this setting, the dynamic personality of Kwame Nkrumah outshone the lackluster images of his opponents. In a sense, voters were consciously tied to their candidates in a personalistic bond based on perceptions of interest, identity, and benefit.

In 1956, the CPP garnered 54 percent of the popular vote and 71 of the 104 seats in the National Parliament. Its achievement may be credited to its position at the forefront of the anticolonial struggle, to the advantages of incumbency, and to the force of Nkrumah's personality. The CPP's youngmen offered something new and exciting, and succeeded in transmitting their message to the countryside. Because the CPP also contested each constituency in terms of local concerns, it could justifiably lay claim to success on a nationwide scale.[7]

The timing and the circumstances of the 1956 elections enabled the CPP and Kwame Nkrumah to assure their predominance on the eve of independence. Nevertheless, the small margin of the CPP victory highlighted the fragile basis upon which this position rested. The 1956 elections, therefore, exposed the multiple rifts within Ghanaian society at the same time as they empowered the new CPP leadership to guide the country through the first years of independence.[8]

Ghana's emergence as the first postcolonial African state, on 7 March 1957, was a watershed in the history of the continent. For Ghanaians, the manner of decolonization determined the framework of public life in the initial years of independence. The constitution designed at this juncture formalized the unitary structure advocated by Kwame Nkrumah. Derived as it was from the Westminster model, it made provisions for parliamentary government based on multiparty competition and continuing participation in regularly scheduled elections. The independence of the judiciary was assured, and essential liberties protected. This formulation represented a compromise between the British desire to perpetuate their own democratic framework on African soil and their recognition of the need to respond to the CPP's imperatives of control. Thus, the constitutional arrangements of the new Ghana exemplified the fact that both the excitement of political emancipation and the promise of a better future were tempered by a growing awareness of the domestic and external constraints that accompanied Ghanaians on the road to independence.

The democratic government of the new state was confronted by a host of problems that had to be confronted simultaneously. These included not only the almost insurmountable challenge of meeting inflated expectations with meager resources, but also the need to assert autonomy from the metropole, to incorporate a diverse population into a workable whole, and to establish policy guidelines for future action.[9]

The significance of workable public institutions was magnified in these circumstances. But the CPP's ruling coalition—made up of the newly forged network of small farmers, workers, clerks, youngmen, and spokesmen for poorer regions and non-Akan groups—was insecure: it did not have access to independent material resources, and its supporters were not well represented in the civil service or the traditional authority structures. It consequently overreacted to opposition activities. When ethnic unrest surfaced in Accra and the Trans-Volta Togoland area, the government responded by prohibiting ethnically based parties. When rumors circulated about plots against the regime, Nkrumah legislated a Preventive Detention Act aimed specifically at his most vociferous detractors (especially J. B. Danquah and K. A. Busia).[10] At the same time, government resources were channeled into party coffers, and the CPP penetrated the rural areas through party appointments of local officials. During its first two years in office, then, the CPP moved further away from the intentions of the farmers of its democratic government.

By 1960, the euphoria of decolonization had begun to wear thin, and the inherited problems of governing a predominantly rural population in an unintegrated economy had intensified. The Westminster model did not seem to provide adequate means either to respond to continuous pressures on the new regime or to stifle discontent within the ranks of the party faithful. Kwame Nkrumah therefore decided to alter the structure of government. In 1960, he introduced a draft republican constitution that augmented the concentration of powers in the hands of a president, to be elected by universal franchise. Careful to abide by legal niceties, Nkrumah presented the new constitution for the approval of the electorate in a nationwide referendum held in April 1960.[11] In this way he hoped simultaneously to eliminate effective opposition and to establish a firmer grip on the reins of government.[12] The amount of competition was therefore carefully circumscribed, while CPP-induced mobilization was actively encouraged.

As expected, the republican constitution received massive approval and Kwame Nkrumah dealt J. B. Danquah, the other presidential contender, a resounding defeat. In effect, the 1960 plebiscite was a carefully engineered executive coup carried out through the ballot box. As a result, the powers of the National Assembly to curtail the presidency were reduced, and the state bureaucratic structure was placed in the hands of Kwame Nkrumah and the CPP. State power was consolidated in an authoritarian mold. A state-centric, party dominated, and highly personalized system was institutionalized and its patronage web expanded.[13] The impulse for control had won over the principle of competition. By 1960, for all intents and purposes, Ghana had become a one-party state.

Ghana's experiment with Westminster democracy was halfhearted and short-lived. Ghanaians had had little practical experience with this model under colonial rule until the postwar period. The independent class structures that buttressed this form of government in Europe did not exist in Ghana at the time. The Westminster construct had not proven its efficiency in the first years of independence. In Ghana, as elsewhere on the continent, a British style of parliamentary democracy retreated quickly along with its colonial originators because the new leaders had little commitment to uphold its precepts.[14]

The First Republic (1960–1966)

The creation of the First Republic was intended to inaugurate a new and permanent set of institutional arrangements that would endure forever. The pivot of the new structure was the state apparatus controlled by the CPP and Kwame Nkrumah.

During the first years of independence, the centrality of the party was consciously augmented. The central committee of the CPP was made responsible for the selection of members of parliament and lower functionaries. The party attempted to gain control over voluntary associations through the creation and control of functional groups such as the United Ghana Farmers Council, the Ghana Trade Union Congress (TUC), the Young Pioneers, the Workers Brigade, and the National Union of Ghanaian Students (NUGS).[15]

Once the party had been consolidated, attention turned to the bureaucratic apparatus inherited from the colonial era. Bureaucratic offices were expanded, new ministries were established a wide array of state corporations was created, and new graduates were incorporated into the civil service. Gradually, two sets of frequently overlapping bureaucratic networks were formed. The party machine continued to function alongside the party-controlled state bureaucracy, thereby institutionalizing a dualistic structure that limited the operational freedom of the technocrats and exposed them to political pressures.[16] Kwame Nkrumah was positioned at the apex of the new edifice. The personality cult that developed with his active support propounded the myth of his immortality in order to underline the durability of the new structure of government.[17]

By the early 1960s, while popular participation in decisionmaking was circumscribed, state institutions charged with the enforcement of decisions were politicized and subjected to direct partisan pressures. Nkrumaism, Ghana's brand of African socialism, was to provide the substantive direction for these structures. Designed to forward what it considered the good of all the people, it rejected both the colonial and precolonial past in an effort to come to terms with demands of social and economic reform.[18] Nkrumaism rested on several distinct pillars: an outright and speedy attack on underdevelopment; industrialization as the key to economic growth; the rapid expansion of state intervention in the economy; and a realignment of foreign contacts.[19]

Nkrumah's "Dawn Broadcast" of 8 April 1961 officially launched the socialist phase of the First Republic, which had been stimulated by the new leadership in the CPP that was composed of a mixture of radicals and opportunists. The cocoa trade was nationalized, heavy emphasis was placed on centralized planning and state ownership, and a shift from investment in infrastructure to industrial production was announced.[20]

The socialist program of the First Republic was predicated on ideological mobilization and the quest for political uniformity. The Kwame Nkrumah Ideological Institute was established at Winneba to propagate the principles of Nkrumaism. The previously free press was muzzled when the state took control over the media, and the activities of nonparty voluntary and religious groups were purposely curtailed. When these actions were challenged in the courts, judicial decisions were openly defied by the regime. The repression of political freedoms was implemented not only by party loyalists, but also by the state security services and by vigilante groups of Party Vanguard Activists charged with policing the new order. Nevertheless, Nkrumah could not silence CPP members of Parliament, who continued to engage in lively debates and to question government actions and authoritarian practices.

Under these circumstances, it is hardly surprising that the performance of the government of the First Republic was unimpressive. The CPP's state entrepreneurs focused their energies on managing the new public corporations and controlling the marketing boards. The state was elevated to the stature of the major employer in the modern sector. State enterprises, however, were expensive, inefficient, and frequently mismanaged.[21] Moreover, they could not always penetrate to the point of production. Thus, farmers at times could be prevented from marketing their cocoa through other channels, but they could not be forced to sell it to the marketing boards.[22] While revenues from public sector firms declined, party officers (including Nkrumah himself) took advantage of their position to enrich themselves and to mollify their followers.

Economic problems began to surface in 1961 as imports and government expenditures rose, while proceeds from exports (cocoa and mining) began to level off. The austerity measures imposed to deal with these difficulties merely intensified public discontent. Between 1962 and 1966, industrial production fell off, prices rose, and, while capital investments remained high, consumption declined and indebtedness grew. The socialist program had clearly not brought prosperity to Ghana. When Nkrumah was overthrown the foreign debt had risen to $768 million. Government plants were operating at 20 percent of single shift capacity. Although cocoa production was up, real urban wages fell.[23] The devaluation announced in early 1966 was a feeble acknowledgement of the sorry performance of the Nkrumaist bureaucracy.

The policies of the authoritarian government evoked strong opposition. Political conflict during the CPP years proceeded in several well-defined stages. First, the party set out to weaken the established intellectuals, chiefs, large cocoa farmers, and professionals—the backbone of the opposition in the 1950's. Vocal dissenters were jailed or exiled. The second stage of conflict commenced in 1961, with the eruption of a series of workers' strikes, spearheaded by the Takoradi railwaymen.[24] Vociferous trade unions were joined by religious groups who opposed the attribution of godly qualities to Nkrumah. Simultaneously, cracks appeared within the party: after an attempt on Nkrumah's life at Kulungugu, moderate elements were purged. The distance between the president and his supporters widened.[25]

The third stage of conflict, roughly between 1962 and 1964, witnessed a generalized wave of protest as students, women's associations, professional organizations, and disenfranchised ethnic groups joined in countrywide protests. By 1964, not one of Ghana's vibrant corporate groups, social formations, or community structures (including many of the original party faithful) openly supported the regime.

The Nkrumaist response was to isolate itself even more from public currents. In 1964, through a manipulated referendum, the government officially transformed Ghana into a one-party state. It resorted to the use of force to achieve compliance, and its officials continued to engage in rampant corruption.[26] By 1965, falling cocoa prices and failing state enterprises combined to make the Nkrumaist experiment a shambles: Nkrumah was isolated, and authoritarian rule had given way to precariously personalized government.

On 24 February 1966, a group of army officers, led by Colonel E. K. Kotoka, Police Inspector J. W. K. Harlley, and A. A. Afrifa, carried out a coup d'état against Nkrumah while he was on a state visit to China. Support for the abrupt overthrow of the Nkrumah tyranny came from all segments of Ghanaian society: the government of the First Republic and its operative organ, the CPP, disintegrated overnight.[27]

There has been a continual debate over the causes for the downfall of Ghana's first authoritarian government. Some have claimed that socialism is unsuitable to the Ghanaian environment. Others stated that the Nkrumaist brand of socialism was inadequate.[28] A few observers have suggested that the president was too weak and inconsistent, while others have decried his unbridled authoritarianism. Whether Kwame Nkrumah was a victim of his domestic and external environment, a true social reformer, or an autocrat, his demise was a consequence of a repressive regime that permitted select groups to pursue their own interests and thereby render popular criticism ineffective.[29] His authoritarian experiment could not even ensure its own survival.[30]

Yet, the First Republic could point to several achievements: the expansion of a universal system of education, the construction of a network of institutions of higher education, the development of impressive medical facilities, a decrease in the rate of infant mortality, and increases in cocoa and other agricultural production alongside a rise in exports. Infrastructural facilities were improved, Tema harbor was constructed, and the Akosombo Dam gave Ghana control over important energy resources. More significantly, Kwame Nkrumah, with his emphasis on improving the lot of all Ghanaians, helped to develop a national consciousness linked to the value of social equality.

The CPP government, however, also left behind a multiplicity of problems. Ghana's foreign reserves had been systematically squandered, a cycle of external indebtedness was set in motion, real urban wages were cut by half in the last two years of CPP rule, and the state had proven to be a poor facilitator of economic development.[31] This record of economic mismanagement placed a heavy burden on Nkrumah's successors.

Kwame Nkrumah's legacy was one of statism and inefficiency. The quest for control, populist pretensions notwithstanding, was pursued at the expense of popular cooperation and participation. The CPP's ideology of socialism denied the representative rights of those who did not agree with its vision. Authoritarianism under Nkrumah rested on repression and the purposeful curbing of civil and political liberties (especially personal, associational, press, and judicial freedoms). The fact that life was not as intolerable as it could have been was due not only to the activities of individual Ghanaians, but also to the inefficiency of the regime. The CPP's authoritarianism bred mismanagement and corruption. The First Republic politicized and personalized the state apparatus in Ghana: it first augmented the centrality of state structures and then allowed for their subversion for private ends.

The National Liberation Council (1966–1969)

The first intrusion of the military into the political arena was intended to clean up the mess left by Nkrumah and hand over government to a new set of responsible leaders. It was therefore temporary in nature and corrective in design.[32]

The ruling National Liberation Council (NLC) was headed by Lieutenant General J. A. Ankrah. Its eight members were mostly Sandhurst-trained, Western-oriented senior military and police officers. Ethnically, however, the NLC was skewed toward Ga and Ewe. The new government relied, at the outset, on broad-based support that came from bureaucrats and chiefs, students and professionals. Civilians were prominently represented on some councils.

The NLC's outlook was pragmatic and pluralistic, reflecting its administrative makeup and its distaste for Nkrumah and his ideology. It sought to promote individual responsibility and reduce state involvement in economic production and distribution. The NLC turned its attention first to eradicating Nkrumaism and punishing its purveyors. Political activity was curtailed and a bewildering array of commissions were established to investigate the wrongdoings of the previous regime.[33] At the same time, an effort was made to restore civil liberties and facilitate civic reeducation. Voluntary organizations were encouraged, some press freedoms were restored (even though censorship continued), and the autonomy of the judiciary was reinstated.

The first military leaders also dismantled several state corporations in an effort to streamline government expenditures. They lifted controls on the private sector, permitted the freer importation of goods from abroad, and avidly courted Western financial concerns. In 1967, the government adopted an IMF stabilization program that commenced with a 30 percent devaluation. The 1967 statistics did show some stability: commodity prices dropped, inflation was checked, and cocoa production was sustained. A year later, these moves were regularized in a two-year development plan. In order to deflect allegations that it favored foreign capital, the NLC also passed the Ghanaian Enterprises Decree in December 1968, which curbed immigration and stipulated that the retail trade be indigenized within five years.[34]

In retrospect, NLC policies gave both Ghanaians and their economy a measure of breathing space, leaving major socioeconomic strategy for its successors. The military government was not, however, without its critics. Ethnic leaders from the forest regions and the north felt that their political access was circumscribed by the coastal complexion of the NLC. Students and displaced politicians were quick to express dissatisfaction with the regime's pro-Western orientation. These strains came to a head in April 1967, when Colonel E. K. Kotoka was killed in an abortive coup. By then, the trade unions were sufficiently disaffected to launch a series of debilitating strikes in 1968 and 1969. At the same time, ethnic tensions within the NLC grew. At this juncture, the NLC leaders decided to hasten the return to civilian rule.

The retreat to the barracks in 1969 was voluntary and planned. The soldiers had intervened to rectify the Nkrumah debacle, and returned to the barracks to maintain their cohesion once they felt that they had accomplished this goal. The National Liberation Council (NLC), although authoritarian by definition, was also more responsive than its civilian predecessor. It lacked the overtly repressive qualities that had characterized government under the CPP. Nevertheless, the NLC set a problematic precedent: it institutionalized the army as a potent political force and an acceptable funnel for political change. It, therefore, set in motion a deleterious cycle of civilian rule and military intervention that has not as yet been halted.[35]

The Second Republic (1969–1977)

The democratic government of the Second Republic came into being by the ballot box at a historical crossroad. The 1969 elections were seen as the culmination of the process of recuperation from the excesses of the Nkrumah period.

They were intended to provide a necessary affirmation of the reconstituted order and an opportunity to reintroduce meaningful popular participation after years of authoritarian rule.[36]

The elections were preceded by a conscious, thorough, and intricate exercise in constitution-making.[37] A constitutional commission was established in September 1966, barely seven months after the coup that ousted Nkrumah. Its seventeen members represented the lawyers, academics, and professionals of the UGCC and the NLM. After a series of consultations with major organized groups, they produced a cumbersome legalistic document characterized by strong platonic overtones. To be sure, provisions for the protection of human and civil rights were everywhere in evidence; particular consideration was given to the position of certain groups (such as the armed forces and the civil service). But limitations were placed on the popularly elected legislature. Although the Westminster-based proposals were endowed with more populist concerns by the Constituent Assembly, the resultant document was heavily influenced by the elitist perspective of its drafters.[38]

Agreement on the rules of the political game prepared the groundwork for lifting the prohibition on political competition. In May 1969, the traditional rivalries dating back to the colonial period were revived in the form of two main parties. The Progress Party (PP) led by K. A. Busia was a latter-day reincarnation of the UGCC, the National Liberation Movement, and the United Party. Unlike its precursors, however, it succeeded in consolidating the coastal and forest Akan-speaking groups within the same umbrella organization. The PP's main opponent, the National Alliance of Liberals, was headed by K. A. Gbedemah, a CPP stalwart who had fallen out with its founder in the early 1960s. The NAL did not enjoy the geographic appeal of the CPP: its backers hailed mostly from the Volta region; its leadership was composed mostly of professionals, but many CPP activists were banned from party politics. These differences aside, the opportunity for political activity saw the resurrection of the two main coalitions of yesteryear. The urban-populist-autocratic construct of Nkrumah's was somewhat recreated in the NAL; the rural-elitist-democratic makeup of the preindependence opposition was more convincingly embodied in the Busia alliance, and was reinforced by the return to political life of some of Nkrumah's main challengers.[39]

The Progress Party offered the voters a free enterprise program and the proven expertise of its leadership. This plan differed in content from the guarded social welfare orientation expounded by the NAL. These platforms were discussed with vigor even though they lacked the bite of preindependence ideological rivalries. Professional associations, religious groups, youth and women's organizations, as well as villagers and traditional authorities, were involved in this debate.[40] The mood in the country was one of reawakening, of a generalized revival of commitment to central government after a stultifying period of political somnolence.

The 1969 elections, therefore, resurrected some notion of competition. Those who were allowed to stand for office generated a new kind of excitement.

The broad coalitions of decolonization were updated; the localized pattern of party partisanship was restored; and elites publicly vied with each other for grassroots support.

Mobilization to party politics in 1969 owed a good deal to the activation of a variety of voluntary associations. Even in areas where ethnic groupings were weak, mutual aid associations were contacted and drawn into the electoral orbit.[41] Local concerns were given expression in party platforms, and appeals were made in the name of traditional symbols, authorities, and interests. In this context, patronage took on a different meaning. The drawing of the informal sector into the electoral process, as in the early CPP years, was carried out by individuals who had high standing in their community or professional groupings.[42] A more personalized type of patronage came to replace the single-party variety.

The localized and group basis of political mobilization almost inevitably highlighted debates over personalities and leaders. Many Progress Party contenders promised moral probity as well as assured access to resources. NAL candidates countered with offers of competence and efficiency. Ironically, this campaign style served to entrench, at least temporarily, the most successful elements of the dominant class.

The 1969 campaign was, to all minds, genuinely open, smooth, and fair. Participation therefore reached a new high (63.2 percent of registered voters). The electorate gave Nkrumah's opponents a resounding 59 percent of the ballot. Busia's party did enjoy the backing of the outgoing NLC, but it also amassed seats throughout the country. A new crop of educated, young political aspirants running under the PP banner made significant inroads into the local scene. The ability of the Progress people to retain a monopoly in all predominantly Akan-speaking strongholds added to their success. The party projected the sense that it had something special to offer both materially and morally.[43]

Thus, the elections brought an Asante and Brong, professional and merchant ruling coalition into power. An unrepresentative, yet popularly endorsed, set of middle class patrons was ushered into office on a wave of popular acclamation.[44] The effect of the 1969 vote was, therefore, to return Ghana to civilian rule under the aegis of a small group of highly educated individuals.

Kofi Busia and the clique around him were undoubtedly committed to democratic norms.[45] They did not aim at total social change, nor—in keeping with the British tradition in which they were educated—were they tied to ideas that foreclosed the rights of others. Nevertheless, both by background and choice, they were aloof from popular currents. Busia, a prominent member of the opposition to Nkrumah, lacked the charisma and organizational activism of his civilian predecessor. His style tended toward the paternalistic.

Thus, while the constitutional provisions for liberal democracy existed and civic rights were protected by law, the party structure was loose. Throughout its short years in office, the Progress Party's internal organization remained underdeveloped, as its opposition in the NAL and small parties was consistently weak. The Busia government consequently had very patriarchal overtones: personal links among the "the big men" of government were more significant than institutionalized ties of a more permanent sort. This structure added to the constraints imposed by previous regimes upon the second experiment in democratic government. These included the continuing need to deal with the political and economic legacy of Nkrumah, the difficulties attendant upon following in the shadow of three years of military rule, and the inflated expectations accompanying the return to civilian government.[46]

Busia's policies, unlike those of the NLC, aimed at gradual reform and rehabilitation. The role of government was consciously limited to constructing a framework within which individuals could fulfill their aspirations. The function of state agencies was defined in regulatory rather than entrepreneurial terms. Compensation was made for the reduction in public resources accruing directly to the state by enhancing the flow of capital from abroad.[47]

The development strategy of the Progress Party followed the path laid down by the NLC: the fortification of the private sector coupled with a renewed stress on agriculture and rural development. The government enacted an Aliens Compliance Order to protect local entrepreneurs and combat rising unemployment, and passed the Ghanaian Business Bill that called for the indigenization of small retail companies. The PP then liberalized imports and undertook a massive increase in government spending at the same time that cocoa prices crashed, nullifying the gains of the NLC's austerity program. A severe balance of payments problem then ensued. There was a 44 percent rise in food imports, much of which could have been produced at home under the right conditions.[48] In 1971, the government adopted an austerity budget to come to grips with its sliding grasp of the economy. Nevertheless, some attention was devoted to the rural sector; a Rural Development Fund was established in 1970. Incentives were given to producers, rural services were upgraded, a rural electrification program was launched, and feeder roads were constructed in the countryside.

In order to carry out these programs, the government attempted to gain control over the civil service, conducting a politically motivated purge of over 500 employees, the bulk of whom were Ewe and Ga (the cabinet, on the other hand, was mostly Asante and Brong). When the Supreme Court ordered their reinstatement, Busia refused. Thus, some of the more important provisions regarding the independence of the judiciary were violated. The bureaucracy also lost much of its professionalism as substantive norms of access to officials gave way to favoritism of the basis of kinship, ethnicity, and friendship.

After dealing with the civil service, the government went on to decentralize administrative tasks, restore national and regional houses of chiefs, and diffuse the functions of ministries. Lines of communication became blurred, and where inefficiency prevailed corruption blossomed.[49] The big patrons of the PP used the freedom they had within the democratic framework to appropriate public resources for private wealth. In fact, they preyed on the state coffers, foreign firms, and even outside governments. Busia, himself probably not entirely free of misdoing, was directly responsible for not stopping the privatization of state resources by others.[50] In an effort to regulate state-society relations, the PP gave preference to its own supporters and allowed them a free hand to implement policy. Many people felt that the government had one set of rules for the common people and one for the big men in government. At the same time that Ghanaians were asked to exhibit restraint, government officials engaged in the worst sort of conspicuous consumption. The performance record of Busia and his cohorts was scarcely encouraging. In two years, the PP government accumulated debts equaling those that Nkrumah had compiled in his nine years in office. The economy, once again, ground to a standstill. The last straw was the sharp decline in cocoa prices, which reduced export revenue. Busia, then, under pressure, was forced to devalue the cedi in December 1971.

Inevitably, these actions led to reactions from different quarters. Besides the Ewe and northerners, who felt that their interests had been neglected, the Progress Party also alienated the workers, students, and small farmers.[51] More ominously, a reduction in the military budget sparked rumblings in the ranks of the armed forces. As voices of opposition grew, Busia struck back by suppressing rural agitation, berating student leaders, quashing strikes, censoring critics, and detaining opponents. In 1971, the students demonstrated and the workers launched a rash of strikes throughout the country. In response, Busia proceeded to disband the umbrella Trade Union Congress (although not the individual unions, which later reconstituted the TUC voluntarily) and to threaten the leadership of the National Union of Ghanaian Students. He also encountered real difficulties in stemming defections from the ruling party.[52] The PP's mishandling of the opposition displayed an authoritarian strain fundamentally at odds with the democratic precepts it espoused.

Within two years of its inauguration, Ghana's second liberal democratic government was floundering. Participation, although ostensibly open, was biased in favor of the middle class and people from the Brong-Ahafo and Ashanti regions. The inequalities of income and wealth so blatantly paraded by PP activists inevitably stirred resentment among workers and small farmers. Even moderate intellectuals voiced concern over the cost to the country of the conduct of its leaders. Warnings were issued about the exacerbation of social and regional inequalities resulting from these actions. Economic performance was, at best, ambiguous. On the other hand, repression under Busia was restrained (press freedom was not significantly curtailed; associational life flourished; personal rights were by and large respected). Moreover, the climate of political debate was far more open than during the Nkrumah days. Thus, while the groundwork for the overthrow of the Progress Party was laid by the government's inability to contain the inequities fueled by its members, when the military intervened once again on 13 January 1972, it did so in advance of a popular demand for Busia's ouster, to advance its own narrow interests. New elections were scheduled for the following year, and the democratic experience, while not particularly auspicious, had not failed.[53]

The demise of Ghana's second democratic effort exposed basic political difficulties that went far beyond the limitations of a single regime. In the first place, a democratically elected government, much like its authoritarian predecessors, had been unable to assure regularized channels of participation and communication. Second, repression, so obvious under authoritarian government, recurred (albeit in much more muted forms) under democratic rule. Third, despite the salience of state structures, these seemed too weak and ineffective to carry out regime policies. And fourth, social and economic inequality was intensified. The departure of Busia heralded the entrenchment of instability and regime fluctuation as the single most prominent feature of Ghanaian politics.

The National Redemption Council/ Supreme Military Council I (1972–1978)

The 1972 coup led by Colonel Acheampong differed from the military intervention of the NLC in several important respects. First, it displaced a popularly elected democratic government, not an autocratic authoritarian regime. Second, Acheampong and his supporters, unlike their more senior military predecessors, came from the upper middle ranks of the officer corps. And third, the National Redemption Council (NRC), in contrast to the NLC, came with the intention of staying in power and undertaking institutional and social reform. Even though the background and experience of its leaders were limited, its ambitions were far grander than those of its military precursors.[54]

The National Redemption Council, between 1972 and 1975, was constructed around a narrow base of six middle-echelon officers and one civilian who expressed distaste for politicians of any sort. The Acheampong clique shunned participatory organs and sought to establish a working coalition between the bureaucracy, the military, and traditional rulers.[55] This bureaucratic-corporatist structure was meant to depoliticize public life and to enable some semblance of functional control through the appointment of military men to key positions in public corporations and government ministries.

In his early years, Acheampong launched a series of self-reliance efforts and tried to reschedule Ghana's external debt.[56] For a while, his government succeeded in allaying populist discontent and increasing food production. Incapable, however, of overcoming the effects of the 1973 oil crisis, and unable to keep his civilian and military partners in check, Acheampong chose in 1975 to reorganize the structure of his government rather than reassess policy.

A Supreme Military Council (SMC), resting entirely on the foundation of the armed forces, was brought into being with Acheampong at its helm. The NRC took on advisory functions; its original members resigned or were forcibly retired. The structure of the SMC reflected Acheampong's aversion to criticism of any sort. Acheampong's response to the dilemmas of rule in Ghana was to institutionalize coercion as a means of control. Stiff restrictions were placed on civic action, the press once again was regulated directly,and heavy penalties were inflicted on those who attempted to express discontent. Consultation in decision making was blocked and no supervision of government practice was entertained.[57]

Acheampong came to power in an atmosphere of dwindling expectations and growing disillusionment. While he declared a goal of pragmatically tackling Ghana's social and economic ills, his proposals were amorphous.[58] Self-reliance was the linchpin of the NRC's policy, but besides the creation of Regional Development Corporations and some expression of concern with handling problems of regional inequality, no real steps were taken even to amplify, let alone implement, this program. For a while, it appeared that this kind of policy might actually work; but an unwillingness to cut populist spending led to economic distress. The year 1975 proved to be a turning point, and by 1977 the economic disorder was unprecedented. Production had dropped significantly in all sectors, shortages were recorded in essential commodities, and inflation soared.[59] Ironically, economic conditions in Ghana worsened at precisely the same time that cocoa prices reached an all-time high. And Acheampong, unlike his predecessors, could not even bring in foreign capital to provide essential goods: the international financial community, aware of Acheampong's inflationary and ineffective policies, responded by withholding funds from an untrustworthy leader. Thus, external neglect exacerbated, but did not cause, the misery of the latter part of the decade of the 1970s.

Not only were Ghanaians confronted with growing scarcities and the discomforts of random military discipline, they were also forced to witness the plundering of their remaining fortunes by those close to "Kutu" and his family. *Kalabule* (roughly, "keeping the lid on" through economic malpractice) was practiced by everyone in Acheampong's Ghana. The SMC, however, was the worst offender, creating nothing short of an official kleptocracy.[60] Acheampong preyed on small traders, extracted bribes from investors, personally controlled desired imports, and set up large bank accounts abroad. Within three years, Acheampong and his wife had amassed a personal fortune that made Nkrumah's misdeeds pale in comparison.[61]

Unquestionably, the reformist promise of the second military government was shamefully squandered by an incompetent and self-serving leader pursuing unrealistic policies. Initial dissatisfaction with Acheampong's intrusion gradually grew into outright civilian revolt. At first, Acheampong enjoyed some respite from civilian dissent, and only the Ewe and some disgruntled politicians objected openly to his actions. In 1975, however, a cycle of ever-widening dissent and protest was unleashed, gradually encompassing virtually the entire politically active portions of the population in all its diversity. Urban elites—mostly professionals organized in the Association of Recognized Professional Bodies (ARPB)—spearheaded the agitation and were joined by students, traders, and even bureaucrats and chiefs.[62]

Acheampong's intolerance of dissent was reflected in his response to the growing tide of civilian unrest. He harassed his opponents, issued decrees prohibiting criticism of the regime, and stifled the press. But repressive measures could not control the public outcry. In October 1976, Acheampong announced his intention of constructing a union government (Unigov), which would include representation of all major groups in the population, including the military, in a nebulous corporate framework.[63]

The Unigov scheme evoked an even wider wave of protest, culminating in a massive countrywide strike in July 1977, organized by the ARPB and encompassing almost all wage earners. The leaders of this strike, which approximated a civilian revolt, issued an ultimatum demanding Acheampong's abdication. Rather than bow to these pressures, Acheampong declared a two-year timetable for return to some form of civilian rule. The first phase in this plan called for a referendum on Unigov. In anticipation, civilian agitation intensified, as anti-Unigov forces coalesced around the People's Movement for Freedom and Justice and the Front for the Prevention of Dictatorship, both led by ex-Progress Party leaders, mostly based in Kumasi. In response, the SMC sponsored the pro-Unigov Ghana Peace and Solidarity Council led by some ex-CPP stalwarts, and mobilized the National Charter Committees to lobby for its plan. The Unigov referendum mirrored the persistence of factional divisions dating back to decolonization.

The campaign was intense and ugly, but most Ghanaians preferred to stand aside and not participate in the race. Only 42.48 percent of the registered voters took part in the balloting. The results of the 1978 referendum gave pro-Unigov forces a narrow margin of victory. The returns, however, were flagrantly manipulated by the regime.[64] They revealed a generalized distate for the SMC, but did not enable its replacement. The Unigov exercise created chaos and brought the country to a standstill. The spring of 1978 was marked by strikes by almost every social group in the country. Ghana was in turmoil. The intervention of Fred Akuffo and a portion of the military, in July 1978, forced Acheampong's abdication and freed the country from his stranglehold.

The coercive authoritarian regime of Ignatius Acheampong was an unmitigated disaster for Ghana. During his six and a half years in office he ignored popular currents, trampled civil rights, ravaged the economy, and transformed Ghana into a private estate for himself and his followers. In this process, he severely undermined the commitment of Ghanaians to their central government. While it is true that Acheampong inherited from his predecessors a failing economy and a set of serious structural problems, under his inept guidance these difficulties intensified and became almost insurmountable.[65]

Supreme Military Council II and Armed Forces Revolutionary Council (1978–1979)

General Fred Akuffo, Acheampong's chief of staff, was acutely aware of Acheampong's shortcomings: therefore he tried to restore a modicum of order and rehabilitate the image of the military in the public eye. Indeed, at first, he suggested a further period of military rule, but then quickly capitulated to civilian pressures and agreed to another transition to full civilian government. This Supreme Military Council (SMC II) was, therefore, a caretaker regime concerned with overseeing another military return to the barracks.

During his short interval in office, Akuffo nevertheless attempted to introduce some measures to stabilize the economy. Stringent regulations were imposed by the government at the demand of the International Monetary Fund. These reduced the monetary supply by holding back increases in government expenditures to 11 percent in the 1978–1979 period and clamped down on government borrowing from the central bank. Akuffo also devalued the cedi, immediately upon his assumption of office, by 58.2 percent.

Nevertheless, inflation persisted, shortages of all basic commodities were recorded, and the price of consumer goods literally doubled. The cedi exchange program, conducted in the spring of 1979, did little to alleviate the public's distress. Although *kalabule* brought in extra money, next to no goods were available in the market.[66] Urban residents most directly affected by these events demonstrated to express their displeasure. The November 1978 strike by the civil service forced Akuffo to declare a state of emergency, which lasted for two months. Throughout this interlude, the hold of SMC II was shaky at best. Even as it hastened the constitutional process and made preparations for the elections that would return Ghana to civilian rule, it overlooked the strains within the army's own ranks and ignored pleas to bring Acheampong to trial for his malfeasance.

The demand for retribution was taken up by the rank and file in the person of Flight Lieutenant J. J.Rawlings, whose first attempt to topple Akuffo on 14 May 1979, failed. But, with Rawlings in jail, his supporters did finally overthrow Akuffo, on 4 June 1979, in a burst of violence heretofore unknown even to Ghana's coup-weary populace.[67]

The Armed Forces Revolutionary Council (AFRC) created by Jerry Rawlings differed drastically from its military predecessors: the ten-member council was drawn almost exclusively from the enlisted ranks, and it was noted for the youthfulness of its leadership, especially in a society that so values age. The AFRC succeeded in molding the have-nots of Ghanaian society into a potent political force by capitalizing on their discontent and speaking on their behalf.

The AFRC intervention was as traumatic as it was brief. At its root was a belief that the formal leaders must be held accountable for their actions, and that more fundamental normative change was needed if Ghana were to recover from years of military misrule. The AFRC set out to attain several objectives. The first was to punish the corrupt leaders of previous military regimes. The housecleaning exercise commenced with the arrest, summary trial, and execution of notable NLC and SMC leaders, including Acheampong, Akuffo, and Afrifa. The executions bore witness to the AFRC's determination to overhaul the power structure. In the following months, the AFRC scrutinized the actions (and bank accounts) of middle-level officers and published daily lists of those who were to appear before people's tribunals for betraying the public trust.[68]

The AFRC then turned its attention to the civil service. Senior office holders, principal secretaries and supervising senior secretaries (commonly held to be the source of corruption) were dismissed, and junior personnel were investigated. Thus, the bureaucrats were served notice that henceforth they would be held responsible for their actions.

The second goal of the AFRC was to pursue a campaign of moral reform. The AFRC hit out at the worst instances of black marketeering, hoarding, and other corrupt practices. There were probes, property confiscations, and tax collection exercises. Those found guilty were fined, flogged, or jailed for lengthy periods. Moreover, Jerry Rawlings reinstituted price controls and vigorously enforced compliance.[69] Finally, after exhortations failed, Makola Market Number 1—the alleged hub of trade malpractices—was razed. Focusing on local distributors, the AFRC succeeded in collecting millions of dollars in back taxes, which it then handed over to its civilian successor. These actions, however, did come at the expense of loss of overseas confidence. The IMF and other external sources of support dried up, and in protest against the AFRC's wave of execution, some suppliers imposed an informal embargo.[70]

Nevertheless, the AFRC's message was unambiguous: the moral rectitude of the servants of the state and popular vigilance were a precondition for laying the foundations for good government. Rawlings, however, in his first intervention, paused short of undertaking a total structural upheaval. The AFRC, not entirely in control and lacking in internal cohesion, was content to wait on the sidelines and watch as the civilians attempted to continue the task of rehabilitation.[71]

The AFRC interlude was as abrupt as it was violent. It interrupted, but did not stop, the planned return to civilian rule. Its significance lies as much in the fact that it constituted a prelude to a more permanent populist takeover as in its actions on the eve of the formation of the Third Republic. It was in this context of turbulence and upheaval that the scheduled elections took place. Much to Jerry Rawlings's credit, he oversaw the balloting despite his antipathy to the political establishment. The proposed constitution of the Third Republic, drafted in 1978 and revised by the Constituent Assembly in early 1979, provided for an executive (rather than a ceremonial) presidency to be elected directly by a majority of the voters. In other respects, the parliamentary structure of the Second Republic was retained, as were key provisions relating to the separation of power and checks and balances.[72] But the new constitution emphasized the creation of safeguards against official abuse of power and highlighted questions of efficiency and effectiveness.

Two dozen parties surfaced when the ban on political parties was lifted; six survived to contest the elections. The People's National Party (PNP) brought together CPP activists, Busia opponents, and pro-Unigov forces. The Popular Front Party (PFP) was composed of lawyers and large cocoa farmers mostly from the Ashanti and Brong-Ahafo regions. Its leaders read like a list of Busia's inner circle. The United National Convention (UNC) brought together Ga, Ewe and coastal Akan leaders who, like their PFP counterparts, had been active in the Second Republic and in the opposition to Unigov. In 1979, more party fragmentation was apparent than at any point in the past, and ethnic tensions were expressed in party constellations. Yet, the new parties constituted updated versions of the CPP-UGCC rivalry under a different heading.[73]

The platforms of these parties did evince some very real ideological differences. The PNP constantly waved the banner of Nkrumaism while also underscoring its leaders' proven capacity to provide the the material needs of their constituents during the relatively abundant years of the first regime. PFP and UNC candidates tried to forward similar arguments, recalling the days of the Second Republic.

The 1979 campaign, however, was a lackluster affair, as people concerned themselves mostly with the more pressing needs of daily survival. Even the presidential candidates lacked spark. Dr. Hilla Limann, a Sisalla from the Upper Region and PNP presidential candidate, was a political unknown. His main opponent, Victor Owusu, was a former Progress Party minister who was as alienating as he was forceful. And Paa Willie Ofori-Atta, the sentimental favorite, was given little chance of success.[74] It is hardly surprising that participation in the elections reached an all-time low: only 34 percent took part in the first presidential elections and 38 percent in the second round.

In June 1979, it was the turn of the CPP inheritors to come back to office. The PNP picked up over half of the seats in the Parliament, and Hilla Limann soundly defeated Victor Owusu. The PNP exhibited electoral strength throughout the country. In some people's minds, this victory followed ethnic lines; but, in all probability, the PNP's appeal lay as much in its ability to present itself as the party of change and to accentuate the vitality of its leaders.[75] By translating these perceptions into locally distinctive images and capitalizing on the fragmentation of the opposition, the PNP parlayed its advantages into a veritable success at the ballot box.

Ghana entered the 1979 elections in a precarious position, and it emerged without the means to repair this condition. The results of the 1979 ballot pointed to a threefold pattern of power peripheralization. For the first time in the country's history, northern leaders held sway in the dominant political party. So, too, did an almost exclusively middle class coalition. It became apparent that the bases of state power had narrowed substantially. Hilla Limann inaugurated the Third Republic poorly equipped to confront the enormity of the tasks relegated to him by his authoritarian predecessors.

The Third Republic (1979–1981)

Rarely has a new democratic government acceded to office under such dismal circumstances as those that greeted the new leaders of Ghana's third liberal democratic experiment. Hilla Limann had to deal simultaneously with an economy that had experienced a 30 percent fall in production in the preceding decade, governmental institutions in disarray, and a public suspicious of all government.[76] The president was further handicapped by the AFRC's transitional provisions to the constitution, which prohibited the new regime from scrutinizing the judgements of the military tribunals.

Nevertheless, Limann proceeded to appoint a cabinet containing an impressive array of academics and technocrats. The elitist composition of Limann's cabinet resembled that of Busia's not only in its class makeup, but also in its ethnic bias (in this case toward the Ga and northern groups). But, unlike any of his predecessors, Limann relied heavily on formal institutions to maintain contact with the population. He took the Parliament and the newly formed Council of State (which was composed of representatives of key interest groups) seriously. Although unable to garner the same degree of cooperation from the civil service and the military, Limann did try to ensure party competition, expand local government structures, and protect a wide range of freedoms guaranteed by the constitution.[77]

The PNP platform had advocated social reform; once in power, however, its policy outlook was extremely cautious. In a piecemeal, pragmatic way, Limann outlined the PNP's concerns and plan of action in the economic sphere. The thrust of the two-year agricultural plan centered on increased food production. It also gave high priority to the improvement of infrastructure in the rural areas, to the alleviation of income discrimination against rural workers, and to industrial rehabilitation.[78] Under the circumstances, much effort was put into finding the necessary capital to underwrite the program. Taxes were raised, restrictions on foreign investments were lifted, an appeal was issued for greater aid allocations, and IMF support was courted.

Limann's economic program was, perhaps, overly hesitant given the depressed state of the economy. He proceeded to enact incremental measures when some of his critics claimed that more drastic action was needed. The government continued to overspend (partly because it tripled the minimum wage), and inflation consequently soared to 70 percent in 1980.

The Third Republic's listless approach to policy formulation was compounded by inadequate procedures. Cumbersome bureaucratic regulations impeded efficient action. The reluctance of producers to cooperate with the government hampered efforts to carry out changes in the rural areas. And, once again, the government's inability to supervise the civil service invited the continuation of oppressive bureaucratic corruption (the AFRC's admonitions notwithstanding).[79]

The results of these halfhearted efforts were meager. Government services and eroded. Acute food shortages persisted. The Food Distribution Corporation could barely keep up with demands for essential commodities. Cocoa production reached its lowest level since decolonization at precisely the time that world cocoa prices dropped to a nadir in the postwar period. Foreign debt consequently increased and external dependency grew. On every conceivable scale, economic performance during the Third Republic was poor.[80] The

Limann administration, like its predecessors, failed to make a significant change in the country's economic morass.

In the prevailing atmosphere of agitation and vigilance, the Third Republic was subjected to a great deal of scrutiny from the start. Rawlings had unleashed populist sentiment, and Limann fell victim to constant criticism from antiestablishment organizations in the form of the June Fourth Movement and the New Democratic Movement (both loyal to Rawlings' vision of a moral revolution). During his short term in office, Hilla Limann also had to contend with labor unrest. Striking workers were dismissed for protesting their low wages (after parliamentarians had awarded themselves a magnificent salary increase). The TUC threatened a nationwide strike to protest reduced subsidies.

Ethnic discontent was not lacking either: the Ewe were unhappy about their poor representation in the government, and many Asante leaders withheld allegiance to the central government. Assailed from all sides, Limann was forced to clamp down: he suppressed student demonstrations, stifled ethnic dissent, and also censored the press. These actions, it appears, went against his grain. He complained that "it is the way people make constitutions work which matter. If people are not prepared to cooperate but tend to tear themselves apart, no particular type of government can do anything."[81]

The real threat to the Third Republic, however, came from the ranks of the military. Barely two months after he assumed office, Limann dismissed the chief of staff and forcibly retired Jerry Rawlings and other members of the erstwhile AFRC. The military establishment had lost much of its standing among the rank and file and could not contain Rawlings, whom they feared and disliked. Rawlings, indeed, remained in the country, granted interviews, and let his opinions be known. The government set out to monitor his movements. But, by linking coup attempts with his name, the PNP bolstered his visibility and enhanced his status. At the same time, the party was wracked by internal dissension after the death of its founder, Imoru Egala. It was forced to take action against corrupt party officials accused of, among other things, accepting a loan from South Africa. "Whatever Limann did—and there was not much he could do with a bankrupt economy—he was compelled to do so under the gaze of the would-be revolutionary who waited, disapprovingly, off stage."[82]

The leaders of the government of the Third Republic operated under severe constraints from the outset. The constitution they had crafted so conscientiously was altered by the AFRC, which also served notice that its patience was extremely limited. The paucity of resources, coupled with Hilla Limann's feeble leadership, however, doomed this experiment to failure. The PNP was not so much mismanaged as it was inept. With people clamoring for a square meal, Hilla Limann's moderation was a poor substitute for the forceful policies needed at this juncture.[83]

On 31 December 1982, Jerry Rawlings carried out his threat to Hilla Limann that he would return if the Third Republic did not pass muster. In retrospect, the two years of the Third Republic were simply an interlude between

Jerry Rawlings's hesitation and his decision to engage in politics on a more permanent basis. By 1981, inflation had soared to 116 percent, and the military was enfeebled: the third democratic government in Ghana was so weak that it could not resist the takeover.

The Provisional National Defense Council (1981–)

The return of Jerry Rawlings differed in design and intent from his first intervention. The Provisional National Defense Council (PNDC) action came against a duly elected civilian government, not against a disdained military establishment. It relied heavily on elements outside the military. The PNDC, regardless of its name, seemed determined to stay in office for as long as it took to effect a sweeping transformation. Unlike other military administrations in Ghana, it actively coopted civilians into the government. The nonestablishment groups that Jerry Rawlings had molded into a political force in 1979 had now come to power.

The return of Jerry Rawlings was greeted with a mixture of enthusiasm, skepticism, and fear. Although Rawlings himself was highly regarded and his youthful ingenuity and honesty widely acclaimed, a few people were pleased about the prospect of another period of military rule. They were also apprehensive about Rawlings's call for a populist revolution.[84]

The initial support for the PNDC came primarily from discontented urban elements: radical left-wing intellectuals, some lower-level trade union leaders, dissatisfied soldiers, students and urban unemployed.[85] The traditional elites of Ghana—the professionals, large entrepreneurs, businessmen, wealthy farmers, and ex-politicians—were purposely excluded from the PNDC coalition. Jerry Rawlings sought to insulate his regime from the patrons. The original PNDC, composed at first of six members, included civilians and soldiers, reform-minded liberals, radicals, and Marxists. Although the membership of the PNDC has changed over the years, it has always comprised a mixture of soldiers and civilians. The PNDC Secretariat (the cabinet) is primarily a civilian institution.[86] Secretaries have been appointed mostly on the basis of their qualifications and their commitment to a national overhaul. Thus, if Rawlings protected his government from the intrusions of the previous establishment, he did not isolate himself from civilians.[87]

Indeed, Rawlings, like other populist leaders, sought to establish direct contact with his followers. The initial vehicles for this task were a series of People's Defence Committees (PDCs) established in each community, Military Defence Committees (MDCs) for the army, and Workers' Defence Committees (WDCs) set up in the workplace. An Interim National Coordinating Committee (later changed to the National Defence Committee—NDC) was established to oversee the activities of the local bodies.[88] Through these committees, the PNDC hoped to link people with the government, create a cadre of loyal supporters, and solve serious problems of penetration.

This general strategy of establishing alternative structures without dismantling existing ones carried over into other areas. New youth organizations, women's movements, and workers collectives were set up. Committees were created to examine a plan for decentralization, deal with long-range economic planning, and investigate possibilities for a return to civilian rule.[89] Interim Management Committees filled the vacuum at the local government level. A National Mobilization Committee was established first to supervise the absorption of Ghanaian refugees after the expulsion of aliens from Nigeria in January 1983 and again in April 1985, and then to encourage rural development.[90]

The vast array of committees and commissions existed alongside regular bureaucratic structures in what was essentially a dualistic system reminiscent of the Nkrumah days. In these conditions, the personality of Rawlings and his personal advisors were crucial as a mobilizing and cementing device. Rawlings and his closest colleague, Kojo Tsikata (who came to control all three security organizations), supervised activities directly and personally. The consolidation of the PNDC during its first year in office thus rested on two quite different foundations: the heterogeneous popular committees and the highly personalistic and, at times, autocratic coterie that revolved around Rawlings's own person.

Radical rhetoric characterized the new government. It attacked old institutions, derided legal niceties, made a plea for moral reformism, and struck out against external forces, imperialism, and foreign subjugation. The PNDC envisaged the creation of a vibrant community based on egalitarian values and guided by people's socialism.[91] In this mood of fundamental change, the first task the PNDC set out to accomplish was a reform in the system of justice. It wanted to make sure that those guilty of corruption would be brought to trial and that public officials would be monitored. Activities of individuals were scrutinized by a series of investigating commissions. Traders, businessmen, journalists, and professionals suspected of flouting revolutionary doctrines were questioned. A National Investigations Commission was set up to oversee public behavior. Citizen's Vetting Committees (CVCs) reviewed the earnings of those with large bank accounts, examined the bureaucracy, retired recalcitrant civil servants, eliminated superfluous positions, and established themselves as the watchdogs of the state apparatus.[92]

People found wanting by these various investigating bodies were brought before newly created public tribunals, which were given broad criminal jurisdiction. These peoples' courts meted out justice quickly and, frequently, harshly. Massive sentences (sometimes amounting to sixty years or more) and fines (in millions of cedi) were handed down to PNP officials, senior civil servants, and officials of public corporations. Army personnel suspected of malfeasance were brought before parallel military tribunals.[93]

By the end of 1982, at least five established courts were shut down, and individual members of the judiciary were subjected to physical intimidation. The murder of three high court judges in August 1982, later officially attributed to an overzealous member of the PNDC, revealed the precarious position of Ghana's judiciary—one of the few public institutions that had maintained a semblance of autonomy over the years.[94] Civil rights were, therefore, subordinated by Rawlings to a nebulous vision of social justice. These moves, however, did not go unanswered. The Ghana Bar Association has refused to appear before the public tribunals, a popular outcry has forced the government to investigate the murder of the judges, and resistance to acts of random violence have persisted.[95] Although the tribunals have not been disbanded and basic freedoms are still not safeguarded by the government, litigation in the regular courts became more commonplace after 1983.

The lack of concern with civil rights stemmed, in part, from a preoccupation with the economy. At first, the PNDC focused its activities on organizing the evacuation of cocoa from the countryside and ensuring the supply of basic foodstuffs. By the end of its first year in office, however, it published an ambitious Four-Year Economic Recovery Program. The initial effort to transform dependency theory into policy failed in Rawlings's Ghana, laying the foundation for the adoption of an economic policy of structural adjustment along IMF guidelines.[96]

The new plan did not bear fruit immediately. 1982 and 1983 were disastrous years for Ghanaians and their economy: the cedi was devalued, and price controls were lifted; production, especially of cocoa, continued to decline; acute shortages were recorded in every single sphere; and unemployment was rampant. As Ghana was hit by the worst drought in years, food shortages reached monumental proportions. In November 1983, the PNDC convened a donor's conference in Paris to help bail the country out of its economic plight. 1984 saw some improvements, and, in 1985, the worse shortages were alleviated and the economy saw some signs of recovery.[97] By 1986, food was abundant, production levels had increased, and overall improvements in infrastructure were visible.

Rawlings's style was not designed to garner support in establishment circles. The urban elite, many Asante and Brong, the clergy, and even the students expressed their concerns about the populist government early on. They were joined by factions of the military, who attempted several coups throughout 1982 and 1983. By the summer of 1983, exiles had established an overseas movement to oust Rawlings: the Campaign for Democracy in Ghana. Another group, the Ghana Democratic Movement, led by J. H. Mensah, was formed in London in 1984 (where Elizabeth Ohene, former editor of the *Daily Graphic*, published her opposition magazine, *Talking Drum*).

At this point, Rawlings decided to pursue a course of moderation.[98] He clamped down on abuses by the armed forces. In December 1984, the PDCs and WDCs were renamed Committees for the Defence of the Revolution (CDRs).[99] These were reorganized, and a new CDR secretariat was created. In the hope of achieving some kind of national reconciliation, Rawlings began to make plans for the establishment of a people's parliament. These and other measures, quite naturally, offended many of Rawlings's early supporters. On the left, Marxist proponents claimed that he had abandoned the revolution and withdrew from any association with the PNDC. The TUC continued to resist PNDC economic policies and several times threatened a nationwide strike.[100] By 1986, many of the original bases of support of the PNDC had eroded, and the future was unclear.

The PNDC government differed dramatically at the outset from its authoritarian predecessors. Its composition was distinctly populist and excluded middle class elements; it surpassed even the young Nkrumah in its reformist zeal and commitment to thoroughgoing change; it was violent, harsh, and particularly repressive. Pretensions aside, its institutions precluded serious debate or criticism. But most significant, the PNDC was able, after a faltering start, to introduce and implement harsh but necessary economic measures that have brought relative yet important improvements throughout the country.

By 1985, however, it was apparent that the regime was having difficulty in translating its economic success into political terms. Although still rhetorically committed to mass participation, the government increasingly downgraded its own populist structures, coopted a new group of technocrats, and insulated itself from public protest. Corruption resurfaced in ruling circles. The contradictions set in motion by the PNDC were unavoidable.[101] The inability of the PNDC to institutionalize itself meant that its control weakened, and that some realignment of institutional processes—whether by design, failure, or transfer—would be imminent.

Ghana's Experiences with Democratic and Authoritarian Government: An Evaluation

Ghana's experiences with a variety of democratic and nondemocratic governments, with the exception of Rawlings's PNDC, have all ended in failure. Each of the country's democratic experiments collapsed after extremely short periods: the Westminster experiment failed because it lacked a powerful constituency within the country; the government of the Second Republic was not given a chance to succeed; and Limann's third democratic experiment was not, despite widespread distaste for military rule, really expected to subsist, let alone prosper. Although each of these governments was different in the circumstances in which it came to power and in its party structure, social composition, constitutional safeguards, institutional arrangements, and specific ideology and practice, they all evinced a marked inability both to manage the economy and to sustain levels of mobilization and participation over time. The ensuing problems of legitimacy were compounded in every case by the consequences of elite disunity and the absence of political acumen.[102]

Authoritarian regimes, whether of a civilian or military variety, have also crumbled under the strains of popular discontent and economic mismanagement, although they could not even claim entry legitimacy. The variety of authoritarianism in Ghana could not obscure its precariousness: singe-party government, military coalitions, coercive personal rule, and even populism have not endured for any reasonable length of time.

Democratic governments in Ghana have failed but they are unlikely to disappear entirely. Although authoritarian regimes, as in the past, will probably be more numerous on the Ghanaian political scene, democratic intrusions may still recur not only because of deeply ingrained democratic values in Ghana's indigenous institutions and political culture, but also because authoritarian solutions in Ghana have proved to be less satisfactory than their democratic alternatives. But, as long as Ghanaian politics remains statist, then these governments will not thrive.[103] Democratic and authoritarian governments in Ghana have replaced each other as a means of limiting political excesses. In the unstable environment of Ghana, democratic rule has failed, but the promise of democracy endures. Democratic pressures persist while authoritarian rule prevails.

• HISTORICAL ANALYSIS: THE FAILURE OF DEMOCRATIC AND AUTHORITARIAN GOVERNMENT•

The chronic inability of Ghanaian governments to achieve a measure of durability and to sustain an equitable and workable system of rule is the outcome of the interaction of a complex set of factors over time. Democratic regimes in Ghana have differed in several important respects from the multiplicity of authoritarian constructs that have emerged in the country. The upholders of liberal democratic values have come largely from the middle class: professional groupings of lawyers, intellectuals, and wealthy businessmen and farmers schooled in the British tradition. The commoners, Nkrumah's "verandah boys," students, the CDRs—the inheritors of the Asafo companies[104]—have consistently voiced populist concerns and propounded statist ideas wrapped in socialist language.[105] Democratic leaders in the country adopted a gradualist approach to development and defended capitalist policies. Authoritarian rulers, at least initially, have been change-oriented. In each democratic regime, some institutional mechanisms were available for competition and participation. Authoritarian governments have not always designed such arrangements. Indeed, these regimes in Ghana have been avowedly statist and they have viewed central government organs not only as a mechanism of control, but as the key instrument for societal transformation. This has not always been the case for their democratic alternatives. Democratic governments in Ghana have, in varying measures, protected civil and political rights and preserved associational freedoms. Authoritarian regimes have been explicitly more repressive and coercive. If these governments have been marked by their excesses, they have sought to sustain—if only rhetorically—egalitarian concerns. Democratic rulers have generally been weaker and less forceful in the pursuit of their goals; they have also, somewhat ironically, supported greater inequalities.

Despite these differences, however, neither type of regime has been able to strike deep roots in the country. Democratic and authoritarian experiments in Ghana have all exhibited an inability to withstand partisan pressures from below. They have been simultaneously too removed and too permeable. While political leaders have curtailed channels of participation, public institutions have been penetrated by every conceivable interest.[106] In a sense, national politics had "come to matter too much, to weigh too heavily on social life."[107] The zero-sum attitude toward formal political life encouraged the personalization of authority in very diverse ruling coalitions; tolerance for opposition has been low. Corruption emerged not only as a device to maintain control and build political support through patronage, but also as an instrument of class formation and power consolidation around the state.[108] Even though corruption has been turned to private ends at many junctures, it has sustained a network of clientelistic attachments underwritten by strong norms of reciprocity. It has also exposed decisionmakers to specific sectional interests. The selective representation of solidarity groups in ruling coalitions has induced leaders to divert state resources, which, in turn, has reduced their performance capabilities. The inability to balance the societal requirement of supervision over policymakers with the bureaucratic need for professional freedom set in motion a counterproductive rhythm, in which increasingly autocratic leaders sought to control progressively unharnessed state officeholders for the benefit of a contracting human constituency.

Ghanaian regimes have, therefore, all been plagued by inadequate mechanisms for policy formulation, decreasing capacity, poor performance records, dwindling legitimacy, and an image of domination and repression. As one government has replaced another with amazing alacrity, the social basis of support for any government has contracted and social regulation has decreased. Prevented from repeating the policies of their predecessors, new leaders have found their range of options progressively constricted. A continual incapacity to solve problems has unleashed greater disloyalty and less attachment.[109] Governments have become more exploitative, society more detached.[110]

Explanations for these political patterns lie in the changing relationships between specific social groups and state institutions. At independence, historical and structural circumstances militated for the concentration of power and authority around the state. Dependence on the state had been nurtured during the colonial period, when land tenure policies were enacted to impede the growth of an indigenous middle class.[111] In conditions where state power was weak and central authority tenuous, democracy yielded to a search for hegemonic domination. In Ghana, as in many other parts of Africa, the state "is sometimes excessively authoritarian in order to disguise the fact that it is inadequately authoritative."[112]

If the initial failure of democracy in Ghana may be attributed to statist tendencies, the instability of authoritarian rule was closely tied not only to political factors and the frailties of leadership, but also to the resilience of associational life and local political cultures.[113] The demise of each of Ghana's governments coincided with its inability to come to terms with a different component of democracy. Kwame Nkrumah crushed competition and then obstructed participation. The Second Republic under K. A. Busia could not meet basic requisites of social equality. The erratic military regime of Ignatius Acheampong was finally removed because of its lack of accountability. Hilla Limann, in a quest for representation, could not ensure the rule of law. And Jerry Rawlings's Provisional National Defence Council has assailed some of the most basic prerequisites of freedom. Whereas other African statist patrimonial systems have survived and even blossomed, authoritarian regimes in Ghana have floundered. The incapacity of political leadership was an important factor in the demise of authoritarian governments, but structural variables have also been significant.

Over the years, Ghanaians have shown that there are alternatives to statism. A deeply ingrained indigenous culture of consultation, autonomy, participation, and supervision of authority, coupled with the continuous existence of vibrant local social structures and institutions, has enabled Ghanaians to combat the uncertainties of state domination and the tyranny of its leaders. Lawyers, students, unions, and traders have also evolved a liberal culture of resistance to interference in their affairs. If democratic government has failed in Ghana, the democratic ethos has proven extremely resilient.

As the process of decline unfolded, Ghanaians developed elaborate means to cope with the exigencies of poverty and the uncertainties of their political environment. Nonformal institutions and modes of economic exchange have thrived in recent years, reinforcing alternative loci of power, authority, and legitimacy.[114] The upshot has been the gradual separation of government institutions and social organizations. Ideas about accountability, good government, and trusteeship have come to the fore. Ghana may be experiencing an evolution away from authoritarian government and the state and toward a more meaningful democracy based on notions of power sharing.

The causes of the crisis of governance in Ghana contain the kernels for its resolution. Although it is correct to assume that no democracy is possible in the absence of governability, Ghana's complex experience suggests that democracy may be the avenue for the reconstruction of government. The key challenge facing Ghanaians today is survival, and there can be no survival without initiative. The issue is, therefore, less one of equality than of liberty: the acknowledgement of liberty may lay the political foundations for the creation of a positive climate that could ease the painful process of economic development and concomitant social change in the years to come.[115]

The Historical Pattern

The first phase in this dynamic coincided with the collapse of the democratic experiment immediately following the transfer of power. The traditional institutions of the peoples of Ghana, many of which possessed strong participatory and egalitarian components, were brought into a common framework by the imposition of colonial rule at the end of the nineteenth century.[116] The British intrusion into the Gold Coast was accompanied by the establishment of a military bureaucratic state apparatus endowed with independent, externally derived resources and capable of controlling some production and exchange. The technological superiority of the British colonial state enabled it to regulate processes of existing social differentiation around the colonial center. Legislation curtailed individual access to land and hampered the emergence of an autonomous middle class.[117] Colonial rule in Ghana, despite the democratic character of the metropole, was bureaucratic and authoritarian.

Colonial economic policy, aimed at the introduction of cash crops for export, helped to incorporate Ghana into the world economy and, simultaneously, guaranteed its unequal position in this system.[118] The economy of the Gold Coast under colonial rule possessed dualistic properties: a small export-oriented sector coexisted alongside a multiplicity of indigenous precapitalist configurations.[119]

The British system of indirect rule preserved traditional authorities and even reinforced localized allegiances. The cultural diversity of the Gold Coast was sustained, if not actively encouraged, by this policy. At the same time, colonial administrators developed a strong network of secondary schools and provided opportunities for the incorporation of educated elites into the margins of the colonial center. This approach enabled the creation of an incipient bureaucratic class during the colonial period.[120] The interests of upwardly mobile groups did not always coincide with those of traditional leaders. Clashes between the youngmen and local authorities were a commonplace occurrence, and laid the foundation for the intensification of nationalist agitation and party conflict after World War II.

The Gold Coast moved toward independence before it had the opportunity to acquire experience with democratic institutions. Competitive structures were designed at the same time as political participation was guaranteed. The preindependence constitution scarcely acknowledged cultural traditions and indigenous political predispositions. More to the point, however, the nationalists inherited weak state institutions lacking in legitimacy and the power to extract, regulate, and effectively use resources or garner societal support. It did not have extensive, binding jurisdiction and was poorly integrated into the global and local economy.[121] In effect, a single political system did not really exist on the eve of independence. The class situation was fluid, and the national social structure was extremely heterogeneous.

These historical and structural handicaps were not insubstantial. They were further magnified during the preindependence elections, as competing elite and populist coalitions appealed to the recently enfranchised masses on the basis of local solidarities or promises of substantial change.[122] In the immediate postcolonial period, the newly independent parliamentary government of Kwame Nkrumah was strained not only by sectional pressures, but also by the vociferous demands of the party's youngmen, who clamored for the promised material benefits of independence.

The Nkrumah government, faced with the negative consequences of the limited pluralism it inherited from the British, had few options under these circumstances. It could either nurture and safeguard democratic impulses at the price of alienating many of its supporters or it could use the public sector to reward its backers and assert control.[123] Kwame Nkrumah chose the latter course. He decided to increase his grasp on the bureaucracy, expand the tasks of state organs, centralize decisionmaking procedures, and nurture and augment the pool of state managers.[124] The selection of this direction was facilitated by the fact that liberal democracy was associated with British colonialism and the middle class opponents of the CPP; that Nkrumah's populist nationalism highlighted unity at the expense of competition; that the notion of state welfare and sacrifice for the public good provided a legitimating formula for the CPP's noncapitalist program of rapid social and economic change; that the utilitarian value of democracy was questioned in Africa; and that Nkrumah had precious few resources and could not rely on the cooperation of key segments of the population.[125] The 1960 referendum was called to sanction the move toward power consolidation and to allow for the closer coordination and extension of the public sector. Its meaning lay in the coalescing of CPP power around the formal bureaucratic structure. Ghana was perhaps the first, but hardly the only, African country to adopt state centrism as a guiding ideology on the continent.

This model placed the public sector at the hub of processes of class formation and made prospects for personal mobility contingent upon proximity to its resources.[126] Its functionaries were the core of the new managerial class. Thus, statism in Ghana came to mean the limitation of pluralism to small enclaves; the linkage of social groups to the state in a "utilitarian knot," which enhanced centralized control but limited participation;[127] the preference for bureaucratic structures and personalized decisionmaking over consultation; and the blurring of the distinction between political and administrative institutions.[128] This construction was as notable for the groups it excluded from its paradigm as for those it allowed access to its resources.

1960 was a turning point in Ghanaian political history. The consolidation of a new managerial elite around the state sounded the death knell for early democratic government in Ghana. The state had effectively detached itself from society. A second phase of authoritarian, and increasingly erratic, rule was about to commence.

Authoritarian rule in Ghana fell victim to progressively more intense periods of corruption, inefficiency, and mismanagement during which economic and external constraints combines with political factors to set in motion a cycle of deterioration. This process began with the First Republic. The pattern of rule laid down by the CPP relied on the consolidation of a corps of state managers. This group politicized public resources and, through its patent corruption, enriched itself and its clients. The demise of the Nkrumaist experiment may be explained by its denial of participation and by the hostility it aroused among a multiplicity of specific groups who objected not so much to the actions of the CPP leaders, but to their privileged access to state facilities. Nkrumah's brand of personal rule linked the CPP leaders with associates, patrons, clients, and supporters. Those left out could not but resent their exclusion.[129]

The return to civilian rule in 1969 was intended to reopen access to the state and its resources and to revive some notion of free competition: those groups that had suffered at the hands of Nkrumah, especially democratically inclined professionals and farmers, wanted to guarantee that their interests would be represented. The 1969 elections consolidated the position of the public sector as an instrument of class interests. The new form of elite politics and the circumstances in which it came to power encouraged the misuse of public office. Indeed, once the democratic government was installed, its leaders began to use their position to repay their supporters and to enrich themselves. A form of "prebendal" politics, the privatization of the state, was conducted under the aegis of Kofi Busia and the Progress Party. By 1972, it was no longer possible to make a sharp distinction between the public and the private realms.[130]

The sorry experience of the short-lived Second Republic proved that high participation in competitive elections in a patrimonial state had a destabilizing effect because too much was at stake.[131] Populist impulses were reawakened by the inequities wrought by the entrenchment of big patrons, whose behavior belied the precepts they espoused and undermined nationalist pride.

Ignatius Acheampong, however, entered the political arena as much to serve his own interests as to rectify the injustices of almost three years of civilian rule. His exclusion of all ex-politicians divided patronage networks and was, in fact, a prescription for the personalization of government resources by Acheampong and his cohorts.

Acheampong succeeded in alienating everyone, including the bureaucrats and his military peers on whom his maintenance in office depended. Some individuals, crushed by the weight of SMC oppression, turned apathetic.[132] But most Ghanaians were angry and they exhibited their frustration in a variety of ways. Over a million people voted with their heels: they simply abandoned the country in search of economic livelihood and a modicum of political predictability. Others followed Acheampong's lead and engaged in trade in the parallel system. Smuggling, hoarding, and black marketeering became rampant as commodities grew scarce and prices soared. The informal economy also, however, provided some new opportunities for independent production beyond the reach of the government. Those Ghanaians who could (mostly in rural communities) simply avoided contact with state institutions. This process was especially pronounced in the wealthier cocoa-growing regions, where local patrons were powerful and relatively self-sufficient.[133]

If Busia's patrons had privatized the state in Ghana, Acheampong's individualized it. He not only fragmented the ruling class in Ghana, but, by his actions, discredited this group. Since few people benefited from Acheampong's quixotic hegemony, he was finally brought down by the force of an almost universal demand that he be held accountable for the plight of the country and the systematic impoverishment of its people.

The Acheampong period unhinged the structure of the patrimonial state in Ghana. Three possibilities existed. First, those patrons who were not disgraced and had an autonomous resource base could simply detach themselves from formal institutions and their vagaries. Since the state had nothing to offer, they had precious little to lose by this course of action. The detachment of these individuals from the central political arena highlighted the precarious nature of legitimacy at the beginning of the 1980s. A second option, favored by the discontented urban masses and the military rank and file, was to pursue the quest for equality by ousting the remnants of the much depleted state managerial class. This path was taken by the AFRC and later, in a more systematic manner, by the PNDC. A third option, followed by those patrons with some attachment to the state, was to reopen possibilities for representation. The creation of the Third Republic was a feeble effort in this direction.

The 1979 elections took place while the country was in a state of almost total disarray. Electoral competition, in any true sense of the term, was notably absent. Many voluntary associations stayed away from the party struggle; others evinced only intermittent interest. The informal sector had practically divorced itself from the institutional framework of the state. This fact was reflected in the low voter turnout. At this stage, politicization, everywhere in evidence, was not being translated into participation at the state level.[134]

The movement of power to Hilla Limann and the PNP mirrored the breakdown of many established patron-client relations. Seven years of arbitrary military rule had wreaked considerable havoc in the personal linkage structure that had flourished during the Second Republic. Dislocations were particularly apparent in the relatively advantaged regions of the forest and the coast. Here, expectations of government were magnified and disillusionment over the performance of state officeholders was also greater. In the north, demands were limited and satisfaction higher. The north stayed in closer touch with both SMC I and SMC II. Their patrons emerged from the period of military rule virtually intact. They, therefore, had a distinct advantage over their rivals: they enjoyed the benefits of both proximity to the state and divergence from its incumbents.

The PNP's ability, despite its seemingly narrow sources of support, to penetrate to the local level may be explained by the fact that, while it could employ its still vibrant patronage networks, the standing of other patrons had eroded. The PNP also benefited from the propensity of patrons with strong local bases to withdraw from national politics. Hilla Limann's success at the polls can be attributed to the fact that his segment of the elite, although drawing on relatively disadvantaged regions, was the only group that could still inspire confidence in central government.[135] In 1979, patrons were more fragmented, more unsure of themselves, and less important than in previous years. Election results confirmed this process of marginalization.

The pattern of PNP rule was marked by its peripheral impact on socioeconomic processes. The patronage structure had declined. The ouster of the government of the Third Republic merely sanctioned what was already known: that state domination was no longer a viable form of government in Ghana.

The final blow to this system was meted out by Jerry Rawlings and the PNDC. The antiestablishment propensities of the PNDC dispersed the few members of the state managerial class who still remained in the country at the beginning of 1982. At the same time, the PNDC's various committees undermined the last cornerstone of the existing system of government: the right of citizens to some minimal protection under the law. The violence that accompanied PNDC actions in the early 1980s was both an important indicator and a contributing cause of the breakdown in civil order.[136]

It is ironic that the populist regime that had come into being out of the contradictions that developed around patron statism in Ghana succeeded in remaining in power not only because of its willingness to employ force and to implement unpopular economic policies, but also because of props from the outside.[137] The IMF and the World Bank prevented the collapse of Ghanaian public institutions by a well-designed rescue operation.[138] The activities of these financial organizations, however, imposed a new form of external control without responsibility. The PNDC has been more effective economically than its predecessors; its legitimacy, however, is meager. The paradox of Ghana's political economy, as accentuated by the PNDC experience, "has been that its own dynamic drives relentlessly toward increased governmental economic control as a response to the state sector's economic failure, while the lack of entrepreneurial autonomy of the state ensures that failure will persist."[139] Ghana in the early 1980s became the prototype of the antidevelopment state.

The instability of authoritarian rule in Ghana can be explained as an outgrowth of both political and idiosyncratic factors and the resistance of local and occupational associations concerned with conserving their scope of action. The selective institutionalization of statist domination by Nkrumah brought about a crisis of participation. The entrenchment of the patrons in office under Busia led to the privatization of the state and the intensification of inequalities. Acheampong's personalization of rule invited plunder, divided the elite, discredited many patrons, and required an accounting. The turmoil wrought by Acheampong's military successors led to the physical or functional disengagement of many other members of the elite. They had denied the legitimacy of the state. Limann's effort to restore representation did not work. And, by dispersing the establishment, the PNDC reduced whatever liberties the state could still guarantee to its citizens.

By the early 1980s the various unsuccessful efforts to concentrate power in the hands of formal officeholders had led to a serious power diminution at its core. State agencies had few resources to dispense; their institutional capacities were close to nil. Formal structures had lost the support of critical groups in

Ghanaian society, and they no longer had a total monopoly on the means of coercion. The breakdown of government coincided with the loss of power. It was also accompanied by the absence of legitimacy and the dwindling of authority.[140]

The corollary of the contraction of authoritarian rule in Ghana has been the assertion by social institutions of some spheres of autonomous action.[141] This pattern has been developing slowly since the colonial period. At independence, some groups, mostly at the local level, were never fully incorporated into the official network. Throughout the Nkrumah years, they protected themselves as best they could from state interference while counting on government agencies to provide goods and services. This pattern had been elaborated upon during the past decade. Relying on kinship networks, local collectivities, and vibrant socioeconomic structures in the urban and rural areas, Ghanaians have gradually found autonomous niches for survival and growth.

One way that some autonomy has been asserted is by resistance to arbitrary and capricious directives. When price controls were put into effect, people preferred to let their crops rot in the ground rather than sell the fruit of their labor at a loss.[143] Many laws were simply ignored and others consciously violated.

Resistance has often implied participation in the illegal, but hardly illegitimate, nonformal sector. During the harsh years of SMC overrule and the drought that followed, those goods that were available had been introduced through the parallel economy. As Richard Sklar notes, "despite the widespread disregard for, and neglect of, informal sector enterprises by officials of third world governments, most of whom favor centralized economic decision-making, a 'symbiotic' relationship between formal sector demand and informal sector supply may be the fundamental fact of life in poor countries. It is also a 'democratic' fact: an expression of the people's will in economic organization."[143] Many products unattainable in the country were smuggled from neighboring states, just as homegrown goods were transferred across the borders to obtain precious foreign exchange.[144] Gradually this network was expanded to include manufacturers and producers. Proceeds from legal enterprises were pumped into small manufacturing firms by Ghana's growing and ingenious indigenous bourgeoisie.[145] Capital accumulation processes and, with them, new patterns of class formation began to emerge.[146] The political base of the managerial elite was being replaced by the material base of a new set of independent patrons.

A third method of establishing freedom has been to engage in productive, but not illicit, economic activities. In the north of Ghana, wage-earners have found refuge in the household economy.[147] In the Brong-Ahafo region, villagers have started cottage industries and provided their own amenities.[148] Petty manufacturing thrives in the cities. When these techniques failed, Ghanaians resorted to the time-proven strategy of escape, propelled by the belief "that no matter how demeaning life might be elsewhere, it cannot possibly be as hard as it is in Ghana."[149] In 1985, after the forced return of millions, fully 1.2 million

Ghanaians still resided outside the country.[150]

These survival strategies not only illuminate direct forms of resistance and confrontation, they also circumvent government agencies and, by providing social networks of support and solidarity, offer an alternative vision of state-society relations. The reassertion of individual and group autonomy away from the vicissitudes of government action and inaction has created new sources of power accumulation in Ghana. Around these foci new norms of behavior, many rooted in the participatory and egalitarian traditions of indigenous cultures, are developing. Today, there may be more legitimacy, authority, and power in these structures than in formal institutions and more lateral transactions between them. There may also be more meaningful democracy. The final stage in the diffusion of politics in Ghana, which commenced with the detachment of the state from society at the beginning of independence, was the disengagement of society from the state three decades later.

The rhythm of national politics in Ghana has revolved around vying populist and elitist notions of government. Statism propensities of authoritarian regimes have been tackled by coalitions committed to liberal ideas of democratic rule. As various attempts to implant these concepts at the center have faltered, Ghanaians, through a variety of social and economic networks, have carved out independent niches for organization and interaction. The state is too narrow a lens through which to grasp the shape of these movements. Viewed from above, Ghanaian politics has been undergoing a process of disaggregation. But, from below, it is possible to trace a process of reaggregation away from monopolistic statism. State structures do not coincide with the multiple power vectors in the society. Thus, while the interaction of central institutions with specific groups and individuals is not always integrating, a distinctive pattern of diffuse democracy has gradually begun to take shape in the country.[151]

• THEORETICAL ANALYSIS OF THE OVERALL HISTORICAL PATTERN •

Structural elements (historical, cultural, and socioeconomic), together with external variables, have interacted with political, idiosyncratic, and normative ones to produce the dynamic process of vitiation of democratic regimes and reinvigoration of alternative forms of democracy in Ghana.

The structural factors that brought about the failures of democratic government begin with the historical developments that preceded the attainment of independence in Ghana. Although British colonialism in this part of Africa was neither particulary harsh nor repressive, the transition to independence relatively smooth, and the colonial regime certainly concerned with the inculcation of liberal norms through its educational institutions, the colonial experience is more noted for its authoritarianism than for its democratic inheritance. Ghanaians were barely given a chance to vote before independence, let alone experiment with different forms of political competition. Democratic government, as it was instituted at independence, was alien to indigenous and historical traditions.

The problems inherent in these historical conditions were compounded by the country's pluralistic national structure. Ghana, like most African states, is culturally heterogeneous. Its peoples have a history not only of interaction, but also of antagonism. Although ethnic conflict has not resulted in significant separatist aspirations, ethnicity has surfaced periodically as a divisive factor on the national scene.[152] Because political mobilization in democratic regimes has rested substantially on local issues and concerns, ethnic differences have been highlighted, especially during elections.

Ghana's class structure, at independence and afterwards, has not contributed to the prospects for stable democratic government. To be sure, class formation is still very fluid, but economic inequalities have always been pronounced, and the disparity between a small group of haves and the have-nots has intensified over the years. While Ghana was endowed with an educated stratum at independence, and it had a multiplicity of trade unions and professional organizations, social differentiation in the postcolonial period has been closely related to proximity to state resources. The absence of an indigenous, autonomous capitalist class impeded the institutionalization of democratic governments in the country.

The domestic constraints placed on Ghana have been compounded by external ones. Ghana, at independence, and to this very day, has been unequally integrated into the global economy and exposed to fluctuations in its fortunes. Although, unlike other African states, Ghana has not suffered from direct external intervention, foreign institutions and governments, especially those with democratic institutions, have constantly tampered with domestic policies. External factors constantly impinge; "when the world economic system catches a cold, Africa catches pneumonia."[153]

These structural forces bred in Ghana, again as in many other African states, a state prominence not always accompanied by dominance. State authority in Ghana was not in the past, and is not today, effectively established. During the bulk of the independence period, regimes consolidated their power around state institutions, centralizing their grip and their almost absolute control over the formal economy. As time went on, successive regimes have been unable to maintain order by either democratic or authoritarian means. The civil service has been overestablished but underbureaucratized.[154] Hegemonic impulses in Ghana have fostered a zero-sum pattern of political conflict at the national level. The fate of democratic government may be attributed not only to the compelling force of these structural elements, but also to their reinforcing nature.

The demise of democratic government, as well as the move away from the formal arena, have also been influenced by actors, beliefs, and choices. Ghana has, unfortunately, had more than its fair share of inept political leaders. Many of its rulers have not had the requisite skills needed for engaging in statecraft, and those who have did not always put them to good use. Many of Ghana's leaders have displayed an intolerance of criticism and a distaste for true consultation and compromise. Although some heads of state—Busia and Limann—have been personally committed to democratic principles, these beliefs have not been put into action once they assumed office, largely because they have not been able to learn from the mistakes of their predecessors. Moreover, most of Ghana's leaders have been corrupt, further eroding the legitimacy of each regime.

During periods of democratic rule, party structures—resting as they did on differing patronage networks and social constellations that embraced varying political worldviews—constituted a serious impediment to the longevity of specific regimes. What is of some significance in this context is the fact that, at every point since independence, major groups were purposely excluded from representation in the ruling coalition, and, consequently, party structures have not been able to mature and institutionalize themselves.

Tension between rulers and the judiciary has paralleled the political evolution of the country, reaching crisis proportions in recent years. And, although Ghana does have an independent press tradition, the media have usually not been allowed to operate freely. The inability of constitutional provisions, the press, and the judiciary to check the power of political leaders has contributed to the record of the failure of Ghanaian democratic regimes.

These factors have nurtured an extractive and utilitarian political culture at the state level, where extensive state corruption has undermined trust in officeholders.[155] Democratic beliefs may be shared by major social groups, but they do not necessarily revolve around central institutions. If anything, the commitment of some leaders, especially authoritarian ones, to the rights of others has been equivocal.[156] When taken together, these political, normative, and idiosyncratic factors have not only suborned democratic regimes, they have deflected attachments away from the state.

Ultimately, however, the dictates of survival and the force of beliefs have propelled the reconstitution of democracy in smaller units. The Ghanaian answer to domination and repression has been a quest for liberty; the reaction to poverty, a reassertion of initiative; the response to injustice, a search for equality. Two factors have enabled this development. The first is a deeply democratic tradition ensconced in local political cultures. As J. R. Lukas states, "Government by discussion depends on people being in the habit of discussing things and being governed by discussion. Democracy can flourish only in a land of puns."[157] Ghana is just such a place. Moreover, as indicated earlier, its associational groups reflect democratic authority patterns that conform to these norms.

The second factor in the democratic reawakening currently permeating the country is the existence of alternative institutions and patterns of interaction separate from those that have developed in the formal arena. Ghana has a vast array of voluntary associations and communal networks that are not only autonomous, but actually flourish when access to the center is denied.[158] These groups, unable to attain or attenuate formal power, have reorganized their activities and established a series of norms to guide their lateral interactions. Led either by disaffected professionals, traditional authorities, independent farmers, students, or members of the country's incipient capitalist group, they have underwritten the parallel economy and laid the foundation for economic survival.[159] At the same time, they have accumulated independent power. Around these institutions, democracy in Ghana is gaining new relevance, even though it is unaccompanied by the apparatus of legal-rational institutions.

The Ghanaian experience with democratic government has several comparative ramifications. Analytically, Ghana highlights the significance of the connection between regime ineffectiveness and the loss of legitimacy; it also underscores the close connection between the viability of democratic institutions and the social composition of their purveyors. The reasons for regime instability highlight the conjunctural nature of explanatory variables. Theoretically and conceptually, events in Ghana reflect the need not only to review the connections between democracy, capitalism, and modes of rule, but also to move attention away from predominantly state-centric analyses. Ghanaian political history is rich in detail and heterogeneity: therefore, it offers subtle insights into the nature of the relationships between power, politics, authority, legitimacy, regimes, and the state.

• FUTURE PROSPECTS AND POLICY IMPLICATIONS •

The nebulous and fluid political environment in contemporary Ghana does not lend itself to facile policy interventions or solutions. The reassertion of the paramountcy of existing state institutions requires massive injections of money and forces capable of maintaining order. There are now some indications that these financial resources are forthcoming. Total collapse is not imminent. As long as subnational units overlap and intermingle, as long as their leaders interact and function, as long as individuals affiliate with a variety of associations to fulfill daily needs, as long as protest persists and thereby lends credence to the significance of the state, and as long as the existing international state system endures, Ghana is likely to persevere.

Without workable common arrangements, however, no capital accumulation is possible, nor are the objectives of the development of an economy of scale, economic specialization, equitable distribution, meaningful cooperation, or an increase in the quality of life attainable. It is, therefore, crucial to design new ways to stem disintegration and guarantee human well-being.

Such a task cannot be carried out by simply reversing the mistakes of yesteryear or by attempting to revamp ailing institutions and endow them with appropriate functional content. It must also deal directly with the structural need to alter the bases of the interrelationship between Ghanaians, their social institutions, and their state. The reconstruction of state-society ties and the regime forms they entail could conceivably draw on the rich array to be found in the careful examination of African history.[160] The reorientation of policies does require a renewed effort at the substantive Africanization and localization of contemporary Ghanaian politics, a task yet to be undertaken on a statewide basis in the postcolonial era.

Possible directions of such a change can be gleaned from current experiences in the country. Economic revival in the nonformal sector carries the seeds of political renewal.[161] The peculiar brand of capitalism developing in the countryside is indicative of the promise ingrained in the freeing of economic activities from political constraints.[162] Herein may lie the foundations for a developmental democracy in Ghana.[163] Existing coping strategies in Ghana have shown how groups and organizations have carved out economic fields in which they can operate. As resources have accumulated and skills honed, these structures have garnered a modicum of economic—and hence also political—space.[164]The linchpin of any reordering program is reformulation of the terms of exchange between these groups and government agencies. The disregard of autonomy led to political dissipation in the past. The precondition for revival is the protection of this independence.

A viable democratic reordering in Ghana could commence with the setting in motion of processes of participation already defined economically and socially. Participation also involves the shaping of equitable channels of access to resources. Another dimension in this reorganization relates to the exposition of political means and to the creation of mechanisms of accountability, adequate checks and balances, and the recognition of social and economic diversity.[165] These issues are currently being discussed in Ghana, where the organization of new forms of democratic government more in tune with existing realities, is a major preoccupation. There is a growing realization that, although the search for social equality and fair representation is not unimportant, political democracy is a precondition for social justice. This cannot be achieved in Ghana without first institutionalizing freedom.[166]

Ghana is in search of a new political vision in line with the economic vision it is currently exploring. As long as power is exercised in hegemonic terms, its articulation will not mirror the web-like structure of Ghanaian social organizations. Solutions to regime instability and illegitimacy may lie as much in rethinking the possible ways of linking social, economic, and political forces as in revising the instruments of control. In this process, Ghanaians may possibly devise "a formula for the decolonization of the state."[167]

Instability makes complete rehabilitation impossible. Ghanaians must be given the opportunity to work out these arrangements over a protracted period of time. For this, a modicum of order is required. To echo Dennis Austin, "I am inclined to believe that the need in post-colonial Ghana is for a settled constitution, settled politics, settled laws and the free deliberation of public opinion rather than revolutionary gestures, People's Defence Committees and military councils."[168]

• NOTES •

Sincere thanks are due to Katya Azoulay and Nozipo Maraire for their meticulous research assistance and to Radcliffe College and the Center for International Affairs, Harvard University, for support that made the preparation of this paper possible. Larry Diamond, Goran Hyden, Jon Kraus, Donald Rothchild, and especially Richard Sklar read an earlier draft and commented extensively. Their help has been invaluable.

1. For more detail, see Deborah Pellow and Naomi Chazan, *Ghana: Coping with Uncertainty* (Boulder, Colo.: Westview Press, 1986) pp. 91–133.

2. Immanuel Wallerstein, *The Road to Independence: Ghana and the Ivory Coast* (The Hague: Mouton, 1964), p. 41. Richard Rathbone, "Businessmen in Politics: Party Struggle in Ghana, 1949–57," *Journal of Development Studies* IX, 3 (1973): pp. 391–402 points out the different economic interests of the bourgeoisie during the period of decolonization.

3. Jon Kraus, in a personal communication, suggests that this figure may have actually reached close to 70 percent when renegade party members are taken into consideration.

4. For a full discussion, consult Dennis Austin, *Politics in Ghana, 1946–1960* (London: Oxford University Press, 1964); and David Apter, *Ghana in Transition*, rev. ed. (New York: Atheneum, 1966).

5. Dennis Austin, "Introduction," in Dennis Austin and Robin Luckham, eds., *Politicians and Soldiers in Ghana*(London: Frank Cass, 1976), esp. pp. 11–12. Also see Dennis Austin, *Ghana Observed: Essays on the Politics of a West African Republic* (Manchester: Manchester University Press, 1976), pp.3–8; Diddy R. M. Hitchins, "Towards Political Stability in Ghana: A Rejoinder in the Union Government Debate," *African Studies Review* 20, 1 (1979): p. 175.

6. Maxwell Owusu, *Uses and Abuses of Political Power* (Chicago: University of Chicago Press, 1970), p. 264.

7. Highlighted in Donald Rothchild and E. Gyimah-Boadi, "Ghana's Return to Civilian Rule," *Africa Today*28, 1 (1981): p. 65 and passim.

8. Kwame A. Ninsin, "Reflections on Socialism and Participation in Ghana" (Mimeo, Department of Political Science, University of Ghana, 12 July 1979).

9. Naomi Chazan, "The Africanization of Political Change: Some Aspects of the Dynamics of Political Culture in Ghana and Nigeria," *African Studies Review* 21, 3 (1978): pp.15–38.

10. Geoffrey Bing, *Reap the Whirlwind: An Account of Kwame Nkrumah's Ghana from 1950–1966* (London: McGibbon and Kee, 1968), gives details of a military plot as early as 1959.

11. Trevor Jones, *Ghana's First Republic, 1960–1966: The Pursuit of the Political Kingdom* (London: Methuen, 1976), esp. pp. 262–268.

12. The best exposition may be found in Richard Crook, "Bureaucracy and Politics in Ghana: A Comparative Perspective: In P. Lyon and J. Manor, eds., *Transfer and Transformation: Political Institutions in the New Commonwealth* (Leicester: Leicester University Press, 1983), esp. p. 207.

13. Benjamin Amonoo, *Ghana 1957–1966: Politics of Institutional Dualism* (London: George Allen and Unwin, 1981).

14. Willie Breytenbach, "From Westminster Systems to Africa Democracy," *Bulletin of the African Institute of South Africa* 5/6 (1976): pp. 222–229.

15. Bjorn Beckman, *Organizing the Farmers: Cocoa Politics and National Development in Ghana* (Uppsala: Scandinavian Institute of African Studies, 1976), provides one example.

16. Amonoo, *Ghana 1957–1966*; and Crook, "Bureaucracy and Politics in Ghana."

17. Basil Davidson, *Black Star: A View of the Life and Times of Kwame Nkrumah* (London: Allen Lane, 1973); T. Peter Omari, *Kwame Nkrumah: The Anatomy of an African Dictatorship* (Accra: Moxon Books, 1970); Henry L. Bretton, *The Rise and Fall of Kwame Nkrumah* (London: Pall Mall Press, 1966).

18. Naomi Chazan, "Nkrumaism: Ghana's Experiment with African Socialism," in S. N. Eisenstadt and Yael Atzmon, eds., *Socialism and Tradition* (New York: Humanities Press, 1975), pp. 173–192.

19. Crawford Young, *Ideology and Development in Africa* (New Haven: Yale University Press, 1982).

20. This program was elaborated in: Convention's People's Party, *Programme of the Convention's People's Party for Work and Happiness* (Accra: n.d.).

21. Douglas Rimmer, "The Crisis in the Ghana Economy," *Journal of Modern African Studies* 4, 1 (1960): pp. 17–32; Tony Killick, *Development Economics in Action: A Study of Economic Policies in Ghana* (London: Heinemann, 1978), esp. p. 93.

22. Beckman, *Organizing the Farmers*, p. 165

23. Young, *Ideology and Development*, pp. 16–44.

24. Richard Jeffries, *Class, Power and Ideology in Ghana: The Railwaymen of Sekondi* (Cambridge: Cambridge University Press, 1978).

25. For a good analysis of internal divisions in the CPP consult: Emmanuel Hansen, "The Military and Revolution in Ghana," *Journal of African Marxists* 1, 3/4 (1980): pp. 4–22.

26. For a comparative view, consult Larry Diamond, "The Political Economy of Corruption in Nigeria" (Paper presented on the Twenty-Sixth Annual Meeting of the African Studies Association: Los Angeles, 1984).

27. A. A. Afrifa, *The Ghana Coup: 24 February 1966* (London: Frank Cass, 1967); A. K. Ocran, *A Myth is Broken* (London: Longmans Green, 1968).

28. Compare Bob Fitch and Mary Oppenheimer, *Ghana: End of an Illusion* (New York: Monthly Review Press, 1966) with Omari, *Kwame Nkrumah*.

29. Robert H. Jackson and Carl G. Rosberg, *Personal Rule in Black Africa: Prince, Autocrat, Prophet, Tyrant* (Berkeley: University of California Press, 1982), p. 19.

30. Ali Mazrui, "Nkrumah: The Leninist Czar," *Transition* 26 (1966). The general significance of the inability of ruling groups to insure the maintenance of their interests over time was pointed out in a personal communication from Goran Hyden.

31. Killick, *Development Economics in Action*, esp. pp. 228–247.

32. Dennis Austin, "The Ghana Armed Forces and Ghanaian Society," *Third World Quarterly* 7, 1 (1985): p. 91.

33. Details may be found in Robert Pinkney, *Ghana Under Military Rule* (London: Methuen, 1972).

34. Pellow and Chazan, *Ghana: Coping with Uncertainty*.

35. Naomi Chazan, *An Anatomy of Ghanaian Politics: Managing Political Recession, 1969–1982* (Boulder, Colo.: Westview Press, 1983).

36. Naomi Chazan, "African Voters at the Polls: A Re-examination of the Role of Elections in African Politics," *The Journal of Commonwealth and Comparative Politics* 17, 2 (1979): pp. 136–158.

37. Based largely on Robin Luckham, "The Constitutional Commission," in Austin and Luckham, *Politicians and Soldiers*, pp. 62–88.

38. Republic of Ghana, *Constitution of the Republic of Ghana* (Accra: Government Printer, 1969).

39. Hitchins, "Towards Political Stability in Ghana."

40. Fred M. Hayward, "A Reassessment of Conventional Wisdom About the Informed Public: National Political Information in Ghana," *American Political Science Review* 52, 2 (1976): pp. 433–451.

41. Jeffries, *Class, Power and Ideology in Ghana*, pp. 182–183.

42. Peter Ekeh, "Colonialism and the Two Publics in Africa: A Theoretical Statement," *Comparative Studies in Society and History* 17, 1 (1975): pp. 91–112.

43. Dennis Austin, "Progress in Ghana," *International Journal* 25, 3 (1970): esp. p. 596. For a more general discussion of Ghanaian elections, see Naomi Chazan, "The Anomalies of Continuity: Perspectives on Ghanaian Elections since Independence," in Fred M. Hayward, ed., *Elections in Independent Africa* (Boulder, Colo.: Westview, 1987), pp. 61–86.

44. This point is reiterated in virtually every case study of elections in Ghana at the local level. For some examples, see John Dunn, "Politics in Asunafo," pp. 164–213; Joseph Peasah, "Politics in Abuakwa," pp. 214–232; Maxwell Owusu, "Politics in Swedru," pp. 233–263; and Mark Graesser, "Politics in Sekyere," pp. 264–299; all in Austin and Luckham, *Politicians and Soldiers*.

45. This interpretation is favored by Emily Card and Barbara Callaway, "Ghanaian Politics: The Elections and After," *Africa Report* 15, 3 (1970): p. 13; and Audrey Smock and David Smock, *The Politics of Pluralism: A Comparative Study of Lebanon and Ghana* (New York: Elsevier, 1975), p. 244.

46. David Goldsworthy, "Ghana's Second Republic: A Post Mortem," *African Affairs* 72,

286 (1973): pp. 8–28.

47. Naomi Chazan, "The Political Economy of Ghana's Foreign Policy," in Timothy M. Shaw and Olajide Aluko, eds., *The Political Economy of African Foreign Policy* (Aldershot: Gower, 1984), pp. 94–121.

48. Thomas K. Morrison and Jerome H. Wolgin, "Prospects for Economic Stabilization in Ghana" (Paper presented at the Twenty-Third Annual Meeting of the African Studies Association: Boston, 1976).

49. Chazan, *Anatomy of Ghanaian Politics*.

50. Richard A. Joseph, "Class, State and Prebendal Politics in Nigeria," *Journal of Commonwealth and Comparative Politics* 21, 3 (1983): p. 30, introduces the term "prebendal" in this connection.

51. Jeff Crisp, "Rank-and-File Protest at the Ashanti Goldfields Corporation, Ghana: 1970–1972," *Labour, Capital and Society* 14, 2 (1981): pp. 48–62.

52. David Brown, "Who Are the Tribalists? Social Pluralism and Political Ideology in Ghana," *African Affairs* 81, 322 (1982): pp. 37–69.

53. Austin, "The Ghana Armed Forces," p. 91.

54. Ahmed R. Dhumbuya and Fred M. Hayward, "Political Legitimacy, Political Symbols and National Leadership in West Africa" (Paper presented at the Twenty-Fourth Annual Meeting of the African Studies Association, Bloomington, Ind.: October, 1981).

55. Donald Rothchild, "Ethnicity and Purposive Depoliticization: The Public Policies of Two Ghanaian Military Regimes" (Paper presented at the Twenty-First Annual Meeting of the African Studies Association, Los Angeles: 1978).

56. Donald Rothchild, "Military Regime Performance: An Appraisal of the Ghana Experience, 1972–1978," *Comparative Politics* 12, 4 (1980): pp. 459–479.

57. Michel Prouzet, "Vie politique et institutions publiques ghanéennes," *Revue française d'études politiques africaines*, 145 (1978): pp. 50–85.

58. Republic of Ghana, *The Charter of the National Redemption Council* (Accra: n.d.).

59. A good summary may be found in Jon Kraus, "The Political Economy of Agrarian Repression in Ghana," in Michael Lofchie and Stephen Cummins, eds., *Agrarian Malaise in Africa* (Boulder, Colo.: Lynne Rienner Publishers, 1986), esp. pp. 1–5.

60. Term used by Richard Jeffries, "Rawlings and the Political Economy of Underdevelopment in Ghana," *African Affairs* 81, 324 (1982): pp. 307–317.

61. Kwame Ninsin, "Ghana: The Failure of a Petty-Bourgeois Experiment," *African Development* VII, 3 (1982): p. 37 and passim.

62. Naomi Chazan and Victor Le Vine, "Politics in a Non-Political System: The March 30, 1978 Referendum in Ghana," *African Studies Review* 22, 1 (1979): pp. 177–208.

63. Maxwell Owusu, "Politics Without Parties: Reflections on the Union Government Proposals in Ghana," *African Studies Review* 22, 1 (1979): pp. 89–109.

64. This fact has been widely noted by all observers and analysts of the referendum. For an excellent summary of this period, see Michael Oquaye, *Politics in Ghana, 1972–1979* (Accra: Tornado Publications, 1980).

65. Jon Kraus, "The Political Economy of Conflict in Ghana," *Africa Report* 25, 2 (1980): pp. 9–16.

66. For one detailed discussion, see Claire Robertson, "The Death of Makola and Other Tragedies," *Canadian Journal of African Studies* 17, 3 (1983): pp. 469–495.

67. Barbara E. Okeke, *4 June: A Revolution Betrayed* (Enugu: Ikenga Publishers, 1982). For one interpretation, rooted in worker anger, see Louise Gore, "The Rawlings Regime in Ghana: The Political Economy of Military Intervention," *Studies in National and International Development* (Occasional Paper no. 84–102, Queens University, Kingston, Ontario: 1984).

68. Emmanuel Hansen and Paul Collins, "The Army, the State, and the Rawlings Revolution," *African Affairs* 79, 314 (1980): pp. 3–23.

69. Richard Jeffries, "Ghana: Jerry Rawlings ou un populisme à deux coups," *Politique africain* 2, 8 (1982): pp. 8–20.

70. Nigeria, for one, imposed an unofficial oil embargo and cut back on credit.

71. "The Economic Consequences of Rawlings," *Legon Observer* 11, 12 (1979): pp. 284–287.

72. Republic of Ghana, *Constitution of the Republic of Ghana, 1979* (Accra: Government Printer, 1979).

73. Donald Rothchild and E. Gyimah-Boadi, "Ghana's Return to Civilian Rule," *Africa*

Today 28, 1 (1981): pp.3–16; Richard Jeffries, "The Ghanaian Elections of 1979," *African Affairs* 79, 316 (1980): pp. 397–414.

74. Naomi Chazan, "Ethnicity and Politics in Ghana," *Political Science Quarterly* 97, 3 (1982): pp. 461–485.

75. Jeffries, "The Ghanaian Elections of 1979," p. 413. This point has been highlighted for Nigeria in Richard Joseph, "The Ethnic Trap: Notes on the Nigerian Campaign and Elections, 1978–79," *Issue* 11, 1/2 (1981): pp. 17–23.

76. Jon Kraus, "Rawlings' Second Coming," *Africa Report* 27, 3 (1982): pp. 59–62.

77. Hilla Limann, *Democracy and Ghana: Select Speeches of President Hilla Limann* (London: Rex Collings, 1983). Also Jon Kraus, "Ghana's Radical Populist Regime," *Current History* 89, 501 (1985): p. 165.

78. Donald Rothchild, "Ghana's Economy—An African Test Case for Political Democracy: President Limann's Economic Alternatives," in Colin Legum, ed., *African Contemporary Record, 1979–80* (London: Holmes and Meier, 1981), pp. A137–A145.

79. "Ghana's 'Holy War,'" *Africa Report* 27, 3 (1982): pp. 12–13.

80. Robert Price, "Neo-Colonialism and Ghana's Economic Decline: A Critical Assessment," *Canadian Journal of African Studies* 18, 1 (1984): pp. 103–193.

81. "Interview with Hilla Limann," *West Africa* (26 August 1985): pp. 1743–1744.

82. Austin, "The Ghana Armed Forces," p. 95.

83. For a comparison with Nigeria: Martin Dent, "Conflict and Reconciliation in Nigeria: The Approach to the Elections" *Conflict Studies* 150 (1983); and Nduko Onum, "Rights, Freedom and Justice in Nigeria," *Africa Now* 18 (1982): p. 8 and passim.

84. *West Africa* 3362 (11 January 1982): p. 70.

85. Kraus, "Ghana's Radical Populist Regime," pp. 166–167.

86. Adotey Bing, "Raising the Black Star," *Africa* 160 (December 1984): pp. 18–22.

87. Henry Bienen, "Populist Military Regimes in West Africa," *Armed Forces and Society* (1985), p. 373.

88. Zaya Yeebo, "Ghana: Defence Committees and the Class Struggles," *Review of African Political Economy* 32 (1985): pp. 64–72.

89. "Interview with Jerry Rawlings," *Africa* 160 (December 1984): pp. 20–22.

90. *Africa* 160 (December 1984): pp. 72–73.

91. *A Revolutionary Journey: Selected Speeches of Flt.-Lt. Jerry John Rawlings, Chairman of the PNDC* (Accra: Ghana Publishing Corporation, n.d.).

92. E. Gyimah-Boadi and Donald Rothchild, "Rawlings, Populism and the Civil Liberties Tradition in Ghana," *Issue* 12, 3/4 (1982): pp. 64–69.

93. Amnesty International, "The Public Tribunals in Ghana" (London: Amnesty International, 1984).

94. Rothchild and Gyimah-Boadi, "Civil Liberties Tradition," pp. 66–69. Also see C. E. E. S. Flinterman, *Human Rights in Ghana* (Arecht: SIM, 1984).

95. Deborah Pellow, "Coping Responses to Revolution in Ghana," *Culture et développement* 15, 1 (1983): pp. 11–36.

96. For an excellent evaluation of Rawlings' early moves, see James C. W. Ahiakpor, "The Success and Failure of Dependency Theory: The Experience of Ghana," *International Organization* 39, 3, (1985): pp. 535–552.

97. *AED*, 3 August 1985.

98. Donald Rothchild, "The Rawlings Revolution in Ghana: Pragmatism with Populist Rhetoric" *CSIS Africa Notes* 42 (2 May 1985).

99. It is interesting to note that other populist regimes (Benin, Burkina Faso) have also chosen to call popular committees CDRs. See Philippe Leymare, "Benin: Une démocratie populaire qui s'estime constamment menacée," *Revue française d'études politiques africaines*, 135 (Mars 1979): pp. 52–58.

100. Adotey Bing, "Popular Participation Versus People's Power: Notes on Politics and Power Struggles in Ghana," *Review of African Political Economy* 31 (1984): pp. 91–104. Also see Donald Rothchild and E. Gyimah-Boadi, "Ghana's Economic Decline and Development Strategies," in John Ravenhill, ed., *Africa in Economic Crisis* (London: MacMillan, 1986), pp. 254–285; and Setorwu Gagakuma, "PNDC and Workers at Odds," *New African* 215 (August 1985): pp. 29–30.

101. The best analysis to date may be found in Donald I. Ray, *Ghana: Politics, Economics*

and Society (London: Frances Pinter, and Boulder, Colo.: Lynne Rienner Publishers, 1986).

102. Ninsin, "Ghana: The Failure of a Petty-Bourgeois Experiment," passim.

103. Richard L. Sklar, "Democracy in Africa" (UCLA: Special Publication of the African Studies Center, 1982), p. 2. Also see Dennis L. Cohen, "Elections and Election Studies in Africa," in Yalamu Barongo, ed., *Political Science in Africa: A Critical Review* (London: Zed Press, 1983), pp. 72–93; and Sholto Cross, "L'Etat C'est Moi: Political Transition and the Kenya General Election of 1979" (Discussion Paper 66, University of East Anglia Development Studies, 1980).

104. The Asafo companies were associations of young men in the Akan-speaking areas, during the precolonial period who were involved in community development functions.

105. This pattern was repeatedly pointed out in a series of interviews held in Ghana, July 1986.

106. Richard Rathbone, "Ghana," in John Dunn, ed., *West African States: Failure and Promise* (London: Cambridge University Press, 1978), pp. 34–35; Price, "Neo-Colonialism and Ghana's Economic Decline," pp. 186–188; and Robert Price, *Society and Bureaucracy in Contemporary Ghana* (Berkeley: University of California Press, 1975), pp. 41–42.

107. Larry Diamond, "Nigeria in Search of Democracy," *Foreign Affairs* 62, 4 (1984): p. 915.

108. Larry Diamond helped me to clarify these thoughts.

109. This is a paraphrase of Austin, "The Ghana Armed Forces," p. 98.

110. Ali A. Mazrui, "Political Engineering in Africa," *International Social Science Journal* 25, 2 (1983): p. 294. Also see Juan Linz, *The Breakdown of Democratic Regimes: Crisis, Breakdown, and Reequilibration* (Baltimore: Johns Hopkins University Press, 1978), p. 50.

111. See Beverly Grier, "Contradiction, Crisis and Class Conflict: The State and Capitalist Development in Ghana Prior to 1948," in Irving Leonard Markovitz, ed., *Studies in Power and Class in Africa* (London: Oxford University Press, 1987), pp. 27–49; Ali A. Mazrui, "The Reincarnation of the African State: A Triple Heritage in Transition from Pre-Colonial Times," *Présence africaine*, 127–128 (1983): pp. 114–115. Also see Gianfranco Poggi, *The Development of the Modern State: A Sociological Introduction* (Stanford: Stanford University Press, 1978), p. 1.

112. Mazrui, "Political Engineering in Africa," p. 293.

113. Dennis Austin, *Ghana Observed*, p. 1.

114. Jean-François Bayart, "La politique par le bas en Afrique Noire," *Politique africaine*, 1, 1 (1980): pp. 53–82.

115. Thomas M. Callaghy, "Politics and Vision in Africa: The Interplay of Domination, Equality and Liberty," in Patrick Chabal, ed., *Political Democracy in Africa* (London: Cambridge University Press, 1986).

116. Ivor Wilks, *Asante in the Nineteenth Century: The Evolution of a Political Order* (London: Cambridge University Press, 1975), summarizes a lot of this material.

117. On aspects of the autonomy of the state during the colonial period, see Beverly Grier, "Underdevelopment, Modes of Production, and the State in Colonial Ghana," *African Studies Review* 24, 1 (1981): pp. 21–43. On the notion of the autonomy of politics, Giovanni Sartori, "What is 'Politics'?" *Political Theory* 1, 1 (1973): pp. 5–26.

118. Rhoda Howard, *Colonialism and Underdevelopment in Ghana* (London: Croom Helm, 1978).

119. Cyril Kofie Daddieh, "The State, Land, Peasantry and the Crisis in Ghanaian Agriculture: Lessons from the Rice and Coconut Industries in the Western Region" (Centre for African Studies, Dalhousie University, October 1982).

120. David Kimble, *A Political History of Ghana, 1850–1928* (Oxford: Clarendon Press, 1963).

121. Richard Crook, "Decolonization: The Colonial State and Chieftaincy in the Gold Coast" (Mimeo, 1985), passim.

122. Crook, "Bureaucracy and Politics"; Also see David Brown, "Who Are the Tribalists? Social Pluralism and Political Ideology in Ghana," *African Affairs* 81, 322 (1982): pp. 37–69.

123. For the general pattern, see Robert H. Jackson and Carl G. Rosberg, "Popular Legitimacy in African Multi-Ethnic States," *Journal of Modern African Studies* 22, 2 (1984): pp. 177–198.

124. On specific aspects, see Jones, *Ghana's First Republic*. There is a fair amount of controversy in the literature on the degree to which the state in Africa was "overdeveloped" at independence. For different views, see Saul, *The State and Revolution in Eastern Africa*, pp. 169–170;

Duvall and Freeman, "The State and Dependent Capitalism"; and Colin Leys, "The 'Over-developed' Post-Colonial State: A Reevaluation," *Review of African Political Economy* 5 (1976): pp. 42–43 and passim.

125. See Harvey Glickman, "Reflections on State-Centrism as Ideology" (Paper presented at the Twenty-Eighth Annual Meeting of the African Studies Association, New Orleans: November 1985).

126. Richard L. Sklar, "The Nature of Class Domination in Africa" *Journal of Modern African Studies* 17, 4 (1979): pp. 531–532.

127. Price, "Neo-Colonialism and Ghana's Economic Decline," pp. 188–190.

128. Callaghy, "Politics and Vision," pp. 4–5; Keith Hart, *The Political Economy of West African Agriculture* (London: Cambridge University Press, 1982).

129. Recognized by Dunn, "Politics in Asunafo," but not spelled out in full.

130. Nelson Kasfir, "State and Class in Africa," *Journal of Commonwealth and Comparative Politics* 21 (1983): p. 14.

131. Ruth Berins Collier, "Parties, Coups and Authoritarian Rule: Patterns of Political Change in Tropical Africa," *Comparative Political Studies* 9, 1 (1978): pp. 83–84.

132. Austin, "The Ghana Armed Forces," claims that society is passive; but this is not necessarily so.

133. Donald Rothchild, "Comparative Public Demand and Expectation Patterns: The Ghanaian Experience" *African Studies Review* 22, 1 (1979): pp. 127–147. David Brown, "The Political Response to Immiseration: A Case Study of Rural Ghana," *Geneva—Africa* 18, 1 (1980): pp. 56–74; and Harry Silver, "Going for Brokers: Political Innovation and Structural Integration in a Changing Ashanti Community," *Comparative Political Studies* 14, 3 (1981): pp. 232-260.

134. Chazan, "The Anomalies of Continuity: Perspectives on Ghanaian Elections since Independence."

135. For background, see Fred Hayward, "Perceptions of Well-Being in Ghana: 1970 and 1975," *African Studies Review* 22, 1 (1979): p. 122.

136. Linz, *The Breakdown of Democratic Regimes*. Also see Rothchild and Gyimah-Boadi, "Civil Rights Tradition in Ghana."

137. Ninsin, "Ghana: Failure of a Petty-Bourgeois Experience," p. 37.

138. Jackson and Rosberg, "Why Africa's Weak States Persist: The Empirical and the Juridicial in Statehood," *World Politics* 35, 1 (1982): pp. 1–24. Also see G. K. Helleiner, "The IMF and Africa in the 1980's," *Canadian Journal of African Studies* 17, 1 (1983): pp. 17–34.

139. Price, "Neo-Colonialism and Ghana's Economic Decline," p. 190.

140. Poggi, *The Development of the State*, pp. 147–149, discusses some options.

141. Richard L. Sklar, "Developmental Democracy" (Paper presented at the Annual Meeting of the American Political Science Association, Washington, D.C.: August 1985), p. 29.

142. Pellow, "Coping Strategies." Also see Jette Bukh, *The Village Women in Ghana* (Upsala: Scandinavian Institute of African Studies, 1979).

143. Sklar, "Developmental Democracy," p. 36.

144. Ernesto May, "Exchange Controls and Parallel Market Economies in Sub-Saharan Africa: Focus on Ghana," *World Bank Staff Working Papers*, no. 70 (1985).

145. Paul Bennell, "Industrial Class Formation in Ghana: Some Empirical Observations," *Development and Change* 15 (1984): pp. 593–612.

146. Nelson Kasfir, "State, *Magendo* and Class Formation in Uganda," *Journal of Commonwealth and Comparative Politics* 21, 3 (1983): esp. pp. 99, 101.

147. Nicholas Van Hear, "'By-Day' Boys and Dariga Men: Casual Labor Versus Agrarian Capital in Northern Ghana," *Review of African Political Economy* 31 (1984): pp. 44–45.

148. Merrick Posnansky, "How Ghana's Crisis Affects a Village," *West Africa* 3306 (1 December 1980): pp. 2418–2420.

149. Pellow, "Coping Strategies," p. 35.

150. *African Business*, no. 84 (August 1985), pp. 38–39.

151. Robert A. Dahl, *Dilemmas of Pluralist Democracy: Autonomy vs. Control* (New Haven: Yale University Press, 1982).

152. One borderline case might be the Ewe. See David Brown, "Borderline Politics in Ghana: The National Liberation Movement of Western Togoland," *Journal of Modern African Politics* 18, 4 (1980): pp. 575–609.

153. Richard Hodder-Williams, *An Introduction to the Politics of Tropical Africa* (London: George Allen and Unwin, 1984), p. 236.

154. John Ayoade, "States Without Citizens: An Emerging African Phenomenon," in Donald Rothchild and Naomi Chazan, eds., *The Precarious Balance: State and Society in Africa* (Boulder, Colo.: Westview, 1987, forthcoming).

155. Compare with Anyang Nyongo, "The Decline of Democracy and the Rise of Authoritarian and Factionalist Politics in Kenya," *Horn of Africa* 6, 3 (1983/84); and G. N. Uzoigwe, "Uganda and Parliamentary Government," *Journal of Modern African Studies* 21, 2 (1982): pp. 253–271.

156. Ekeh, "Colonialism and the Two Publics in Africa."

157. J. R. Lukas, *Democracy and Participation* (Harmondsworth and Penguin, 1976), p. 264.

158. Sandra T. Barnes and Margaret Peil, "Voluntary Association Membership in the Five West African Cities," *Urban Anthropology* 6, 1 (1977): p. 101.

159. Hart, *West African Agriculture*, p. 103.

160. One example may be found in S. N. Eisenstadt, Michel Abitbol, and Naomi Chazan, "Les origines de l'état: Une nouvelle approche," *Annales économies, sociétés, civilisations*, 6 (1983): pp. 1232–1255. Also see Chazan, "The Africanization of Political Change."

161. Kenneth M. Dolbeare, *Democracy at Risk: The Politics of Economic Renewal* (Chatham, N.J.: Chatham House Publisher, 1984), p. xii.

162. The same point is raised for Nigeria in Larry Diamond, "Cleavage, Conflict, and Anxiety in the Second Nigerian Republic," *Journal of Modern African Studies* 20, 5 (1982): pp. 687–688.

163. Sklar, "Democracy in Africa," p. 15.

164. Frank Holmquist, "Defending Peasant Political Space in Independent Africa," *Canadian Journal of African Studies* 14, 1 (1980): pp. 157–167.

165. Sklar, "Developmental Democracy."

166. Callaghy, "Politics and Vision."

167. Crawford Young, "The African Colonial State and its Political Legacy," in Rothchild and Chazan, *The Precarious Balance*, p. 64.

168. Austin, "The Ghana Armed Forces," p. 101.

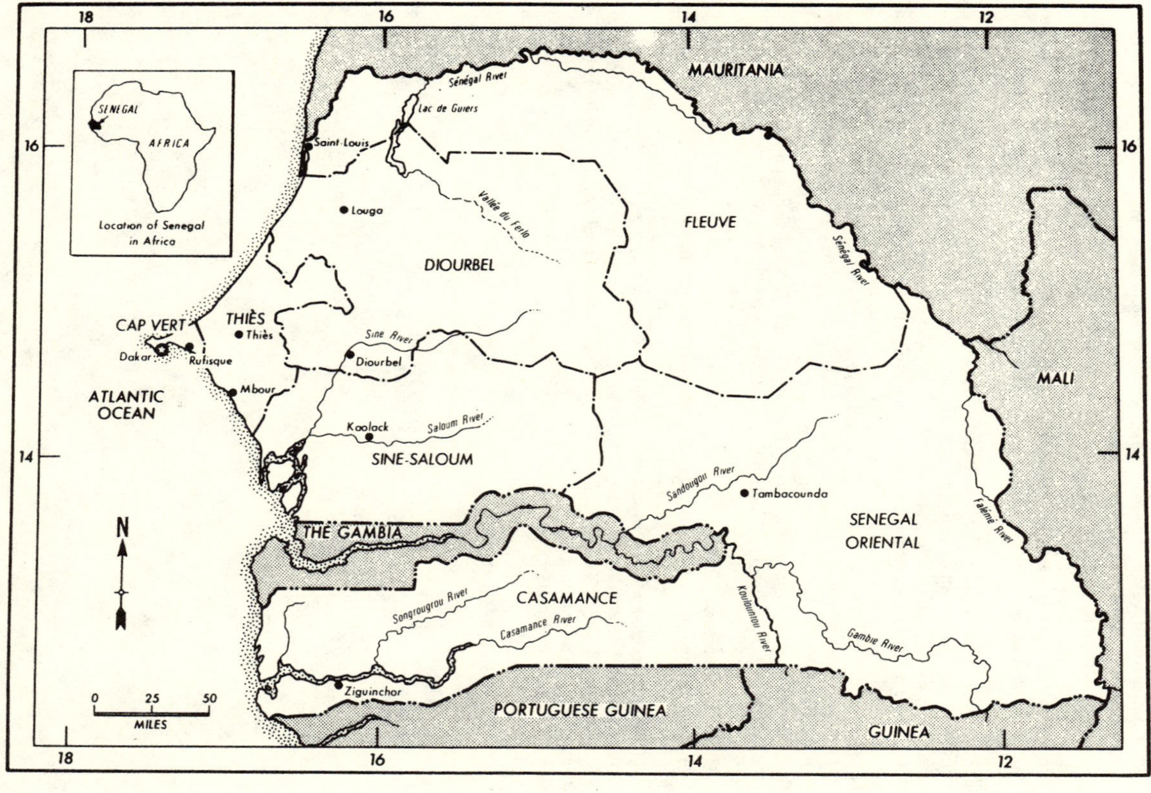

MAURITANIA
MALI
FLEUVE
DIOURBEL
THIÈS
CAP VERT
SINE-SALOUM
THE GAMBIA
CASAMANCE
SENEGAL
ORIENTAL
PORTUGUESE GUINEA
GUINEA
ATLANTIC
OCEAN
Sénégal River
Lac de Guiers
Saint-Louis
Louga
Vallée du Ferlo
Thiès
Dakar
Rufisque
Mbour
Sine River
Diourbel
Kaolack
Saloum River
Sandougou River
Tambacounda
Falémé River
Koulountou River
Gambie River
Songrougrou River
Casamance River
Ziguinchor
Location of Senegal
in Africa
SENEGAL
AFRICA
N
0
25
50
MILES
18
16
14
12

SENEGAL

• CHAPTER FOUR •

Senegal: The Development and Fragility of Semidemocracy

CHRISTIAN COULON

• THE ROUGH ROAD TO DEMOCRACY •

A survey of historical experience in Senegal shows that democracy has had mixed success in that country. To facilitate analysis, three periods, with their own specific characteristics, have been singled out. The first covers the period from the beginning of the century to independence (1960). It is characterized by the progressive extension of rights and liberties within the framework first of colonization and then of decolonization. The second period extends from independence to 1976 and is set off by a *de facto* one-party state. Since 1976, Senegal has embarked little by little on an experiment in democracy that seems daring indeed when compared to the political situation of most countries in black Africa, but which, as will be seen, has had its limits.

It is important to emphasize, as will be pointed out later in more detail, that each of these periods is mixed in nature. Although the "democratic" periods are not lacking in restrictions concerning civil and political liberties, the era of the one-party state cannot be compared to a tyrannical regime, and even less so to a totalitarian one.

Conquering Liberties

Senegal became independent in 1960—at about the same time as most of the other countries in black Africa. Decolonization was brought about quasi-naturally, without violence or revolution, and with the agreement of the various interests. It was the culmination of a political process that began before World War II, tending to reduce political inequalities by encouraging the ever-widening participation of Africans in public matters. On this point, it is necessary to emphasize the specific nature of Senegal's political experience. In Senegal, as elsewhere in Black Africa, political parties came into being after World War II. Unlike in other countries, however, "modern" political practices and elections were not unknown in Senegal before this date, at least for the (very small) percentage of the population that enjoyed French citizenship. Indeed, it is not possible to understand postindependent political development without taking into account this heritage, which has influenced the style of Senegalese political culture.

It is not our purpose here to undertake an analysis of French colonial politics in Black Africa.[1] The ideology of and the experiments in assimilation, however, have left their mark on Senegal. Since the middle of the nineteenth century, a small number of Africans held French citizenship and, as such, participated in the election of a deputy to represent Senegal in the French National Assembly. A little later, when Saint Louis, Dakar, Gorée and Rufisque became townships with full political rights *communes de plein exercice* their inhabitants were called to the polls to elect members of the municipal councils. In 1879, the government set up a General Council in Senegal to be elected by the inhabitants of the four towns.

Democratic rights were limited to the famous four townships. To be a citizen and to participate in these different elections, one had to show proof of having been born in one of the four towns or of having resided there for at least five years. Such people were considered French, enjoyed the right to vote, and were subject to the French civil and penal codes. The other Africans in Senegal were French "subjects" with no political rights. They came under the jurisdiction of customary or Islamic law, as interpreted by the French, which did not prevent colonial administrators from inflicting sentences and fines on these "subjects" without any form of trial. In addition, these "natives" could be enrolled by force in public works projects. Up until the period just after World War II, the number of Africans who could claim citizenship was very small. In 1922, there were 18,000 *originaires* out of a total of 66,000 inhabitants in the four towns and 1,200,000 in the country.

However limited this experience was in terms of the numbers of people concerned, it clearly had an important impact on Senegalese political life. It fostered the habit of political competition, mobilized social forces (business establishments, religious organizations, ethnic-based groups, etc.) around political clans, and, above all, allowed a few Africans to be members of consultative bodies. In the nineteenth century the political class was made up mainly of Europeans and people of mixed blood. After World War I, however, and particularly after the election of Blaise Diagne, the first authentic African to reach the French National Assembly, African leadership became more pronounced and gradually conquered the different representative institutions.[2] In 1931–1932, Blaise Diagne became the first African to hold a cabinet position in a French government (as undersecretary of state for the colonies).

Thus, a class of African politicians developed in Senegal much earlier than in most colonies. They were true political entrepreneurs who controlled important support networks and appeared as real political bosses. If conflicts about factions and money issues often prevailed over questions of electoral platforms, these politicians, nonetheless, had to justify their positions before their African constituencies and defend their specific interests, which were sometimes opposed to the interests of the French colonial office. This democracy "of the few" set the tone for Senegalese political life and contributed to the creation of a class of professional politicians.

After World War II, the French Fourth Republic gave new impetus to the process of democracy in the colonial situation. In 1945, forced labor was abolished. The following year, the status of "native" was dropped and French citizenship granted to all former "subjects." The French constitution of October 1946 that created the French Union called for participation of overseas territories in the central institutions. Henceforth, Senegal sent two deputies to the National Assembly and three senators to the Council of the Republic and to the Assembly of the French Union. Like other territories, Senegal was given a territorial assembly and was included in the regional Council (the Grand Council of French West Africa)—with limited powers, however. Universal suffrage was adopted only progressively, and it was not until 1956 that all adult citizens, male and female, had the right to vote.

Important modifications to this political structure were made when the law of 1956 (called the *loi cadre*) was passed. The law called for a government council in each territory to be elected by the territorial Assembly and to be made up of a number of ministers, one of whom had the title of president of the government council. The road to autonomy was now open.

These constitutional modifications allowed for greater participation and more democratic management of public affairs by Africans. Rural inhabitants who had played no role in public life up to then could, henceforth, participate in public affairs. The sweeping social changes going on in the country—urbanization, upheavals in the rural areas as a result of the development of peanut farming, the emergence of a working class and of a middle class of civil servants—created new situations and new demands that engendered new organizations: associations of all sorts, trade unions, and political parties. Despite the diversity of their aims and ideologies, these movements had the common goal of promoting and defending the interests of Africans. At this time, the trade union movement began to develop, although the unions, and in particular the Senegalese branch of the French General Confederation of Labor (Confédération générale du travail—CGT), had already made themselves felt before the war in fierce strike actions like that of the railway workers in 1938. Regional and ethnic-based movements also started to bloom.

Above all, during these final years of colonial rule, political parties began to flower as well: the Rassemblement démocratique africain, which was the Senegalese section of the SFIO (the French International Socialist Labor Party), and the Mouvement nationaliste africain. At first, it was the SFIO of Lamine Guèye, Blaise Diagne's former lieutenant, that dominated political life. But very quickly, Léopold Sédar Senghor, a young politician who had been elected as deputy to the French National Assembly as a member of Guèye's party, set himself off from his former boss. Senghor accused Guèye and his party of being too tied to the interests of continental France and the French Socialist party, of encouraging assimilation, and of favoring the old elite of the four townships. In 1948, he founded an independent movement, the Bloc démocratique sénégalais (BDS), which wanted more autonomy for overseas territories, sought to pave the way for an "African socialism," and defended the interests of peasants, whom the old politicians of urban areas had tended to treat as second-class citizens.

Senghor's BDS rapidly became the dominant party. It was more rooted than its rival in the rural areas, and although Senghor was a Catholic, it was much closer to the Muslim brotherhoods (*tariqa*) who held tight control over much of the peasantry. It was also much more open to currents of African thought, like negritude and African socialism, with which trade unionists and the new elite of young intellectuals and civil servants easily identified. In 1951, the BDS won the two seats in the French National Assembly. The following year, it carried forty of the fifty seats to be filled in the territorial assembly elections. The elections of 1956 confirmed this position.

The BDS gradually tried to gather rival political movements under its banner. A first attempt in 1956 brought several minor parties into the BDS, which now became the BPS (Bloc populaire sénégalais). The year 1958 witnessed the birth of a "unified party," the Union progressiste sénégalais (UPS), which absorbed Lamine Guèye (who had become reconciled with Senghor) and his partisans.[3]

In was in this context, and after General de Gaulle came to power (1958), that the referendum of the project of the French Community took place. Under this project, African territories were to be granted extensive autonomy. The UPS suffered its first division over this issue. The majority of the party was in favor of de Gaulle's project, but the left wing broke off and founded the Parti du regroupement africain (PRA). The split did not affect the UPS unduly, however, and it won a massive victory in the referendum (92 percent of the votes), thanks to the support of rural leaders and marabouts (Muslim religious leaders). During the 1959 elections for the Senegalese National Assembly, the opposition was completely divided between the Marxist element, the Parti africain de l'indépendance, and the more conservative forces, the PRA and the Parti de la solidarité sénégalaise, and did not win a single seat. With 82.7 percent of the votes, the UPS's victory was absolute.

Thus, when Senegal became independent in 1960, first within the framework of the Federation of Mali and then as a sovereign entity, the UPS had a strong hold on the new country.

The long period we have just surveyed was essentially as a time of formal questioning of the colonial order. To explain these political gains, one must focus mainly on the struggles of the elite and the different movements that sought to give Africans elementary democratic rights—to elect their representatives, to form associations, trade unions and parties, and to have adequate protection under the law. These struggles, of course, were led by a minority—those whose ambitions were frustrated by a colonial situation that only very reluctantly and incompletely encouraged the appointment of Africans to positions of responsibility. In contrast to what happened in Algeria, or to a lesser extent in Cameroon or in Madagascar, there was never any mobilization of the masses against the colonial regime, and even less so any attempt to take up arms against the colonizer.

One of the main explanations for this was that Senegalese peasants, particularly in the regions where peanuts—"the great wealth of the country"—were grown, were under the control of Muslim religious leaders, who exerted a sort of formal and indirect rule over the rural world in their role as middlemen between the "center" and the "periphery." The ties of these very popular religious leaders—and peanut producers—to the colonial system were strong enough to act as a kind of safety valve. The marabouts rendered services of all kinds to the peasants. They also had the charisma (*baraka*) that made them leaders whose protection was sought not only in the here and now, but also in the afterlife. In addition, because of their religion, the marabouts felt very little attraction for white culture and were, therefore, very reluctant, if not hostile, to accepting any form of assimilation. This religious power was a definite factor of political stability, and the success of Senghor and his party can be explained to a great extent by the relationship of trust he was able to cultivate among this class of religious leaders.

Léopold Senghor, who came from an ethnic group in the interior of the country and loudly proclaimed his African culture, appeared to be the natural spokesman of the marabouts and the peasants. Moreover, his status as an intellectual,[4] his active involvement in the African culture and literary movement of the time, as well as his pioneering efforts to defend "African socialism" attracted the sympathy of a great number of the young elite who could not identify with the older, urban-based leaders whose attitude they felt to be too "French."

Other explanations for the above political gains can be found in the age of political traditions in the country. Despite its status as a colony, Senegal was the only overseas territory to enter into modern political life at such an early date. as early as at the beginning of the century, a number of Africans had begun participating actively in electoral competition and acquired the habit of political debate. African politicians knew how to manage townships, how to make themselves heard in assemblies, and how to build a support network. At the outset, only a minority of the population was involved, and political struggles resembled private quarrels more than ideological debates. But, largely because these political activities took place in the urban arena, they had an impact that extended far beyond the few thousand people who were directly concerned. Hence, when political participation was widened, political "games" were not something new in Senegal. At the time of independence, a great number of leaders were immersed in the culture of political machinery, even if they endeavored to give it a new meaning. This was an inheritance that very few ex-colonies could claim. It made it very difficult to impose restrictions on a people who, for more than a century, had been used to political battles.

From a Dominant Party to a Single Party (1960–1976): Moderate Authoritarianism

In the period following independence, as a result of a series of crises, the regime sought to reinforce its control over society by strengthening the executive and the centralized power structure, and by developing a mass party. This authoritarian tendency was accompanied by restrictions on civil liberties, but, unlike many African countries, the regime never developed into a police state or promoted a situation of state-inspired political violence. Despite the UPS's monopoly over political life, despite many violations of civil liberties, and despite the personalization of power, freedom of speech in Senegal was never throttled. Social and political life in the country was constantly enlivened by debates on issues, by the voicing of opposition, and by the confrontation of clans and of ideas.

Senegal became a sovereign state in September 1960 after a short-lived attempt at union with the former French Sudan (April-August 1960) as the Federation of Mali. Ideological and personal antagonism, as well as differences in history and social structures between these two countries, explain the failure of this experiment.[5]

In August 1960, Senegal adopted a constitution that was inspired, both in spirit and largely in letter, by the French constitution of 1958. The text granted political parties the freedom to compete for the people's vote, on the condition that they respect "the principles of a national sovereignty and democracy." It called for a bicephalous system of executive power, with a president of the republic to be elected for seven years by an electoral college made up of parliamentarians and representatives of municipal and regional councils. As guardian of the constitution and supreme arbitrator, the president insures the continuity of the republic and the regular working of institutions. The president of the Council, or prime minister, determines and carries out national policy and is responsible to the Assembly. Legislative power is invested in a single chamber, the National Assembly, whose members are elected for five years by direct, universal suffrage. The constitution recognized the independence of the judicial branch and set up a Supreme Court that, aside from being the highest administrative jurisdiction, ensures that the Constitution is respected. In sum, then, the constitution called for a liberal, parliamentary democracy in which power is shared and civil liberties are guaranteed.[6]

Such a democratic foundation, however, hardly prevented the authoritarian evolution of a regime that was confronted, from the start, by major political crises. The most important was that of 1962, which brought into conflict the president of the republic and secretary-general of the UPS, Léopold Senghor, and his prime minister, the party's assistant secretary-general, Mamadou Dia. This conflict provoked a profound split between the UPS and the National Assembly that fast turned into a struggle of clans and clienteles, as had always been the case in Senegalese political life. Above and beyond any question of personal or factional rivalry, however, fundamentally different ideological options explain the uneasy co-existence of these two men.

Mamadou Dia supported a strong socialist line and urged rapid, radical reforms in economic and social matters. He wanted to put a stop to the all-powerful French interests, which were backed by their African clients. His idea of democracy was based not on institutional pluralism, but on grassroots action that gives initiative to the "powerless masses" through cooperatives and rural organizations. In order to bring about these changes, he thought it was necessary to build a party of the masses that would have preeminence over constitutional powers. Dia was not so attached as Senghor to the former "motherland," and encouraged the diversification of Senegal's foreign relations, particularly with Eastern bloc countries. His populist brand of socialism drew the favor of young civil servants and rural organizers—in short, of the "radical" wing of the UPS. Conversely, he met with the hostility, not to say hatred, of French businessmen and most Muslim religious leaders and traditional political authorities, who did not take kindly to the idea of radical changes that would reduce their own power. This power elite placed their faith much more in Senghor, whose humanistic form of socialism did not call for such rapid or profound changes. Senghor's lack of dogmatism, his concept of Negritude that encourages cultural contact, and his less "authoritarian" view of the party not only reassured businessmen, but also the marabouts and the dignitaries with whom he had been dealing for so long.

After a series of complicated events, a motion of censure was voted against Mamadou Dia by forty-seven members of Parliament on 17 December, 1962. He was accused of restricting parliamentary liberties and abusing power. Dia tried in vain to put down this parliamentary rebellion by force. The following day, he was arrested by the forces of order loyal to Senghor. In 1963, after a public trial, Dia was sentenced to life in prison, and several of his political friends also received prison sentences of varying lengths. In the period that followed the regime hardened. Executive power was reinforced and the opposition tamed. The man who had given the image of moderate and democratic leadership, who had criticized his adversary's dictatorial tendencies, gradually turned more authoritarian in order to rectify the situation.

After Mamadou Dia was arrested, Senghor initiated a constitutional reform, changing the regime from a parliamentary to a more presidential type. Henceforth, the president of the republic was to be elected by universal suffrage. Presidential power was extended, and in "exceptional circumstances" and for a limited time, the president was enabled to govern without the Assembly. He also had recourse to referenda in order to have legislation approved.

The basis for election to the National Assembly was also modified. Senegal was transformed into a single constituency, and parties were authorized to present candidates at an election only if they offered a complete list of candidates. As G. Hesseling noted, "For the authorities, the ballot by list was supposed to encourage national unity. In reality, it meant that only one party could sit in the Assembly."[7] In 1967, another constitutional reform further increased the powers of the president by giving him the right to dissolve the Assembly.

Opposition groups were gradually eliminated, either by integration into the government party or by repression. The Marxist-oriented Parti africain de l'indépendance (PAI) had been outlawed in 1960. In 1963, Senghor began a major campaign to woo the Bloc des masses sénégalaises (BMS), a party that stood under the banner of African nationalism and was favored by some marabouts of the powerful Muslim brotherhood, the *mourides*. In exchange for two ministerial appointments and some seats in the Assembly, Senghor proposed a merger of the BMS and the UPS. A few members of the BMS accepted the offer, although others refused, including Senghor's great intellectual rival, the historian Cheikh Anta Diop. On October 14 the BMS was outlawed by decree. Its leaders refused to be intimidated and decided to found another political movement, the Front national sénégalais (FNS).

In January 1964, a new law went into force requiring political parties to request a "receipt" from the minister of the interior to be authorized to carry out their activities. A few months later, the FNS was dissolved, having been accused of encouraging violence and of being a cover for the activities of the partisians of Mamadou Dia.

Still, the Parti du regroupement africain (PRA), which had splintered off from the UPS at the time of the 1958 referendum (see above), continued to exist. The PRA was solidly anchored in a few places like Casamance, in the south of Senegal. Senghor attempted to buy out the PRA, and, in 1963, a minority group of the party swallowed the bait. Those who held back were taken to court. But, in 1966, the two parties reached an agreement: in exchange for three ministerial appointments and a few seats in the controlling organs of the UPS, the PRA merged with Senghor's party.

All the parties belonging to the legal opposition had now disappeared. From this point on the "unified party" was a *de facto* single party. In the legislative elections of 1968, the UPS was the only party to present candidates and it obtained 99.4 percent of the ballots cast.

The opposition now had a choice between two channels of expression: clandestine political activity or trade union organizations. But here also, the trend was to unification. In 1962, all Senegalese trade unions had been regrouped into the Union nationale des travailleurs Sénégalais (UNTS), which was linked organically to the UPS. Despite having been bought out in this way, some union organizers did not hesitate to stir things up. Serious strikes took place in 1968 and 1969 as the result of pressure from the membership. Unable to control its rank and file, the UNTS was dissolved and replaced by a union more loyal to the government, the Confédération nationale des travailleurs du Sénégal (CNTS).

In 1973, by virtue of the 1965 law on seditious associations, the government abolished the Syndicat des enseignants du Sénégal (SES), the teachers' union and the second legal organization to openly attack the politics of the government.

The replacement, not to say monopolization, of political power by decisionmaking institutions had its effect on the management of the state and the society. As Sheldon Gellar writes, after Mamadou Dia's departure from power, "the technocratic perspective gained ground over the agrarian socialist perspective of the early 1960's."[8] The cooperatives and the rural organizations that were supposed to revolutionize social and economic relationships in the country were not done away with, but efforts were made to reduce whatever dysfunctional features they might have that would threaten the established order. On the other hand, centralized control of the marketing of peanuts was reinforced through the state marketing agency (set up at the time of independence)—for the simple reason that the sale of peanuts furnished most of the funds necessary for the functioning of the state and the salaries of its civil servants.

By the same logic, the state took steps to extend its control over the governing bodies on the local level. The Ministry of the Interior's power over townships was consolidated, and the latter's budgets were limited. The powers of regional governors were reinforced, and the regional assemblies were reduced to being organs to relay decisions and programs coming from the central state. In short, as Gellar concludes, "the subordination of local government to administration control coupled with the elimination of opposition political parties marked a sharp setback to democratization of Senegalese politics that was not reversed until the mid-1970's."[9]

Thus, throughout this period, one can observe in Senegal, as in most African countries, the setting into place of an authoritarian state and a one-party regime, aimed at concentrating all decisionmaking powers in the hands of the central authorities and at eliminating any group liable to oppose the established power structure. However, in Senegal this process never went so far as to set up an arbitrary or absolute dictatorship. If there were arrests, unlike in Guinea, there were never any concentration camps, nor were politial opponents physically eliminated. Having lived in Senegal during this period, I can testify to the fact that people did not hesitate, even openly, to criticize the government. The political atmosphere was tense at times, but there were no reactions of fear, of silence, or of secrecy. Those who were arrested were regularly tried, even if the courts leaned to the side of the government. The attitude of the government toward the opposition was strict, for Senghor's policy was to "unify" all parties and movements; but such a policy implied the use of the carrot as well as the stick. After all, there were many more leaders of the opposition who chose to join the party in power than those who chose to go into hiding.

Furthermore, the government was (relatively) amenable to negotiation and power plays. In 1968, under pressure from the UNTS, the government agreed to talks on a tripartite basis (government, employers, unions) that resulted in an increase in wages and an attempt to lower the price of staple foods. The principle of authoritarianism never excluded the idea of maneuvers and tactics to come to terms with difficult situations. The strategy of defusing conflicts was not only used for parties and trade unions, but also for Muslim religious leaders who "held" (and who still hold today) much of the country. Rather than eliminate the "feudal enclaves" of the marabouts as Sékou Touré tried to do, the Senegalese government preferred to win them over by meeting some of their demands (particularly in agricultural matters) and by using them to govern the peasants, as the French had done. Such policies lessened, to some extent, the effects of centralization, which, on the other hand, the regime was attempting to reinforce. Strangely enough, the marabouts were an obstacle to the state's absorption of civil society.[10]

Finally, the progressive elimination of the opposition did not prevent power struggles within the government party. Much more than a mass party, the UPS was (and is still) composed of clientele networks that compete for control over the local, regional, and national organization of the party—and, thus, for control of the political resources attached to them. There is a long history of such struggles in Senegal, and they can be violent. This is the case, in particular, when choosing candidates for elections to the National Assembly. The UPS's timid attempts to centralize the mechanisms of the party and to introduce a code of morality were not strong enough to resist this fundamental characteristic of Senegalese political culture. The UPS has remained a political arena in which bosses compete with one another not out of any ideological motivation, but for the spoils they expect to pick up.

Thus, the existence of a single party did not stifle political life, and competition continued to prevail in the choice of party officials. It was very difficult in Senegal for the central party organ to impose a leader on a constituency if he had no local power base. Such practices had no ideological dimension and were but a fiction of real democratic proceedings, but they did serve to limit the all-powerful tendencies of the party and the state. They functioned both as safety valves for the regime, by preventing the crystallization of more radical tendencies, and as obstacles to the abuse of power.[11]

From independence to the middle of the 1970s, Senegal was characterized by a modified one-party state. The government had set up a regime that could be called authoritarian, but the process was never complete because the government either could not or did not want to do so. What factors explain this situation? We will first take into account elements that arose from the situation itself and examine later the structural features of the Senegalese political system.

At the outset, one has to stress the importance of the personality of President Léopold Senghor, the "father of the nation," who left such an indelible mark on the first years of independence. His regime reflected the leadership of a man who is both a great intellectual—one of Africa's most well-known writers and the pioneer of African socialism—and a first-class politician, skilled in political maneuvering and shrewd in his ability to adapt to situations or to predict them.

Senghor can in no way be defined as a dogmatic intellectual or politician. The father of "negritude" is also the man who promoted such ideas as *métissage culturel* (cultural crossbreeding) and *dialogue des cultures* (cross-cultural communication). He borrowed part of his socialist ideas from Marx, but he also endeavored to adapt such ideas to Africa, and even to go beyond them. His humanistic socialism is a far cry from the combative Marxism of someone like Sékou Touré. If he was in favor of the creation of a "unified party" and worked to bring it into being, he never conceived of the party as a monolithic institution, even if he always denounced the "fratricidal" struggle of factions within the UPS. While arguing that the absence of real social classes in Africa (a proposition one could debate) and that the need to promote national unity justified the existence of a single large national party, he never rejected the idea of pluralistic democracy—when circumstances allowed it. And, as we will see, he became the promoter of pluralism in the middle 1970s.

Senghor's international status and his prestige as a writer were important factors in his moderation and liberalism. It was very difficult for the man who has long been thought of as a future Nobel prize winner in literature to behave as a tyrant and as a violator of civil liberties. He has always been very sensitive to the image that Senegal projected abroad, and he did not want to appear as the oppressor of the country's intelligentsia—remarkably large and lively for such a small nation. Whatever love-hate relationships he may have had with fellow artists like Sembène Ousmane, the filmmaker, or Cheikh Anta Diop, the historian—people who did not hesitate to voice their criticisms—Senghor endeavored to turn Senegal into a "black Greece." Such an ideal was incompatible with a hard-line regime suspicious of artistic creation and criticism.

Senghor also turned out to be a first-rate politician who could be firm when he felt it was necessary, but who was amenable to discussion and negotiation. His authority and his "untouchable position," to use a term coined by G. Hesseling, were as much the result of his political art as they were of his intellectual aura.[12] Two very good examples of this political know-how were the ways in which he was able to win the backing of Muslim brotherhoods, despite being a Catholic himself, and to "convince" many opposition leaders to rally to the cause of the government or the UPS.

If Senghor had so much authority and prestige, it was because a whole class of political and intellectual elites identified with him in a certain way, even if a few members of this group had uneasy relationships with him. Senghor was the the "ideal portrait" of the Senegalese elite of the time. A brilliant craftsman of both the written and the spoken word, he was the best symbol of the all-important "master" figure in Senegalese culture. In the subtle and efficient way he played the politician's game, he was a real political boss, a most worthy heir of the great Senegalese politicians who preceded him.[13]

Under these conditions, it is easy to understand why the UPS never became a monolithic party. Local leaders in Senegal were too used to political competition (the "natural" mode of selecting leaders) and to the process of creating a clientele to agree to unite within a closed organization, where they would have to be at the leader's beck and call and where they would have to accept decisions from the top without complaining. Whatever authority Senghor had over his party, he was never able to turn the UPS into a mass party of ideology that toed the line behind him. The UPS remained a political machine, or rather, the sum of a number of political machines.

Nevertheless, Senegal's political and economic situation in the first years after independence gave rise to political and social tensions that pressed toward a hardening and a centralization of power. Although the country appeared to be much further along the road to "political modernization" than many other African countries (with its skilled political elite, electoral tradition, and experience in the management of public affairs, etc.), it was not saved from the structural problems that shook most of these new nations, even if it coped better than the others with these problems.

Between 1960 and 1970, Senegal was buffeted by three major political crises, which resulted in a redefinition of the structures of power and of the state along more authoritarian lines. The first was the short-lived Federation of Mali, whose demise not only put an end to the hope of achieving regional political union in West Africa, but also took its toll on Senegal's political climate. The impossible entente with Modibo Keita's Soudan (now Mali) created tensions within the UPS that led to sanctions against party officials and members who were suspected of encouraging Keita's plans. Emergency measures were taken to "set things in order": the Law of 7 September, 1960 authorized the government to legislate in effect by decree in certain areas. The Decree of 10 October, 1960 restricted the freedom of movement in the country for any person whose actions were judged to be a threat to public order and safety.

The second major crisis was the conflict between Senghor and Mamadou Dia, mentioned earlier. This rift, as well, was followed by purges in the party, a reinforcement of executive power, and the gradual elimination of the opposition. Senghor's aim was to get rid of the rival political clan that was guilty of questioning his supremacy. If the rules of the game of Senegalese political culture allow for struggles between factions, such conflicts must never reach the top of the political pyramid so as to threaten the position of the supreme leader, who is conceived as the ultimate arbitrator. In this sense, one would have to say that competition between political clans cannot lead to any true choice or even to any true alternative sharing of power.

In 1968 and 1969, it was not any struggle at the summit that shook Senegal, but rather a movement of revolt on the part of students and unions. Initially inspired by the French "revolution" of May 1968, the events provoked violent clashes involving a great number of intellectuals, civil servants, and workers who protested price increases and who felt their careers were stifled by the government's timid measures of Africanization in the public and private sectors. As we have seen, the government's response was to pull in the reins on the workers' movements.

Essentially urban phenomena, these crises masked the profound malaise in rural areas resulting from the deterioration of the situation of peanut farmers. Peanut production had declined sharply after the agreements signed between African countries and the European Economic Community, putting an end to the preferential prices France granted Senegal. Moreover, the years of chronic drought in the Sahel had not helped matters any.

The peasants were losing their enthusiasm for growing a crop that paid them less and less and were increasingly devoting their efforts to the cultivation of staple foods. The state, however, was dependent on peanut farming to furnish an important share of its budget. Thus, the government cultivated the influence of local political and religious leaders to hold the rural world in line, but it did not hesitate to resort to force if necessary, carrying out veritable "dragon hunts," in the words of René Dumont, to collect taxes and to force peasants to pay their debts.[14] All these methods served to alienate the state from the rural population, who felt they were being taken back to the worst days of colonization. Thanks alone to the marabouts, who played the role of middleman and safety valve, this situation of structural conflict did not degenerate into a full-scale peasant revolt.[15]

In the final analysis, the growing authoritarianism (in relative terms) of the regime corresponded to the elite's inability, or at least its difficulty, in holding the civil society and its movements in check. It was to correct these shortcomings that the regime changed its course.

Democratic Renewal (1974–1985)

In 1974, Senegal began setting into action a series of institutional reforms that were to modify the nature of the regime profoundly by opening the political arena to multi-party competition, first on a somewhat timid basis and later in total freedom. Judged by outsiders to be exemplary in Africa, these initiatives did not solve the more structural problems of the country. They did, however, guarantee the stability of the political system, at least for some time. But closer analysis shows that this transition to democracy corresponded to an acute crisis between the state and the society that was masked by the often naive expectations generated both inside and outside Senegal by these reforms. Liberalizing the regime was an attempt—whose success must be qualified—to give new life to a state that was up against social, economic, and political constraints that it could hardly control.

This new chapter in the history of Senegal is marked, in the main, by the personality of Abdou Diouf, the chosen successor of President Senghor, who voluntarily resigned from office in 1981. Senghor's decision was motivated by his desire to be seen as a fighter for democracy. More a high-level civil servant than a politician, and more a technocrat than an intellectual, Abdou Diouf had carried out his career in the shadow of Senghor, first as first secretary to the president and then as prime minister. The date of his later appointment, 1971, coincided with a constitutional reform that reinstated the function of prime minister as a means of diluting executive power.

Abdou Diouf's role in the democratization of the country cannot be denied, but it was Senghor who initiated the reforms as early as 1974 by officially recognizing lawyer Abdoulaye Wade's Parti démocratique Sénégalais (PDS), a party that proclaimed its allegiance to the tenets of social democracy. In 1978, a constitutional reform was adopted which put into place a system of "controlled democracy." The number of parties was limited to three, and they were required to belong to one of the following three systems of thought: (1) liberal and democratic; (2) socialist and democratic; (3) Marxist or communist. These restrictive measures were aimed at fostering political rigor and stability and discouraging opportunism and anarchy.

The UPS voted to become a socialist party at its 1978 convention and chose the second option. The PDS agreed, although reluctantly, to define itself as "liberal and democratic." As for the old African Marxist movement, the Parti africain de l'indépendance, it much more willingly accepted the communist label, although internal divisions within Senegal's extreme left wing had led to the proliferation of rival clandestine or semiclandestine groups.

On the other hand, the Rassemblement national démocratique, the party of Senghor's old rival, Cheikh Anta Diop, was rejected from the official political scene. The party had been founded in January 1976 under an essentially nationalistic platform. In 1978, a fourth "conservative" option was recognized, thus allowing Boubacar Guèye's Mouvement républicain Sénégalais (MRS) to participate openly in political life.

The legislative and presidential elections of 1978 were a great success for the Socialist party (which received 81.7 percent of the ballots cast and 82 of the 100 seats in the Assembly) and for President Senghor personally (who won 82.5 percent of the vote). But they also gave the country an official opposition, the PDS, which won eighteen seats in the Assembly, while Abdoulaye Wade received 17.4 percent of the presidential vote. It must be emphasized, however, that the elections were held in a tense climate and organized in a way that threatened the secrecy of the ballot. Furthermore, the rate of participation (63 percent of registered voters) showed a lack of enthusiasm on the part of the people for this experiment in democracy. This allowed the "illegal" opposition—particularly the RND, which had called for a boycott—to claim success in the elections.

With the arrival of Abdou Diouf as head of state in 1981, Senegal seemed to undergo an even greater renewal. While claiming to be Senghor's heir, Diouf set out to give new impetus to political life and to provide better management of state affairs. In his own words, they were to be "transparent" and more open to democatic debate.

Four months after coming to power, Diouf proposed a constitutional reform abrogating the law of 1976, which had set limits to the number of parties and the number of possible ideological banners. This liberalization, to which Senghor declared his opposition, brought forth a multitude of political movements, including Cheikh Anta Diop's RND and the Movement démocratique populaire of ex-Prime Minister Mamadou Dia. Thus, today there are more than fifteen officially recognized political parties in Senegal, including a number of small Marxist groups. This adventure in democracy had its counterpart in the labor movement, and there are currently four trade unions in Senegal: the CNTS, "affiliated," although no longer "integrated" with the Socialist party; the Union des travailleurs libres du Sénégal (UTLS), which has close links to the PDS; a teachers' union, the Syndicat unique et démocratique des enseignments du Sénégal (SUDES), a powerful opposition movement to the government; and the Confederation Générale des travailleurs démocratiques du Sénégal (CGTDS). Likewise, there has been a proliferation of political journals, some more long-lived than others. However, all this has had little effect on either the television authority, the Office de la radiotélévision sénégalaise (ORTS), or on the country's only daily newspaper, *Soleil*, both of which show little tendency to voice other than official opinions.

President Diouf did not stop at the lifting of restrictions on political life that had been initiated by his predecessor. He also wanted to renew both the style and the political practices that had prevailed among the old Senegalese political elite. Speaking first in front of the National Council and then before the convention of the Socialist party, he denounced the corruption, opportunism, and influence peddling that was so common in the party and invited it to open up to "all the winds blowing in from afar" and to the "quickening forces" of the nation. He urged party officials to encourage the initiatives of members, who were often treated as simple clients and who were "glorified in periods of renewal [of party leadership] and pushed to the sides afterwards." In Diouf's view, the free political competition that had been inaugurated should, in turn, incite the Socialist party to renew itself in order to keep its dominant position.

At the same time, Abdou Diouf and his government adopted a policy of dialogue and reform with respect to the social groups that had long been on uneasy terms with the state. Turning to the rural world, he put into place a more liberal policy, less controlled by the state and more heavily dependent on private business. This was designed to appease the peasants, who had become discouraged by unwieldy and ineffective production and marketing structures that were more useful in serving personal and political aims than those of development.[15] In August 1980, when he was still prime minister, he had replaced the official marketing board with a more flexible and less bureaucratic organization. All these measures had the effect of restoring the confidence of both peasants and traders and of encouraging their initiative.

The problems of education on primary, secondary, and university levels were also taken up. These issues had been responsible for much violent discussion, agitation, and unrest since independence. In January 1981, Diouf invited the teachers and their unions, including the SUDES—which accepted despite its well-known hard-line attitude—to attend a vast forum to debate the question of education. The long-running conference led to an extensive, if gradual, reform of the educational system. Politically it reduced tension, for some time, between the government and the teachers and students. For Diouf, it was also a step toward what he called "national reconciliation" as a means of "overcoming old ideological reflexes."[16]

Finally, for the new president, the extension of democracy also called for a healthier management of public affairs in a country that was ailing from corruption, misdoings, and frequent misuse of public funds. It was a question of creating an image of rigor and clarity in the business of running a state. Toward this end, a law was passed in July 1981 punishing the accumulation of illicit wealth. Although few people were actually prosecuted, the law did have the effect of bringing about a rumor campaign against a certain number of politicians, including some ministers, who had no recourse but to resign.

In short, Diouf and his new team projected an image of liberal leadership that aimed to put the affairs of state in order and that was open to dialogue with the social forces in the country.

The legislative and presidential elections of 1983 were to be the most patent sign of democratic renewal in Senegal, as well as a popularity test for Senghor's successor and for his policy of change. Diouf won a large victory over the five rival candidates (receiving 83.5 percent of the ballots cast) and the Socialist party kept absolute control of the Assembly with 80 percent of the votes and 111 seats. The opposition was left with only ten seats (nine for the PDS, one for the RND). But the participation of voters was even lower than in 1978 (58 percent of those registered), and many irregularities in balloting procedures were also officially noted, pointing to the limits and the difficulties of democratic renewal in Senegal.[17]

The fact is, although Diouf has given new life to the regime, many problems remain up in the air and much tension still exists. The enthusiasm generated by the new president and his ministers when they first came to power five years ago has dampened somewhat, and the honeymoon period is over. The liberalization of the economy and, in particular, of the marketing networks for peanuts, have not brought about the hoped-for results, nor have they been able to prevent the illegal sale of seed stock on a large scale. Dialogue and democracy have been powerless in the face of violent regional outbursts in Casamance, the southern part of the country (in 1980, 1982, and 1983), which represent a challenge to the Senegalese nation-state. Nor has the new team managed to channel and control increasingly restless Islamic forces. It would seem as though social forces, expectations, and grievances have been unable to find a means of expression in the structures and organizations that Senegalese democracy has made available to them—a significant reminder (to which we will return) of the gap between civil and political society. Moreover, the Senegalese military expedition into Gambia in July 1981 (in order to save a regime that was up against the wall and to set up a confederation of the two countries) had all the appearances of a power play to gain control of the former British colony. Even if this move plucked a thorn from Senegal's side, one would be hard put to say that it grew out of an authentic democratic desire for regional unity or that it was the result of free choice by the interested groups.

One should, nonetheless, beware of underestimating the extent of the reforms undertaken by Abdou Diouf. Two facts help to explain why the democratic structures that he tried to put into place did not always produce the expected results. First, Senegal's democratic experience is one of the most daring that Africa has seen. Second, many of the obstacles encountered were due to an established political culture and to structures that were based on political bargaining and on networks of clientelism—patterns of behavior, in other words, that are resistant to innovation. To understand the nature, scope, and limits of this experiment in democracy, it is necessary to focus more closely on the factors that explain Senegal's recent evolution, as well as the obstacles encountered.

It is important to recall, briefly, Senegal's situation on the international scene. We have already seen how aware Senegalese leaders (Senghor in particular) were of their country's international image. The reputation of the poet-president's regime, despite efforts at moderation, was a bit tarnished as a result of the *de facto* outlawing of opposition parties and trade unions and the repression of student strikes. Senghor wanted his country to be a model of liberty and democracy for Africa, and he counted on this prestige to attract Western aid and investors, who could not but be impressed by the example of Senegal in an Africa characterized by the widespread degradation of living standards and political mores. Similarly, Senghor wanted his party to be recognized as a full-fledged member of the International Socialist Movement that included many social democratic parties in Europe and Latin America. This membership required the liberation of all political prisoners and the official acknowledgment of a pluralist state. Senghor's idea was that Africa should add its brick to the construction of the socialist ideal in the world. A short time after tri-party structures were set in place, Senegal's Socialist party joined the International Socialist Movement, in which Senghor took on important responsibilities.

Above and beyond the international ambitions of this little country, internal factors led the regime to modify the political structures and climate of a state that was increasingly powerless to do anything, either about the crisis in the countryside or uncontrolled urban development. By 1981, an estimated 31 percent of the population lived in urban areas, especially in Dakar and its outskirts. This had given rise to a veritable parallel society that the political system was not able to keep in check.

Léopold Senghor had managed, by charm or threat, to integrate into his government and his party most of the opposition forces, and, thus, to establish the great "unified party" that he had dreamed of. However, this personal success also had its shortcomings. Far from injecting new strength into the party, the state, and the government, these political maneuvers had the effect of encouraging the growth of clientelism, crony networks, and inefficiency. In the words of Pierre Biarnes, "Senghor found himself at the head of a weakened political movement that was threatened with sclerosis, and the disease finally infected the apparatus of the state itself."[18]

In such conditions, Senghor and his successor were intelligent enough to attempt to regenerate a political system that was running out of breath and increasingly cut off from the realities of the country. Senegal's enormous economic problems made it even more urgent to carry out reforms and to call forth the "living forces" of the country—the class of African businessmen and young managers—that political democratization had neglected up to then. It was also urgent to find new forms of organization and control for this society that were more pluralist in conception, less rigid, and more open to local initiatives. Moreover, the renewal of democratic processes and the reworking of state structures were meant not only to loosen the lines of communication between the government and the civil service on the one hand and the citizens on the other, but also to boost the economy by reinstating confidence in producers.

Reform had also become necessary to deal with the challenge of growing Islamic mobilization. During the 1970s, Islam served as an ideology that mobilized and structured social groups who could not find the answers to their problems and expectations elsewhere. This was all the more true in that the *turuq* (brotherhoods), which were traditionally rooted in the rural milieu, had succeeded in adapting themselves to the urban context. Pushed forward by their followers, the marabouts had become more of a threat to a state that sought, in vain, to isolate them.

Thus, the democratic renaissance must be seen in a much wider context than simply an isolated response to a state of crisis. Democratization and liberalization of the regime and the state are attempts to strengthen the social foundation of the state, to ensure that the legal country and the real country coincide. Political stability in the past had been guaranteed by a mixture of bureaucracy and clientelism that allowed for political communication between the "center" and the "periphery," each of which checked the excesses of the other.

However, the system was less and less able to cope with the changing reality in the country. Challenged by the rise of a young, dynamic elite, old political bosses clung to their positions and privileges. Confronted by rural exodus, economic collapse, and the tragedy of drought-stricken rural areas, as well as by the government's grand development schemes (like those of the Diama and Manatali dams), these older men were drained of their "resources" and left helpless. As for the central government and the civil service, they had gradually given up bureaucratic control of the economy (as we have seen with the reform of peanut-marketing networks) and adopted a new ideology and new institutions aimed at organizing society at the local level and incorporating citizens directly into the state—meaning doing without middlemen such as political "bosses" and marabouts.

In the minds of Abdou Diouf and his "Young Turks," renovating the Senegalese Socialist party, giving free rein to different currents of opinion, and attacking the bureaucratic rigidity of the state were all means of restructuring, within a single, established framework, the centrifugal or parallel forces and movements that the authoritarian and clientelist state had impelled away from the political arena. In so doing, the state also became the main spokesman for both urban and rural masses.

It remains true, however, that the new generation of leaders cannot claim to have the same political backing as the "old barons" of the regime they are replacing, even if the older generation, as we have seen, was somewhat on the decline. Gellar writes:

> Technocrats spending most of their time running the state bureaucracy, they had few close ties with the party faithful at the grassroots levels. The lack of contact with the less educated and more traditionalist rank and file members of the party was largely due to the fact that Diouf and the relatively young, well educated cosmopolitan group around him, defined themselves as members of a national intellectual elite rather than the representatives of local, regional, and ethnic constituencies.[19]

Thus, it is easy to understand that democracy had not become part of everyone's belief system in Senegal. It is identified with the intellectual and professional elite of the country. A large percentage of the people do not play the game at all. They are not interested in partisan competition and channel their demands through other social institutions (religion, local associations, music)—or through violence (the revolts in Casamance). The authoritarian and clientelist, but inert, state counted on middlemen to preserve stability. The new technocratic, democratic, and more ambitious state can no longer call upon these local resources to maintain itself. That makes it all the more vulnerable.

• THE SEARCH FOR EXPLANATIONS •

Having traced the different historical stages of Senegalese politics, we can now step back to consider the explanatory factors behind the regime's mixed success. We will be better equipped, as a result, to open the perspectives that seem to be the most plausible.

Political Culture

Just as the democratic performance of the regime has been a mixed success, so Senegalese political culture partakes of a mixed nature. It is a combination of rather authoritarian values and beliefs, compensated for by a propensity for debate, political gameplaying, and a conception of power that depends more on the interdependence of actors (even if the relationships are unequal) than on organized violence.

It must first be emphasized that the traditional political culture of Senegal's ancient local political systems was far from being locked up in a rigid authoritarianism, even if it was based on political and social hierarchies. Political competition between clans was indispensable for the exercise of power, and the Senegalese certainly did not wait for the birth of modern politics to discover the virtues (and the shortcomings) of political contests—they belong to their "natural" political universe. Moreover, among the Wolof (as among the Tukulor), political power holders were chiefs who were closely watched over by dignitaries, by the people, and, above all, by a whole political code that required them to work for the commonwealth. The Senegalese historian Cheikh Anta Diop has spoken in this regard of "constitutional monarchies."[20] The power of the "king" was limited, shared, and decentralized. It was governed by a political culture that defined a chief as a *samba linguer*, that is, as a man of honor who was supposed to protect those who were living under his authority and to be generous toward them. Dominant groups could not totally exploit or tyrannize their subjects without losing their favor. The "king" had duties toward his people, and if his power became too arbitrary, he could expect to be unseated and replaced. Power was thus held in check, if only because of its potential danger. As a Wolof proverb says, "A king is not a parent"; this means that the self-interested nature of power can lead its holder to sacrifice the interests of his family to his own interests.[21]

If traditional chiefdoms have disappeared today, this political culture has not disappeared with them. It survives, in particular, in the Muslim brotherhoods, whose leaders are viewed on the popular level as the holders of "good power," people whose "resources" profit those who are lacking in them.

The modern political elite has also been marked by these values. Of course, such values have become somewhat twisted in the system of patronage and clientelism that is the backbone of contemporary Senegalese political culture. One has to admit, however, that these kinds of behavior are ambivalent. It is true that they are responsible for the corruption, the prevarication, or at the very least, the manipulation of institutions for personal aims that are features of modern political life. On the other hand, they are also a way to control power. A "boss" who is unable to furnish the benefits expected will be disowned by his rank and file (his clients) in favor of a rival who appears to be more generous.

But the political elite of the present day have not only been nourished by these traditions and experiences. They have also been schooled in the ways of Western democracy. Senegalese leaders, more than others in Africa no doubt, are sons of France. They have learned from the former motherland the arts of politics on the most pragmatic level (political maneuvering), but also on the most noble. Hence, for Abdou Diouf, "knowledge of the other, the refusal to wear ideological blinkers, the search for the truth which leads one to listen to others, the expression of all opinions on acts of power, and the safeguard of the social and moral values of the country are all indispensable conditions for any pluralist democracy."[22]

Modern political culture in Senegal is thus a mixture of *liberalism*, which delights in discussions of philosophy and doctrine and which is hardly compatible with ideological dogmas, combined with a propensity for the *accumulation of power* (the more resources one has, the larger one's clientele, and the means to achieve such ends include compromise, as well as the crushing of rivals). A final element of this combination is the constant concern to convey an *acceptable image to the outside*, for Senegalese politicians have also conceived of their experiences as being models.

These values, however, appear more and more artificial or theoretical to segments of the population whose daily problems have not been solved by the intellectual debates, games of patronage, and pursuit of international prestige of the Senegalese political class. This explains the tendency for some to turn toward other systems of reference, such as militant Islamic organizations that purport to solve the county's problems through ideals of rigor and nationalism. The lack of interest in elections and the growing development of different Muslim brotherhoods and associations attest to an evolution that could lead, in the long run, to radical transformations.

Historical Developments

The historical developments that have left their mark on the Senegalese political system have been noted and analyzed in the preceding pages. The essential features can be summarized here.

Traditional political systems in Senegal, although articulated around unequal power relationships (except in the south, in Casamance, where acephalous types of societies predominate), can be defined more as "constitutional monarchies" that allow for some political competition and control of power. We have shown what remnants of this remain in contemporary political life.

Second, if the colonial experience had sometimes been brutal (slavery, economic, social and political destruction), it was nevertheless conditioned—one is tempted to say "softened"—by two elements: the existence, in the rural world, of a sort of system of indirect rule, based around Muslim brotherhoods that had taken on the role of the precolonial aristocracy; and, in the urban world, the existence of democratic institutions that mobilized the African elite and allowed it to gain access to certain positions of responsibility. This explains to a great extent why independence was acquired without revolutionary struggle. Structured as Senegal was by the marabouts, who had the confidence of the peasants, and by a class of experienced politicians, the conditions were not present for violent anticolonial sentiment to develop—contrary to what happened in the Portuguese colonies or in Zimbabwe, for example. Indeed, one could say that the absence of revolutionary and violent anticolonial struggle in Senegal helped to generate democracy by limiting violence as a method of political expression.

Class Structure

The structure of social classes in Senegal is extremely unequal. Nevertheless, certain social and political mechanisms have limited up to now the disruptive effects of this inequality.

It must be remembered that inequality was an inherent feature of traditional societies in Senegal. Such societies were divided into "orders" (free men, castes of craftsmen, slaves), which themselves were subdivided into several categories (noblemen or simple commoners in the first group, for example). An exception to this, as we have seen, was the south, where the idea of hierarchy in social structures was practically nonexistent, particularly among the Diola. These traditional social distinctions are far from having disappeared. Members of inferior social groups have, of course, been able to climb the social ladder to positions of leadership. But they remain the object of prejudices that depreciate them socially, and it is often difficult for them, in particular, to marry outside the social group from which they originate. In a 1977 interview, Léopold Senghor admitted it was a delicate issue that did come up when making appointments, although he always tried to play down the phenomenon.[23]

Social inequality is, thus, not new in Senegal. However, whereas traditional social ranks were based on differences of social status and not necessarily on wealth, modern hierarchies are much more a matter of differences in income. These gaps are particularly acute between the urban and the rural worlds. The average income of wage earners in the public and private sectors is estimated to be ten times higher than that of farmers, and the income gap between town and country is widening despite the higher prices growers have been getting for peanuts in the last few years.

The upper classes are dominated by the bureaucrats of the civil service, who make up the class of power wielders. "Senegal's proliferating state administration, accounting as it does for almost half of the national total of wage employees and for more than half of the national budget, may properly be called [in local terms] a ruling class."[24] Furthermore, the income the state uses to pay civil servants derives, in part, from trade in peanuts, for "the export monocrop has remained the nation's most readily taxable resource."[25]

Under the influence of the International Monetary Fund, however, the expansion of the public sector has slowed down of late. Since 1980, the Senegalese government has taken a number of measures to limit public spending, creating problems, in turn, for young university graduates who are finding it increasingly difficult to procure employment—although job offers in the private sector have been on the rise in recent years.

The class of Senegalese merchants and manufacturers is still relatively small compared to the powerful foreign interests in the country. During the early years of independence, the state directed its efforts more to expanding the public or semipublic sectors rather than to developing domestic capitalism. It has had to change its position somewhat since the beginning of the 1970s in response to demands from Senegalese businessmen who felt their margin of maneuver between state-run companies and foreign interests was much too narrow. It is a growing category nonetheless—although very dependent on the state—not only for the supply of credit, but also for the marketing of goods.

Many of the most successful businessmen are merchants belonging to the *mouride* brotherhood. Religious networks have been put to use parallel to political networks. Thanks to these two factors, for example, the *mourides* have managed to gain control of the main market in Dakar, Sandaga.

Also among the *mourides* (and, to a lesser extent, the other Muslim brotherhoods) can be found a bourgeoisie of rural religious leaders. Marabouts in Senegal are the only big growers. They have at their disposal a free labor force to work their fields—that of their faithful (*taalibe*)—not to mention the Islamic tithe (*zakat*) that brings to them a share of the harvest from the private farms of other disciples. In exchange, the marabouts must take care of the moral, as well as the material, well-being of their followers: help them in time of need, supply them with fields to work, find them wives, and defend their interests (meaning the price of peanuts) before the state.

Up to now, these structures of patronage between unequal categories have contributed to the stability of the country, for they have allowed a certain redistribution of wealth. If these structures continue to govern the relationships between marabouts and *taalibe*, however, they work less and less well in the modern sector, even though it is customary in Senegal for a wage-earner to come to the aid of a great number of people. The urban explosion and the crisis in the rural world no longer enable these mechanisms to function on a large scale. Given the degree of peasant discontent, one cannot be sure that the marabouts will be able to continue to act as effective buffers. As "peasant leaders" of rural revolts, they may be tempted to make political use of discontent. They may even be led to instigate such revolts.

Ethnicity and Religion

For a long time, Senegal was free of any ethnic and religious tensions that might present a threat to nation building. However, the conflicts that have arisen in Casamance since 1980 are such that, in the long run, ethnic stability might well be upset.

With the ethnic equilibrium that seemed to prevail for many years, Senegal had been relatively privileged compared to other African countries. The Wolof group, with 41 percent of the population, appeared to be the keystone of the edifice. Indeed, their language had gradually become the medium of communication in the whole country. There were several reasons for this: the great number of Wolof living in towns, their weight in the civil service, their dominant position among African traders, their geographic mobility, and their positions of leadership in Muslim organizations. Their domination was often viewed as intolerable by other ethnic groups, but at the same time, they appeared as models of social promotion for non-Wolof elites. Moreover, the Wolof domination did not prevent other groups from being present in representative institutions, including the head of the state. Senghor himself was a Serer (14 percent of the population).[26]

Also contributing to the reign of ethnic peace was the fact that the government never sought to impose Wolof as the only African language. Along with French, the official languages included six national languages: Wolof, Fulani,

Serer, Malinké, Diola, and Soninké. But, on the question of introducing these languages into the educational system, the attitude of the government was much more reserved. The prestige of French was admittedly an inhibiting factor, but so was the Wolof question. Teaching African languages would naturally mean putting Wolof in a privileged position, not only because of the extent to which it is spoken in the country, but also because it has been studied more by linguists and could be immediately operational in school curricula.[27] And although non-Wolofs might well be able to function in that language, they would certainly object to any attempt to impose Wolof as a compulsory official language—for which certain Senegalese nationalist (Wolof) groups have been clamoring.

Another element that must be weighed is the overwhelming presence of Islam as the religion of 90 percent of the Senegalese people. Aside from the question of unifying customs—a point that is too often raised—there is no denying that the Muslim religion has, at the very least, inspired new feelings of belonging to a national and even an international community. The celebration of major Muslim feast days, for example, or the participation of the brotherhoods in the pilgrimage to Mecca, are ways of uniting people of different ethnic origins around common experiences and common symbols, even if, here again, Wolof leadership is an obvious element.

One could point out, of course, that Senegalese Muslims are divided into several brotherhoods (*murridiyya, tijaniyya, qadiriyya*), not to mention the groups of reformists or Islamists who reject or criticize these traditional religious orders and advocate the unity of Islam. However, if such marginal beliefs have sometimes led to friction or even violent outbursts, particularly inside mosques, there is no seed here of any religious war. The leaders of brotherhoods meet upon occasion and adopt common attitudes from time to time. The authorities of the muridiyya do not cry out that the tijanes or the qadirs are heretics. None of these groups excludes the others from the world of Islam. The only problem would seem to arise from the dynamic nature of *mouride* activism, which inspires a great deal of jealousy among the other brotherhoods.

Christians (mainly Catholics—about 5 percent of the population), are found primarily among the Serer and the Diola. Islamic renewal movements in Senegal might raise problems for them one day, if those who advocate an Islamic republic were heeded or came to power. But for the time being, and despite strong pressure from Muslim groups, the government remains firmly attached to the notion of the separation of religion and state.

Religion is a prominent aspect of the specific identity of the people in Casamance. The Diola dominate groups that defend regional interests. Very few Diola are Muslims, and where conversion has taken place, it is often only very superficial. Traditional religions and Catholicism (led by clergy who have a strong sense of ethnic membership) are ramparts against Islamization and militant Islamic movements. Other differences derive from the social and political organization of these societies, which are radically different from those of the northern part of the country. Wolof and Tukulor societies are characterized by the tradition of a central state and by social systems based on a strict hierarchy. Diola society, on the other hand, like that of neighboring peoples, the Balante and Manjaque, is acephalous and egalitarian.

Other factors contribute to the strong sense of frustration in Casamance and the drive to actively proclaim local identity in the face of "internal colonialism." There is Casamance's geographic isolation. It is separated from the rest of Senegal by Gambia. The infrastructure, in matters of health and education particularly, is much less developed in Casamance. Finally, local commerce and civil service jobs are dominated by "northerners." All of this has created, as D. Darbon has written, "a general incapacity of communication between the Senegalese state and the people of Casamance."[28]

The specificity of Casamance was first expressed through the blossoming of prophetic movements, then by the development of opposition parties in the region (the PRA was, above all, a Casamance party, and more recently, the PDS has chalked up much higher scores in Casamance than its national average). Recently, regional demands have become much more radical and violent, and serious troubles have broken out in Zinguinchor and Oussoye resulting in several dozen deaths. On a number of occasions, Casamance was in a state of seige. A Casamance flag appeared along with a clandestine political movement, the Mouvement des forces démocratiques de Casamance (MFDC), led by a Catholic priest, Father Augustin D. Senghor, who is in prison.

In my opinion, there is a real regional movement in Casamance today. It is an expression of the difficulties of communication and presents a real challenge to the Senegalese state. But, above and beyond Diola ethnic identity or Casamance regional identity, what is finally at stake is the kind of relationship that exists between a powerless central state and a "periphery" that has brought a number of mechanisms into play in its efforts to repel an intruding "center" whose actions are perceived as negative.

In sum, Senegal's relative ethnic equilibrium and religious homogeneity have allowed the country to avoid conflicts that would have undermined the political stability necessary to democracy. But, on the other hand, groups who are outside this "natural" national unity, like the Diola, might feel drawn to commit acts of violence to express themselves.

State and Society

The Senegalese state is heir to the French tradition of centralization. Senegal's administrative structures, as well as the national ideology that governs them, have been modeled on the French Jacobin state. Regions are void of power and autonomy, and any manifestation of ethnic difference is rejected, on principle, as being an obstacle to national unity. This tendency to centralization has also been reinforced by the colonial tradition. Finally, Senegal's leaders justify the state's domination as a condition for development. According to them, in order for development to be effective, efforts and initiatives must not be spread out too thinly.

All of these factors, in addition to the state's role as the main employer and the means by which the class of politicians and bureaucrats can accumulate wealth, have resulted in an administration that is omnipresent and that employs a great number of people. With independence, Senegal adopted a system of national planning and set up many state-owned companies, particularly after 1970 (between 1970 and 1975 approximately seventy-five state companies were created). A nationalized system for marketing farm produce was also erected. The central role played by the state in the organization of society, added to the "resource" it commands, has contributed to the forging of a political system based on clientelism and patronage.

The policy of centralization, however, has not been completely effective. First, the state does not have the material means to carry it out. Its budget is not big enough to allow effective presence in all sectors of the society. Its capacity to control and organize society is also limited by the vitality of so-called traditional societies and the presence of local leaders (like the marabouts), who either ignore or marginalize the role of the state or who refocus and deform the structures and initiatives of the "center" that might threaten their autonomy, in order to turn them to their own advantage.

When confronted with such "peripheral" forces, the state is often obliged to make concessions to local systems, for its political legitimacy depends to a very great extent on the support of these middlemen. This is what J. S. Barker calls the "paradox of development": the government is torn between the need for political support that requires it to listen to the demands of the local community and the need to carry out a policy of development that drives it to transform the community.[29] Nevertheless, we have already noted the increasing tendency of the state to do without these middlemen and to communicate directly with the people. As we have seen in Casamance, the political risks of such an undertaking are enormous because of the danger of direct conflict breaking out between the state and the local community.

Recent reforms have attempted to lessen the weight of the administration, particularly in the realm of the economy. The signs of impotence were all too clear. Already heavily in debt, the public sector was also having to pay heavy costs for mismanagement, corruption, and absence of clear lines of responsibility. The IMF agreed to a loan of $66.1 million conditioned on certain reforms: the structure for marketing peanuts was redesigned, subsidies for state companies (almost all in the red) were curbed, and civil service hiring was brought to a halt.

If these measures liberalized the economy, they did not fundamentally change the nature of the Jacobin model. Although a failure from the political and economic point of view, it remained part of the political culture of the power elite. Unable to control society, the state has managed all through this period to maintain order. To be sure, discounting recent events in Casamance, it has never had to deal with any subversive or terrorist movements. But this absence of destabilizing forces is also because of the relative freedom of expression that political movements enjoyed in Senegal and the concern of Senegalese leaders to accept the principle of dialogue with members of the opposition. This is what President Diouf calls a "national consensus." If, in certain circumstances and at certain points in time, the government took a hard line and made decisions that were antidemocratic, the use of force was never looked upon as a *long-term* means of solving problems.

Another consequence of political stability is that the role of the army is much less noticeable than in the rest of Africa. The government has sometimes turned to the army for help (in Gambia and in Casamance), but in the last analysis, it does not owe its survival to military intervention. There is in Senegal today a tradition of nonintervention by the army in political life (members of the armed forces do not have the right to vote) that could only be brought into question in the event of grave difficulties.

Although this tradition is conducive to the consolidation of democracy, the centralizing ideology of the state is a major obstacle in this regard. The failing is one of communication. Paradoxically, the more the state becomes centralized, the further away appears to be from society, and the greater is society's tendency to act autonomously. The Senegalese state is not an expression of the Senegalese society. It aims to control society without taking into consideration its specific features, its ethnic and cultural diversity, and the movements that society has engendered. From this point of view, one might agree with Mar Fall that the Senegalese state is, indeed, sick. It is suffering from the disease of isolation.[30] And the democratic renewal has done very little to modify the situation.

Political Institutions

As we have observed, presidential power has grown since independence. In Senegal, it is the executive that governs. For many years, the Assembly was a body where decisions were simply registered. The presence today of a number of opposition parliamentarians has made the Assembly a political forum, but its capacity for initiative to legislate or to control the government is extremely limited—in fact, if not by law. All powers are concentrated in the hands of the Socialist Party, the government, and the president. The judiciary would also seem to be subservient to the executive branch, even if it appears to have some margin of maneuver compared to other African states. Here again, there is no contrast between the two periods. Trials are conducted in a relatively unrestricted manner, but as Gellar notes, "the courts have rarely ruled against the government in important constitutional cases or political trials."[31]

In the party system, there have been some important changes with the evolution of a *de facto* one-party state to first a limited multiparty structure and then a totally unrestricted multiparty system. The government party, however, continues to play a dominant role in political life, and opposition parties remain marginal. But distinctions must be made on this point. The PDS and the RND are both movements with a wide social base (their clientele has about the same social profile as that of the Socialist party) and a wide geographical base—although their position is stronger in regions with problems, like Casamance for the PDS. The political philosophy of both parties is also rather moderate. It is, in fact, quite close to that of the Socialist party on many issues, their principal criticism being the Socialist party's incompetence or its unwillingness to carry out its program. The small parties of the extreme left, on the other hand, are much more ideologically oriented and divided by points of doctrine. Their social base is very narrow (teachers, students, and trade unionists), and their influence is practically nil outside of the towns. Yet, all of these groups have contributed in a big way to the development of a very active political press that enjoys great freedom compared to the systematic repression it experienced in the past.

Despite the apparent vitality of political life in Senegal, the party system still remains relatively impervious, as has already been noted, to movements in the rest of society. Politics is much more an arena for politicians than a channel for the expression and defense of new social interests and forces. The low voter participation in elections is one sign of this crisis, and the difficulty of Senegalese political movements in coping with Islamic mobilization is another.[32]

Political Leadership

This last commentary underscores the limits of political innovation in Senegal, as well as the gap that exists between political leaders and the masses, who are looking outside official or institutionalized political channels for solutions to the problems they face. We can see taking hold and developing in Senegal today an informal political system that aims to compensate for the failure of the political system to adapt to social changes—but that also is an obstacle to the initiatives of political leaders. There is a sort of vicious cycle in the dichotomy between the "center" and the "periphery," between the state and what can be called *grassroots movements of political action*. Such movements are channeled through structures like Muslim brotherhoods or village development associations. Their strategy consists either in bypassing official institutions by creating their own organizational networks and schemes of action, or in recouping the benefits of initiatives from on high. Violence sometimes breaks out, as in Casamance, when problems of divison and incomprehension fail to be overcome by passive resistance or manipulation.

It is not a question here of the democratic bent of Senegalese leaders. We have seen throughout this chapter that, even in the authoritarian period, the Senegalese government has been open to dialogue and negotiation. For the most part, compromise and consensus have always been the rules of the game, at least in the long term. They are part of what can be called the political art of

Senegal. The problem is much more that of a state whose centralizing ideology does not mesh well with grassroots dynamics.

Socioeconomic Development

The distance between the state and the society is a factor that has hampered development in the country. Since independence, the Senegalese government has endeavored to carry out what it calls "great development projects" (the building of dams and petrochemical plants, for example). It has given itself the tools that were supposed to free the country from dependence and underdevelopment through the creation of a whole series of state companies and strictly controlled peanut-marketing mechanisms—leaving the door open, however, for foreign investment. But these measures were undermined by bureaucratic structures that left no room for responsible participation on the part of producers or wage-earners. They also carried the threat of gigantic production structures that were not compatible with local traditions, particularly in rural areas. The outcome of these efforts was often financial disaster. In the final analysis, those who profited from these schemes were, above all, the experts hired as advisors and the technocrats. As Donal Cruise O'Brien puts it, when there were profits in the agricultural sector, "instead of being used to support modernization and increased productivity in the rural sector, the surplus was absorbed into costly services, state enterprises and the civil service."[33] And René Dumont, one of the most astute observers of Senegal's economy, has observed:

> What is called rural development seems to have been the development of the bureaucracy rather than of the peasantry. The civil service widened its hold to serve the interests of the various organizations of control or intervention, more than that of peasants who were only alibis . . . In wanting to organise peasants along strict lines without consulting them, the state turned them into welfare cases.[34]

Development has also been hampered by the chronic drought that has prevailed in Senegal for fifteen years, bringing about drastic fluctuations in agricultural production and accelerating the country's food dependency.

It is true that other sectors have been relatively more successful: the phosphate mines, the petrochemical industry (with the refinery at M'Bao), and tourism. But this has not been enough to offset the effects of the slump in agricultural production, which remains the cornerstone of Senegal's economy. The situation is all the more serious in that the sharp rise in the price of oil (a twentyfold increase between 1960 and 1980) has sent the country's national debt skyrocketing.

A few statistics are enough to demonstrate the poor performance of the economy. Between 1965 and 1984, Senegal's annual growth rate of per capita GNP was minus 0.5 percent; and between 1973 and 1984 the GNP grew by 2.6 percent (minus 0.2 percent in agriculture and 6 percent in industry). The deficit in the balance of payments went from $16 million in 1970 to $274 million in 1984. The external debt, which was $131 million in 1970, rose to $1,565 million in 1984.[35]

As Gellar concludes, these development schemes "have failed to raise living standards for most Senegalese or to redistribute wealth and services in favor of the poor."[36] As indicated in Table 4.1, improvements in the quality of life for the average Senegalese over the last two decades have been more modest than the average for low-income countries in the Third World, or even for those in sub-Saharan Africa. In fact, by such revealing measures as life expectancy, infant mortality, and adult literacy, Senegal remains among the poorest countries in the world, with a literacy rate of 10 percent and a life expectancy below fifty. Not only has the economic situation worsened since independence, but inequalities have increased.

Faced with such a disastrous situation, yielding to the pressure of the IMF, and aware also of the political dangers of rural discontent, President Diouf has embarked upon a program of reform and austerity. The state marketing board has been abolished, limits have been set to the growth of state enterprises and of the public sector in general, and their structures have been reformed to make them more competitive and efficient. A liberal economy is supposed to come to

Table 4.1 Socioeconomic Development in Senegal and Other Low-Income Countries

	Senegal		Sub-Saharan African Low Income Countries[a]		Low Income Countries[a]	
	1965	1984	1965	1984	1965	1984
Male life expectancy (in years)	40	45	41	47	44	50
Female life expectancy (in years)	42	48	43	50	45	52
Infant mortality (per 1000 live births)	172	138	155	129	147	114
Adult literacy (percent)[b]	6	10	—	—	23	40
Primary-school enrollments[c] (as % of school-age population)	40	53	37	76	44	74
Secondary-school enrollments[c] (as % of school-age population)	7	12	4	13	9	20

Source: World Bank, *World Development Report 1986* (New York: Oxford University Press), and for literacy, *World Development Report 1983*.

[a] These figures are the averages for each group of countries, weighted by population. The category "Low-Income Countries" includes all 36 countries classified by the World Bank as low-income in 1986, excluding China and India, which are more developed.

[b] These figures are for 1960 and 1980.

[c] These figures are for 1965 and 1983.

terms with all of Senegal's problems—and a liberal philosophy in politics to be a safety valve for the regime.

It is too early to measure the effects of such policies. It is not certain, however, that such measures will not be detrimental to the lower classes and provoke, in turn, more unrest and other forms of inequality (the development of a business bourgeoisie). This is all the more probable, as a policy of "truth in prices" will no doubt increase the price of staple foods—and wage earners of the public sector will not remain indifferent to an erosion of their purchasing power.

To conclude on this point, it is nonetheless surprising to note that, in spite of this disastrous economic performance, Senegal has experienced continuous political stability. This is no doubt because of the function of mediation played by the Muslim brotherhoods and, on a wider level, the practice of clientelism, which has acted as a safety valve. But, as the gap between the state and society grows, one cannot be sure that these networks will continue to maintain a relative and fragile communication between the top and the bottom of the political and social system. One may well ask if the democratic renewal will be able to cope with these frustrations.

International Factors

International relations in Senegal are characterized by two tendencies that, at first sight, are contradictory. The first is the country's extreme dependence on the outside. Despite the efforts of its government to diversify agricultural production and equip itself with a dynamic industrial sector, Senegal's monocrop economic structure remains typically colonial. Seesawing agricultural output (508,000 tons in 1977 and 1,145,000 tons in 1982, for example) and the fluctuating world price of peanuts are grave threats to economic stability and an important contributing factor to Senegal's rising national debt. The situation has been aggravated, as seen above, by the rise in the price of oil. In such a context, French aid, which had solved the problem for a long time, is no longer adequate. To improve matters, Senegal must appeal to the IMF—and agree to its conditions—as well as to other outside sources. Hence, as Gellar notes, "at the beginning of the 1980's the Senegalese economy was more than ever hostage to external economic forces."[37] If France has remained the first supplier of technical assistance (63 percent of such aid in 1980) and Senegal's first trading partner, more and more financial aid and investment comes from other sources, including the European Development Fund and the IMF. The United States is also visibly present in Senegal through USAID and U.S. commercial banks. The aid of Arab countries, in the form of bilateral agreements or multinational business interests, is also on the increase.[38] The influence of France, however, remains preponderant on the political and cultural planes. France still has a military base in Dakar, and Senegal's intelligentsia is the most Parisian in all of Black Africa.

This dependence on the outside is matched by extremely active diplomatic involvement in Africa and the rest of the world. From this point of view, the Senegal of Abdou Diouf is as enterprising as that of his predecessor. Senegal has played a pioneering role in setting up regional economic bodies. The country has been a mediator in many inter-African conflicts (recently in the Western Sahara), and has made important contributions to the Organization of African Unity. Moreover, Senegal has been one of the initiators of the French "Commonwealth" (*francophonie*) and has always been an active participant in international institutions like the United Nations and UNESCO. In the eyes of the world, Senegal is one of the leaders of moderate Africa. If it leans more to the West than to the East, with whom relationships are somewhat distant, Senegal also aspires to be nonaligned.

Senegal's leading role in international relations implies the existence of a political regime that is stable and respectful of human liberties. We have already seen how important Senegal's international image was for Senghor in the past, and how important it still is for Diouf today—particularly as it concerns Western countries that are important sources of aid. This image has two complementary functions: it allows Senegal greater influence on the international scene than its demographic and economic weight would merit; and, by offering reassuring guarantees on the nature and stability of the regime, it helps attract international assistance and private investment.

With Abdou Diouf, however, another image has grown up around Senegal, that of an Islamic country. Senghor developed close ties with certain Arab countries (Saudi Arabia, Kuwait, Iraq, and the Gulf States), and in 1973 he authorized the Palestine Liberation Organization to open an office in Dakar. But, as a Muslim, his successor can go even further in this direction, and Diouf's participation in January 1981 at the Islamic Conference in Saudi Arabia, combined with his pilgrimage to Mecca, have had a considerable echo in Senegal. In openly underscoring Senegal's Islamic character, Abdou Diouf has aimed to encourage Arab aid. At the same time, such moves are also symptomatic of internal aspirations in Senegal, where Islam is increasingly active. But Diouf also wants to control and contain the phenomenon of Muslim renewal, and in 1984 he did not hesitate to close down the Iranian Embassy, just as Senghor, a few years before, had not hesitated to break off diplomatic ties with Libya when it was accused of meddling in Senegal's internal affairs. Thus, as we can see, Senegal's relationships with the outside are closely linked to its internal problems.

Summary

In the last analysis, Senegal appears today to be a semidemocracy. The factors that have played in favor of democracy relate to Senegal's history and political culture, as well as to its relative ethnic equilibrium and religious homogeneity. In addition, one cannot overlook the international image that this little country has tried to project. On the other hand, the weight of the state, economic—and, to a certain extent, political—dependence, and the phenomenon of clientelism have functioned as limits to democracy.

• FUTURE PROSPECTS •

Formal democracy is a political tradition in Senegal, despite a period of about ten years during which some violations were committed. More than elsewhere in Africa, Senegal has used pluralism and negotiation (sometimes accompanied by threats, it is true) to overcome the difficulties it has encountered. There is no doubt that the majority of the political elite strongly favors democratic government. The problem is whether democracy can solve the fundamental issues facing the country.

The first of these concerns Senegal's economic survival. As has been pointed out, despite its efforts to take better advantage of its (scarce) resources, Senegal has been hit head-on by the world recession and the drought. It has also had to face the consequences of the neocolonial structure of its economy, as well as the shortcomings of its political and administrative apparatus—its unwieldiness and lack of flexibility and its clientelist practices. Up to now, public funds, international aid, and foreign investment have served to develop the ruling elite and the bureaucracy rather than the country's productive forces. In such conditions, democracy is fragile and artificial. It can benefit, at the very most, certain elites by giving them channels to express their opinions, but it has not changed the living conditions of the majority of the people. This explains their growing mistrust of institutions and political parties and their lack of interest in electoral, political and public affairs. The success of ideologies and movements outside the formal political scene is thus not very surprising, and the renewal of Islam has to be seen in this light.

Here, then, is the second big issue facing Senegal. It is one of utmost importance, for it reveals the existence of another political culture that may not be fundamentally antidemocratic, as is often thought, but which brings into question the political heritage and traditions that have dominated the intelligentsia and the ruling elite up to now. For a long time, Islam, and especially the brotherhoods that structured it, served as institutions of social, political, and economic mediation. Today, however, Islam has become an ideology of mobilization and protest. The failure of modernization has contributed to the rise of a religion that appears as a weapon in the combat against the West and its values as expressed by the elite of the country. Henceforth, the marabouts are no longer simple clients of the ruling elite and of the state. Riding on the wave of popular opinion that sees Islam as a universal remedy to poverty and decadence, the marabouts have become more demanding partners of the state, setting themselves up as lesson-givers, or even as a counterelite. In this sense, Islam is no longer simply an element of popular culture. It has become an ideology aiming to remodel society and the state. The young, and particularly young intellectuals, as well as members of the frustrated petty bourgeoisie, no longer identify with the values of the West, or with Marxism, but have thrown themselves into Islamic movements.[39]

It is very difficult for the state and for democracy to cope with this dynamic social force. What we are witnessing is the transition from a relatively tolerant and open kind of Islam to an Islam that is setting itself up as an autonomous political force. Whereas the first type was compatible with democracy, the second is more of an obstacle, for it implies a totalitarian vision of society.

The problem of Casamance represents a third challenge for the regime. The revolts that have shaken the southern part of Senegal in the last five years cannot be stopped by mere administrative reforms. I have tried, briefly, to give reasons for this. It must be emphasized that this is not just a rebellion of a particular ethnic group. What is being questioned, above all, is the kind of communication that exists between the "center" and the "periphery." It is the culture of the Jacobin state itself that is under fire, particularly by a people who do not live in the same social and cultural universe as those of the rest of the country and feel they have been ignored for too long.

In short, these three critical issues show the limits of a democracy that has been too much the exclusive concern of a relatively privileged minority and that remains cut off from the realities of the country. The inhabitants of Senegal will only be able to feel concerned about pluralism and liberalism if this minority is able to provide for their security and dignity. As of now, the above problems not only impose limits to the liberalization of the regime, but threaten the country's political stability.

It would be presumptuous of us to claim to have lessons to teach or to have miracle solutions to the crisis facing Senegal today. However, in light of the above analysis, it is possible to indicate a few directions that could allow Senegal to consolidate its democratic gains and to make these gains more meaningful for a greater number of its inhabitants.

The most fundamental point concerns the economic survival of the country, and, more specifically, that of its most underprivileged categories. On the whole, massive state intervention and huge agroindustrial complexes have been failures. Not only have such schemes prevented any grassroots initiative, but they have failed to improve the income of the social groups they were meant to benefit. Worse, the effects have often included a profound breaking down of the groups concerned—and erosion of the legitimacy of a regime that has been unable to meet people's expectations and fulfill promises made.

The recently adopted state policy of economic liberalism is certainly a step forward, but only if two conditions are maintained. First, as proclaimed in a recent government report, it must indeed encourage "real participation on the part of rural inhabitants as well as sharpen their sense of reponsibility."[40] Next, it has to achieve food self-sufficiency for peasant communities and make them less dependent, not only on the state, but also on the world market. This is also the only approach that can stop the rural exodus and the uncontrollable urban spread, both sources of anomie and social frustration and factors of political fragility.

Such steps cannot be carried out simply by limiting the role of the state. It is necessary, above all, to invent a new means of communication between the "center" and the "periphery." And that means that the state has to be more open to local realities. I believe that only a policy of decentralization would be able to put such dynamics into motion and reestablish confidence between the summit and the base, for political pluralism will function in a vacuum if it is not anchored in local societies. Unfortunately, both the Jacobin tradition and the monocratic presidential system work against such transformations, justifying the monopolization of power in the name of "the greatest good." In his contribution to a debate on democracy in Senegal, Pathé Diagne observed that democracy loses much of its meaning when it is structured around a monocratic and centralizing power system that prohibits people "from achieving their full material and cultural potentials by refusing to allow them to set up their own assemblies and local administrations in their own specific context and geographic space."[41]

Decentralization is certainly not a panacea for all the problems in Senegal, and it might even be a threat to national unity, but it can bring institutions closer to the people and thus prevent disastrous clashes, such as might well occur one day in Casamance.

Finally, if decentralization really is to work, both the state and the forces behind it have to anchor themselves more deeply in Senegal's cultural environment. The elite's Westernized consumption patterns and concept of the state only serve to widen the gap between the ruling class and the majority of the people, who live in another universe and who have no means of gaining access to the "superior" culture. Muslim nationalism feeds on this gap. And refocusing the political culture around "indigenous" values, practices, and realities would help narrow and, finally, close this gap, which is detrimental to democracy.

What national or extranational forces might foster such changes?

I have emphasized already the rather large consensus that exists in Senegal around the concept of pluralism. Such orientations, however, could be brought into question by the rising forces of Islam, which are gaining support among certain elites seeking new forms of action and legitimacy. Among the social categories mobilized by the Islamic revival can be found the young intellectuals and, to a lesser extent, the business class, no doubt because they perceive the Muslim religion as a way of setting themselves off from the political and administrative elite that governs the country. As for the latter, it is undermined by a conflict of generations that pits the former political bosses and dignitaries against young technocrats. The older generation has strong local backing but it is incapable of coping with the mutations the country is undergoing, and the younger generation is more competent but less rooted in the "real country."

What they do share, however, is their mutual support for the democratic form of government.

The values and institutions of democracy find much less favor, on the other hand, among the lower social classes, who do not perceive their utility, or rather their effects, on daily life. For these classes the state is often a foreign entity that is ineffective and oppressive. Competition among political parties is a game that does not concern them directly because it cannot solve their problems or fulfill their aspirations. In such conditions, democracy lacks pertinence and cannot throw down roots in the "real country."

The most important task on the international level, I believe, is not merely to consider Senegal as a politically strategic region for the West, but to try to overcome the difficulties that restrict the impact of democracy. From this point of view, any action that limits the state is a necessary, although insufficient, condition, for there is the everpresent risk that giving free rein to economic forces would create new forms of inequality and reinforce the neocolonial structure of the economy. International aid must not only help to develop an entrepreneurial class in the strictest sense of the word. It must allow local communities to have control of their own affairs and give them the means of innovation. Thus, heavy capital outlay or aid schemes for "massive development projects" should give way to an aid emphasis on smaller-scale and intermediate technology, featuring projects that are less ambitious but closer to the people. It bears repeating that any policy that tends to bring the "center" closer to the "periphery" promotes stability and democracy.

On a strictly political level, it is also vitally important that Senegalese political parties not be isolated, but be in constant contact with democratic movements in the world. To be shut off from the outside carries with it the threat not only of political sclerosis, but also of authoritarianism. Anything that facilitates the exchange of experiences and ideas encourages the development of democracy and renewal. Dialogue of this sort could not but help to widen the perspectives of Senegalese political parties.

Finally, the industrialized nations of the West must be reminded that they should not set themselves up as the supreme models of democracy. African history has shown us that the dynamics of African politics can also invent original forms of participation and pluralism. Nothing is more dangerous for the West than to appear to be the sole source of democracy. The West should content itself, on a much more modest level, with facilitating the changes that propose an alternative to authoritarianism and tyranny. From its contact with Africa, the West could also learn to respect differences, which is the very core of the concept of democracy.

• NOTES •

1. On this subject, see Michael Crowder, *Senegal: A Study in French Assimilation Policy* (London: Oxford University Press, 1962).

2. See J. H. J. Legier, "Institutions municipales et politiques coloniales: Les communes du Sénégal," *Revue francaise d'histoire d'outre-mer*, no. 201, p. 445. On this period see also the fundamental work of G. Johnson, Jr., *The Emergence of Black Politics in Senegal: The Struggle for Power in the Four Communes, 1900–1920* (Stanford: Stanford University Press, 1971).

3. On the political life in Senegal in this period, the following works can be consulted: R. S. Morgenthau, *Political Parties in French West Africa* (Oxford: Clarendon Press, 1964); K. Robinson, "Senegal: The Elections to the Territorial Assembly," in J. W. Mackenzie and T. Robinson, eds., *Five Elections in Africa* (New York: Oxford University Press, 1960); P. Mercier, "La vie politique dans les centre urbains du Sénégal: Etude d'une période de transition," *Cahiers internationaux de Sociologie* 6, no. 17, (1959).

4. Senghor was the very first African to pass France's prestigious *agrégation* examination, which allows successful candidates to teach at the higher levels of the lycée and is often a stepping stone to a university career (translator's note).

5. See W. F. Foltz, *From French West Africa to the Mali Federation* (New Haven: Yale University Press, 1965).

6. Among the many studies of this constitution and its different reforms, one may consult the following works: J. C. Gautron and M. Rougevin-Baville, *Droit public du Sénégal* (Paris: Pedone, 1977; 1st ed. 1970); D. G. Lavroff, *Le Sénégal* (Paris: Librairie générale de droit et de jurisprudence, 1966); G. Hesseling, *Histoire politique du Sénégal* (Paris: Karthala, 1985).

7. G. Hesseling, *Sénégal*, p. 247.

8. Sheldon Gellar, *Senegal: An African Nation Between Islam and the West* (Boulder, Colo.: Westview Press, 1982), p. 31.

9. Ibid., p. 41.

10. On this subject, see. my own work, *Le marabout et le prince: Islam et pouvoir au Sénégal* (Paris, Pedone, 1981).

11. On clan struggles, see. in particular, F. Zucarelli, *Un parti politique africain: L'union progressiste sénégalaise* (Paris: Librairie générale de droit et de jurisprudence, 1970); and C. Coulon, "Electious, factions et idéologies au Sénégal," in Centre d'étude d'Afrique noire et Centre d'études et de recherches internationales, *Aux urnes l'Afrique* (Paris: Pedone, 1978), pp. 149–186.

12. G. Hesseling, *Sénégal* p. 137.

13. On Senghor, the following works will be found very useful: J. L. Hymans, *Leopold Sedar Senghor: An Intellectual Biography* (Edinburgh: Edinburgh University Press, 1971); I. L. Markovitz, *Leopold Sedar Senghor and the Politics of Negritude* (New York, Atheneum, 1964).

14. R. Dumont, *Paysanneries aux abois* (Paris: Editions de Seuil, 1972).

15. For a very skillful analysis of peanut-growing policies in Senegal, see N. Casswell, "Autopsie de l'ONCAD: La Politique arachidière au Sénégal," *Politique africaine* 14 (1984): pp. 38–73.

16. See A. Sylla, "De la grève à la reforme: Luttes enseignantes et crises sociales au Sénégal," *Politique africaine* 8 (1982): pp. 61–73.

17. Donal Cruise O'Brien, "Les élections sénégalaises du 27 février 1983," *Politique africaine* 11 (1983): pp. 7–12.

18. Pierre Biarnes, *L'Afrique aux africains (Paris: A. Colin, 1980), p. 130.*

19. S. Gellar, *Senegal* p. 119.

20. Cheikh Anta Diop, *L'Afrique noire précoloniale* (Paris: Présence africaine, 1960).

21. In addition to Diop's work mentioned above, see also A. Sylla, *La philosophie morale des Wolof* (Dakar: Sankore, 1978).

22. Abdou Diouf in the preface to J. M. Nzouankeu, *Les partis politiques sénégalais (Dakar: Edition clairafrique, 1984), p. 7.*

23. *Jeune Afrique*, no. 834–855, 1977, quoted in G. Hesseling, *Sénégal* p. 82.

24. Donal Cruise O'Brien, "Ruling Class and Peasantry in Senegal: 1960–1976," in Rita Cruise O'Brien, ed., *The Political Economy of Underdevelopment: Dependence in Senegal* (London and Beverly Hills: Sage, 1979), pp. 213–214.

25. Ibid.

26. W. J. Foltz, "Senegal," in James S. Coleman and Carl Rosberg, Jr., *Political Parties and National Integration in Tropical Africa* (Berkeley: University of California Press, 1964), pp. 16–64.

27. See Donal Cruise O'Brien, "Langue et nationalité au Sénégal," *Année africaine* (1979) pp. 319–338.

28. D. Darbon, "Le culturalisme des Casamançais," *Politique africaine* 14 (1964): p. 127.

29. J. S. Barker, "The Paradox of Development: Reflections on a Study of Local-Central

Relations in Senegal," in Michael F. Lofchie, ed., *The State of the Nation: Constraints of Development in Independent Africa* (Berkeley: University of California Press, 1971), pp. 47–63. On the same theme, see also the work by Jean-Louis Balans, Christian Coulon and Jean-Marc Gastellu, *Autonomie locale et intégration nationale au Sénégal (Paris: Pedone, 1975).*

30. Mar Fall, *Sénégal: L'état est malade* (Paris, L'Harmattan, 1985).

31. S. Gellar, *Senegal*, p. 37.

32. I have analyzed the attitude of political movements towards Islamic renewal in my article, "Sénégal" in "Centre des hautes études d'Afrique et d'Asie modernes," *Contestations en pays islamiques* (Paris: CHEAM/Documentation française, 1984), pp. 63–68.

33. Rita Cruise O'Brien, *Dependence in Senegal*, p. 30.

34. René Dumont and M. F. Motin, *Le défi sénégalais* (Dakar: ENDA, 1984), p. 9.

35. World Bank, *World Development Report 1986* (New York: Oxford University Press, 1986).

36. S. Gellar, *Senegal*, p. 63.

37. Ibid., p. 52.

38. Between 1974 and 1981, Senegal ranked fourth among African countries (after Guinea, Zaire, and Mali) in aid received from Arab countries ($397.7 million).

39. I have analyzed the reasons for the nature, and the extent of Islamic renewal in my book, *Les musulmans et le pouvoir en Afrique noire* (Paris: Karthala, 1983).

40. "New Agricultural Policy," report by the Ministry of Rural Development, 1984.

41. Actuel Tekkrur, *Quelle démocratie pour le Sénégal?* (Dakar: Editions Sankore, 1984), p. 48.

• CHAPTER FIVE •

Botswana: A Paternalistic Democracy

JOHN D. HOLM

A liberal democratic political system has existed in Botswana for the last two decades. National and local elections have taken place every four to five years. The Botswana Democratic Party (BDP) has carried a substantial majority each time; however, it has always faced a multiparty opposition able to win as much as a third of the vote. This string of contested partisan elections is unmatched in the rest of Africa, where in almost every case various forms of authoritarian rule are, at best, punctuated by occasional and usually short periods of democracy.

This chapter explores the origin, stability, and dynamics of Botswana's experience with democracy.[1]. Three themes are developed. First, many of the classic facilitating forces of democracy have not existed. The indigenous polity was highly authoritarian, and the country's social class structure has always been one of the most inequalitarian in Africa. The forces of social mobilization that are usually thought to promote democracy are less substantial than in most parts of the continent. Finally, the international context of Southern Africa has provided severe and prolonged threats to Tswana sovereignty, which could easily justify suppression of citizen rights.

The second thesis is that democracy persists in Botswana because it provides an effective context in which to resolve two political conflicts that critically influence the exercise of sovereignty in the country. On the one hand, democratic practices serve to resolve intense conflict between the ruling political elite, the leadership of the Botswana Democratic Party, and a highly trained and effective state bureaucracy. Equally important, democracy provides a means for recognizing the powerful decentralizing forces resulting from the size of the territory, the need for ethnic political autonomy, the continuing political influence of traditional chiefs, and the extent and variety of foreign influences.

Finally, Botswana's democracy is still not institutionalized, so that its future is by no means certain. Most important, there is minimal organized interest group activity; traditional political rights are abridged sometimes by the political elite when it feels threatened; the Tswana chiefs appear to be waiting for a

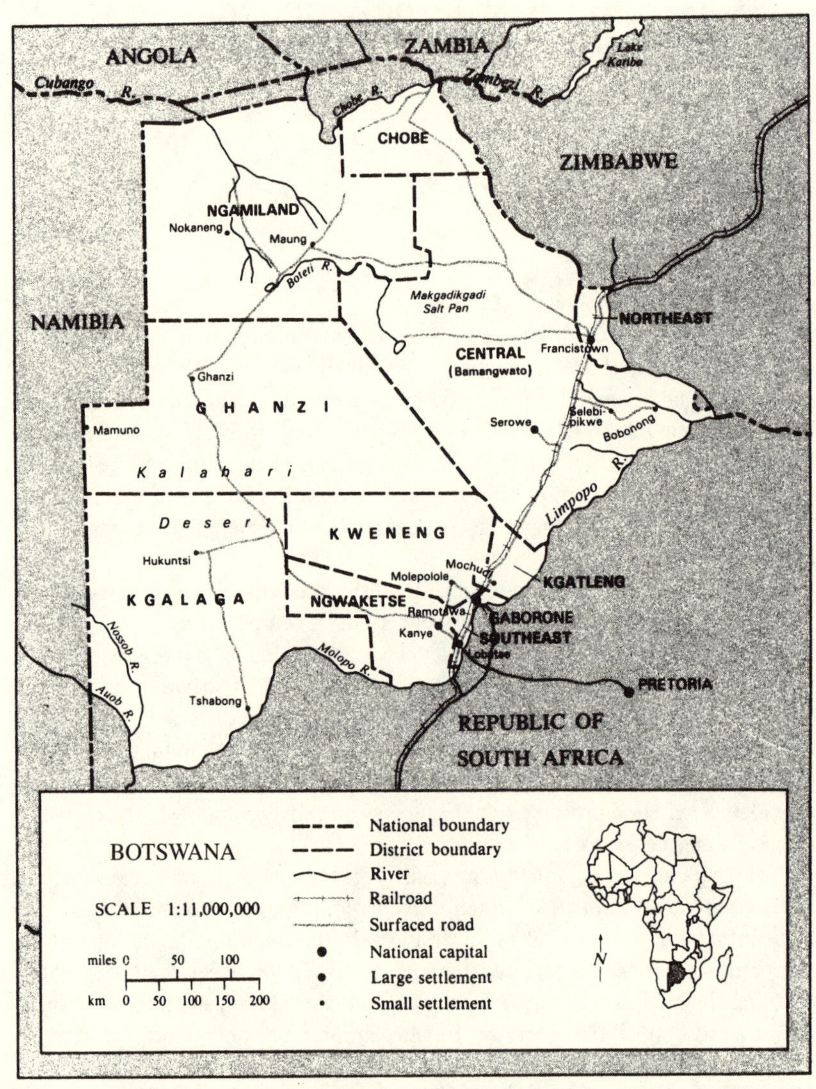

Reprinted from Fred M. Hayward, *Elections in Independant Africa*, Westview Press

chance to regain their previous authority; and the overflow of South Africa's racial turmoil may give the military a dominant position in Botswana's domestic politics.

• HISTORICAL REVIEW •

The political history of Botswana provides little evidence of a trend toward democracy until the nationalist movement began in the sixties. To detail this thesis this section looks briefly at the structure of politics in the tribal polities, the colonial period, and within the nationalist movement.

The Tribal Polities

The Tswana chiefdoms emerged during the eighteenth and early nineteenth centuries from a large number of smaller groups in the area that is now eastern Botswana and northern South Africa. Of the eight that came to locate in modern Botswana, Bamangwato became the largest. This tribe now includes somewhere over 35 percent of the total population of the country. Three others, the Bakwena, Bangwaketse, and Bakgatla, were initially fairly effective competitors with Bamangwato politically and economically. The first two now each constitute 15 percent of Botswana's population while the latter, in part because it was divided with South Africa, makes up only 8 percent. Four other Tswana tribes—the Barolong, Batlokwa, Bamalete, and Batawana—have remained small. Today they collectively constitute not more than 12 percent of the total populace.

Three factors seem to have been critical in the growth of the four larger states: war, trade, and strong leadership by the chiefs. These states successfully defended themselves against the Zulu armies moving up from the southeast in the 1820s, and, in the middle of the century, parried attacks from Afrikaners trekking northward to escape British colonial rule. This constant need to protect against outside military threat both required and legitimated the growth of autocratic leadership.

This period of warfare coincided with the emergence of the Tswana states as centers of trade in southern Africa. The Tswana chiefs found themselves strategically placed to control movements of goods to African peoples north and east of their area. From the beginning of contact with the Europeans, the chiefs enhanced their power by granting licenses and otherwise manipulating the transit of goods for their profit.[2]

The ability of the Tswana chiefs to expand their states through war and trade undoubtedly stemmed from the fact that they were already very powerful rulers. Obtaining their position did not normally require public support; it was passed from father to senior son. The scope of their authority had few limits. As Schapera says, the chief was "at once ruler, judge, maker and guardian of the law, repository of wealth, dispenser of gifts, leader in war, priest and magician of the people."[3]

The chiefs dominated the tribal economy, and they allocated land for all purposes. Until the end of the nineteenth century, they controlled or owned all cattle, the most prominent form of wealth in society, which were lent or allocated in chains of clientage to subordinates. The chiefs also maintained large fields of arable crops that members of the tribe cultivated as part of their civic duties. From his wealth in crops and cattle, the chief not only supported a large household, but also provided for tribal festivals and fed those in need during a drought.

The chief dominated all important forms of collective action in the community. He controlled the tribal age group regiments, which were the primary vehicle for military action, public works, hunting, and other community functions. As the community's religious leader, the chief not only practiced various forms of traditional medicine himself, but also supervised others in the community who worked with the world of the spirits. When Christian missionaries moved into the Tswana areas in the middle of the nineteenth century, the chiefs very quickly gained control of this new religious force in such a way that conversion of part of the tribe to the new religion did not undermine chiefly authority.[4]

Within this social and economic structure, the chief was well positioned to dominate community decisionmaking. According to custom, he was obliged to consult two groups: his senior relatives and headmen of the major foreign groups within the tribe. Members of both groups held their positions by virtue of birth, but were expected to consult with family heads living in their areas of authority.[5] On important matters, the chief called all adult males to an assembly. There the chief and his advisors pressed for acceptance of a particular course of action. In rare cases where his advisors could not agree, the chief took a vote. While not obliged to accept the results, Schapera contends that the chief usually did.[6] For the most part, the chief used this assembly, the *kgotla*, to consult with the public and mobilize popular support for a desired action. There is no indication that the public was allowed to set the agenda of issues. It played a veto function at best, and this was not easily done, since those who opposed him had to fear reprisals from their leader.

The real constraints on the chief were twofold. First, his immediate relatives might usurp his authority by deserting to another tribe with followers, refusing to follow orders in a military campaign, assassinating him, or, in the last resort, establishing a new chiefdom. The chiefs themselves, from time to time, would urge such insurrection in the other tribes. The resulting fluidity of chiefly power appears to have insured a certain amount of concern for opinions of those with more social status.[7]

A second constraint on the Tswana chiefs was a highly developed practice of traditional law. Still today, the Batswana highly valued obedience to the law, viewing the community as a broad set of legal obligations binding on public and private life.[8] Even the chiefs, who were the heads of the tribal court systems, were expected to abide by the law. In each tribe a group of elders advised the chief as to what the law was in a given situation; a chief who did not follow this advice most of the time was vulnerable to insurrection.

In sum, the Tswana political systems had little semblance of democracy. One authority ranked them as among the most rigidly stratified of any in southern Africa.[9] There was, however, sufficient conflict within the ruling class to encourage the more astute chiefs to seek public support. A fairly developed system of law also provided a basis for agreement between ruler and ruled as to what was acceptable chiefly behavior. Needless to say, certain groups, most particularly women and slaves, were excluded from any right to have a say in the system.

At the village level or in wards within the highly populated capital towns, somewhat more democratic practice seems to have existed. Certainly this was true of some Sotho peoples such as the Kgalagari. Adam Kuper contends that the Kgalagari headmen had no authority in a situation unless they spoke for something close to a consensus of the village. The advisory council that discussed policy always included persons representing family groups opposed to the headman. Majorities emerged from constantly changing coalitions of kinship groups.[10]

A dual legacy of this political system remains to this day. First, there is a feeling that policy issues relating to the larger social system are matters of concern for the political elite and not something that the average citizen can easily influence. Second, in so far as these larger matters of policy are discussed, it is to be done within the tribal community. Outside the tribe, the only issue is protection of its interests vis-à-vis competitors. We will return to both these considerations later.

The Colonial System

Colonial rule in Botswana had a very minimal impact compared to most of Africa.[11] To counter increasing Afrikaner threats, the Tswana chiefs collectively invited the British to declare a "protectorate" over the area. London agreed to the arrangement because it wanted to "protect" a road link with its colonies to the north, but the degree of sovereignty the British chose to exercise was so mild that even the term "indirect rule" would be an exaggeration.[12] The chiefs ruled with a few added constraints: they could no longer make war; they were supposed to collect a small hut tax to support the colonial administration; and they had to curb certain practices that offended British sensibilities, like slavery and polygamy. The more progressive undertook projects like road building and formal education.

The British lack of interest in effecting any direct control over Botswana was evident from the beginning, when they set up their administrative headquarters across the border in South Africa. Only at independence did the administrative seat of government move to the Botswana town of Gaborone. With the formation of the Union of South Africa in 1910, London's policy looked to incorporation of Botswana within the union, an objective that was rejected only in the late 1940s.

In the meantime, the chiefs were left to rule as they always had, backed by the prestige of British protection. They even exercised substantial control over the entry of European influences in their areas and administered local development projects such as boreholes, dams, churches, schools, and roads.[13]

Some argue that the chiefs became more autocratic during this period than they had been previously. Only prolonged appeals to the British resident commissioner could bring relief from the most abusive traditional authorities.[14] On the other hand, the mass of the population in some instances chose not to obey the chief, and there was little he could do, given the limited means of coercion available to him. In many cases, there seemed to be simply a breakdown of political authority.[15] Chiefs who abused their powers ultimately undermined their own legitimacy. Only those chiefs who recognized this reality curried public support so that their policies would be obeyed.

The colonial government did little to promote the development of democratic procedures. They created a Native Advisory Council in 1920.[16] Only in 1939, however, were all the major Tswana tribes represented in this assembly. Membership was roughly proportional to each tribe's size, with one-quarter of the members being official representatives of the resident commissioner. The council's function was to advise the resident commissioner on issues affecting *African* interests. It had no power to take binding action, or to consider matters related to the small European population. Eight members were chiefs. The rest were supposed to be selected by the tribe at a public meeting, but, in practice, those present ratified the chief's selection. The territory did not obtain a legislative council until 1961. Even then, only one-third of its members were Africans, who were selected by the chieftaincy-dominated African Council. In 1963, three years before independence, the colonial government began to develop plans for internal self-rule with a legislative council elected on the basis of universal adult suffrage. The elections took place in October of 1965, less than a year before the British withdrew.

In effect, Botswana became independent without any sustained experience with a democratically elected government. The chiefs provided representation at the national level, such as it was. There were not even any local councils in the urban areas with elected representation. This rather extraordinary inertness of political action can be explained by two factors. First, the chiefs did not hesitate to speak for nationalist objectives. Thus, it was difficult for potential nationalist politicians to find an issue with which to launch a movement. Second, there were few economic opportunities in Botswana for those who sought jobs outside the traditional structure. As a result, most of the educated who were not teachers migrated to South Africa in search of jobs and advanced education. Thus, this vanguard group was not available for political action.

The Nationalist Period

The catalytic event for nationalist politics in Botswana was the South African government's banning of the two main African parties at the time of the Sharpeville massacre in 1960. In four years, over 1,400 refugees crossed the border into the protectorate. Many of the founding members of the first nationalist party, the Botswana People's Party (BPP), came from this infusion of the politically aware. The South African orientation of the BPP was also evident in the fact that five of its twenty-two branches in 1961 were in Johannesburg.[17] Most of the remaining members were in urban areas of Botswana. The party's attacks on the racist character of colonial rule had little attraction in the rural areas where chiefly government largely held sway. As one authority comments, the independence movement in Botswana turned out for many of the politically active rural population to be as much a movement against chiefly rule as against foreign domination.[18]

The BPP did serve an important function during the early 1960s. Through the BPP's demonstrations and appearances before the UN, the colonial government and rural elites soon recognized they would need to prepare for political independence or face the consequences. The party's energies were quickly spent, however, as its leaders fought among themselves, eventually splintering into two parties by 1964. One segment, still calling itself the BPP, under Philip Matante, found its popular support among the Kalanga population in the Francistown area. Motsamai Mpho led a second branch, renamed the Botswana Independent Party (BIP). This has been popular among his Byei people, a non-Tswana group that had long lived under Tswana domination in northern Botswana.

As the BPP's internal conflict boiled on, Seretse Khama, Quett Masire, and a number of other rural-based activists began organizing another party, the Bechuanaland Democratic Party (BDP). Khama's varied background reflected dramatically the powerful Botswana social groups that came to back the BDP.

Khama was the first-born son of a chief who ruled Bamangwato until 1925. He should have become chief of the tribe when he returned from school in the late 1940s, but the British, bowing to pressure from the new Afrikaner government in South Africa, in 1949 denied him his rightful position because he had married a white woman the year before. Most members of the tribe deeply resented this decision and quickly came to look on the BDP as the vehicle that would bring their chief to power. Khama was also part of the territory's educated elite. He had gone to secondary school in South Africa and then attended Oxford before becoming a law student at the Inner Temple in London. He came out of this experience committed to promoting the modernization of his people.

Upon returning from England, Khama concentrated first on developing a commercial ranching enterprise with his father's cattle. In this connection, he associated both with other Africans beginning to do the same thing and a small community of white, mostly Afrikaner, ranchers who were buying Tswana cattle and fattening them for sale in South Africa. When Khama launched his political party, many in the cattle sector, white and black, moved to back him. Since cattle-ranching was the only major productive sector of the Botswana economy before independence, this meant that Khama was in a very strong position to secure financial support.

Khama cultivated the colonial regime as a supporter of his political career. It quickly came to view him as much more attractive than the more radical leadership of the BPP. In 1961, the British named him as one of the two Africans on the Executive Council, where he gained experience supervising the operation of government, as well as the prestige that accompanied this role. Thus, Khama gained the respect of four very influential groups: traditional authorities, the educated elite, cattle ranchers, and the colonial civil service. Under his leadership, the BDP served as a coalition bringing these four groups together. The BDP overwhelmed its opponents in the first election in March 1965.[19] It won 80 percent of the vote and twenty-eight out of the thirty-one parliamentary seats. The BPP under Matante won the other three seats, two in the Francistown area where his Kalanga tribe was the major ethnic group. Mpho's BIP could only come close to carrying his home district.

Conclusion

Although the colonial period ended with an election, there was no reason to believe that Botswana was going to become a democracy. Popular control, at best, was something that was practiced in terms of a consensus style of decision-making at the village level. At the tribal and territorial level, no citizen influence had been institutionalized outside of occasional assemblies wherein those with social status tended to dominate. In this regard, Botswana had a very different experience from the elected urban and territorial councils that prevailed in most of West Africa toward the end of colonial rule.

• THE STRUCTURE AND FUNCTIONING OF DEMOCRACY IN BOTSWANA •

National Government

Botswana is governed by a parliamentary system. One house of Parliament, the National Assembly, has power to make laws and approve appropriations and taxes. It consists of thirty-four persons chosen by popular elections, four members selected by the elected members, the attorney general, and the speaker of the Assembly. The elected members of the Assembly select the president, and he retains this office until the Assembly is dissolved or he receives a vote of no confidence. The president appoints the members of the cabinet, including the vice-president. The other branch of Parliament is the House of Chiefs. It only has the power to advise the Assembly or the president on matters that relate to the interests and organization of the country's tribes.

The government structure varies from the Westminster model in that all executive power is vested in the president. The cabinet advises the president, while the president only has an obligation to consult with the cabinet. Each minister has such responsibility as is assigned to him by the president. The cabinet is also required by the constitution to be collectively responsible to Parliament for actions of the president. The president also has a privileged position relative to the National Assembly in that he can dissolve it, and the Assembly cannot consider a bill that increases taxes or appropriations or alters the terms of the government debt unless the bill has been recommended by the president.[20]

The Parliament's role in national policy making is a fairly passive one. Backbenchers and opposition MPs ask questions about particular policies, especially with regard to adversities caused to their constituents. Occasionally an uproar in Parliament can bring down an important official.[21] For the most part, however, the MPs serve as a forum wherein bureaucratically generated policies are publicized and ratified. The serious debate about policies occurs in the cabinet, where important changes are sometimes made.

Local Government

The centerpiece of Botswana democracy is the local council system. The BDP promised in its 1965 platform that it would transfer most of the chief's authority at the local level to district councils directly elected by the voters. By the next June, elections for the new councils were held. The BDP again scored a decisive victory, winning almost three-quarters of the seats and a majority in all councils except two, Francistown and the North East District, where the BPP triumphed on the Kalanga vote.[22]

The councils were given many of the chief's powers, including responsibility for constructing and operating primary schools, maintaining public water supplies, building and repairing rural roads, licensing private businesses, and supporting such development projects deemed necessary. In the rural areas, they also took over collection of stray cattle, which had been a source of income for the chiefs. Further compromising the traditional authority, in 1969, a new land law created district land boards that assumed the chiefs' land allocation function (although chiefs were included as board members). In essence, these changes left the chiefs with basically ceremonial duties of representing the tribe and control over traditional courts.

Within three years, the BDP government moved local government from a monarchy of sorts to a form of majority rule. The change was not as radical as it seemed in that the central government could appoint up to four councilors besides those elected by the public. It used these appointments to provide additional leadership responsive to Gaborone's directives and to override the BPP's majority in the North East District and Francistown.

The central government also manipulated the councils by providing funds for much of their budgets that were not covered by school fees. The result is that councils end up, much of the time, petitioning the central government on behalf of the local population for particular programs. Further limiting the councils is the fact that their civil servants and those of land boards are part of a "national" local government service, headed and administered by a high official in Gaborone. Supposedly, this service was created to upgrade the level of local government staff, but, in fact, its members must be very sympathetic to central government directions if they are to succeed in their careers.[23]

In reality, the local councils act as intermediaries between the central government and local communities. Officials in Gaborone want the councilors to explain, defend, and mobilize support for national programs. Councilors are, moreover, to concentrate on the technical questions of implementing policies already broadly determined in the capital and "not to entertain their political inclinations in council meetings."[24] The same behavior is sought from the local land boards, which can modify central bureaucratic decisions on the creation of private leasehold ranches only if the minister of local government and lands approves. Thus, both local government bodies are part of the national bureaucracy rather than providing a counterpoint to it.

Community Participation

The Botswana government has also encouraged local communities to take initiatives in development projects in a number of ways. Almost all have started out as avowedly democratic structures but have tended to evolve into appendages of the government bureaucracy. Probably the most prominent is the Brigade Movement. Its objective was to provide a means by which students could receive an education in the construction trades, automobile maintenance, and agricultural production, and, at the same time, earn their tuition through labor in their trades. The democratic character of the schools was reflected not only in the fact that teachers, students, parents, and community leaders were to be involved in policy making, but also that various brigades sought to launch new forms of cooperative economic organization in the community. A number of other attempts have been made to foster community participation in economic organizations, including the cooperative movement, management of community water sources, and range management.[25]

All these experiences have tended to follow a general pattern. The government seeks to create democratic structures when it promotes development at the community level. A few people are enthusiastic, but the group, as a whole, lacks many of the requisite resources and skills to perform the required tasks on anything but a minimal basis. In addition, the organizations created are short on funds for investment and lack a national organization to fight for their interests vis-à-vis government. Finally, local communities are not familiar with a decisionmaking process based on elected representatives. Previously, the chief or local headman would either appoint the leadership or himself direct the operation. When a conflict becomes severe or the responsibilities grow very complex, the new organizations usually collapse, and national officials have the choice of either allowing the project to die or attempting a rescue that greatly reduces local participation. This pattern has been repeated so many times that, increasingly, the government is looking for other approaches that involve market or administrative controls.

Parties and Elections

The first elections after independence were held in 1969. The Botswana National Front (BNF) emerged as a new opposition party. It was founded by Kenneth Koma, who had just returned from Moscow where he had received a doctorate. He had definite socialist sympathies but recognized that he would need the support of traditional authorities to challenge the BDP successfully.[26] Despite the general resentment of the chiefs over the dissipation of their powers, Koma could only entice the Ngwaketse Chief Bathoen to join his party.[27]

The BNF's challenge did little to shake the ruling party's popular support, which only slipped from 80 percent in 1965, to 69 percent.[28] The BNF won three parliamentary seats, all in Bathoen's tribal homeland. There, even Quett Masire, the vice-president and chief architect of the BDP's organization, went down to defeat. The BPP held its three districts and the BIP picked up one, to give the opposition a total of seven seats out of thirty-one. The three opposition parties increased their presence in district and town councils at the same time, obtaining at least half the seats in five out of twelve and being one short in another.

In the two elections of 1974 and 1979, the opposition parties suffered serious setbacks. After the second contest, they only had three seats in Parliament out of thirty-two. Their strength on local councils was cut in half. Most impressive were the clear majorities the BDP won, for the first time, in the Gaborone and Francistown town councils. The BDP even triumphed in the urban working class areas, a surprising achievement given its conservative orientation.

The 1984 election brought a reversal of the opposition's decline. The BNF secured five seats in Parliament, the BPP one. The BDP still attracted 68 percent of the popular vote in parliamentary contests. In the local government elections held at the same time, the opposition parties won majorities in five local councils out of fourteen, whereas in 1979 they had not won one. The BNF gained a particularly impressive win in Gaborone, where it took both parliamentary contests and ten of the fourteen seats in the town council. The BDP did everything it could to resist this challenge to its dominance in the capital, running most prominent cabinet members for these seats and financing their campaigns at a level never seen before in Botswana.

In all these elections, the parties have shown little interest in raising and debating issues. In the 1965 contest, the BDP vaguely presented itself as a party that would abolish the rule of chiefs and replace them with local councils and a new national bureaucracy providing basic services. Subsequently, the BDP's election manifestos have been little more than a digest of the latest development plan, which government planners have prepared with minimal attention to political realities.[29] The only other major BDP theme is to attack the BNF incessantly as a radical party that is pledged to abrogate democracy and launch socialism.[30]

The BNF started off projecting a radical image in 1969, identifying with socialism and revolution in Southern Africa. However, in part, because of the party's alliance with traditionalist elements and also for practical political reasons, the BNF has rejected both socialism and revolution in favor of pragmatism in recent campaigns.[31] The BNF now attacks the BDP for the poor quality of the services provided and its favoritism toward the rich. The BNF campaigners claim the party is a coalition of many different groups in society, from chiefs to Marxists, all of whom are seeking more government services for the people (e.g., free education), no taxes for the poor, and rapid localization of the government bureaucracy.[32] For all practical purposes, the BNF does not appear much different from the BDP in policy terms other than having a somewhat more equalitarian program.

The other two opposition parties make even less of a distinction between themselves and the BDP. Mpho openly admits that his BIP simply pushes the BDP to fulfill its campaign promises. The BPP does about the same, although it has raised some issues specific to the Francistown area, including a demand that the schools use the Sekelanga language as the medium of instruction.[33]

Issues, if anything, have played a declining role in Botswana elections. Both the BPP and BNF started out as radical parties that would bring socialism and help end white rule in Southern Africa. Both now play down these appeals. They have, rather, sought to challenge the BDP on ethnic and class grounds.

Class, Ethnicity, and Party Conflict

The BDP's success rests on an effective use of class and ethnic factors. Organizationally, it makes a pretense of being a mass-based organization ranging from branches to a National Congress. In point of fact, the party is a collection of local notables whose prestige derives from their traditional status, cattle holdings, or involvement in private enterprises and local voluntary groups, including churches. In most constituencies, these notables mobilize a fairly effective campaign organization, including hired organizers, motor vehicles, bicycles, loudspeakers, posters, and party manifestos.[34] The financing for this campaign organization comes from a number of sources including dues, voluntary contributions, and profits from renting out office space in Tsholetsa House, the party headquarters, to the government.

The other parties give little evidence of having the money to mount a broad-based campaign of public meetings and written appeals. They rely much more on small gatherings of neighbors and door-to-door canvassing to reach their supporters. In addition, there is some evidence that opposition candidates, who are also local notables for the most part, end up paying for more of their campaigns out of their own pockets.[35]

Equally critical to the BDP's success is its ethnic base. It is perceived by the Bamangwato and the Bakwena tribes as representing their people. As we have noted, when Khama took the lead in forming the party, his fellow Ngwato tribesmen viewed it as an instrument by which their rightful chief would acquire political authority. The BDP has never lost a parliamentary seat within Bamangwato. In eight of the twelve districts, it has gained at least 90 percent of the vote in every parliamentary election. In only five cases, since 1965, have the BDP candidates received less than 75 percent of the vote in the Bamangwato districts. Khama's death in 1980 does not seem to have changed the tribe's attitude, even though the new president, Quett Masire, is an Ngwaketse and not of royal background.

In Kweneng, the BDP has an equally strong ethnic base. Englishman Kgabo has, from the beginning, headed a BDP organization which is viewed as effectively representing the Bakwena.[36] Since 1966, the BDP has won with at least 73 percent of the vote in every parliamentary context. At the council level, the BDP has won by equally large margins.

In effect, within these two tribes (which together constitute almost a majority of the population) a vote for the BDP is an affirmation of ethnic membership. Opposition candidates are not seen as offering a significant choice. This is not to say that important segments of the local elite are satisfied with BDP policies. In both areas, many believe that government departments have implemented major land- and cattle-marketing policies in a totally unsatisfactory manner. Nevertheless, no major BDP notable has publicly suggested bargaining with the BNF for a better deal; that would be an act of communal disloyalty. The sixteen seats that the BDP gains in these two areas are two short of a parliamentary majority. The BDP thus starts with an advantage that virtually assures it of government control. In the rest of Botswana, the party generally faces serious competition. In 1969 and 1984, it only secured 54 percent of the vote in these areas.[37] By contrast, in Bamangwato and Kweneng, the BDP took 88 percent of the combined vote in 1969 and 85 percent in 1984.

Outside of Bamangwato and Kweneng, the BDP plays down its ethnic base. Almost without exception, the ruling party has distributed the results of government programs highly equitably in regional terms. One expert examining the drought relief program went so far as to conclude that the government was so obsessed with the political need not to appear to favor a particular region or ethnic group that it was impossible for policy makers to target the "most vulnerable" groups.[38]

Because of this strategy of treating all ethnic groups alike, the BDP secures a healthy following even when the opposition wins. The BDP succeeds by gaining the support of critical notables and offers them patronage to distribute to their supporters. Even in strong opposition areas like the two BNF districts in Ngwaketse, the BDP was able, in the 1984 election, to accrue over 40 percent of the vote. The result is that the opposition parties, while they too seek ethnic support, have been unable to attain the total community identification that the BDP does in Bamangwato and Kweneng.

A question political analysts have not effectively answered is the extent to which social class considerations affect elections in Botswana.[39] There is clear evidence that the BDP has made an appeal to bourgeois groups throughout the country. Its Tribal Grazing Land Program (TGLP) is designed to give the more entrepreneurial farmers a chance to acquire the financing and land tenure to start privately owned ranches. Previously, the tribes had held all grazing land communally. Recently, the Financial Assistance Policy has provided resources for Tswana wanting to set up their own businesses in other sectors of the economy, although this is rationalized as job creation.

The BNF has appealed to working-class groups by criticizing the BDP for not allocating a sufficient proportion of the country's increased income to wage earners. Whether or not this message has mobilized target voters has not been documented in a convincing way. Parson, for instance, tries to make the case that, since the urban areas are working class and these areas supported the BNF, it can be concluded that the BNF has a working class base in the cities.[40] However, several critical pieces of evidence are missing to make this point. First, there is no analysis of the individual voter's perceptions and behavior to determine whether those with different class associations actually do behave differently. Further, the aggregate data that are available do not confirm that the two parties mobilize much support on the basis of class appeal. One highly working-class town, Selibe Phikwe, has continually supported the BDP (in 1984 by almost a two-to-one margin over the BNF). In two Gaborone polling districts populated by wage-earners and unemployed living in a shanty town (i.e., Naledi), the BDP has consistently performed well. In the last election the BNF only obtained 54 percent of the town council vote. In the previous two elections, the BDP actually won the Naledi contest.[41] These are hardly the landslides that one would expect if the urban areas were voting from a class perspective.

Finally, the argument that a class-based vote exists ignores the extent to which the urban vote is an ethnic vote. The BDP's strength in Selibe Phikwe reflects the fact that most of the workers come from the surrounding Bamangwato area. The BDP's popularity in Gaborone probably results from fact that many working-class migrants are Bakwena and Bamangwato. The BDP's increased support in the Francistown district over the last decade is very likely the result of the fact that 58 percent of recent migrants have come from Bamangwato areas, thus reducing the previous dominance of the area by the BPP's Kalanga supporters.[42]

In sum, there is evidence that the BDP and BNF make opposing class appeals. Both are trying to move beyond their ethnic bases. The BDP has succeeded in securing a firm base of local notables throughout the country to provide its organizational base. The BNF, on the other hand, has yet to pick up any sort of commanding support among the urban working class.

Democratic Rights in Practice

A democratic system rests on the commitment of, at least, the elite and, ideally, the masses to certain essential rights. At a minimum, these values entail freedom to run for office, equality of franchise, freedom of press, speech and assembly, secret ballot, and rule by elected representatives. The Botswana government, in principle, accepts the idea that political rights ought to be respected. It has, however, been hesitant to apply them in practice too extensively. Rather, it is inclined to restrict their application for fear that not all of the population, particularly those with little education, can be trusted. Complete democratic rights are only enjoyed by a small group that is educated and privately employed.

The freedom to run for office in Botswana is, in theory, very great. Anyone who can raise the necessary deposit may contest a seat.[43] There are, however, several important restrictions. Most significantly, no government employee can run for office. This includes civil servants, teachers, and employees of parastatals. They cannot even take a leave of absence during the campaign. Since this group constitutes two-thirds of the wage- and salary-earning public, this means that most who are financially able to run for office cannot do so without resigning from government, hence bearing not only the costs of the campaign, but also the risk of a career change. For the society as a whole, this restriction effectively excludes most of those who are informed and articulate on policy questions.

Chiefs are also barred from seeking elected positions. If a chief wants to run, he must resign his position. Only one chief, the BNF's Bathoen, has thus far stepped down. Hence, while many in the population still regard the chief as the person who should speak for the tribe on political issues, most do not have the option of selecting him to be their representative in the National Assembly or local councils.

A third limitation applies in the case of parliamentary candidates. They must "speak, and . . . read English well enough to take an active part in the proceedings of the Assembly."[44] Practically, this limits eligibility for office to those who have completed primary school—only about 18 percent of the voting age population.[45] Since cultural norms generally exclude women from holding public office, slightly less than half (45 percent) of those with a primary education are effectively eligible.[46] If we then remove those who hold government jobs, this leaves not many more than 10,000, out of a total population of almost one million, in the pool from which parliamentary candidates can come.[47]

The rights of speech, assembly, and press are generally protected in Botswana. The opposition parties regularly make serious charges against the BDP's rule: that it is neocolonialist, favors the rich, mismanages various programs, and even that it rigs the elections. Privately owned newspapers also attack government programs and practices.

However, the government places some limits on these freedoms of expression, so that its critics must continually take some care in what they say. Every few years, the government prosecutes one or more opposition politicians for statements made in the course of political debate. The secretary-general of the BNF was actually convicted in 1979 of being abusive of then President Khama.[48] In the most recent campaign, the deputy chairman of the BNF was charged with attempting to incite the Botswana Defense Force to "unlawfully unseat the Government."[49] His words were relatively harmless, and in this case the magistrate found the defendant not guilty.[50]

All urban political meetings are registered with the police. At least one officer is then present to tape-record the speeches and any questions and answers. Although the BDP meetings in the towns are also monitored, it is the opposition politicians who must take care that they do not say things that could provoke an indictment. In effect, the government shows itself fearful that the opposition will use public meetings among the more socially mobilized urban residents to subvert the democratic process.

Although there is freedom for the press to report political debate, there is only one daily newspaper within the country, the *Daily News*, and it is owned by the government. It reports the news that is made available; it does not try to find stories, particularly those that would embarrass the government. The other newspapers are weeklies. Currently operating are *Mmegi,* the *Guardian* and the *Gazette*. They are much more aggressive, sometimes reporting stories exposing and angering the BDP leaders. Their ability to do so on a consistent basis is compromised by several factors. First, they have been able to garner sufficient income from advertising and subscriptions to sustain only a few experienced reporters. In fact, some have temporarily ceased operating or failed altogether due to lack of funds. The government's insistence on subsidizing the *Daily News* (which permits it to be distributed free of charge) is part of the reason why these independent newspapers are hard-pressed to survive. Second, the leadership of all three papers is in the hands of expatriates who have little political support in the country. Except for *Mmegi*, they appear consequently to be subject to effective informal pressure when they become too aggressive for the government. For example, the *Guardian*'s publisher sacked his editor after the latter began to offend the government too much. Such manipulation and financial pressure mean that *de jure* press freedom has not yet been realized or even tested in a *de facto* sense.

An important aspect of a democracy is that elected representatives determine policy. If this is not the case, a voter's choice of candidates is meaningless. At the local level, this political right had been seriously compromised until recently. As noted earlier, the minister of Local Government and Lands regularly appointed up to four additional members to each local council, thus assuring that the councils were compliant with BDP wishes. However, after the opposition parties won control of five councils in the last election, the government decided not to try to overturn the results, in most cases, by its appointments. Where the opposition was in the majority, it was allowed to name some of the appointed members. For the first time, thus, there are some councils dominated by the opposition, among them those in the two largest cities—Gaborone and Francistown. This change could herald a step toward an independent local council system. The real test, however, will be the extent to which the BDP allows the opposition to determine its own budget priorities. Top officials of the Ministry of Local Government and Lands have spent considerable time, of late, lecturing the opposition councils on the need to conform.[51]

With each of the above rights—freedom to run for office, freedom of speech and press, and rule by an elected majority—the BDP elite has taken a paternalistic approach. They see themselves as educating the public and changing its opposition to the democratic way. They are not at all certain that the chiefs cannot seduce the public to give back its freedom to its former rulers. Local councils cannot be trusted to know what is good for their constituents. There is also a fear that the people cannot be trusted to select the best persons for Parliament. The choice is to be only from among those literate in English. The overall BDP attitude toward democratic rights bears some similarity to that of the founders of the U.S. federal government, in that they want to limit the extent of participation by the uneducated masses but, otherwise, recognize the need for constitutional rights. Thus, when the courts say the government has gone too far, it accepts the decision without feeling a need, as so often happens in South Africa, to write new legislation to overrule the decision.

Democratic Values in Practice

Stable democracy depends on more than the fulfillment of minimum legal conditions. It also requires a sense of comity and compromise among the parties struggling for power. Politics must not be a winner-take-all game. In this regard, traditional Tswana political norms have greatly facilitated the BDP's democracy. The BDP has been most assiduous in preserving the tradition of the *kgotla*, a community meeting in front of the chief's or headman's residence and presided over by him. Traditionally, these leaders did not make major decisions without consulting the *kgotla* and, if possible, achieving a consensus. The BDP has, if anything, amplified on this tradition in that government officials—both civil servants and politicians—discuss all new policies with the local community in *kgotla* before any local implementation. They also seek to get a consensus behind their proposals. If one does not emerge, the program is likely to be reformulated or sometimes terminated.[52]

This consensus aspect of Tswana culture is also reflected in the relative absence of political violence. For the first decade after independence, the country had a police force but no military organization. In response to incursions from first Rhodesia (subsequently Zimbabwe) and now South Africa, the government has moved to create a military force. This force functions basically to control the movements of freedom fighters moving through Botswana on their way to South Africa. Ideally, the Botswana government would prefer to keep these forces out of Botswana. Barring that, it seeks to frustrate this transit sufficiently to keep the nervous South African military from taking matters into its own hands. Also, the Botswana government wants to make sure that the freedom fighters do not become a disruptive force in Botswana's politics.

Otherwise, the only significant violence in the last two decades has been police action to control two strikes—one at the big abattoir in Lobatse and the other at the copper mine in Selibe Phikwe. In both cases, government leaders moved to bring a negotiated settlement. Subsequently, they have sought to avoid a similar confrontation by a twofold strategy of keeping the union leadership weak and buying off the workers with generous wage and benefit packages.

The culture of the Tswana seems to be more antithetical to physical violence than many others in Africa. Alverson remarks that Botswana place a particularly high value on peaceful social relations.[53] They "commemorate the virtues of propriety, tranquillity, and a peaceful approach to interpersonal relations. The peacemaker, the wise man of words, and the conciliator are as likely candidates for herodom as the warrior . . . physical and verbal aggression . . . is sanctioned in very few contexts in current communal life."[54]

Tswana political culture does not support extremist organizations. As we have noted, both the BNF and the BPP started out with radical socialist and antiracial platforms. Both soon concluded that such politics would not gain them popular support. Even opposition to South Africa has been handled in a very low-key fashion.

These traditional Tswana values of public discussion, community consensus, nonviolence, and moderation are critical elements of a democratic political culture. In some respects, they compensate for the lack of rigorous support for the legal rights of speech and press already mentioned. On the other hand, there is little in the traditional culture that supports the idea of popular election of leaders. There is a presumption, particularly in the rural areas, that males from the royal families ought to rule. As a consequence, outside the cities, the public shows little concern about the central government's appointments to local councils. It is presumed that the central government has the real power, that it is the new chief.

Democracy and the Economy

In Africa, democracy has suffered particularly from economic stagnation and mismanagement. Even where there has been growth, the masses resent manifest elite corruption and waste. The BDP government has not only enjoyed two decades of growth, but has managed the economy in a way that gains the party a broad base of support. Most prominently, no group has been able to profit inordinately.

Since 1965, the GNP has increased in real terms at an average of 11 percent per annum.[55] The basis for this growth has been the building of a copper-nickel mine in the early 1970s and, subsequently, two large diamond mines. Also making a marginal contribution has been the expansion of overseas markets for the country's beef products. By the early 1980s, Botswana had a per capita national income of just over 900 dollars compared to 100 dollars in 1968.[56] In a decade and a half, Botswana has moved from being one of the poorest countries in Africa to one of the richest.

The state has maintained tight and effective control over this growth process. Its bureaucracy has taken an aggressive role in planning investment. In most sectors, government either provides the funding itself (e.g., water and electricity) or does so in conjunction with foreign or domestic private capital (e.g., mining and agriculture). Well over four-fifths of all fixed capital formation is subject to fairly direct government control.[57] The control exercised is considerable. No government development expenditure may occur on a project until it has been included in the approved development plan. After inclusion in the plan, which usually takes over a year, the ministry involved must draw up a detailed implementation plan and obtain approval from the Ministry of Finance and Development before decisions are made on either foreign or domestic funding. Once a project is launched, the MFDP scrutinizes each payment. A recent report by a World Bank mission has praised the civil service for its "commendable attention to detail, discipline, and dedication," and rated Botswana's public sector management of development "one of the most successful in Africa."[58]

The economy's growth has fueled a dramatic expansion in government programs. At independence, the government had a very meager budget. Moreover, Britain still covered 57 percent of the total outlays.[59] A more favorable customs union agreement with South Africa, negotiated in 1969, provided the funds to erase the recurrent deficit. Subsequently, the revenues from the diamond mines and increased taxes derived from economic growth have led to a substantial expansion of government programs. Between independence and 1981, total expenditures have grown annually by an average of 15.7 percent and revenues by 23 percent.[60] Government employment has more than tripled since 1970.[61] Development expenditures have averaged between 43 percent and 45 percent of total government expenditures.

This surge in government activity has touched all sectors of society. Much of the development expenditure has gone into basic infrastructure such as transportation, communication, and public utilities. But heavy expenditures have also been made in programs that affect the mass of the population. In the government's recurrent and development budgets, close to a third annually goes to education, health, social services, housing, and regional development. The police and the military receive 10 percent of these same budgets.[62] Particularly impressive, in terms of social justice, was the relief effort the government mounted to combat the recent drought. In the years 1984–1985, relief was budgeted at over 20 million dollars, most of which appears to have reached the poor. The result was only a slight increase in malnutrition and almost no evidence of starvation.[63]

One of the reasons government programs reach out to such a large segment of the population is the politics of elections. The BDP wants to keep its voters. For instance, it was the politicians in the cabinet who pushed to increase the drought relief effort to the levels it reached in the 1984–1985 budget. The mass demand for more schools has made high expenditures in this area mandatory as well. Such political spending is, however, kept under bureaucratic control for the most part; overspending on a budget line almost never occurs. Indeed, the government seeks to maintain a surplus for bad times.

Botswana's rapid economic expansion has provided opportunities for a certain amount of fraud involving powerful economic and political figures.[64] Relative to other African countries, however, the elite keeps the lid on corruption and other forms of influence peddling through a fairly rigorous system of accounting controls, which allows quick tracing of misused funds to the officer responsible. In addition, there is an independent audit under the supervision of the National Assembly that is extremely aggressive in demanding an accounting of expenditures. Even the parastatals are sufficiently well managed so that few require any subsidy, and some actually produce a tidy profit. None of the parastatals can borrow funds without the approval of a supervising minister.[65] Elite economic restraint is also evident in civil service salaries, which have been kept relatively modest. Indeed, total civil service salaries are less than 30 percent of recurrent revenues.[66] The life styles of top government officials are equally modest in everything from office space to homes and cars.

The government's rhetoric of development constantly emphasizes the twin goals of growth and equity. Many observers, particularly outside consultants, have argued that most of the population has benefited very little in income terms from the first two decades of independence. The fact of the matter is that there are very little reliable data on which to build a case either way. Certainly a good share of the economy's growth has accrued to expatriates who have provided the necessary expertise and capital. Estimates of the income they receive range from 20 percent to a little over 45 percent in the formal sector.[67] For citizens in this sector, the distribution of wages and salaries as a whole appears to have become more equal.[68] This may account, in part, for the generally peaceful quality of labor relations in Botswana. Moreover, the number of jobs in the formal sector has steadily increased, from 37,520 in 1971 to 97,400 in 1981.[69]

The incomes of the rural populace have increased little in real terms with the economy's growth. Several studies around 1980 indicated that rural laborers made between 5 and 10 pula (P) per month.[70] In contrast, the private sector minimum wage outside of agriculture was 2.88 pula per day at the same time.[71] A study of rural income distribution in the middle 1970s showed that the main rural source of wealth, cattle, was highly unevenly distributed, with 5 percent of the households owning 50 percent of the cattle surveyed.[72] Some would argue that rural cattle-holding has been becoming more unequal over the last quarter-century as a consequence of government programs.[73] The evidence presented is by no means convincing, if only because there is little comparative data available.[74]

There is little doubt that the rural population remains relatively poor in spite of the growth in national income; however, the prediction that political unrest will result overlooks critical aspects of the rural social structure.[75] Many in the rural areas are, as Cooper puts it, part of "supra-households" in which some are at work in the city, one or several are herding the cattle, still others raise crops and tend to small stock, and some are away at school and will shortly gain employment in the government.[76] This network, which encompasses extended family and, possibly, several neighbors, provides many rural households protection from the fluctuations in the economy. A good number of rural families share in the expansion through a relative who has regular employment. Many workers in the city also benefit in that they have access to land and cattle in the rural areas to which they can return if they cannot find a job.[77] Thus, economic inequality, which certainly is considerable, does not automatically create intense feelings of alienation and political dissent in either the urban or rural areas.

The BDP policies enhance this suprafamily security system. The government has preserved the communal land holdings of the rural areas for both crop production and grazing of cattle and small stock. Its drought relief program reduces the pressure to come to the cities in search of a more reliable source of income. Also, a large crop extension program provides the medium farmers (i.e., those with ten to forty cattle) with financial and technical aid designed to keep them interested in crop production.[78]

In economic terms, the BDP's programs have reinforced its legitimacy. It has not squandered the expanding national income so as to generate a public disrespect for a corrupt leadership. Democratic politics have not been intensified by a struggle for the spoils of development. Rather, virtually all sectors of society—politicians, civil servants, businessmen, large cattle-holders, and the middle strata of peasants—have received some of the benefits allocated by a bureaucratic planning process. Even the poorer peasants are likely to feel that they benefit through their suprafamilies and drought relief.

Democracy and the Chiefs

This chapter began with a discussion of the overwhelming power of the tribal chiefs during the precolonial and colonial periods. The BDP's democratic structure has only been in place for two decades. Not surprisingly, the chiefs and their headmen still survive as a potent force in politics. The government is very aware of their popular status; it uses them to legitimate its new structures, to lead community meetings where government policies are discussed, and to urge the community to go along with the local development program. For this assistance, the politicians and civil servants tolerate idiosyncrasies of individual traditional authorities, even when they involve rank insubordination.

Some consultants have proposed that the government return several powers to the chiefs so that their authority could be utilized more extensively to realize government objectives. Among the powers suggested for return are control over grazing lands, adjudication of land disputes, and chairing of local councils.[79] The BDP elite has rejected most such ideas outright. It is not about to reverse the process it has set in motion of taking power away from the chiefs. In this sense, the elite is firmly committed to maintaining its democratic base.

The chiefs deeply resent being reduced to the role of legitimating the new political structure. A number have been a source of continual difficulty for the government. Often, village development projects have floundered because of the disinterest or even opposition of a headman or chief. Even when chiefs are willing to help the government, they hesitate to support projects that only benefit a segment of the community, e.g., cattle owners, since they perceive themselves as speaking for the whole community.[80]

Most difficult for the BDP has been Linchwe II of the Bakgatla. In the first two elections, he allowed his sister effectively to mobilize a willing vote for the BPP. The BDP then bought Linchwe off for a while by making him ambassador to Washington, but he has recently fallen out with the government again and, in a number of ways, has shown his support for the BNF. Early in 1985, his activity became too much for the government, which put pressure on him to withdraw from politics.[81]

The BDP has been effective in keeping most of the other chiefs in a ceremonial role. How long this can continue remains to be seen. The former president's son, Ian Khama, was recently installed as chief of the Bamangwato. He is politically ambitious. Should he and Linchwe decide to side with the BNF, the BDP could be in serious trouble.[82] In general, the chiefs can still pose, at least, a serious threat to local level democracy. Should they support a BNF victory, they would want a revival of their role in local government. For this reason, the BDP's new democratic regime cannot yet be said to be on a firm foundation.

The International Factor

Botswana is a country deeply penetrated by foreign influence. Most prominent over the last century and a half have been the Europeans, especially the British and the Afrikaners. At best, Botswana politicians have succeeded in playing off various European interests against each other. The rise of the Afrikaners to power in Pretoria, the retreat of British colonial power, and the rapid growth of the Botswana economy have further complicated Botswana's position in Southern Africa. On the one hand, Botswana needs the South African connections in order to continue to grow economically. On the other, for almost all Tswana, their neighbor's racist policies are an outrageous evil that must be overturned. Achieving a palatable balance among these competing concerns is next to impossible; the compromise, for the most part, has been to keep the issue off the agenda. The opposition parties rarely try to score points by condemning the government for being soft on South Africa. Indeed, in the last election, the supposedly radical BNF suggested that more concessions be made to South Africa.

Another important foreign influence in Botswana is private capital. With the exception of the Botswana Meat Commission, every enterprise of any significant size is owned wholly or in part by outside investors. Amax and Anglo-American own controlling shares in the copper mine, and De Beers runs the diamond mines through a local company it owns with the government. The government is currently discussing inviting capitalist agrobusinesses to set up large irrigation schemes as a means of coping with the food shortage. The opposition has taken relatively little advantage of this prominent role of foreign capital to charge that the BDP is allowing the country to be exploited by outside investors.

A third source of foreign influence is with the expatriates who play critical leadership roles in many programs. Over half of the professional and close to one-third of the technical cadres in government are expatriates.[83] While the opposition has emphasized the need for localization, it has more pursued the point that Tswana are being cheated out of jobs rather than that slow localization allows foreigners to influence policy.

All these foreign influences have an undemocratic potential. To cope with various aspects of the South African situation, the government must build a military organization that could easily seize power. Foreign capital in the private economy and expatriates in government often promote programs that have little relevance to the local population. On the other hand, some of this European influence has clearly promoted the development of democracy in Botswana. Expatriates provided the leadership, particularly in the early years, for the Brigade Movement and the cooperatives. Foreign aid organizations have put large sums of money into the development of the local council system. Foreign consultants have often been the strongest advocates of policies designed to promote social equality. Since they have often held policymaking positions, their voice has sometimes been decisive. In sum, idealistic Europeans have provided a good deal of the intellectual leadership for Botswana's experiments in democracy over the last twenty years.

A Summary Evaluation

Locating Botswana on the summary matrix used in this study is not clear-cut. With regard to the dimension of democracy, the country fits somewhere between the democratic and semidemocratic levels. Civil and political liberties generally exist, and there is substantial group and individual competition for power. However, there are limits in terms of who may run for office, the degree of criticism of the government, and the extent to which citizens are able to think in other than tribal terms. It is questionable, as a consequence, that the competition for power produces results that reflect meaningful policy preferences. The competition is more between ethnic leaders for a "fair" distribution of the nation's resources.

With regard to stability, a placement on the matrix is also not without question. Botswana is the only country in Africa to have almost a quarter-century of unbroken electoral democracy. It is hard to say yet that this system of leadership selection is "deeply institutionalized," given the fact that several centuries of autocratic political practice predated the present regime. The country is making progress toward institutionalizing a democratic approach. Thus, Botswana is probably best categorized as partially stable.

• THEORETICAL REVIEW •

Particularly striking about the development of democracy in Botswana is that it has been occurring in a political community lacking many of the classic preconditions for polyarchy. As detailed earlier, traditional political structures at the tribal level were highly authoritarian. Colonial rule did almost nothing to encourage or provoke new forms of citizen political organization. The social class structure is highly skewed, with a large low-income category, a small middle class, and a minuscule group of wealthy cattle owners. South Africa poses a severe outside threat that could justify the suppression of political liberties. Approximately 80 percent of the population is not literate. Transportation and communications are poor. The press, while relatively free, is almost nothing but an occasional critic of the government. The economy is dominated by state planning and foreign investment. Since independence, only a very small number of politically active interest groups have developed outside of, possibly, the trade union area. The main economic interest group—cattle owners—do not have any sort of organized voice.[84] How, then, do we explain the development and persistence of relatively democratic institutions in Botswana?

Two considerations seem to be particularly dynamic and central in shaping Botswana's democracy: (1) the struggle between the BDP and the bureaucratic state and (2) powerful decentralizing tendencies in society. Many other factors have undoubtedly facilitated the growth of democracy. The ruling BDP elite has generally employed democratic practices in building its broad-based ruling coalition, which transcends tribal divisions, economic groupings, and political concerns. Democratic consultation is consistent with the traditional Tswana consensus style of politics. The resulting distributionist politics also fit in comfortably with the elite's concern to govern through the existing tribal communities. However, the first two factors seem to have tipped the scales away from an authoritarian approach.

Democracy and the Bureaucratic State

Weber observed that mass democracy fostered the modern bureaucracy in Western Europe and North America.[85] The enfranchised public demanded equality before the law and an absence of privilege, which only the bureaucratic approach to public administration could provide. In Botswana, the relationship seems to be the reverse in many respects. A relatively efficient bureaucratic state requires mechanisms of democracy to assure its legitimacy.

In most African states, bureaucratic domination has not been seriously attempted. Rather, political leaders have created patrimonial forms of rule in which public office is treated as a personal right. By this means, the state secures sufficient legitimacy to survive and carry on some of its functions, but at severe cost to other social and economic organizations, as well as the state's own effectiveness.[86]

The political elite in Botswana has set out on a different path for a number of reasons. Its own background is particularly critical. The BDP leadership consists predominantly of owners of large cattle herds. Almost all cabinet members, for instance, own over two hundred head and are assured of deriving sufficient income from this enterprise to pay for a good share of their living expenses. In contrast to the typical Tswana owner of a large herd, who is satisfied to bask in the status his possessions give him, most of the BDP politicians come from a small but growing number of cattle owners who seek to build commercial operations. Their model is in the large ranches run by whites both in Botswana and across the border in South Africa.

For these Tswana entrepreneurs, the state at the time of independence provided fairly effectively for their critical needs: it offered veterinarian services at minimal costs and it drilled a large number of boreholes for cattle in communal areas, particularly during periods of drought. Most important, it sponsored the building of a large and efficient abattoir that effectively assured a steady and rising price for cattle. There was, in short, reason for these nascent ranchers to believe that the small bureaucratic state the British had created could be a worthwhile instrument to service not only the cattle industry, but the rest of the country as it sought to develop.

However, there was a serious problem with trying to maintain the bureaucratic approach in the postindependence period. The colonial government had made almost no attempt to develop a Tswana bureaucratic class. There were nowhere near the number of secondary and university graduates required to fill the needs of the expanding civil service, let alone other sectors of the economy. Hence, the BDP decided to pursue a process of only very gradual indigenization, hiring expatriates to staff most decisionmaking positions up to the highest level. Today, two decades after independence, middle-level bureaucratic positions have the same percentage of indigenes as in the early 1970s. Even in the superscale grade, where Botswana have increased in numbers, expatriates in 1983 continued to fill 22 percent of the 183 positions.[87] In the parastatals, the top executives are still mostly European.

Using expatriates in policymaking positions brought the BDP a number of benefits. While such staff costs more than locals, it also has the experience, in most cases, to produce more. This has contributed to the government's ability to sustain rapid economic development. In addition, expatriates in the line of command are more effective trainers than temporary advisors because they control important sanctions such as pay and promotion. Finally, expatriates provide a second channel of information for top policymakers as to what is going on down below in the bureaucracy. Because they do not plan to make their careers in Botswana, they do not hesitate to blow the whistle on problems they see.

However, this slow indigenization strategy entailed some serious risks for the BDP. Such a large foreign cadre renders the bureaucracy more insensitive to public opinion. Also, expatriates can easily behave in a manner that offends local custom. The government could thus lose its legitimacy by being perceived as a neocolonial enterprise. The various democratic structures, from Parliament to community participation, often seem to function to counter this possibility. They serve to put the BDP on notice when the bureaucracy does not understand the political environment in which it has launched a particular program. If the discontent appears sustained and serious, the cabinet tells the civil servants to see what can be done to redraft the offending policies. The public consequently has a sense that it is choosing its leaders and having an input into government programs that affect it directly, and hence that excessive foreign influence can be corrected. This sense of control is crucial in sustaining the legitimacy of the BDP's bureaucratic state.

Civil servants are not simply on the receiving end of public opinion. They have learned to use the *vox populi* both to test the acceptability of different approaches and to buttress ends they have decided upon. For this reason, the bureaucracy has itself been one of the prime promoters of a democratic approach. The Ministry of Local Government and Lands has been particularly effective in this regard, mobilizing local councils, which it supervises, to promote or reject programs in other ministries. For instance, it has repeatedly urged local councils to ratify its demand that the Ministry of Agriculture mount programs to assist the rural poor in producing more food. Officials in Local Government and Lands have also most effectively stalled and reshaped Agriculture's TGLP ranch program by encouraging local land boards and councils to speak out on their particular objections to private ranch sites. The Ministry of Agriculture, in turn, has developed a very large group extension program to demonstrate popular support for its programs.

Many of these attempts to use democratic methods result in questionable outcomes. Local communities and civil servants often seem to be talking past each other. Moreover, there is a highly manipulative quality to much of the consultation. For example, on the nationwide consultation regarding TGLP, the public was never asked whether it wanted the program but, rather, whether certain parts would be acceptable. Nevertheless, the Botswana public has numerous opportunities to use mechanisms of democratic control, and politicians are concerned about seeking public support for their reelection with certain policies. In Dahl's terms, there is a certain amount of polyarchy, that is "opportunities for contestation and participation in the processes not only of the national government but of various subordinate governmental and social organizations."[88]

Political Decentralization

A second force propelling democratic development in Botswana is the highly decentralizing character of the political community. Two considerations seem most important. One is the long history of political independence of the nine Tswana tribes. Each has jealously guarded its territorial boundaries. In terms of language and many cultural traditions relating to family, religion, and economy, all the groups are relatively similar. Moreover, there has been a certain amount of migration among the various tribes, as well as intertribal marriage. Nevertheless, the legitimacy of the Botswana state requires that these separate entities be recognized. The elections for Parliament and the local councils provide a graphic recognition of this fact. Each group can point to its own representatives in Parliament, and each can see that it has its own local government.[89]

Decentralization is sustained by the great distances over which sovereignty must be exercised. It is true that most of the population maintains a residence along the narrow corridor of land that runs up the eastern side of the country. But many only remain there part of the year. The rest of the time, they are out at their cattle posts, working at their lands, or off laboring at local mines or in South Africa. The cattle industry is particularly spread out over the country because grazing in arid areas requires a very low stock density. Of late, there is growing evidence that even those engaged in arable farming are spending more time at their fields, which are often great distances from their village residence. The chiefs traditionally fought this balkanizing tendency by requiring their subjects to spend certain periods of the year in the villages. The modern BDP state is simply not able to exercise this sort of control. The easiest way for it to obtain control over this fluid society in such a vast territory is to seek popular consent for its policies.

Other forces of decentralization have been added in recent times, tending to further check and disperse state power. One is that the chiefs remain a means of political mobilization even if stripped of many of their original powers. They are the keepers of tradition for many and legitimaters of change for the government. They also stand as potential leaders of a tribal opposition to national policies.

Trade unions are emerging in mining and manufacturing. While not militant in their demands, they must be dealt with. For union leaders, elections provide another means of expressing their dissatisfaction with the country's low wage structure. Thus far, their support has not added much to the opposition's electoral strength (as we noted earlier) but, as the industrial sector expands in size and becomes more militant, this could change.

Still another force for decentralization is the extensive foreign influence in the form of foreign aid projects, expatriate personnel, and private capital. The homogeneity of British rule is being replaced by a great variety of ideas and programs. Because these forces are driving and managing much of the economic development, they are having a profound impact on the way society is organized or disorganized. Democracy both allows for this new diversity and provides a means to keep the Tswana influence felt, particularly through the use of *kgotla* discussions at the community level.

A final decentralizing element is the continual bureaucratic struggle over the direction of central government policy. The politicians have been willing to give the civil servants considerable latitude to initiate and develop most programs of government. The result is that each ministry and its various subdivisions contest one another for both funding and policy influence. A ministry often seems like a political party seeking to mobilize popular support: several have their own community groups scattered throughout the countryside to attract the public to their side.

In sum, the BDP elite uses democratic structures as a means of harnessing all these fissiparous tendencies. Much of this decentralization is similar to that found in other African countries, such as the varying origins of foreign aid personnel, but its scale in Botswana is more extensive than in many. Other forms may be fairly unique to Botswana, like the combination of cultural homogeneity and tribal independence. Certainly, democracy in itself is not the sole cohesive factor. There is also the dominance of the president over the parliamentary system, the strength of the BDP's ethnic coalition, and the power of the Ministry of Finance and Development Planning in directing the government's policies.

Sustaining Factors

If the factors of bureaucracy and decentralization propel the development of democracy in Botswana, a myriad of other considerations have rendered the political system susceptible to such development. Probably, of most importance in this regard is the relative underdevelopment of the country at the end of the colonial period in terms of the formal educational system, transportation and communication systems, and economic productivity. Thus, the advent of elections did not bring a rush of socially mobilized groups to join in political conflict. There was no need for departicipation because social change was not yet inspiring mass political action. The small group of educated commoners and relatives of the chiefs and headmen who were interested in politics found they could compete with each other without fear that the mass of the population would be mobilized to drastically alter the character of government.

Also facilitating democracy is the high degree of legitimacy the system has. In part, this flows from the fact that the various local councils reflect longstanding tribal identities. Thus far, the BDP has also been able to coopt the chiefs to support the government policies in various ways. Also, the new political elite has taken over the traditional *kgotla* from the chiefs and allowed citizens to use it to voice local concerns relative to the implementation of national programs. Consequently, elected officials and civil servants appear to be acting like the chiefs in that they regularly consult the *kgotla*. Finally, the government has managed the economy in a way that has not only brought an incredible record of growth since independence, but also insured that the results are being enjoyed to some degree by all social groupings.

Reinforcing this legitimacy is the congruence of certain aspects of democratic practice with traditional culture. The new system encourages moderation and compromise, behavior traditionally highly respected in Tswana culture. Also, the rule of law, which is a requisite of a stable democracy, is greatly admired by all Botswana as a value that must be upheld by political elites. Another sustaining factor is elite attitudes toward the state. Major political and bureaucratic actors do not look on the state as the area in which they can or should enhance their personal income; rather, economic security is to be achieved in the private sector. At the time of independence, most elites expected that wealth was to be acquired through cattle. Recently, commerce and employment with the new mine corporations are looked upon as additional avenues to economic success. The rigorous enforcement of civil service codes requiring honesty have further protected the state from being perceived as a source of personal income. The result is that political contestation has not involved the sustained struggles for personal enrichment that have characterized other African states. Finally, two critical institutions of the state have remained largely independent of politics. The courts have regularly stepped in to protect the political rights of opposition politicians and newspapers when the government has sought to prosecute its critics. The military has likewise stayed out of domestic political conflict. More important, there has been no indication that the military leaders have given any thought to staging a coup.

All of the above factors—underdevelopment, state legitimacy, adherence to traditional norms, economic opportunity outside of the state, and independence of the courts and the military—have served to make possible the development of democracy in Botswana. The principle forces driving democratization forward, however, are the myriad of conflicts between the political elites and the state bureaucracy and the mass of decentralizing forces in society with which the centralized state must contend.

• FUTURE OPTIONS •

Until Botswana's constitutional structure has been tested in one or more severe crises, we cannot determine the degree to which it has been institutionalized. In the short run, potential crises are twofold: the chiefs in the rural areas are a threat for mobilizing their followers to reject the existing system, and the workers in the cities could challenge the existing allocation of national income. In the long run, more serious confrontations may arise if the intellectual elites remain isolated from the ruling class, and if the influx of freedom fighters seeking to overthrow white rule in South Africa promotes the militarization of Botswana politics.

The chiefs remain among the most respected political figures in the country. While they have been stripped of all but their judicial powers, most Batswana still consider their chief the rightful head of their tribal community. Since ethnicity remains the most powerful source of political cohesion, especially in the rural areas, the chiefs are potentially a source of serious challenge to both the government and the democratic structure itself. Under exactly what circumstances the chiefs would launch such a challenge is not at all evident. The young and obviously ambitious chiefs of Kgatleng and Bamangwato are the most obvious threats in this regard. If they were openly to reject their tribes' present support for the BDP, the party's leadership would face a whole series of difficult problems in trying to control the chieftaincies without further alienating its rural constituency. The resulting conflict could well force the BDP to choose between losing the parliamentary elections and abandoning elections as a method of leadership selection. Given the paternalistic attitude of the BDP from President Masire on down, the latter choice would not be surprising.

The growth of the economy over the last two decades has led to the rise of a sizeable working-class population in the urban areas of the country. Labor relations have remained generally peaceful because of the steadily increasing income from diamond and beef exports, opportunities even Botswana's gradual localization presents for the more ambitious to assume staff and management positions, and the tight controls maintained by government on trade union leadership.[90] However, the future is likely to be more conflictual. There is every indication that the country's income from beef and diamonds will level off. The Botswana Meat Commission (BMC), one of the largest employers in the country, has overextended itself in terms of capital investments and has moved to cut back on worker benefits. If the diamond or beef markets go into a slump, the political elite would have no choice but to make politically explosive cuts in either workers' income or rural services, or to find some balance between the two. Reduction of rural services is particularly unattractive in that it would hit at the heart of the BDP's electoral majorities. The government's reaction to the present financial crisis at the BMC is probably indicative of its inclinations.[91] It has insisted that the BMC retain the price paid to farmers for beef and that it cut its expenses for labor. Any sustained decline in export income could thus lead to serious working-class anger in the cities if a similar approach were taken.

Needless to say, the BNF—which appeals to both the chiefs and the working class—is well-positioned to take advantage of either potential crisis. It certainly has the organizational capacity in the cities to move when the time is right. It need only wait. In the rural areas it could be dramatically strengthened with more chiefly support.

In the long term, two other crises could emerge. One concerns the need to develop a native intellectual class that can influence the political process. Thus far, Europeans have assumed most intellectual roles in Tswana society. They have been hired on contracts to provide ideas about what directions the government should take. They have tended to think in European terms, often with little sensitivity to local perceptions or experiences. Since government pays these intellectuals, the BDP manipulates them or eases them out if they become too critical. Consequently, the BDP operates without any very significant indigenous intellectual class to criticize and inspire it. In time, if the BDP does not turn to such a class for policy direction, it may need to adopt an increasingly patrimonial approach to retain its legitimacy.[92]

Probably the more serious long-term crisis is that Botswana could become embroiled in the civil strife emanating from white-ruled South Africa. Pretoria wants Botswana to expel any public supporters of political organizations seeking to overthrow white domination in South Africa. The BDP has been partially compliant, only allowing nonmilitary persons to remain. But, Gaborone's ability to enforce even this policy is less than completely effective. South Africa has thus launched a number of cross-border raids when it perceived that Botswana was not doing enough. If the Botswana government is to protect its sovereignty against such aggression, it has no option but to substantially augment its military and police. Such dependence on violence will have several destabilizing consequences for Botswana democracy. Of necessity, the military and police will become more influential as they come to control a greater share of the budget. Also, military and police pursuit of South African freedom fighters could bring a state of virtual war in which citizen rights are suppressed.

None of the above crises is imminent. All require a train of events. The political leadership will have time to conjure with the challenge to its system of rule. There are a number of factors that could help insure that most of the country's democratic practices survive. One is the tradition of civility and consensus that pervade Tswana decisionmaking. A consensus will be sought. In addition, there are a number of institutional forces that should help preserve democracy during a crisis. The various ministries will probably enter on different sides of the issue. The opposition will have a voice through the local councils it controls. Foreign aid donors will continue to provide substantial funds that can be used to alleviate many problems that could precipitate one of the above crises. Financially, the government also has considerable flexibility to reallocate appropriations to problem areas because close to half the total state budget goes for development projects, which could be delayed or even canceled.

Probably, the most vulnerable aspect of democratic practice in Botswana is the electoral system itself, which has only been in place for twenty years. There is little indication that the mass of the population has much faith in this means of controlling its leaders. The public tends to see policymakers as outside its influence. From the Tswana perspective, the more important democratic practice is decisionmaking by communal discussion that seeks a consensus. If the BDP elite faced defeat at the polls, it could well abolish elections while continuing to operate by this *kgotla* style and succeed in convincing the population that a government by consent was operating.

On the other hand, any number of transformations in the social, economic, and political structure could enhance the legitimacy of the electoral system. Politically, the more the government gives policy independence to the local councils, the more the local communities are likely to value their elected representatives in council as means to protect and promote their communal interests. The BDP elite gives much evidence of wanting to grant such independence so that each ethnic group will have a sense of participation in the political system, thus increasing the regime's legitimacy.

Another political change that could strengthen the electoral system would be the establishment of a private newspaper capable of competing with the government's *Daily News* two to three times a week throughout the country. One of the BDP's advantages is that there is no mass medium that investigates, exposes, and analyzes government practice or policy. Scandals go almost unnoticed. Most important, as far as threats to democracy are concerned, is that the public be given some warning by the mass media. Thus far, private newspapers have only been able to survive on a weekly basis. The emergence of a strong private daily within the foreseeable future is not likely without considerable foreign investment. Such investors, however, would be hard-pressed to justify the outlay of capital required, given the limited literate public and the competition of a government paper distributed free of charge.

Still another political change that is needed to institutionalize democracy in Botswana is the development of organized interest groups that support political parties. In the urban areas, there is an organizationally extensive union movement; its leadership, however, is not yet very aggressive politically. Otherwise, very few sectors of society are organized for political action. In this sense, Botswana is quite different from the Ghana that Chazan describes: there is not a maze of interest group leaders lobbying the government officials for action.[93] Even the major Tswana cattle producers are without an organization to represent themselves.

Over several decades, the government's attempts to promote community participation may pay off in the institutionalization of a range of strong community groups in villages and towns. Thus far, this movement lacks a basis of community demand. Rather than articulating their own interests, communities are mobilized to serve the objectives of particular government ministries. If some of these groups produce payoffs genuinely sought by the communities they serve, this could end the current void in group political action.

Extensive group politics must ultimately await the development of a larger commercial bourgeoisie that can provide the leadership and financing for this form of political activity. The government itself has inhibited the politicization of the middle class in Botswana by insisting that civil servants stay out of politics. This aids the development of the bureaucratic state but limits the personnel available to lead social groups, particularly for political purposes. The development of a nonbureaucratic bourgeoisie will not occur as long as the state continues to dominate the development of the economy. Hence, some privatization of the economy is needed to foster a bourgeoisie, which could sustain independent and politically active interest groups.

The survival of democratic politics in Botswana in the face of one of the major crises already mentioned is most questionable. The local councils show considerable potential for enhancing the viability of polyarchy. Otherwise, a free press that effectively scrutinizes the government is not likely, and a healthy range of interest groups lobbying politicians is a long way off.

• NOTES •

1. My essay, "Elections in Botswana: Institutionalization of a New System of Legitimacy," in Fred Hayward, ed., *Elections in Independent Africa* (Boulder, Colo.: Westview Press, 1986), pp. 121–147, concentrates on the electoral system, whereas this analysis is concerned with the broader social, economic, and historical context within which democracy developed in Botswana.

2. See Neil Parsons, "The Economic History of Khama's Country in Botswana, 1844–1930," in *The Roots of Rural Poverty in Central and Southern Africa*, edited by Robin Palmer and Neil Parsons (Berkeley, Calif.: University of California Press, 1977), pp. 113–143; and Gary Y. Okihiro "Resistance and Accommodation: baKwena-baGasechele, 1842–1852," *Botswana Notes and Records* 5 (n.d.): pp. 109–116.

3. I. Schapera, *A Handbook ofTswana Law and Custom* (London: Frank Cass, 1970), p. 62.

4. Anthony Sillery, *Founding of a Protectorate: History of Bechuanaland, 1885–1895* (London: Mouton & Co., 1965), p. 35.

5. Schapera, *A Handbook*, pp. 75–80.

6. Ibid., p. 83; I. Schapera, *Tribal Innovators: Tswana Chiefs and Social Change, 1795–1940* (New York: Humanities Press, 1970), pp. 189–227.

7. Sillery, *Founding of a Protectorate*, pp. 27–28.

8. Hoyte Alverson, *Mind in the Heart of Darkness*(New Haven: Yale University Press, 1978), p. 135.

9. Monica Wilson and Leonard Thompson, eds., *The Oxford History of South Africa*, vol. I, (Oxford: Oxford University Press, 1969), p. 155.

10. See Adam Kuper, *Kalahari Village Politics: An African Democracy* (Cambridge: Cambridge University Press, 1970).

11. The British referred to the territory now called Botswana as Bechuanaland. For consistency, I will only refer to the territory as Botswana.

12. See Lord Hailey, *Native Administration in the British African Territories* (London: HMSO, 1953).

13. See Schapera, *Tribal Innovators: Tswana Chiefs and Social Change, 1795–1940* (New York: The Athlone Press, 1970).

14. Schapera, *A Handbook*, p. 86.

15. Schapera, *Tribal Innovators*, p. 79.

16. In 1941, it was renamed the African Advisory Council and, in 1951, it became the African Council.

17. Richard P. Stevens, *Lesotho, Botswana, and Swaziland: The Former High Commission Territories of Southern Africa* (London: Pall Mall Press, 1967), p. 143.

18. See R. Nengwekulu, "Some Findings on the Origins of Political Parties in Botswana," *Pula: Botswana Journal of African Studies* 1, no. 2 (June 1979): p. 71.

19. For the final election results, see *Bechuanaland Daily News*, 1 March 1965, "Supplement," pp. 1–3.

20. See Republic of Botswana, *Constitution of Botswana* (Gaborone: Government Printer, n.d.), chaps. IV and V.

21. A recent example was the retirement of Titus Madisa as executive chairman of the Botswana Meat Commission, a parastatal, after the BMC became subject to severe criticism in Parliament led by a BDP member. See *Daily News*, 1 April 1985, p. 1.

22. *Bechuanaland Daily News*, 15 June 1966, pp. 1–2.

23. For a discussion of the consequences of the nationalization of the local government service, see E. B. Egner, *District Development in Botswana* (Gaborone: Government Printer, 1978), pp. 7–8, 51–55.

24. These are the words of Assistant Minister Chilume of the Ministry of Local Government and Lands to a workshop for councilors. Quoted in *Botswana Daily News*, 1 April 1985, p. 5.

25. On the history of cooperatives see J. Stephen Morrison, "Cooperatives and the Liberal State in Botswana" (Paper delivered at the annual meetings of the Midwest Political Science Association in Chicago: April 1984); and Richard G. Morgan, "The Evolution of Agricultural Cooperatives and Government Policy in Botswana," *Botswana Notes and Records* 14 (1982): pp. 35–45. For agricultural organizations, see A. B. J. Willett, *Agricultural Group Development in Botswana*, 4 vols. (Gaborone: Ministry of Agriculture, 1981).

26. Botswana National Front, *National Front Pamphlet No. 1: The Botswana National Front, Its Character and Tasks*(Typed copy, BNA Unit BNB 1090, 1965).

27. James H. Polhemus, "Botswana Votes: Parties and Elections in an African Democracy," *Journal of Modern African Studies* 21, no. 23 (1983): pp. 397–430.

28. Sources for election data reported in this section and the next are as follows: Supervisor of Elections, *Report on the General Elections 1969* (Gaborone: Government, 1970); Supervisor of Elections, *Report to the Minister of State on the General Elections, 1974* (Gaborone: Government Printer, n.d.); Supervisor of Elections, *Report to the Minister of Public Service and Information on the General Election, 1979* (Gaborone: Government Printer, n.d.); and Supervisor of Elections, *Report to the Minister of Public Service and Information on the General Elections of September 8, 1984* (Gaborone: Government Printer, n.d.).

29. To be sure, most plans are prepared long before potential political issues could be identified. For example, the 1970–1975 plan came out in September 1970, one year after the 1969 election, the 1976–1981 plan appeared in May of 1977, over two years before the 1979 contest; the 1979–1985 plan was published in November 1980, one year after the 1979 election; and the 1985–1991 version appeared in 1985, one year after the most recent election.

30. See, for instance, Botswana Democratic Party, *Election Manifesto 1984* (Gaborone: Botswana Democratic Party, 1984). In order to appreciate how little the platform has changed, see Botswana Democratic Party, *Election Manifesto 1969* (Gaborone: Botswana Democratic Party, 1969).

31. In the last election, it went so far as to support the signing of an accord similar to the Nkomati Accord signed by Mozambique with South Africa.

32. See interview of Kenneth Koma in the *Botswana Guardian*, 27 July 1984, p. 8; and *Daily News*, August 1984, p. 2. Polhemus, "Botswana Votes," provides a good summary of BNF programs for earlier elections.

33. Jack Parson, "The 1984 Botswana General Elections and Results: A Macro-Analysis" (Paper prepared for presentation at the workshop on preliminary results from the 1984 Election Study Project at the University of Botswana, Gaborone: May 1985), pp. 50–51.

34. Jack Parson, *Botswana: Liberal Democracy and the Labor Reserve in Southern Africa* (Boulder, Colo.: Westview Press, 1984), pp. 49–50.

35. Ibid., p. 48.

36. See Richard Vengroff, *Local-Central Linkages and Political Development in Botswana* (Ph.D. diss., Syracuse University, 1973). In recent years, the sparkplug of the Kwena BDP organization has been Daniel Kwelagobe, currently also minister of agriculture.

37. These calculations are based on a total of fifteen constituencies. One, the Kgalagadi, was excluded in both elections because it was uncontested.

38. Steven Tabor, *Drought Relief and Information Management: Coping Intelligently with Disaster* (Gaborone: Government Printer, 1983), p. 37.

39. It is generally agreed that the BPP and BIP have only been effective in making an ethnic appeal. See, for instance, Jack Parson, "The 1984 . . . Elections," p. 86.

40. Ibid., pp. 52 ff.

41. Prior to 1984, there was only one council constituency in Naledi.

42. On migration patterns in Botswana, see Central Statistics Office, *Migration in Botswana: Patterns, Causes and Consequences*, vol. II (Gaborone: Government Printer, 1982), pp. 107–120, 213–223.

43. Currently, the deposit is 100 pula (55 dollars) for parliamentary candidates and 20 pula (11 dollars) for local council. The deposit is returned if the candidate obtains 5 percent of the vote. The supervisor of elections has recommended doubling the fee for parliamentary elections and requiring political parties to pay a 500 pula registration fee in order to discourage small parties. Supervisor of Elections, *Report . . . 1984*, pp. 7–8.

44. Republic of Botswana, *Constitution*, article 62, d.

45. Central Statistics Office, *Census Administrative/Technical Report and National Statistical Tables* (Gaborone: Government Printer, n.d.).

46. Only 14 percent of the candidates surveyed in the 1984 election were females. See J. Kimble and A. Molokomme, "Gender and Politics in Botswana: Some Thoughts on the 1984 Elections" (Paper delivered at the Election Study Workshop held at University of Botswana, Gaborone: May 1985).

47. This is up from a figure of 1,000 at the time of the 1970 census. See John D. Holm, "The Meaning of Democracy in Botswana: An Exploratory Essay" (Paper delivered at the African Studies Association Meetings, Los Angeles: 1984), p. 4.

48. Louis Picard, "Bureaucrats, Elections and Political Control: The District Administration and the Multi-party System," in Louis Picard, ed., *The Evolution of Modern Botswana*. (Lincoln: University of Nebraska Press, 1985).

49. *Guardian*, 17 August 1984, p. 4.

50. He asked, "If the Nigerian soldiers can see all [the] . . . faults by their Government, what about our soldiers . . . when the wealth of this country is amassed by only a few people?" Ibid.

51. See the statements by O. Chilume in *Botswana Daily News*, 1 April 1985.

52. See my "The State, Social Class and Rural Development in Botswana," in Picard, *Evolution of Modern Botswana*.

53. This is the plural noun in Setswana for persons of the Tswana culture.

54. Alverson, *Mind*, p. 142.

55. Stephen R. Lewis, Jr., "Botswana: Diamonds, Drought, Development and Democracy," *CSIS Africa Notes*, no. 47 (11 September 1985): p. 1.

56. John R. Lewis and Valeriana Kallab, eds., *U.S. Foreign Policy and the Third World: Agenda 1983* (New York: Praeger Publishers, 1983), pp. 210–211; Donald G. Morrison, Robert Mitchell, John Paden, and Hugh Michael Stevenson, *Black Africa: A Comparative Handbook* (New York: Free Press, 1972), p. 51.

57. See, in this regard, Ministry of Finance and Development Planning, *National Development Plan, 1979–85* (Gaborone: Government Printer, 1980), p. 56.

58. Nimrod Raphaeli, Jacques Roumani, and A. C. MacKellar, *Public Sector Management in Botswana* (Washington, D.C.: World Bank, 1984).

59. F. G. Mogae, "A Review of the Performance of Botswana's Economy," in M. A. Oommen, F. K. Inganji, and L. D. Ngcongco, eds., *Botswana's Economy since Independence* (New Delhi: Tata McGraw-Hill Publishing Company Ltd., 1983), p. 19.

60. S. R. Lewis, Jr. and D. N. Mokgethi, "Fiscal Policy in Botswana, 1966–81," in *Botswana's Economy*, p. 81.

61. Employment Policy Unit in Ministry of Finance and Development Planning, *National Manpower Development Planning 1983* (Gaborone: Government Printer, n.d.) pp. 10, 21.

62. Republic of Botswana, *Financial Statements, Tables and Estimates of Consolidated and Development Fund Revenues, 1984/85* (Gaborone: Government Printer, 1984).

63. See John D. Holm and Richard Morgan, "Coping with Drought in Botswana: An African Success," *Journal of Modern African Studies* 23, no. 3 (September 1985): pp. 463–482; John D. Holm and Mark S. Cohen, "Enhancing Equity in the Midst of Drought: The Botswana Approach," *Ceres* 19, no. 6 (November–December, 1986): pp. 20–24.

64. Even President Masire has been implicated. For instance, one report recently documented how his brother obtained at least three ranches under the TGLP program when he should not have been able to obtain more than one. See Republic of Botswana, *Commission of Inquiry into the Allocation of Ngwaketse First Development Area Ranches* (Gaborone: Government Printer, 1980). The report was discussed a number of times by the cabinet, but it refused to take action because of the potential political embarrassment. Nevertheless, the fact that the government both examined the situation and debated it gives evidence of the extent to which violations of the law by high political officials are taken seriously. At the time, Masire was still vice-president.

65. See Raphaeli, *Public Sector Management*, pp. 17–36.

66. Ibid., p. 16.

67. See M. A. Oommen, "Growth with Equity—Some Explanatory Hypotheses Based on the Structure and Pattern of Distribution in Botswana," in Oommen, *Botswana's Economy*, pp. 31, 34.

68. Oommen says that the Gini coefficient from 1974 to 1979 came down from 0.496 to 0.452. Ibid., p. 43.

69. Employment Policy Unit, *National Manpower*, p. 10.

70. See Robert Hitchcock, *Kalahari Cattle Posts* (Gaborone: Government Printer, 1978); and J. S. Solway, *People, Cattle and Drought in Western Kweneng District* (Gaborone: Government Printer, 1980). The value of the pula has dropped with the South African rand. It has fluctuated from approximately 1 dollar in 1982 to between 65 cents to 45 cents in the last few years.

71. Oommen, "Growth with Equity," p. 45.

72. Central Statistics Office, *The Rural Income Distribution Survey in Botswana, 1974/75* (Gaborone: Government Printer, 1976), p. 112.

73. Emery Roe, *Development of Livestock, Agriculture and Water Supplies in Botswana Before Independence: A Short History and Policy Analysis*, Occasional Paper (Ithaca, N.Y.: Rural Development Committee of Cornell University, 1980); Steve Lawry, *Land Tenure, Land Policy and Smallholder Livestock Development in Botswana* (Madison: Land Tenure Center of the University of Wisconsin, 1983).

74. Oommen does present Gini coefficients for the years 1968–1969 and 1980; the figures are 0.688 and 0.699. See his "Growth with Equity," pp. 37–38. These are hardly evidence of much change over a decade, especially in light of the fact that small holders have lower cattle holdings after a drought, as was the case in 1968. Indeed, this small difference could result from the poor quality of the data on which the analysis is based.

75. This belief is particularly widespread among European consultants, e.g., Michael Lipton, *Botswana: Employment and Labour Use* (Gaborone: Government Printer, 1978).

76. David Cooper, *How Urban Workers in Botswana Manage Their Cattle and Lands: Selibe Phikwe Case Studies* (Gaborone: Government Printer, 1980).

77. Ibid., pp. 133–136.

78. Johannes B. Opschoor, "Crops, Class and Climate: Environmental and Economic Constraints and Potentials of Production in Botswana," in Oommen, *Botswana's Economy*, pp. 159–179.

79. O. Gulbransen, *Agro-Pastoral Production and Communal Land Use: A Socio-Economic Study of the Bangwaketse* (Gaborone: Government Printer, 1980); Republic of Botswana, *Report of the Presidential Commission on Local Government Structure in Botswana* (Gaborone: Government Printer, 1979), pp. 3–5.

80. Chris Brown, *Local Institution and Resource Management in the Communal Areas of Kweneng District* (Gaborone: Government Printer, 1983), pp. 18–25.

81. *Daily News*, 2 April 1985, p. 1.

82. There was considerable rumor in the last election that Khama was flirting with the idea of becoming active politically. The government has Khama somewhat more effectively trapped than Linchwe in that he is a brigadier in the army.

83. Raphaeli *Public Sector Management*, p. 43.

84. A classic statement of these preconditions is provided by Robert Dahl, *Polyarchy: Participation and Opposition* (New Haven: Yale University Press, 1971).

85. Max Weber, *Economy and Society*, vol. II, Guenther Roth and Claus Wittich, eds., (Berkeley: University of California Press, 1978), pp. 956ff.

86. Thomas M. Callaghy, *The State-Society Struggle: Zaire in Comparative Perspective* (New York: Columbia University Press, 1984); Robert Jackson and Carl Rosberg, *Personal Rule in Black Africa* (Berkeley: University of California Press, 1982).

87. Raphaeli, *Public Sector Management*, p. 44.

88. Robert Dahl, *Polyarchy*, p. 12.

89. The most recent delimitation commission in 1982, as all previous ones, refused to create any electoral districts that crossed tribal boundaries. See Republic of Botswana, *Delimitation Commission 1982* (Gaborone: Government Printer, 1983).

90. The government has the power to require unions and/or management to submit their dispute to an arbitrator appointed by the president. It is not yet clear how extensively the government will use this power. See *Trade Disputes Act of 1982*. Also, the government can refuse to allow a person to be a candidate in a trade union election.

91. This crisis is more a consequence of poor management of the BMC rather than of a decline in export income from beef. See Steven Morrison, "Dilemmas of Sustaining Parastatal Success: The Botswana Meat Commission," *IDS Bulletin* 17, no. 1 (August 1985).

92. There is evidence that President Masire is trying to involve at least a few urban-based intellectuals in the party. In the last election, the BDP nominated an elected to Parliament two such individuals who were former civil servants. Subsequently, the president appointed both to his cabinet.

93. Naomi Chazan, "The New Politics of Participation in Tropical Africa," *Comparative Politics* 14, 2 (1982). See also her chapter in this book.

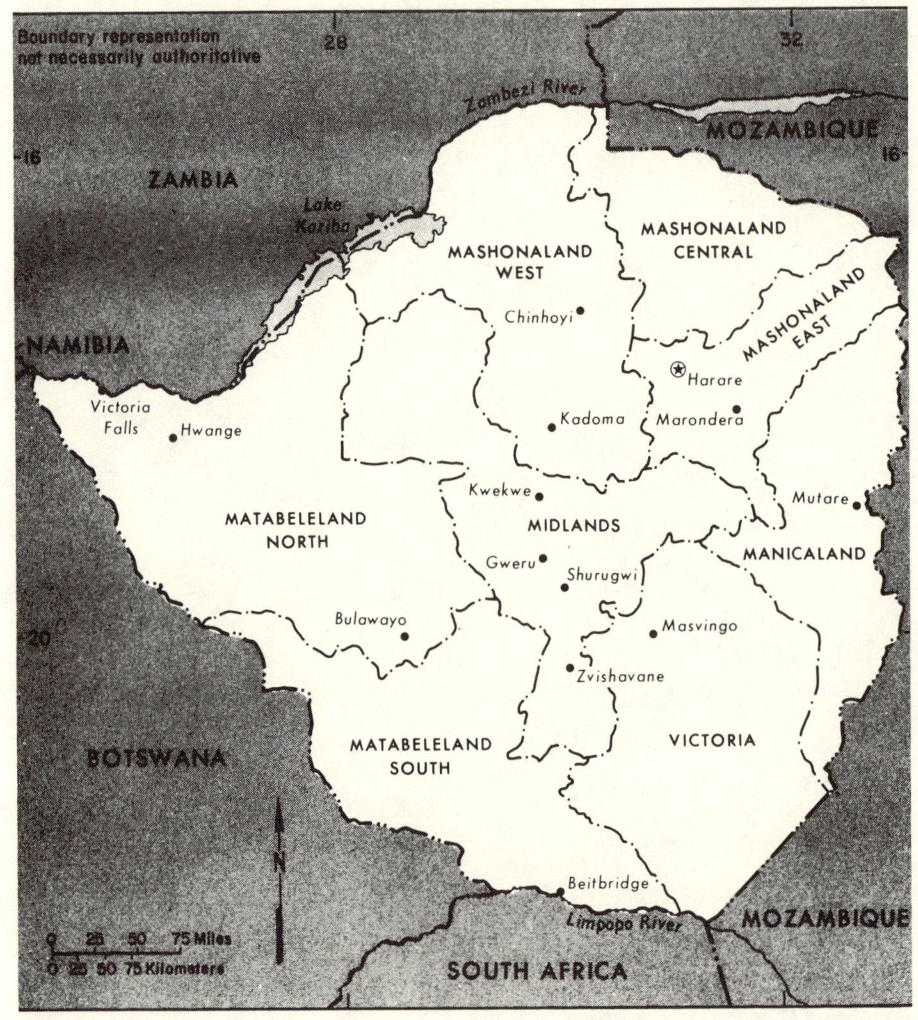
Boundary representation not necessarily authoritative
28
32
16
16
20
Zambezi River
MOZAMBIQUE
ZAMBIA
Lake Kariba
NAMIBIA
MASHONALAND WEST
MASHONALAND CENTRAL
MASHONALAND EAST
Chinhoyi
Harare
Victoria Falls
Hwange
Kadoma
Marondera
Kwekwe
Mutare
MATABELELAND NORTH
MIDLANDS
MANICALAND
Gweru
Shurugwi
Bulawayo
Masvingo
Zvishavane
BOTSWANA
MATABELELAND SOUTH
VICTORIA
N
Beitbridge
Limpopo River
MOZAMBIQUE
0 25 50 75 Miles
0 25 50 75 Kilometers
SOUTH AFRICA

ZIMBABWE

• CHAPTER SIX •

Zimbabwe: In Search of a Stable Democracy

MASIPULA SITHOLE

While there often is disagreement on whether capitalism is good or bad, as well as on the virtues and vices of socialism or communism, there seems to be universal consensus that democracy is good and dictatorship bad. Where dictatorship is spoken of with any virtue, it is with reference to the dictatorship of the proletariat, or the people, or the majority over the minority. Democracy, however understood, universally connotes a positive value, something to aspire to, or at least to identify with. No contemporary leader, no political regime, and no individual will answer kindly to the description, "dictator." Even those who are dictators and autocrats will, more often than not, seek to justify themselves by the exigencies of the times or situations and not on the argument that dictatorship in itself is not bad. Moreover, the term democracy has fallen victim to the emotive stances adopted in the international ideological and intellectual discourse so that it has come to mean whatever those who have spoken the loudest have wanted it to mean.

In discussing democracy in Zimbabwe, it is important to note that there is no consensus yet as to the meaning of the term. The debate surges about whether the democracy Zimbabwe should have is the Western libertarian type, or the Leninist vanguardist type, or the Third World mass mobilizational type.[1] It is not the place here to discuss these three types of democracy, or which is preferable for Zimbabwe. For one thing, I do not think that MacPherson's three typologies, although of heuristic value, are necessarily legitimate, nor do I accept the implicit and derived suggestion that, *ipso facto*, Zimbabwe is experimenting simply with Third World democracy. Democracy must mean government with the consent or mandate of the governed, whether in the East, West, or the Third World. The tendency to call every political system a democracy deprives democracy of meaning and interferes with its growth and development in those areas of the world where there is dictatorship and tyranny. Democracy's universal character is that those who exercise political authority do so with the explicit consent and genuine electoral mandate of their subjects. This is the criterion I use in assessing the democratic project in Zimbabwe. Thus, where Zimbabwe is a success, it succeeds in democracy and not just in Third World democracy.

Similarly, where Zimbabwe is a failure, it fails in democracy and not just in Third World democracy.

In discussing the democratic experiment in Zimbabwe, one is visited with an immediate problem: where to begin. The easy way out is to start from 1980, when Zimbabwe was born following a "one man, one vote" election. In this way, one would conveniently cover six years of experience with democracy in Zimbabwe. In a way, this is largely my intention. However, anything born is born of something, and this weighs heavily on its potential. To that extent, some historical background as to how democracy in Zimbabwe was born is necessary. As with individual human beings, the past experiences of nations heavily affect the way they see and deal with the present, and this further affects, in some ways, what happens in the future.

Many of the problems and, indeed, prospects for Zimbabwe's experiment in democracy that seemed to emerge after independence were not entirely new. They were either a resurfacing of earlier tendencies or they emanated from the political arrangements that brought independence, and were, themselves, the result of various factors with a long history. This chapter, therefore, reviews the experiences with democracy in both the colonial and the postcolonial periods. The first section reviews the history of intrawhite democracy in the Rhodesian settler state, the development of the African nationalist movement, and the postcolonial democratic regime. The second section analyzes the above historical developments. The third discusses the several theoretical assumptions of this chapter about democracy in an effort to isolate those factors that seem, hitherto, to have been more salient in explaining Zimbabwe's experience with democracy. Finally, the last section considers the future prospects for democratic government in Zimbabwe.

• HISTORICAL REVIEW •

The country known today as Zimbabwe was first organized as a single nation-state and named Rhodesia in 1890, following the conquest of its Ndebele and Shona inhabitants by Cecil John Rhodes's Pioneer Column of the British South Africa Company. Rhodesia was a British colony for the ninety years between 1890 and 1980, when the African people won their struggle for independence and majority rule and renamed the country Zimbabwe. Prior to 1980, white settlers ruled Rhodesia without the consent of the conquered African majority, who were deprived of practically all civil and political liberties. Open competition with African leaders and political parties was so restricted as to be denied. Looked at from the standpoint of the African majority, white Rhodesian settler rule was not democratic; it was an imposed dictatorship of the few over the many, an oligarchy based on color. Whatever African participation there might have been was marginal and peripheral.[2] However, our intention here is not to discuss how whites ruled without the consent of the Africans but, rather, to outline white politics in a Rhodesian settler state that was an "intrawhite" democracy.

Intrawhite Democracy

Many accounts of white Rhodesian settler political history have been written. It is not necessary to detail all of them to establish the point we want to make. But, of particular note for our purpose, is Larry W. Bowman's *Politics in Rhodesia: White Power in an African State*[3]. Bowman's work, more than any before, demonstrates that intrawhite political conflict took place "within a 'democratic' political process."[4]

By the Southern Rhodesia Order in Council of 1898, the British government established a partially elected legislative council for the white settler community. Thus, whites in Rhodesia enjoyed representative government almost from the outset. From 1922, when the settlers opted for self-government under British tutelage instead of joining the Union of South Africa, to 1979, when a short-lived accommodation with the less militant element of the nationalist leadership was reached, the white electorate took part in several crucial decisions regarding the future of Rhodesia. Seven national referenda were held during this period. In 1922, whites voted 64 percent in favor of federation with Northern Rhodesia and Nyasaland (two other British possessions to the north); and, by an impressive 89 percent vote, the white electorate tacitly approved the impending unilateral declaration of independence in the referendum of 1964. In 1969 and 1971, respectively, the white electorate (now with characteristic enthusiasm) approved a republican constitution, and settlement proposals negotiated between Ian Smith and British Foreign Minister Sir Alex Douglas Home. Finally, in 1978, they approved terms of the "internal settlement" negotiated between the Smith government and a "moderate" African nationalist element that, once very popular, was becoming increasingly marginalized.

In addition to national referenda, general elections were held periodically and at regular intervals during the period of colonial rule. There were fourteen such elections between 1924 and 1977. From 1933 to 1962, Rhodesian politics were dominated by a "liberal" element of the settler community led by the United Rhodesia Party (URP), renamed the United Federal Party (UFP) during the period of the federation, 1953–1963. Two personalities, Sir Godfrey Huggins and later his deputy, Sir Roy Welensky, dominated white settler politics during this decade. The URP won the two successive federal elections in 1954 and 1958, and, while federation lasted, the leadership of Huggins and Welensky after him was rarely challenged in intrawhite settler politics. Welensky was seriously and successfully challenged only toward the last years of federation, when the right wing was gaining ascendency in Rhodesia.

The period of federation, however, also witnessed intense factional fights among white politicians within Rhodesia itself. While, in 1953, the quarrel was over the prudence of the proposed federation, in 1958, Garfield Todd, who had become Rhodesia's prime minister in 1953 succeeding Huggins (now on the federal mantle), lost his position as a result of an internal leadership crisis. The government of his successor, Sir Edgar Whitehead, was defeated in the 1962 election for vacillating on African suffrage, and a completely new party, the right-wing Rhodesia Front (RF), assumed control. In 1964, after just two years in power, the RF founding leader Winston Field was replaced by his more militant deputy, Ian Smith. A year later, the latter issued the Unilateral Declaration of Independence (UDI) when negotiations with Britain proved unfruitful. Under the RF, the right wing thus held sway in Rhodesian politics from 1962 to 1978, the eve of black majority rule.

Rhodesia had five prime ministers from 1933 to 1978. However, thirty-six of those years were dominated by two personalities: Sir Godfrey Huggins, who ruled for twenty years before taking on federal politics in 1953, and Ian Smith, who ruled Rhodesia for fifteen years until 1978, when he began to give in to black majority rule—a prospect, ironically, he had sprung to the forefront of Rhodesia politics in 1964 to prevent. The eleven years between Huggins and Smith witnessed leadership instability in white politics: there was, on the average, a new government every three and a half years. By contrast, prefederation and postfederation white politics in Rhodesia suggested a tendency toward one-man rule and, therefore, the one-party state. In 1965, and again in the subsequent and final three elections under white minority rule (1970, 1974, and 1977), the RF captured all fifty white seats in Parliament. In each election, it increased its vote, completely eclipsing white opposition parties.

The period of RF rule under Ian Smith saw the breakdown of democracy within the white community. Although parliamentary elections continued and the regime sought the mandate of white public opinion before taking important political decisions, political repression increased and was extended to the white community. For the first time, white opponents of the government were openly harassed, and organs of the state were used against them. Any white perceived to be sympathetic to black rule was denounced as a "traitor to the white race." Former federal Prime Minister Sir Roy Welensky was denounced as "a bloody Jew, a communist, a traitor, and a coward," and his "liberal" inclinations appeared to compromise white interests.[5] Former Rhodesia Prime Minister Garfield Todd was put under house arrest many times. Many white intellectuals and clergymen were arrested and several were deported during this period. The frequency of these arrests and deportations increased in the 1970s as nationalist guerrilla activity intensified.[6]

Rhodesia's relationship with Britain likewise deteriorated under RF rule. The self-government constitution granted to Rhodesia in 1923 provided for reserved clauses that gave Britain a limited but critical right to monitor constitutional developments in Rhodesia, particularly in those matters affecting Africans. This relationship with Britain progressively became a contentious issue in the late 1950s onwards, when successive white governments in Rhodesia demanded total independence before the African majority was enfranchised.

In 1961, Britain granted Rhodesia a multiracial constitution, which gave Africans fifteen elective seats in a sixty-five-member parliament. In addition, a Chief's Council was created to advise the white government on matters affecting Africans in the so-called "tribal trust lands." Of special note is the fact that the composition of the Chief's Council was based on the principle of ethnic or regional parity between the Ndebele and Shona despite the fact that only about 20 percent of the population was Ndebele (see below). "Liberal" and "conservative" governments alike inflated the political importance of the chiefs throughout the colonial period, in particular during the period of the nationalist movement in the 1960s and 1970s, in an unsuccessful bid to undercut that movement. Moreover, the chiefs were granted representation in all successive attempts to settle the Rhodesian constitutional problem. Even the final solution at the 1979 Lancaster House constitutional conference gave the Chief's Council power to appoint ten chiefs from their members to represent them in the thirty-member Senate. And, significantly, parity was still maintained between Ndebele and Shona representation.

While Britain would not grant sovereign independence to the white minority government in Rhodesia, it did not intervene to prepare Africans for an eventual takeover. Hence, African political advancement practically depended on the attitudes of successive white settler governments, which differed only in minor details of strategy on the question of how best to preserve white supremacy. The "liberals" came up with a deceptive middle-class strategy designed to enfranchise "civilized" and "responsible" Africans who had acquired substantial incomes and a certain level of education while, at the same time, limiting African access to both education and, therefore, to high incomes. The "right-wing" element that dominated Rhodesian politics after federation did not see any virtue in liberal pretentions. The RF leadership was forthright. Ian Smith spoke of "no African government in my life-time," and "not in a thousand years."[7] He went on to declare UDI in 1965, plunging the country into fifteen years of international isolation and bloody civil war. During the 1970s, nationalists hardened their demands as the liberation war expanded.

When Britain would not recognize UDI, it suited the Smith government to continue to seek accommodation. Four unsuccessful attempts were made in 1966, 1968, 1972, and 1978. In late 1979, however, a successful settlement to the Rhodesia impasse was reached at the Lancaster House conference, in which all the parties to the dispute participated.

The Development of the Nationalist Movement

At this point, we outline the historical development of the nationalist movement, its internal and external dynamics, and its outcome to this day with direct implications for democracy in Zimbabwe.

Zimbabwe is racially and ethnically a plural society. Blacks are by far the majority, 97.6 percent of the country's population of over 7.5 million (1982 census estimates); whites constitute 2 percent, while the rest, 0.4 percent are coloreds and Asians. The black population belongs to about forty different ethnic groups. However, Murphree and his associates note that "on the basis of ethnic, cultural and linguistic affinities," the Shona (77 percent) and Ndebele (19 percent) can be further subdivided into several subethnic groups by linguistic dialect and subculture characteristics.[8] Below is a graphical presentation of the various ethnic and subethnic groups by percentage of the total population.

The Karanga are the largest of the major black subethnic groups in the country, while the Ndau are the smallest. The Zezuru are the second largest group, and the Ndebele, Manyika, and Korekore are intermediate in size. Often, the Korekore have been submerged with the Zezuru, making the Zezuru the largest subethnic group. Also, the Kalanga in Zimbabwe politics were practically considered Ndebele, thus making the Ndebele the third largest group. Further, the Ndau were generally grouped with the Manyika, making the latter group fourth largest. The Rozwi, constituting 9 percent of the population, were the sixth largest group. However, unlike the other groups, the Rozwi are scattered in smaller communities all over the country.

Historically, the Rozwi are believed to have been the ruling class among the Shona groups before the advent of the Ndebele, followed by the white settlers in the nineteenth century. It is the Rozwi, more than any other Shona group, who are closely associated with the Monomatapa kingdom and the Great Zimbabwe ruins from which the country gets its name. The Rozwi are therefore the remnant of a Shona imperial royalty. While the Shona in general did not have centralized political institutions and authority, but rather were what Fortes and Evans-Pritchard called "stateless societies,"[9] Rozwi political organization was highly centralized.

Figure 6.1 The Ethnic Composition of Zimbabwe's Population

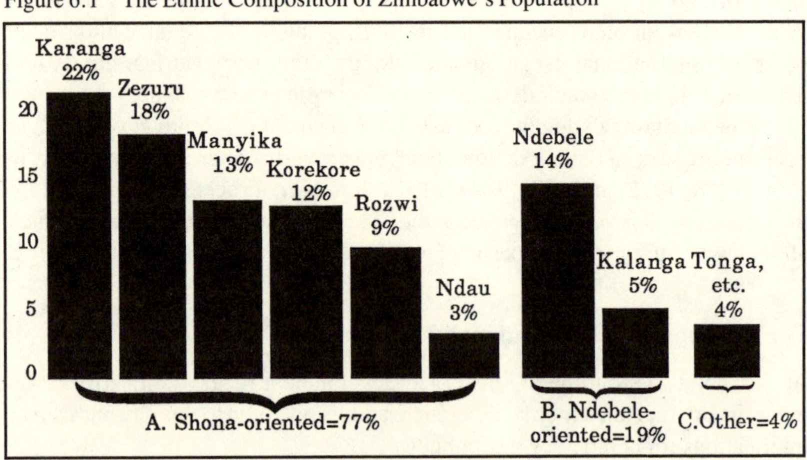

Source: Adapted from M. Sithole, "Ethnicity and Factionalism in Zimbabwe Nationalist Politics, 1957–79," in *Ethnic and Racial Studies,* Vol. 3, No. 1 (January 1980), p. 23. Based on 1969 Census.

The Ndebele migrated from South Africa in the 1930s. Mzilikazi, one of the Zulu King Tshaka's rebellious generals, fled Zululand and led his followers to settle near the present-day city of Bulawayo. It is from this base that he, and later his son Lobengula, conducted further expansionist raids on the surrounding Shona, establishing present-day Matebeleland.

Unlike the Shona, the Ndebele were highly organized around a centralized authority, much in the manner of the Rozwi. They had a highly stratified social system at the top of which was an aristocratic caste, the *zansi*, who were the direct descendants of the original Zulu immigrants. Below the *zansi* were the *enhla*, a group of acculturates whom Mzilikazi accumulated on the long march from Zululand. They were entitled to some limited rights and privileges. The lowest caste was the *holi*, the servant class. These were recruited from among the Shona upon settlement. Until well after the advent of white settlers, "intercaste marriages and intercourse were forbidden."[10] The Kalanga were incorporated into Ndebele society, largely as the *holi* caste, although some became "religious leaders" within the Ndebele superstructure.

Thus, at the time of British occupation in 1890, an unsettled dispute prevailed between the Ndebele and Shona groups over suzerainty and control of the area. This quarrel faded into the background during the period of colonial consolidation and black acquiescence to white rule (roughly 1900 to 1945) but would resurface, albeit in more disguised and subtle forms, during and after the liberation struggle (roughly from the late 1950s to the 1980s).

A nationwide struggle for majority rule in Rhodesia began in earnest in the late 1950s, and, from its very inception, the nationalist movement was conscious of the Ndebele-Shona dichotomy. At a meeting in Harare (then Salisbury) in 1957, the Bulawayo-based African National Congress of Southern Rhodesia, led by Joshua Nkomo, merged with the Harare-based Youth League led by James Chikerema to form a new and expanded organization that retained the name African National Congress (ANC) of Southern Rhodesia.[11] A conscious effort was made to achieve regional or ethnic balance between the Ndebele and the Shona. As such, the reconstructed ANC executive committee was evenly divided between the Ndebele and the Shona. Joshua Nkomo became president of the new organization, and James Chikerema vice-president. An observer of this early balancing act noted that "the Zezuru [Shona] founders of the old African National Congress had invited [Joshua Nkomo] in a bid for unity."[12] The ANC and two other successor organizations, the National Democratic Party (NDP) and the Zimbabwe African People's Union (ZAPU), were banned within a year of each other, notwithstanding the fact that the so-called white liberals were then in power.[13]

The nationalist movement remained united until 1963, when the first major rift occurred. A group of prominent ZAPU executive members led by Ndabaningi Sithole lost confidence in Nkomo's leadership and asked him to step down. When Nkomo refused, they formed their Zimbabwe African National Union (ZANU), which today is the ruling party, ZANU (PF).[14]

The ZAPU-ZANU split of 1963 had far-reaching consequences for politics in Zimbabwe. First, the nationalist movement would remain divided throughout the liberation struggle and after on basically ZAPU-ZANU lines. Second, while it did not take on clearly Ndebele-Shona tribal lines, the split latter degenerated to that, particularly since the 1970s, when intra-ZAPU and intra-ZANU subethnicity was politicized. Although earlier deviant splinter groups were often castigated as "stooge" and "sellout" parties, the ZANU split from ZAPU earned the same labels plus more. Violent methods and tactics were used by ZAPU to liquidate ZANU, and the latter used similar methods to survive. Since then, the use of violence against the opposition has become part of the Zimbabwean political culture. This has implications for democracy in Zimbabwe, which we consider in a later section.

Suffice it to emphasize now that the 1963 split was accompanied by fierce factional fights in most major cities. The ensuing violence involved fists, stones, sticks, knobkerries, knives, axes, and homemade petrol bombs—the only weapons of war readily available to the feuding factions at the time. In the 1970s and after, the feuding factions added to their war paraphernalia all modern weapons of war readily available to them, including armored vehicles. Those factions that did not use modern weapons of war did not have them.

During the mid-1960s, following the ban on ZAPU and ZANU, the theater for Zimbabwe nationalist politics was transferred to exile and progressively took on a new orientation in the form of armed struggle and varying shades of socialist and Marxist-Leninist commitment, particularly in the 1970s. The period between 1965 and 1971 saw a lull in nationalist activity inside the country. However, from 1972 onward, Bishop Abel Muzorewa's African National Council (ANC) filled the apparent vacuum.

What gave rise to Bishop Muzorewa and the ANC was the presence in the country, in March and April of 1972, of the Pearce Commission, which was canvassing African opinion on the acceptability of the 1971 Smith-Douglas Home proposals for a settlement of the Rhodesia independence issue. This event is worthy of note for three reasons. First, it was the first time in the history of colonial Rhodesia that either the British or the white settlers ever sought to sound African opinion on the political future of the country. Second, it was the first time since 1963 that supporters of ZAPU and ZANU united in a joint effort, albeit under a different leader. Third, the subsequent political demise of Bishop Muzorewa, after the release of the better known nationalist leaders, lends credence to our earlier assertion that the fundamental split in the nationalist movement and in Zimbabwe politics has thus far been the ZAPU-ZANU split.

Muzorewa was approached in late 1971 by a team of ZAPU and ZANU officials to lead a new organization in an effort to reject the settlement proposals. He was to be leader *pro tem.*[15] However, after the release of the nationalist leaders in 1974, Muzorewa stayed on at the helm of an independent organization, a gladiator in his own right, until his total eclipse in the 1985 election.

In exile in 1971, the African nationalist movement split further when the Front for the Liberation of Zimbabwe (FROLIZI) was formed amid recriminations in both ZAPU and ZANU involving threats and use of arms to resolve the political difference that had arisen. Important in the formation of FROLIZI was the fact that, for the first time, ethnic conflict between the Shona and Ndebele and among the Shona subethnic groups openly surfaced. Violent exchanges and denunciations of "tribalism," "meetings of clansmen in the dark," and "tribal corruption and nepotism" were openly leveled by principal political gladiators against each other.[16]. When, because of the events of 1971, Chikerema and several other ranking ZAPU officials (mainly Zezuru) left ZAPU, that party then became virtually a Ndebele party. It has retained this stigma ever since and has paid heavily for it at the 1980 polls, and more convincingly in 1985, as we shall demonstrate later. This split also destabilized the political equilibrium in ZANU in a way that has taken that party a long time to recover and to reestablish a new balance of ethnic forces within it.[17] In 1976, in a belated bid to recover his lost support among the Shona, Nkomo asked Robert Mugabe, then on the ascendant in ZANU, to join him in a Patriotic Front that existed tenuously for only three years until the end of the Lancaster House talks in 1979—dashing hopes for a joint campaign in the 1980 election. In his political biography, Nkomo laments that Mugabe abandoned him at the last moment.[18]

By the time of the Lancaster House conference in 1979, there had been a proliferation of political parties on the Zimbabwe political landscape. At their most numerous, they numbered nine. Yet, when the dust finally settled, the residue showed the former ZAPU-ZANU split. Now, however, the scales of dominance had shifted in favor of ZANU, and the leading personality was Mugabe, not Sithole. This proliferation of parties resurfaced on the eve of the 1985 general election, but again the residue showed the centrality of the ZAPU-ZANU cleavage.

Postcolonial Politics

Zimbabwe was born on 18 April 1980, when independence was proclaimed following a general election based on the principle of "one man, one vote," which had long been the basis of the conflict between blacks and whites throughout the political history of white-ruled Rhodesia. In 1979, as a result of the Lancaster House conference involving all the parties to the Rhodesia power dispute, a consensus was reached on a constitution for the new republic. This was the first time that democratic rule in its inclusive sense was established.

Although Zimbabwe is a competitive multiparty state with a single dominant party, there are indications that it is moving to a *de jure* one-party state. The possibility exists, however, that Zimbabwe may still opt to remain a *de facto* one-party-dominant state. We shall discuss this in the concluding section, when we examine future prospects for democracy in Zimbabwe. At this point, we turn to political developments since independence, focusing in particular on the three general elections since 1979 based on the principle of "one man, one vote."

The first one-man, one-vote election was held during the period of Zimbabwe-Rhodesia in 1979.[19]. These elections were held amid both local and international controversy about their authenticity. This stemmed from the questionable legitimacy of the "internal settlement" that authorized the elections while, ironically, excluding the nationalist guerrillas who had brought about the necessary pressure for change.

Following the failure of the 1976 Geneva Conference on Rhodesia, and under increasing pressure from nationalist guerrillas, Ian Smith identified those nationalist factions that appeared out of favor with either the frontline states or the guerrilla forces.[20] He enticed them into a political deal that he hoped would enable them to supersede the Patriotic Front Alliance of Mugabe and Nkomo (then based in exile) while, at the same time, keeping the political outcome securely under white control. This led to the "internal settlement talks," culminating in the "March 3rd Agreement" of 1978 between Muzorewa's United African National Council (the UANC renamed from the ANC of 1971), Sithole's faction of ZANU, and Chief Chirau's ZUPO, on the one hand, and Ian Smith's RF on the other.[21]

The Zimbabwe-Rhodesia constitution spawned by this settlement provided for a president and a Parliament, comprising a House of Assembly and a Senate. The president, who acted on the advice of the prime minister and the Executive Council, was appointed by an electoral college consisting of all the senators and all members of the House of Assembly. The Senate consisted of thirty members, of whom ten were blacks elected by seventy-two black members of the House of Assembly, ten were whites elected by twenty-eight white members of the House of Assembly, and ten were African chiefs elected by the existing Council of Chiefs. Of these chiefs, five were to be from Mashonaland and the other five from Matebeleland—a sort of ethnic balance.

The House of Assembly consisted of 100 members, seventy-two of whom were elected by blacks on a party list system, and twenty-eight by whites on a single constituency basis. At the end of ten years or after the second Parliament, whichever would come later, a commission was to be established to review the question of the retention of the twenty-eight white seats. The franchise was extended to all persons eighteen years or older who were either citizens or had been permanently and continuously resident in the country for at least two years before the election. Provisions were also made in the constitution for the first government to be a government of national unity. To this end, any party winning five seats or more in the House of Assembly was represented in the cabinet in proportion to its seats in Parliament.

In all three elections, parties were represented on ballots by name and by a symbol distinctive to each party. Prior to each election, the government instituted a widespread information program to encourage people to vote and to explain the election process (and, in the case of the 1985 election, the voter registration procedures). Elaborate election procedures were set up for all three elections. Hundreds of polling stations (including mobile units) were established in urban and rural locations to provide as wide a spread of polling as possible. To check that a person had not voted previously, each voter had to dip his fingers in a colorless liquid containing dye visible under ultraviolet light and that stayed on a person's fingers for a week or more. Polling officials were empowered to explain the ballot paper and how a vote should be indicated. Representatives of the competing political parties, international observers, and the press were able to enter polling stations at any time and scrutinize the voting process. They could also be present at the sealing and reopening of ballot boxes and to affix their own seals if they so desired.

An electoral Supervisory Commission was established for all three elections and was charged with ensuring that the elections were free and fair. This feature was required by the constitution, and persons making charges of election fraud were asked in press notices to communicate their information to this commission. It was a democratic process.

Although five political parties ran in the 1979 general elections, only three won seats, with Muzorewa's UANC winning fifty-one of the seventy-two African seats, Sithole's faction of ZANU twelve, and Chief Ndiweni's United National Federal Party (formed only three months before the election) winning nine seats. The voter turnout was 65 percent of the voting population, estimated at 2.9 million.

Although there was disruptive pressure from the Patriotic Front guerrillas, these elections were pronounced to have been "substantially free and fair" by the electoral Supervisory Commission and several international "observer" groups who filed similar reports approving the conduct of the election.[22] All competing parties but ZANU(Sithole) concurred with this assessment. ZANU(Sithole) alleged "gross irregularities" in the conduct of the elections and lodged an unsuccessful petition with the authorities.

The twelve ZANU(Sithole) members initially boycotted Parliament but later took up their seats when it became apparent that no one in the system really believed their story. Also, it became clear that, if they maintained their boycott, they would be excluded from a Zimbabwe-Rhodesia delegation to possible constitutional talks in London. Contrary to expectations, the government formed by Bishop Muzorewa failed to gain international recognition and attracted intensified guerrilla pressure until he and his internal settlement colleagues were summoned to London by the British Government to discuss a new constitution with the leaders of the Patriotic Front late in 1979.

The 1979 Lancaster House conference gave Zimbabwe its current constitution. Thus, since 1980, and most likely until 1990, Zimbabwe government and politics have operated within the framework of a constitution agreed to by all the parties in the dispute. The governmental and electoral provisions of this constitution were similar to those of the Zimbabwe-Rhodesia constitution, already mentioned. There were, however, some important exceptions.

Although the House of Assembly still consisted of 100 members, eighty rather than seventy-two were to be elected by the common roll, while the white seats were reduced to twenty. Further, while the Zimbabwe-Rhodesia constitution required formation of a government of national unity (with proportional representation in the cabinet), the composition of the cabinet was now entirely the prerogative of the prime minister. However, he was still required to choose his cabinet from among those elected to the House of Assembly or Senate.

Another critically important innovation was the way in which nationalist guerrillas were to be handled in the transitional period. During Zimbabwe-Rhodesia, the guerrillas were required to "surrender" to the Rhodesian security forces, but now they would go into "assembly points," where they would remain for the duration of the election. From their number, and from the former Rhodesian army, a new Zimbabwean national army (ZNA) would be created with the help of British military experts. During the transition in early 1980, there were several assembly points throughout Zimbabwe's countryside: in Mashonaland, these assembly points housed ZANU's ZANLA guerrillas, and in Matebeleland, ZAPU's ZIPRA. Eventually, some of these guerrillas were brought into makeshift barracks located within the major cities of Harare and Bulawayo and housed right across from each other in the high-density suburbs of these cities. This worsened existing tensions between the two groups.

Also significant in the Lancaster House agreement was the provision of a British governor charged with responsibility for administering the country during the transition period, supervising the conduct of the elections, and asking the leader of the winning party to form a government. In Zimbabwe-Rhodesia these procedures had been the responsibility of Ian Smith's Rhodesia Front governmental machinery.

Finally, there was the provision of subsection 2, section 75, chapter VII of the constitution, which says:

> The President may give general directions of policy to the Public Service Commission with the object of achieving a suitable representation of the various elements of the population in the Public Service and the Prison Service.

Known locally as the "presidential directive," this clause allowed for the appointment of personnel and lateral entry into any section of the public service if the president (on the advice of the prime minister) deemed it necessary in order to redress past imbalances. This device was particularly important since key public service posts had, hithereto, been staked with "old order" types whom it would take decades to replace on the basis of the normal course of experience.

"Presidential directives" have been utilized to full effect since independence. Ibbo Mandaza, a commissioner on the Public Service Commission observed that, "Were it not for the Presidential Directive, and the fact that qualified Zimbabweans returned home in their numbers at independence, there would have been little change in the structure and direction of this important component of the State machinery."[23] The presidential directive clause not only provided the new leadership with constitutional means for redressing past imbalances, but, more significantly, it enabled the new rulers to meet the aspirations of a highly qualified (if politicized) and potentially critical element of the African intelligentsia. In this way, animosities between blacks and whites were obliterated almost immediately after independence. This facility arrested revolutionary pressures and redirected their energies into implementing bureaucratic procedures in the service of the state.

Among the more significant features of previous constitutions retained in the 1979 Zimbabwe (Lancaster) constitution were the Senate and Presidency. This meant that Zimbabwe would continue to have a parliamentary system, with a two-tier legislature and a basically ceremonial president, much like the British monarchy. Like the House of Lords in relation to the Commons, the Zimbabwe Senate was essentially a vetting, if rubber stamp, body on legislation passed by the House of Assembly. Also noteworthy was the retention of the provision for parity of representation between Ndebele and Shona in the Senate, and the fact that none of the nationalists at the Lancaster talks either advocated or criticized retention of this structure. Once presented, it was accepted as if by conditioned habit.

The 1980 independence elections were held over a period of three days, 27–29 March, with a total of nine political parties contesting (three more than in 1979). However, only three nationalist parties won seats in the 100-member Parliament; Mugabe's ZANU(PF) won fifty-seven, Nkomo's PF(ZAPU) twenty, and Muzorewa's UANC three. The twenty seats reserved for whites were all captured by Ian Smith's Rhodesia Front, which ran unopposed in fourteen of the twenty constituencies. Following his overwhelming victory, Mugabe was called upon by the British governor to form a government.

There were allegations and counterallegations of violent intimidation by all political parties, particularly among the major ones—ZANU(PF), PF(ZAPU), UANC, and ZANU(Sithole)—with the latter three complaining that they could not campaign in any of the rural areas formerly controlled by ZANLA guerrillas. ZANU(PF)'s complaints were mainly directed at Lord Soames (British governor in charge during the transition to majority rule). Soames was accused of bias against ZANU(PF) in favor of the UANC in particular and the other parties generally.[24] Moreover, there were several attempts on Mugabe's life during the 1980 campaign.[25] On the complaint that other parties could not campaign in former ZANLA areas, the ZANU(PF)'s typical attitude was: "Why should any party go where it is not wanted? Why should any party wish to go and reap where it did not sow?"[26] ZANU(PF) was not about to give rival parties safe passage into its areas of dominance. In the big cities, there were numerous clashes between parties and a number of fatalities during the election campaign. However, notwithstanding the various accusations of intimidation and violence, the elections were pronounced by Lord Soames, the electoral Supervisory Commission, and international observers to be a fair reflection of the will and choice of the people.

The independence election of 1980 produced a clear-cut ZANU(PF) victory. But, instead of forming an exclusively ZANU(PF) cabinet, Prime Minister Mugabe invited his former Patriotic Front partners of ZAPU into a government of national unity in an effort to create harmony and a stable democracy. The ZAPU president, Joshua Nkomo, was first offered the position of president, which he turned down, preferring the more powerful post of home affairs minister, responsible for the police. Whites were also included in Mugabe's cabinet in an effort to foster reconciliation between the races. Everything seemed in place for national reconciliation.

Suddenly, in 1982, fighting broke out between former ZANLA and ZIPRA guerrillas stationed around Harare and Bulawayo, culminating in a showdown between the defense forces and former ZIPRA guerrillas in several parts of Matabeleland and the Midlands. Many former ZIPRA personnel defected from the newly integrated national army to form the nucleus of the present dissident activities in Matebeleland. Subsequently, arms caches were uncovered in several ZAPU-owned farms in Matebeleland, whereupon all ZAPU cabinet ministers were sacked, and involved ZAPU properties were confiscated by government authorities. Several ranking former ZIPRA officers in the army were arrested as some defected to join the ranks of dissidents. A renewed state of emergency has existed in many parts of Matebeleland since 1982, the start of serious dissident activities. This remains the biggest threat to the democratic project in Zimbabwe, a theme we shall explore in the next section.

Independent Zimbabwe's most important experience with democracy to date was the general election held on 1–4 July 1985. This election was significant in many respects. It was the first general election Zimbabwe had held as an independent sovereign state; the 1980 election having been held under British supervision. Second, with the exception of some parts of Matebeleland, the 1985 election, unlike the earlier ones, was largely held in an atmosphere of peace. Third, like the 1979 and 1980 elections, the 1985 election was held in a multiparty context, notwithstanding suggestions by the ruling party for a one-party state. Fourth, while the two previous elections were based on the party list electoral system, the election of 1985 was conducted on a single-constituency basis. Finally, although a separate election was again held for the white electorate, the 1985 election brought the end of white unity and fifteen years of Rhodesia Front hegemony in white politics. For the first time in a long while, two white factions (both with a Rhodesia Front background) competed in the white roll elections in 1985.

In 1980, ZANU(PF) had its first experience in running an election campaign; then it was a party out of government. In 1985, it had two onerous responsibilities. As the party in government, it was responsible for the administration and conduct of the general election while, at the same time, it was also responsible for its own campaign for reelection in a contest in which five other parties also sought office, although with varying degrees of vigor and appetite. This dual responsibility placed ZANU(PF) both at an advantage and disadvantage. For the first task, it had gained enormous experience from years of mobilization during the liberation struggle, as well as from the actual election campaign of 1980. For the second task, that of administering a national election, ZANU(PF) had very little prior experience. It had to take the blame for anything wrong about the elections. Moreover, while the black population had prior experience with the party list system of election (1979 and 1980), they had not experienced a constituency-based election. The need for prior administrative experience in conducting elections was manifest throughout the exercise. It was a learning experience.[27]

ZANU(PF) came on top with another brilliant victory. It picked up seven more seats, increasing its 1980 total to sixty-four. It took all the seats in Mashonaland Central, East, West, and Masvingo, as well as in the Midlands, where in 1980 PF(ZAPU) had managed to win four out of the twelve seats. In Manicaland, ZANU(PF) won all but one seat in the Chipinge constituency, stronghold of Sithole's faction of ZANU. PF(ZAPU), shut out in six of the eight provinces, swept all fifteen seats in Matebeleland North and South, defeating two incumbent ministers in Mugabe's cabinet. In the white elections, Ian Smith's Conservative Alliance of Zimbabwe won fifteen of the twenty seats, and the more conciliatory Independent Zimbabwe Group won four seats. One seat was won by a "left-of-center" candidate.

The elections were pronounced "free and fair" by all international observers who came in their private capacities. Independent groups within Zimbabwe itself passed similar judgment of approval, although Nkomo did express disappointment with the results.[28] The electoral Supervisory Commission was also pleased with the conduct of the election. Its chairman, Professor Walter J. Kamba, vice-chancellor of the University of Zimbabwe, commented:

> We were satisfied, beyond doubt, that the elections were conducted fairly at every stage of the process. My commission visited many places in the country observing the election preparations, during the polling period and the counting of votes. We are satisfied that the officials acted and behaved with probity and impartiality. I have no doubt that the electorate expressed its choice at the polls freely. In every area, and in every constituency, people voted for the party or candidate of their choice.[29]

The actual conduct of the election on 1–4 July was peaceful and civil. Everything possible was done to ensure voter secrecy. For four full days, the people quietly cast their secret ballots. Even in dissident affected parts of Matebeleland, relative quiet reigned. According to the registrar-general, the success and orderly conduct during the polling days was attributable to the "prohibition of certain activities, including the wearing of Party Uniform, the banning of canvassing and political activities within 100 meters of the polling stations."[30]

The irony of the 1985 election, however, was the almost unbelievable reaction of many ZANU(PF) supporters, especially women and youth in the urban areas. A few days after the news of the victory, they went on a rampage beating up and evicting members of minority parties from their houses. Whole families and their belongings were thrown out on the streets, and several people were killed in this postelection violence.

Further, there were very strong, if unfamiliar, anti-Nkomo manifestations in several urban communities by some party officials and enthusiasts. At several places, mock funerals were held with people carrying "coffins" of Nkomo and ZAPU for burial. At one such mock funeral in Kadoma, a live bull (the ZAPU election symbol) was actually axed to death in front of a huge crowd to symbolize the death of ZAPU. Although other minority parties were also the objects of similar ridicule, the anti-ZAPU manifestations were many and more pronounced.

Since independence, politics has also been waged at the local government level. The Zimbabwean constitution provides for the establishment of locally elected district and city councils. City mayors are elected from the councils. At the district level, however, district administrators are appointed by the minister of local government. A significant postindependence development was the creation of provincial governorships, one in each of Zimbabwe's eight regions. These governors are appointed by the president on the advice of the prime minister. They coordinate and oversee implementation of government policy in the provinces.

Important to note about politics at the local level is its marked repetition of attitudes shown at the national level. Thus, city and district council elections in Matebeleland tend to be dominated by ZAPU while ZANU controls local councils in the rest of the country. The story is different, however, when it comes to appointive posts such as district administrators and provincial governors. Here they tend to be predominantly ZANU members. In Matebeleland, such appointees have often been targets of dissident violence.

• ANALYSIS OF HISTORICAL DEVELOPMENTS •

At this point we seek to explain the developments outlined above, namely: intrawhite democracy, the development of the nationalist movement, and the development of democracy in Zimbabwe since independence.

Analysis of Intrawhite Democracy

Several questions come to mind regarding intrawhite democracy. Why, in the first place, was there intrawhite democracy in the Rhodesian state? Second, both Godfrey Huggins and Ian Smith ran exceptionally long, uninterrupted regimes—one liberal and the other right-wing. What explains the longevity and stability of these seemingly "different" regimes, in contrast to the apparent regime instability from 1958 to 1964? Finally, why did successive efforts at a peaceful democratic settlement between Ian Smith, the British government, and the African nationalists fail? In other words, could democracy have been achieved without a violent liberation struggle?

Until independence, white Rhodesians were always the more educated and prosperous of the country's population. Moreover, culturally, they were predominantly the offspring of British traditions; as such, the politics of contestation were no stranger to them. The settler economy was basically a free enterprise economy. Most white politicians were wealthy, and had independent status before they rose to preeminence in politics. Huggins, Welensky, and Whitehead were knighted well before entering politics. Todd, Field, and Smith were prosperous farmers long before they became prime ministers of Rhodesia. Politics among whites, therefore, was a vocation rather than a means of livelihood. Among them, it was not a "do-or-die" affair. As each man retired or lost to the other, he had a viable livelihood to return to. Hence, losing an election did not mean losing everything; politics was not a "zero-sum game."

There was, however, a sense in which whites did view politics in Rhodesia as a zero-sum game; this was when politics was perceived in a racial context. Here whites were basically one; regardless of class, ideology, or whether of English or Afrikaner extraction. They all saw African majority rule as inimical to white interests. Thus, the fundamental issue of intrawhite political conflicts concerned the best strategies and policies to follow in order to preserve the system of white privilege through dominance. Decisions to achieve these ends, however, were made in the most democratic way possible within the white community. But why was intrawhite democracy important?

Democracy was important for white Rhodesian politics because it narrowed the perceptual gap between the white political elite and their followers in understanding interests and the strategies necessary to achieve them. This explains why whites were able to maintain unity among themselves, unity that could be broken only after African majority rule had been achieved. Given, in particular, the British cultural legacy and its democratic ethos, democratic consultation was necessary to produce goal consensus and regime legitimacy among whites as they confronted a common enemy in what was perceived essentially as a "do or die" contest between black and white. Without periodic consultations, goal consensus, and regime legitimacy, white rule in Rhodesia would have not lasted as long as it did, and as cohesively.

A second issue of note is the lengthy tenures of the Huggins and Smith regimes. Right from the inception of white rule in colonial Rhodesia, whites saw themselves as a distinct group potentially threatened by Africans. As such, they maintained a basic consensus in the perception of their position throughout the period of white rule. Up until 1958, this consensus was on a philosophy and strategy that viewed relations between black and white in some sort of strange paternalism. Huggins characterized the relationship as one between "junior and senior partners."[31] Whites believed that Africans, formerly a primitive people, felt themselves privileged to be ruled by Europeans—that white rule was a blessing. The fear of the African began during the Federation of Rhodesia and Nyasaland, when the nationalist movement in the two northern territories became increasingly successful amid British acquiescence and an increasingly anticolonial international environment following World War II. White Rhodesia then abandoned its formerly carefree paternalistic disposition and reached a new consensus in the right-wing drift of the RF election of 1962, which was solidified in Ian Smith's ascendency in 1964. The apparent leadership instability of the 1958–1964 period suggests an adjustment period as the white community moved to a new consensus.

It remains to explain why several successive attempts to resolve the Rhodesian constitutional impasse failed until 1979. The simple answer is that the British would not give or recognize independence in Rhodesia based on a constitution that denied the franchise to the African majority. But why would Britain take such a stance, yet not take any tangible steps to enfranchise the Africans?

First and foremost, the international climate after World War II, as we have noted, was hostile to colonialism and racism—both of which Rhodesia typified. Embodied in the United Nations, the international community became activist with regard to democratization and self-determination in the colonies. From the 1960s, the Organization of African Unity (OAU) and other British commonwealth countries effectively discouraged British inclinations to recognize the Unilateral Declaration of Independence. Moreover, Britain had already embarked on granting independence to the other two countries of the federation on the basis of African majority rule, although African resistance there had become more aggressive, and the white population and interests were much less than in Rhodesia. At any rate, Britain could not do otherwise in Rhodesia without being seen as racist in such a double standard.

Finally, and more important, throughout the 1970s, the Zimbabwe African nationalist movement had matured in sophistication and effectiveness and would not settle for any independence formula short of immediate total transfer of power to the African majority. For instance, in 1971, Ian Smith and the British government agreed on a formula for gradually accelerated majority rule. When African opinion was sought by the Pearce Commission in 1972, the proposals were overwhelmingly rejected. Similarly, the 1978–1979 "internal settlement" was denounced by a mainstream nationalist opinion to which the international community now listened.

Given the previous white intransigence, why, then, was 1979 successful? By then, a complex combination of factors had coalesced to induce the white oligarchy to accept inclusive popular democracy. Cumulatively, the international isolation, economic sanctions, intensified nationalist guerrilla effectiveness, political pressure from the African "front-line states" on the nationalists, and from South Africa on the Smith regime all contributed to a conducive climate. Further, there was in London, by 1979, a rather decisive Conservative government with an activist foreign policy. Moreover, there was also that element of luck in the circumstances of the Lancaster House conference whereby all the major power aspirants perceived themselves the likely victor in the proposed elections. Even the whites believed their "black candidates" of the "internal settlement" would win and combine with them in a coalition government.[32]

Finally, was it inevitable that white Rhodesian politics turn to the right as they did, and, therefore, that majority rule be achieved only after an ugly armed struggle? Following the accession to power by the RF in 1962 and by Ian Smith in 1964, it was clear from Smith's pronouncements of "no African government in my life-time" and "not in a thousand years" that armed struggle was inevitable. Simple and "unserious" as they may appear, these statements had tremendous impact on both black and white. The whites received them with reassurance, thereby making them blind and intransigent for fifteen years. On the other hand, such unyielding pronouncements forced African nationalists to reassess their method of struggle, which hitherto had been peaceful and constitutional.[33]

Thus, from 1962 to the attempts at an internal settlement in the 1978–1979 period, Rhodesian politics were extremely polarized between black and white. The two worked at cross-purposes and could find no common ground for a settlement. This, however, suggests that an accommodation was possible earlier, during the "liberal" period. There are two views that suggest why early accommodation did not occur and how such an accommodation might have been achieved, thereby averting further polarization and the escalation of violence.

Early peaceful accommodation presupposes that the liberalism/paternalism of the Huggins, Todd, and Whitehead period was substantially different from the right-wing tendency of the Smith period; that the liberals had it in the back of their minds to see eventual black rule and an independent Zimbabwe. In 1962, right before his electoral defeat, Edgar Whitehead, the last of the "liberals," publicly declared that "there is no doubt that the African will have a majority within 15 years.[34] (Ironically, African majority rule did come soon thereafter, but as the result of armed struggle and not gradual improvements on the 1961 constitution.) However, observers of white Rhodesian politics have commented that the apparent shift to the right was not at all a shift but part of a "continual process of white reassessment" of strategy and tactics in pursuit of white supremacist goals.[35]

We should not, however, lose sight of the possibility that paternalists like Todd, Whitehead, or Welensky might have been philosophical liberals, believing that, ultimately, white interests could only be served by an inclusive multiracial polity. They and others never joined the RF nor were they prominently identified with RF rule. For that reason, one could argue that the fifteen years of polarization and civil war could have been avoided. If, for instance, the British government of the time had been resolute in its commitment to majority rule and had sent unambiguous signals to white settlers that UDI would be treated as treasonable rebellion against which British troops or any other (UN, Commonwealth, etc.) would be unleashed in support of the constitution, the liberals, and other democratic forces, it is conceivable that white opinion in Rhodesia would have been a lot more cautious on UDI. Instead, the British government went on record publicly stating that it would not use force against UDI, and that it opposed the use of violence against an illegal regime by the African nationalists. At UN and Commonwealth forums, the British blocked resolutions to send international troops; such a policy was not attractive to the British government and public because most white Rhodesians were British "kith and kin." Lack of strong commitment to majority rule by the British then fueled tendencies towards further polarization between black and white in Rhodesia. Race interfered with Britain's democratic inclinations.

Analysis of the Nationalist Movement

We have seen that Zimbabwe nationalist movement was fraught with splits and factional in-fighting from the ZAPU-ZANU split of 1963 throughout the liberation struggle. Starting with one organization in 1957, there were nine different parties at independence in 1980. Should this be celebrated as a manifestation of a tendency toward multiparty democracy in the Zimbabwe political culture? Yet, only two of these parties, ZANU and ZAPU, now remain viable. But shall we then celebrate a flourishing of, or prospects for, a two-party democracy in Zimbabwe? No, we cannot, least of all because of the drive toward a one-party state by the present ruling party. What then explains factionalism in the nationalist movement during the liberation struggle and the persistence of division between ZANU and ZAPU after independence?

One theory argues that the incumbent colonialists engineered division and factional in-fighting in the movement to weaken it so that they would either remain in power or in neocolonial control of the emergent government. This is an aspect of the classical "divide-and-conquer" theory. It is difficult, however, to demonstrate how the ZAPU-ZANU split of 1963 was the work of either the white settlers in power or elements external to the movement itself. There were suggestions of "enemy agents" involved in some of the splits in exile in the 1970s.[36] And suggestions that all the "internal settlement" parties of the 1978–1979 period were sponsored, to varying degrees, by the Smith regime have not been disputed. Moreover, more than achieving ethnic parity in the Council of Chiefs, the settler regime hoped to develop or retain Ndebele and Shona consciousness in the polity by always creating structures that weighted the Ndebele as numerically equal to the Shona. But the uneasy relations between these two groups, as we saw, predate colonialism.

It is doubtful that, left to themselves, African nationalists would have inclined toward unity in one party during the liberation struggle. The ZAPU-ZANU split of 1963 was caused neither by white settlers nor by external imperialists. Nationalist leaders disagreed among themselves, and, when they could not resolve their differences, they split and ZANU was formed. Moreover, the major factions involved in the "internal settlement" did not, as we have seen, originate from Ian Smith. They were the result of earlier developments in the nationalist movement itself. In any case, a divided movement, like a divided country, often attracts the attention of its enemies.

A second school of thought argues that factionalism and infighting in the Zimbabwe Nationalist Movement was caused by "unprincipled," "petty bourgeois" politicians hungry for power. According to this argument, as long as the petty bourgeois class led the liberation struggle, splits and factional infighting were inevitable.[37] The suggestion here is that when leadership stems from the working class, splits and factional infighting stop. Such a romantic view of the proletariat is sentimental nonsense.[38]

Finally, a third school of thought argues that a better explanation of factionalism and infighting in the liberation movement and the continued strife after independence is tribalism or the ethnic factor in power contestations.[39] The leaders of political parties and factions within the parties have tended to have an ethnic power base. Hence, when ZANU split from ZAPU, it never made any headway in Matebeleland, Joshua Nkomo's home area. This situation obtains to this day. ZAPU's support among the Shona was mainly among the Zezuru (a Shona subgroup). This was because Zezuru leaders of the Youth League, led by James Chikerema and George Nyandoro, who had formed the ANC with Nkomo in 1957, remained loyal to ZAPU until 1971, when Chikerema and Nyandoro (now in exile) left ZAPU to form FROLIZI. From then on, ZAPU became the largely Ndebele party that it is today. Moreover, when the ZAPU-ZANU split occurred in 1963, Chikerema and others were in detention after the ban on the ANC in 1959. In the 1970s, Chikerema and the bulk of the FROLIZI element rallied behind Muzorewa. As Mugabe (himself Zezuru) emerged as the leader of ZANU in the late 1970s, ZANU became the dominant party for the first time in all Shona-speaking regions.

The three elections we outlined indicate the preponderance of the ethnic factor in postcolonial Zimbabwe politics. The 1985 election epitomized this when the voting patterns revealed an even stronger manifestation of the Ndebele-Shona ethnicity than in 1980. Joshua Nkomo's party won all the seats in Matebeleland, but not because workers and peasants in Matebeleland mistook Nkomo for a worker or peasant. Together with the Ndebele bourgeoisie, they have always known Nkomo loved capital. Similarly, ZANU(PF)'s overwhelming victory in the Shona-speaking areas was not a vote only from Shona peasants and workers. The Shona bourgeoisie also voted ZANU(PF) knowing fully well that Mugabe inclined toward peasants and workers. It could hardly be convincing to argue that the Shona bourgeoisie decided to commit class suicide while Ndebele peasants and workers were not aware of their real class interests.

Further, we have seen that there were subethnic groups among the larger Shona and Ndebele groupings. To what extent has subethnicity been a factor in intraparty infighting? In the 1970s, the internecine fights in the ZANU-in-exile were blamed on emergent hostilities between the Karanga and Manyika Shona subethnic groups. When Chikerema broke away from a coalition with Muzorewa in 1979, he accused the latter of running his party, with a "Manyika

Mafia," while Muzorewa's group denounced Chikerema as leader of a Zezuru "Zvimba clique."[40]. Thus, interethnic alliances in the Zimbabwe nationalist movement have been dynamic and not permanent. If properly understood, such dynamism augurs well for pluralistic democracy in Zimbabwe.

Analysis of Postcolonial Developments

Political developments in Zimbabwe during the postcolonial era were as much a product of the past as they were of new developments. We seek now to explain why democracy has endured in Zimbabwe, however tenuously, over the first six years of independence. But first, let us explain the stresses and strains on democracy during this period.

The first six years of independence were trying times for the new government. Like most countries, Zimbabwe's economy was affected by the world recession, but more important, it was hard hit by a three-year drought (1981–1983) that was the worst in many years. Further, during the same period, Zimbabwe had to deal with a costly conflict in Matebeleland to the west and maintain a military presence to the east, in an effort both to guard a strategic oil pipeline and assist Mozambique's government in its war effort against South African-assisted insurgents destabilizing that country. These were hardly small challenges for people just learning not only how to govern, but also how to lead normal lives after some fifteen years in exile or in detention. Moreover, there was deliberate scrutiny by both the international community and the internal opponents of the new rulers to see how well the new rulers were succeeding in gluing together a country hitherto torn apart by war with its attendant lines of cleavage along race, ethnic, and party-cum-military lines.

However, by far the most difficult and costly problem for the new government was the conflict in Matebeleland. This conflict, as we have seen, dates not only back to the liberation struggle, but into the nineteenth century. It is the central thesis of this chapter that, ultimately, democracy in Zimbabwe depends largely on the resolution of the conflict in Matebeleland.

We stated earlier that a conquering people, the Ndebele, by and large dominated the Shona before the advent of colonialism. This Ndebele dominance in one form or another persisted for some time during the colonial period. It was the result both of history and psychological inertia, as well as settler manipulation of the polity. In Matebeleland, for instance, many Shona families adopted Ndebele names while Ndebeles in Shona communities did not. Further, the deference to and tolerance for nationalist leader Joshua Nkomo among the Shona during the early part of the nationalist movement derived, in large part, from the previous Shona deference to the Ndebele. It is largely this inertia that underlay the conflict in Matebeleland in postcolonial Zimbabwe.

Moreover, ZANLA and ZIPRA, the guerrilla armies of ZANU and ZAPU respectively, developed along ethnic-regional lines. Had the Lancaster House conference not occurred when it did, and had the Smith regime been run out of

Salisbury by ZANLA guerrillas, it is conceivable ZIPRA would have occupied Bulawayo and the two forces would have engaged each other in the Midlands, beginning a worse civil war than the scattered skirmishes witnessed in Matebeleland. ZANLA and ZIPRA guerrillas often wasted their strength upon each other during the liberation struggle. Moreover, it was common knowledge in Zimbabwean liberation circles during the 1970s that ZAPU had adopted a strategy of not engaging its forces in an all-out fight against the Smith regime so that they could engage a worn-out ZANU army at the end of the war. The ZANU leadership had always been suspicious of ZAPU strategy and intentions. Thus, after independence, military maneuvers in ZIPRA assembly points, discoveries of arms caches, and ZIPRA defections from the national army were not only predictable, but anticipated and prepared for by a ZANU leadership that had no reason to trust the ZAPU leadership.[41] A showdown between ZANU and ZAPU was, therefore, inevitable.

Right after the signing of the Lancaster House agreement, ZANU pulled out of the Patriotic Front alliance with ZAPU, dashing Nkomo's hopes that the two would campaign jointly in the impending elections. Why did Mugabe pull out of the alliance, and why was Nkomo interested in running jointly with Mugabe? There are several explanations, but the following we find plausible.

In his political biography, Nkomo argues that he wanted to run jointly with ZANU in order to foster unity and thus prevent the current conflict in Matebeleland, which he foresaw.[42] For its part, ZANU pulled out because it did not trust Nkomo, and, more important, many in ZANU believed ZANU did not need the alliance to win the election and that such an alliance would even be a liability. ZAPU, however, needed the alliance.[43] When this first option was denied, ZAPU then hoped to forge an alliance with the 1978–1979 "internal parties" in a "ganging-up" coalition government in which it would be dominant. Given the possibility that ZANU could well win the election against any other electoral combination and permutation, a third strategy, it would appear, became necessary for ZAPU. This took the form of military confrontation after independence. This would explain the arms caches and defections from the national army.

Several reasons point to why ZAPU strategists would entertain the third option. There was the perception first (not entirely incorrect) that, although extremely popular with the masses, ZANU had been an unstable party suffering more frequent and serious squabbles than ZAPU; second, that Mugabe, who had only just emerged as ZANU leader, had yet to gain control of his fractionalized and unstable organization; third, that the entire former Rhodesian security apparatus, as well as the whites generally, would, under the circumstances, support a move against an infant ZANU government; and fourth, that ZANU's former ZANLA forces would be caught "napping," celebrating their victory and "tired" of war, as had been expected. Moreover, throughout the liberation struggle, ZAPU's ZIPRA army was often cited as "Soviet-trained" for "conventional warfare," as "more disciplined," and, by implication, superior to ZANLA, which was regarded as rather chaotic but whose strength lay in morale and numbers. In addition, there was often a misperception of the Shona of the twentieth century as basically the same as those of the nineteenth century—peaceful and shy of war. Traditionally, fighting was not in the Shona way of life. They belonged to what Ali Mazrui has called the "palaver tradition," while the Ndebele, with their Zulu background, belonged to the "warrior tradition."[44] This misperception has proven costly.

The Shona of the twentieth century is qualitatively different from the Shona encountered by Mzilikazi in the nineteenth century. He is a Shona who believes that he was largely responsible for the defeat of white settler rule with its sophisticated organization and newest weapons of war. Thus, we may be witnessing in the conflict in Matebeleland violence that always arises when society must accept a new balance of forces and a new power equilibrium, much as Marx depicted for changes in modes of production and relations of production.

However, with an arsenal of arms buried in various places in Matebeleland, and a cadre of young men aching to fight, ZAPU had not only the will, but also the capacity to test both Mugabe's will to rule and ZANU's capacity to survive. Postindependence dissident activity then must be seen in terms of this decisive test. It is a test that those intimately connected with the development of the liberation struggle could see coming, and that must fade away as Mugabe's will and ZANU's capacity are effectively demonstrated. It is this conflict in Matebeleland that has threatened the development of democracy in newly independent Zimbabwe as the government has resorted to authoritarian and repressive methods to deal with dissident activity. The agenda to discontinue the state of emergency, introduced during white settler rule, was deferred on account of this conflict. Ronald Weitzer has argued that the repressive powers and institutions of the white Rhodesian state were perpetuated and utilized by the postindependence government.[45] Moreover, the human rights organization, Amnesty International, which frequently cited the Smith government for human rights violation during the liberation struggle, now accuses Prime Minister Mugabe's government of similar infractions.[46]

While Weitzer's well-documented argument cannot be denied by common experience during Zimbabwe's first years of independence, it misses an important point. The Mugabe government faced cruel dangers right from its inception. As shown above, ZANU (PF) came to power in an atmosphere of fear, uncertainty, and mutual suspicion between blacks and whites, as well as among the various black factions. Significantly, the various contending groups had the requisite coercive instruments with which to seize power in pursuit of their aims. Under these circumstances, a premature dismantling of the coercive instruments of the former Rhodesian state was ill-advised. Such a step would have created a power vacuum deliciously attractive to the various centers of power already armed to step in. The alternative to maintaining the instruments of the former Rhodesian state was to create new ones in their place. What, in fact, happened is that new instruments of coercion, such as the Fifth Brigade, were added. This raises the question of whether such an additional instrument was necessary. Here again, it does not help much to examine the events and passions of the present without being sensitive to those of the past.

Although Prime Minister Mugabe's government came to power via an election, this was preceded by a war with fractional armies. The creation of a new Zimbabwean national army from these formerly warring armies meant that its political neutrality and loyalty to the new government could not be simply assumed, at least not in the short run. Such an assumption would have been a textbook approach to power. Dissident activity in Matebeleland started almost immediately after independence, and it became necessary for the new government to create the Fifth Brigade because it could not rest its fortunes on an army initially plagued with mutual distrust. Thus, the observations made by many that the brigade (or, as it is emotionally called, *gukurahundi*—"the storm that gathers and clears everything") is highly politically motivated are not mischievous. At independence, Mugabe's government needed the brigade to deal with an equally politically motivated dissident element.

Yet, repression, like many bad things, is habit-forming. There is the real danger in postindependence Zimbabwe that, the longer the state of emergency in Matebeleland continues, the good life and democratic values for which the nationalist struggle was fought might begin to fade from memory and be replaced by a culture of authoritarian rule and violence. Moreover, those involved in prolonged violence are eventually forced to develop a stake in it. Once this happens, there is no end in sight, much like the situations in Northern Ireland and Lebanon. Herein lies the danger for the development of democracy in societies that allow themselves to resort to protracted armed struggles in settling political disputes (a possible lesson for South Africa).

At this point, we attempt to explain why the Zimbabwean government has survived the severe tests of the past six years, and why competitive multiparty democracy has persisted, however tenuously. A number of factors explain why Mugabe's government has survived and stayed committed to democracy during the past six years. First is its *legitimacy*. Mugabe's government is widely viewed as legitimate. It was twice elected by the people in elections internationally acclaimed as "free and fair." Prime Minister Mugabe has ruled much according to the "social contract"—the Lancaster House constitution to which all parties agreed. Any changes to the constitution have been made within the law, and any changes the ruling party might have wanted (such as the one-party state) but that the law does not allow, have not been made. The political elite thus seems committed to the rule of law. The state of emergency the government declared in parts of Matebeleland was generally understood and accepted by the public, given the nature of the problem as outlined earlier. Moreover, the state of emergency was debated and passed by Parliament in accordance with the constitution.

As the government is regarded as legitimate, so the dissidents and the party associated with them, ZAPU, are perceived by the public—particularly the Shona—to be engaged in illegitimate and unacceptable methods of acquiring power, given that ZAPU has always been allowed to participate in the electoral process. It should be remembered that dissident activity started after ZAPU lost the 1980 elections and long before the elections of 1985. This suggests to many that the insurgents are saying that, unless ZAPU is voted into power, they will fight any other duly elected government. Such an attitude is unacceptable.[47]

Further bolstering the legitimacy of the regime is the fact that it has demonstrated its effectiveness not only militarily, but also administratively. It has penetrated many parts of the country with impressive programs, particularly in health, education, and agriculture. As a result, the majority of the population, especially in the countryside, appears today to agree with the statement, "We are better off today than we were five years ago."[48] This view was expressed throughout the country with 78 percent of those asked saying they were better off.[49] Of note is the fact that 69 percent of those sampled in Matebeleland gave the same evaluation. This suggests that the Mugabe government has not been discriminatory in its development and welfare assistance to the various regions, notwithstanding dissident activity. Moreover, it is conceivable that a strategy to win the hearts and minds of the people of Matebeleland would have involved development and welfare assistance. Disaffection in Matebeleland is often expressed against the high-handed methods the army has used, but not that government has neglected the people of Matebeleland in the highly valued areas of agriculture, health, and education.

The ruling party, too, has successfully penetrated the country very effectively, except in Matebeleland where both the carrot and the stick have failed to produce electoral support for it. Sustained effectiveness in the rest of the country is likely to further strengthen the legitimacy of the government. Such sustained effectiveness might also signal a "lost cause" to the disaffected areas. But the reverse is also true. Any loss of ground by the government and the ruling party would encourage dissidents and other sections of the country to question the legitimacy of the government. Thus far, the ZANU (PF) regime has moved from strength to strength both electorally and in maintaining a stable and coherent administration.

Another factor behind the persistence of the democratic system relates to the above. Contrary to expectations, ZANU(PF) has emerged fairly united and cohesive after years of fratricidal tendencies in exile. Moreover, the more ZAPU and the dissidents continue posing a threat, and the more their methods are perceived as illegitimate, the more likely ZANU(PF) will be to sustain its unity and cohesiveness. Related to this is ZANLA unity. Contrary to expectations, former ZANLA fighters now in the national army were not necessarily weary of war. In fact, they had anticipated the conflict in Matebeleland, given the nature and direction of the liberation struggle.

The white community, which largely accepted the hand of reconciliation extended at independence, is another factor encouraging democratic persistence. This removed a sensitive and dangerous strain on the new government. Whites played a critical role in the fairly sophisticated economy the new government inherited at independence. While collapsing economies give rise to revolutions, once they are successful, revolutionary governments are sustained by sound economies. In the short run, the contribution of the whites to economic stability and sustained growth in Zimbabwe was necessary. This could not be achieved by a reckless policy of reprisals against them. On their part, whites accepted Prime Minister Mugabe's hand of reconciliation more readily than did ZAPU and other black parties. The reason for this is obvious. After the struggle for majority rule was won, the question no longer was, "Who will govern, blacks or whites?," but rather, "Who among the blacks will govern?" At this stage, whites were largely peripheral to the arena of politics. However, their role in the economy has been an important stabilizing factor.

Democracy is also commonly associated with a *free press*. In Zimbabwe, radio and television are largely controlled by government as parastatals. The print medium is, however, free in that, unlike radio and television, individuals or companies are free to establish their own newspapers. Moreover, political parties as well can publish their own periodicals.[50] There are two privately owned major journals, *Moto* and *Prize*, which often engage in "constructive criticism." *Moto*, associated with the local Catholic organization, has earned a reputation as probably the most independent and unbiased newspaper in the country. It is widely read by all sectors of the society.

However, Zimbabwe's two main newspapers, the *Herald* and *Sunday Mail*, are owned by the Zimbabwe Mass Media Trust, a parastatal created after independence. The trust bought up South African shares in both newspapers and other regional dailies like the *Bulawayo Chronicle* and *Manica Post*. Yet, although the editors of these newspapers liaise closely with the Ministry of Information, they are not government or party employees and are free to take an independent line on various issues of policy and public concern. The executive director of the newspapers, Elias Rusike, described the relationship with government and the party as follows: "We make a very serious distinction between the government and the ruling party. Though we might support the government, we are not the mouthpiece of the ruling party."[51] However, editors in a fairly ideological and young country might feel obliged to support government and party policy even when this is not demanded by either government or the party. On balance, press pluralism in Zimbabwe augurs well for democracy.

The heterogeneity of the Zimbabwean social milieu is yet another important factor that has helped to sustain some form of pluralist democracy in Zimbabwe. Here, ethnicity has been a contributory factor. In a real sense, continued Ndebele support for Nkomo's ZAPU has slowed down ZANU's speed toward countrywide hegemony and the one-party state. In addition, intra-Shona ethnicity has also kept the ruling party busy patching up differences that have periodically visited it, such as the Hove-Ushewokunze "diatribe" that errupted in the Parliament early in 1986.[52] Moreover, whites still retain residual political influence. Besides their guaranteed twenty seats until 1990, at the latest, opinions of whites and what happens to them invariably catches international attention, particularly in the West, to which Zimbabwe pays particular attention, given the country's colonial history, and sociocultural and economic links.

Further, Zimbabwe lacks class homogeneity, notwithstanding socialist rhetoric. The political class has shown a highly developed appetite for accumulation. Since independence, high-ranking party officials have acquired substantial personal wealth in violation of the party's leadership code, which strictly limits the amount of wealth party leaders may acquire. This embourgeoisement process could, in due course, produce politicians more dependent on their own means of survival and less on the party, thereby increasing independent political opinion. Related to this issue is the peasantry and proletariat, who constitute roughly 74 percent and 20 percent, respectively, of the population. Peasants, more than workers, featured prominently in the liberation war. Although, after independence, the government has paid a lot of attention to the rural areas, peasant policy preferences have, in some instances, tended to contradict party socialist policy preferences. They have, for instance, been more enthusiastic about state-assisted individual peasant farming than collectives.[53]

The labor movement in Zimbabwe is weak and somewhat defensive, feeling guilty for not participating fully in the liberation struggle. There was a wave of strikes in many cities after independence. The workers were quickly silenced and reminded of their complacency during the liberation struggle. Since then, the government has taken what appears to be a corporatist approach to the country's trade union movement. The Zimbabwe Congress of Trade Unions (ZCTU), formed in 1981 with encouragement and assistance of the government, works closely with the Ministry of Labor and Social Services. This is both its source of strength and weakness in that, on the one hand, its favored status gives it advantage over unaffiliated unions, while, on the other, such status compromises workers interests in negotiations with either government or private employees. However, the fact that other independent trade unions can exist gives workers alternatives. This should encourage more dynamism in the ZCTU even under the present corporatist arrangement—a development descernible with the recent election of a new ZCTU leadership. Thus, notwithstanding its initial weakness, there is potential for the trade union movement in Zimbabwe to play a significant role independent of the government or ruling party.

The initially "friendly" attitude of the international community also contributed somewhat to the persistence of democracy in Zimbabwe during the first six years. None of Zimbabwe's neighbors, including South Africa and the superpowers, were overtly hostile to the new government. When not supportive, they adopted a wait-and-see attitude. Moreover, Zimbabwe was well aware it was the focus of attention and scrutiny by the international community, whose principal actors had doubted if democracy in this newest of African countries could endure. Thus, commitment to constitutional rule and to free and fair elections would retain international respectability for Zimbabwe.[54] However, the recent (1986) commando raids by South Africa into Zimbabwe (as well as into Botswana and Zambia), the withdrawal of economic assistance by the United States under the Reagan administration, and, more important, the escalating war in neighboring Mozambique are all likely to frustrate and drive the Zimbabwean government into the authoritarian rule characteristic of any country on a war footing.

Finally, and more important to sustaining democratic rule in Zimbabwe, is Prime Minister Mugabe's personality and leadership ability. Structural factors notwithstanding, personalities matter a lot and may even be the key factor in determining the success of regimes, including democratic regimes. They may prove decisive, for example, in generating loyalty to the system and in getting things done.[55] In contrast to the naive Marxist once jeered at by Nkomo during the liberation struggle as "an upstart who thinks he can win Zimbabwe with a Marxist textbook," Mugabe has emerged as both more pragmatic and shrewder than all his opponents, including Smith, Sithole, Muzorewa, and Nkomo himself—all of them skilled politicians.[56] He is a man of acknowledged integrity who scorns corruption and indiscipline. He respects the country's political institutions, and has not unduly interfered with the country's press or the system of justice.[57] He has allowed the Public Accounts Committee of Parliament to function—investigating, and thus embarassing, some of his cabinet ministers and high-ranking party officials.[58] And, significantly, Mugabe has earned the respect of Zimbabwe's intellectual community; he is one himself in his own right.[59] The support and confidence of the intellectual community is critical for the survival of any regime, even in this age of populism.

• THEORETICAL ANALYSIS •

Zimbabwe, six years after independence, is far too young to fit into theoretical frameworks of democracy in any definitive way. Although the present Zimbabwe government is the result of "free and fair" elections held within a competitive pluralistic party framework, Zimbabwe cannot be classified as completely democratic. The conflict in Matebeleland has resulted in a state of emergency that has placed limitations on civil liberties in the region for a sustained length of time. Zimbabwe can therefore be classified as "semidemocratic" and "partially unstable" because of the conflict. This classification is similar to that by Freedom House's 1985–1986 survey of freedom in the world, which lists Zimbabwe as "partly free."[60] Yet, one must account for the relative success of democracy during Zimbabwe's brief period as an independent state.

This chapter has identified race and ethnicity as the primary factors that have influenced political behavior and, therefore, the experience with democratic politics, first in colonial Rhodesia and then in independent Zimbabwe. While theories of democracy associate it with economic prosperity, this can hardly be said to hold in all cases. Moreover, it is often difficult to establish causality. There may be an association, but causal relationships have not been established. In circumstances where the polity is subjectively divided along lines of race, ethnicity, religion, or any other form of so-called "false consciousness," the dominant group may deal with subordinate groups in an authoritarian manner to preserve its dominant position, whether or not the economy is growing. This, in fact, is what happened during the period of colonial rule in Rhodesia. The economic prosperity of the days of federation did not lead to the liberalization/democratization of an essentially racial, authoritarian settler rule; it led, instead to a right-wing trend. Even intrawhite democracy gave in to Rhodesia Front hegemony and authoritarianism within the white community, notwithstanding the white prosperity of the time.

Neither can the performance of the economy be easily linked to the fate of democracy. After independence, Zimbabwe enjoyed a booming economy, followed in 1981 through 1983 by a severe drought and world recession. As it happened, Mugabe proclaimed a policy of reconciliation between races, parties, etc., from the outset in 1980. Later, however, he sacked ZAPU from his cabinet, and authoritarian rule followed in parts of Matebeleland. This happened in the middle of the drought and economic hardships for the country. However, it would be far-fetched to link dissident activity and repression in Matebeleland to the distressed economy of this period, or the accommodating approach at independence to the prosperity of the time. Rather, ethnic and political factors were driving these developments. Similarly, it is not the economy (declining or expanding) that continues to induce the electorate in Matebeleland to vote ZAPU and in Mashonaland to vote ZANU. Economic hardships were countrywide. Moreover, Matebeleland received special attention from Mugabe's government in the drought relief effort, indeed because of both political and humanitarian dictates. Thus, the electorate in Matebeleland may prosper from government development programs, but still vote ZAPU. The problem between ZANU and ZAPU is not economic. It is at the subjective level.

Neither has class been a salient factor to date in Zimbabwe's political experience. It was not only the lower classes among whites who favored racial domination and authoritarian rule to preserve it, but all classes of whites. Nor was black resistance identified with any particular class; it cut across class lines. The nationalist movement was led by a petty bourgeois element excluded from positions of power and prestige not on account of ignorance and poverty, but because of color. Prior to independence, authoritarian rule and the resistance to it were based on race. Economic inequalities only enhanced the capacity to repress. Since independence, the central political conflict that threatens the democratic experiment has been based on ethnicity, not class.

As mentioned before, however, there is one sense in which economic performance has affected democracy. The relative effectiveness of the Mugabe government in delivering the goods of development in health, education, agriculture, and so on, has increased its legitimacy and, by extension, that of the democratic system.

With respect to the relationship between state and society, democracy in Zimbabwe has benefited from the lack of coincidence between wealth and one's position in government in Zimbabwe thus far. Zimbabwe's richest African is not in government, but in the private sector. In fact, in the eyes of many upwardly mobile Zimbabweans, the private sector has more status. Also, one's position in the private sector has, thus far, not been affected by membership in the ruling party. Moreover, opposition ZAPU politicians are not the poorest in the country. Nkomo himself, hardly a peasant, drives in a dark, bulletproof Mercedes-Benz similar to that of the prime minister. (This caught the attention of one of my students who observed: "We are so free in this country that even a leader of the opposition drives like a prime minister!") On the other hand, there is the danger in any society that the private sector could become too powerful vis-à-vis the state and then undermine its authority in the eyes of the people.

In terms of powersharing, the postindependence political structure has not been a salient factor. As noted, Nkomo refused the presidency, which, in fact, pays more than the prime minister's job. When he finally accepted other cabinet posts, he did not complain that they were too few. The problem is neither economic nor structural; it is psychological and, therefore, political. It is mainly at that level that efforts should be concentrated. A very key point to appreciate in this regard is that Nkomo and his ZAPU organization had expected to be in power at independence. They had a central committee and an army ready to govern the whole country, not just part of it in the context of local government. Therefore, not until ZAPU is convinced its goal of winning national power is futile can we expect its leading politicians to take a personal interest in local government.

Structures gain salience when perceptions of their importance crystallize at the local and regional level. To this end, elective governorships would be enhanced in being perceived as powerful and, therefore, attractive to politicians now so focused only on power at the national level. Directly elected mayorships could also be similarly affected.

Political culture is, however, a significant and important variable in Zimbabwe's search for a stable democracy. Zimbabwe's political culture is a product of several factors that weigh differently in influencing political attitudes for or against the politics of contestation. Traditional political attitudes and norms tend to be supportive of one-man and, therefore, one-party state tendencies in politics.[61] This is likely to be stronger in the more rural than urban areas where, prior to colonial rule, no organized political parties existed, and there was only one leader (the traditional chief or monarch). People knew the next chief would come from the royalty, and any competition was therein confined. A sitting or aspiring chief did not go around campaigning among his subjects every five years. Political parties as legitimate means of contesting for power are relatively new in Zimbabwe—only twenty-five years old. Further, they developed under circumstances of white settler rule, which normally would manipulate any otherwise legitimate differences between nationalist leaders and parties. Hence, the various factions and personalities often suspected and denounced each other as enemy agents. Moreover, each believed in the correctness of their approach to decolonization, finding the other's deviation unacceptable.

Colonial authoritarianism itself left an oppressive inheritance that it would be a mistake to downplay. Ninety years of colonial rule must leave a type of mental outlook and political style on the colonized. Common sense should prevent us from expecting Zimbabwe to have rid itself of the psychological burden of a century in only five years. In particular, the intolerance manifested by white settler governments of (black) opposition mobilization, as well as the inclination to repress rather than negotiate, have left their mark on the contemporary political culture. And, as noted earlier, instruments of control and coercion, including some of the institutions, laws, and personnel, were inherited and maintained.

The liberation struggle also left a significant mark on Zimbabwe's political culture. The commandist nature of mobilization and politicization under clandestine circumstances gave rise to the politics of intimidation and fear. Opponents were viewed in warlike terms, as enemies and, therefore, illegitimate. The culture from the liberation struggle was intolerant and violent. Enemies were to be killed; hence, in 1985, a caricature of Nkomo was put in a coffin to the delight of crowds who were quite unaware that tomorrow it could be a party colleague who has a different point of view.

Another factor with impact on the political values of Zimbabwe is the climate of international ideological discourse. The Zimbabwean political elite and cadre consumed a large dose of Marxist-Leninist and Maoist thought during the liberation struggle, particularly in the 1970s. Thus, ideas of the Marxist-Leninist one-party state after independence do not come by accident and without reflection. In addition, the African environments in which the liberation movements were based during exile—mainly Zambia, Tanzania, and Mozambique—were themselves one-party states with variations of socialism, Marxism, and Leninisn. This environment had an impact on the emergent Zimbabwe leadership. Moreover, Marxist-Leninist regimes elsewhere have tended to emphasize political conformity rather than diversity.

Religion is another factor affecting Zimbabwe's culture. Zimbabwe is multireligious and multidenominational. Probably, 60 percent of Zimbabwe's population is traditional in its religious outlook. However, the political elite has been exposed to Christianity. For instance, Sithole and Muzorewa were ordained ministers; Nkomo is a lay preacher; and Mugabe is a practicing Catholic. Despite these differences, Zimbabwe is one of the most religiously tolerant societies. In fact, there has never been a reported case of interreligious fighting. Cooperation between church groups of different denominations has been quite high, notwithstanding the fact that Christianity, like political parties, came in the colonial package. This suggests that the lack of interparty tolerance may have very little to do with the novelty of political parties among Africans. Rather, it is rooted in the perception of politics as a zero-sum game.

Most of these factors—the lack of experience with party politics, the authoritarian colonial legacy, the nature and exigencies of the liberation struggle, the climate of ideological discourse, and, not least, the depth and long history of ethnic divisions—have produced a cultural tendency to view politics as a "do-or-die" struggle, a zero-sum game.

The perception of politics as a zero-sum game is not without limits. After Mugabe had won in 1980, he did offer Nkomo the presidency; when that was declined, he nonetheless included Nkomo and other ZAPU leaders in the first cabinet. Similarly, in 1979, Muzorewa invited Sithole to name four persons for cabinet posts as was then required by the Zimbabwe-Rhodesia constitution. Yet, in both instances, as we have seen, there was a tendency for the main opposition not to cooperate fully with an inclusive approach. It is doubtful whether ZANU(PF) would have cooperated fully had it lost the election to either ZAPU or to some coalition. In fact, given that its guerrilla force controlled a good three-quarters of the countryside, it is reasonable to predict that all hell would have broken out. This tendency thus supports the thesis that, when politicians do not play according to the rules, democracy is greatly compromised.

• FUTURE PROSPECTS •

In conclusion, let us consider future prospects for democracy in Zimbabwe. In the foregoing discussion we have shown how the Rhodesian state practiced democratic decisionmaking within the white community, and argued that such consultation narrowed the perceptual gap between the white elite and their followers, to the effect that they maintained goal consensus and unity until the day of African majority rule. But, because the bulk of the African people were governed without their consent, the legitimacy of the white settler state was challenged, and it was eventually overthrown in hopes of an inclusive and more stable democracy. To be underscored here is the fact that goal consensus between leaders and followers facilitates the stability of regimes. Such consensus on values derives from honest consultation with the people at all levels. As such democracy facilitates rather than undermines the stability of regimes.

Perhaps the most important development in postcolonial Zimbabwe politics has been the continued antagonistic relations between ZANU and ZAPU. Because of this, the new democracy in Zimbabwe remains unstable. In a continuing search for stability, the new leaders have actively advocated a one-party state. To that end, unity talks have been held on and off between ZANU and ZAPU since 1983; the latest in early 1986. Should they succeed, one mammoth party is the likely outcome. Thus, looked at through these events, Zimbabwe's days as a multiparty democracy are narrowly numbered. This, however, need not be the only scenario.

Unity between ZANU(PF) and PF(ZAPU) is an imperative that most people in Zimbabwe welcome. As has been shown, the ZANU-ZAPU division has been the most serious and persistent in the nationalist movement. However, unity between these two parties need not lead to the one-party state. Instead of a *de jure* one-party state, Zimbabwe could have a *de facto* one-party-dominant state as in Botswana or Senegal. In such a system, opposition parties would be free to organize, criticize, and compete for power, even though the breadth of the ruling party's base would assure its electoral dominance.

There are several factors that favor democracy in contemporary Zimbabwe. Ironically, one is the multiethnic nature of its society. Considered in subethnic terms, there are two ethnic groups in Zimbabwe large enough to combine into a majority. There would have to be at least three groups in combination to form a political majority. An awareness of this reality would foster intergroup tolerance as each major group realizes that, by itself, it cannot form a majority. Even in a one-party-dominant context, this multiethnic reality would provide some basis of pluralism, and could enhance tolerance and, therefore, democratic tendencies.

Second, Zimbabwe came to independence six years ago with a fairly sophisticated intelligentsia well aware of the paucity of miracles of the one-party state elsewhere in Africa. Thus, the one-party state is less likely to be accepted with the previous enthusiasm. Moreover, the expanding literacy level is likely to enhance a questioning outlook in the mass public. Under the circumstances, and in the long run, an imposed one-party state is not likely to receive the good will of the intelligentsia, and could survive on fear only temporarily.

Third, the experiences of one-party regimes in the region, as elsewhere in Africa, has put the local political leadership under intellectual strain to advance a coherent argument for this anachronism. The one-party state is no longer as popular an idea today in Africa as it was in the initial period after independence. It has not lived up to its promise of unity, stability, economic equality, and development. Moreover, the seeming move away from the one-man syndrome in Africa—if Senegal and Tanzania are any cases to go by—would suggest that the one-man/one-party tendency may no longer be as popular. Abandoning power might become the more fashionable thing to do. Those willing to relinquish power have no stake in perpetuating the one-party anachronism.

Fourth, leadership is often a critical factor in the genesis of one-party regimes in Africa and elsewhere. Zimbabwe's luck, at least for the time being, is that Prime Minister Mugabe himself shares democratic values and is often acknowledged to be a consultative leader. This characteristic in Mugabe is not new. During the struggle, he was acknowledged as being democratic to the point of weakness. Yet, the manner in which he has consolidated power and steered a precarious state since independence would suggest that the "to the point of weakness" image might have been more circumstantial than substantial. Mugabe has, thus far, been successful in observing key social forces and social-psychological trends and has been fairly good in his choice of action and the timing of it. But there is often the danger that popularity and success in politics can lead to a false confidence, which invariably blinds the good and the well-intentioned. An uncritical commitment to the one-party idea, at this hour in Africa's postcolonial history, would be an error. But, to the extent that the issue of a one-party state and the form it takes is still under open debate in Zimbabwe, it is an error that the ZANU(PF) leadership has not finally committed. And, most important, it is an error that there is no need to make.

Fifth, a continued embourgeoisement of the political class bodes well for the emergence of politicians of independent means; they will be consulted by the leader more on a give-and-take basis, whether in the context of achieving national unity and stability or in maintaining unity within the party itself. This is healthy because it facilitates collective leadership. Also in this group should be included personalities outside the party with independent means and religious leaders who periodically voice a constructive opinion, even in criticism. Moreover, a sustained growth of the middle class increases the number of those with a stake in maintaining stability and democratic values. The expansion of the bureaucracy (bureaucratic bourgeoisie) since independence, and the concomitant Africanization of the private sector, favors the continued growth of the middle class in Zimbabwe.

Sixth, Zimbabwe's nonaligned pluralist approach to relations with other countries, particularly the assortment of countries with which economic, cultural and political relations have been established, has increased pragmatism at the expense of dogma. To the extent that such diversity includes countries committed to democratic values, it reinforces Zimbabwe's own commitment to democracy. This should be encouraged.

Seventh, political tolerance, and therefore democracy, tend to be associated with levels of literacy. Zimbabwe's level of literacy has jumped by leaps and bounds from 25 percent at independence in 1980 to 64 percent in 1985, only five years after independence. This is good for democracy in Zimbabwe. However, here a question is often asked: "Will the government have employment for its thousands of school-leavers every year? Would this not lead to revolutionary pressures and, therefore, to authoritarian responses?" This unfeeling question can be taken to suggest that the masses should remain ignorant. Yet, it is when people are educated and enlightened that they can deal more effectively with both their personal problems and those of the nation. In the long run, democracy is more secure in the hands of people sophisticated enough to know how and why it works.

Finally, let us consider ways of enhancing democracy in Zimbabwe. We have argued that there exists in Zimbabwe a political culture that, because of colonial authoritarianism and circumstances of prosecuting the liberation struggle, tends to be "commandist" and politically intolerant. But, since this political culture was "learned," it can be "unlearned," over time, through efforts by government and other agencies deemphasizing the "commandist" and "subject" political orientations that colonial authoritarianism and the liberation struggle left in Zimbabwe's political culture. A more tolerant "civic" culture, respectful of both legitimate authority and the civil rights of citizens (including minorities), could be inculcated through the school system and other agencies of political socialization such as the family, churches, trade unions, and, indeed, the political parties themselves (both ruling and opposition).

Further, the international community can assist in Zimbabwe's democratic evolution. The international community matters for Zimbabwe as it does for other Third World countries. Both government and those who oppose it read international attitudes and signals, and often count on them. With regard to Zimbabwe, those in the international community (the United States and Britain in particular), who have favored multiparty democracy have tended to be more concerned about the ruling party's pro-one-party state pronouncements than about the illegitimate methods of the opposition, which are clearly outside the Lancaster House constitution they helped to formulate. When the makers of the rules do not disdain those who violate them, they only encourage the culprits to play outside the rules even more. A clear stance by international actors in favor of constitutional government and electoral democracy would, therefore, dispel possible misperceptions. Also in this vein, the escalating civil war in Mozambique has serious implications for democracy in Zimbabwe. There is the real danger that conflict could lead to the introduction of a state of emergency the areas on Mozambique's border. The international community could intervene positively to end that conflict before the arena of democracy in Zimbabwe shrinks further on account of that conflict.

But, more than anything else, the dissident element mentioned earlier militates against democratic prospects in Zimbabwe. In the face of violent dissident activities challenging the authority of a democratically elected government, frustration affects decisionmakers who, in search of possible solutions, are tempted to try the one-party formula. In this way, illegitimate or disloyal opposition tactics often contribute to one-party ideas within ruling circles. The opposition often exaggerates its claim to a share of power, the oppressive activities of the regime in power, and its own superior ability to bring manna from heaven once in power. In Zimbabwe, it is rare to hear the opposition praising anything government does.[62] In its bid to gain power, the opposition in Africa has often overlooked constitutional provisions and tried shortcuts, which turned out to bring very long terms in jail or exile. At worst, they have brought unending civil strife to society.

Authority in the new nations is often nervous. Hence, it tends to be intolerant and perceives deviations as threatening the very survival of the regime. The opposition must appreciate this nervous state of the new rulers. Thus, if the opposition were more constructive in its criticism and more responsible in its posture, it could help to build a climate of mutual trust and tolerance between the parties, which would enhance the prospects for democracy. Most of all, it is imperative that the opposition reject any actions or strategies disloyal to the democratic constitution.

Furthermore, opposition parties have had a propensity for flirting with foreign opponents of the state, and the latter, being precarious, has been extremely sensitive and quick to respond. Moreover, the opposition has often lacked tact in its conduct of relations with the enemies of the state. For instance, in Zimbabwe, one opposition leader, when questioned by state security officials about what he had been doing in South Africa, is said to have replied that it was none of the state's business since, as a Zimbabwe citizen, he was free to go anywhere and to see anyone.[63] Such an insouciant attitude invites authoritarian responses.

The future of democracy in Zimbabwe must lie, in large part, in the resolution of the conflict in Matebeleland. It has been argued in the foregoing pages that a showdown between ZANU and ZAPU had to occur sooner or later, (a) to test the theory that ZANU was an unstable party fraught with factional infighting, and therefore could be toppled, and (b) to test Mugabe's and ZANU's capacity and will to rule. All of this was to test an old hypothesis between the Ndebele and Shona. It is the impression of this author that both tests have been passed. Misconceptions and misperceptions between ZAPU and ZANU had to be settled sooner or later. They had to scale each other in a match of sorts. Two matches have occurred electorally. A military match was, perhaps, also necessary to scale things once and for all—and better sooner than later.

With the resolution of the conflict in Matebeleland, however, a *de jure* one-party state seems neither necessary nor obligatory. If the people in Matebeleland want their own party they should have it, but society obligates them to operate within the law. ZAPU's attitude to constitutional and electoral democracy will help, to a great extent, in deciding where Zimbabwe goes from here. My observation is that the Zimbabwe leadership is committed to observing the rules of the game. I have tried to show how, in fact, it has tried to do so. Hence, once the opposition has reconciled itself to accepting and actually playing according to the rules of the game, Zimbabwe—the whole of it—will be a much freer society.

Still, the ZANU leadership has the ultimate responsibility for steering the young nation along a democratic path. To this end, it should resist the temptation to wield more power than is necessary to run the country. There are a number of instances in the Zimbabwe party and political system where improvements could be made to enhance democracy. Clearly, the selection of district administrators and provincial governors are two such instances. The election of provincial governors would make them accountable to the local provincial electorate. Governors could then appoint district administrators. Such devolution of power would expand the arena of politics, thereby reducing the present fixation with politics at the national level.

Also, in the event of Zimbabwe becoming a one-party state, there is need for institutionalizing democratic mechanisms in the one party. In 1984, ZANU(PF) adopted, for the first time, a Politburo in its structure. The Politburo is the organ that wields any substance of collective power in the party, and can take decisions and make policy on behalf of the party and its Central Committee. It is, however, appointed by the first secretary of the party with advice by the second secretary. Its selection from and by the Central Committee could give it broader accountability.

There is no doubt, even among many in the opposition in Zimbabwe politics, that Prime Minister Mugabe's leadership of both his party and the country has been exercised with outstanding skill. But herein lies the danger. What happens when someone else who is less able and democratically committed inherits strong and powerful institutions that could be easily abused? The concern, therefore, should be with constructing institutions in such a way that they cannot be readily abused.

Most important, the ZANU leadership must accept the task of including all major sectors of society in all important structures of power. In doing this, it may be obligated to include the opposition (ZAPU) in structures of power, whatever the difficulties of the past, because ZAPU represents an important and visible constituency. After all, national unity and consensus must ultimately come from a feeling of belonging. The opposition must be made to feel it belongs. To this end, Dunduza Chisiza's diagnostic prescription made a quarter of a century ago is instructive:

> The main explanation for the friction hinges on the sharing of gratitude and prestige. Before independence, foreign rulers occupy the topmost rungs of the social ladder. With the coming of independence, however, they step down and leaders of parties which have triumphed at the polls step up to fill the vacant rungs, thereby becoming the recipients of gratitude and admiration from their fellow-countrymen for having liberated their countries. Leaders of the opposition parties who may have fought for independence just as valiantly as anyone else find themselves the recipients of practically nothing. Herein lies the rub. It is only human for these people to feel that they have been given a raw deal.[64]

This is to underscore that democratic politics cannot be a zero-sum game and be stable. But, while the opposition must be given a stake in the system, the new rulers must equally be given assurance of the loyalty of the opposition. Precisely because the new rulers are new and the system is not secure, this assurance is most important in the early years of the regime. If neither side will see the necessity of playing its part, then, in the phrase of the Ghanaian writer Ayi Kwei Armah, "the beautiful ones are not yet born."[65] There is need for both the rulers and the opposition in Africa to recast and reorient their thinking regarding relations between them. Otherwise prospects for democracy on the continent are remote indeed.

• NOTES •

1. This distinction is suggested by C. B. MacPherson in his book, *The Real World of Democracy* (London: Oxford University Press, 1966).

2. White settlers never, in fact, intended that Africans should be trained for eventual takeover. Such, however, remained the British policy over which disagreement with the settlers widened in the 1960s onward.

3. Larry Bowman, *Politics in Rhodesia: White Power in an African State* (Cambridge, Mass.: Harvard University Press, 1973).

4. Ibid., p. 3.

5. Reported in the *Rhodesia Herald* (Salisbury), 22 September 1964.

6. Reports on Rhodesia by Amnesty International and the Zimbabwe-based Catholic Commission for Peace and Justice document many of the arrests, detentions, and deportations during this period.

7. These inflammatory statements became part of the political vocabulary of the UDI period in the 1960s and 1970s. See the *Herald* (Salisbury), 11 May 1964, also 6 June.

8. Marshall W. Murphree, et al, *Education, Race and Employment in Rhodesia* (Salisbury: ARTCA Publications, 1975), p. 30.

9. M. Fortes and Edward E. Evans-Pritchard, eds., *African Political Systems* (Oxford: University Press, 1940).

10. Marshall W. Murphree, *Education, Race and Employment*, p. 32.

11. For a discussion of the early African National Congress up to 1959, see Tapera O. Chirau, *The African National Congress of Zimbabwe* (Ann Arbor: University Microfilms International, 1986).

12. From an article "Tribalism on Trial" in the *Sunday Mail* (Salisbury) 10 June 1979, p. 13.

13. For a discussion of the development of the Zimbabwe Nationalist movement, see Wellington Nyangoni, *Zimbabwe African Nationalism* (Washington, D. C.: University Press of America, 1978).

14. For a detailed discussion of the ZANU-ZAPU split, see Nathan Shamuyarira, *Crisis in Rhodesia* (London: Andre Deutsch, 1965), pp. 173–193; and M. Sithole, *Zimbabwe: Struggles Within the Struggle* (Salisbury: Rujeko Publishers, 1979), pp. 27–46, especially the document by Ndabaningi Sithole quoted on pp. 31–34.

15. For an account of the formation of the African National Council, see Abel Muzorewa, *Rise Up and Walk* (Nashville: Abington Press, 1979), p. 94; and Joshua Nkomo, *Nkomo: The Story of My Life* (London: The Chaucer Press, 1984), p. 141.

16. Most literature on the Zimbabwe liberation movement on this period will more likely than not cite such exchanges. See the chapter, "Contradictions in FROLIZI" in M. Sithole, *Zimbabwe Struggles*, pp. 88–97.

17. Ibid., pp. 67–87.

18. See the account in *Nkomo: The Story of My Life*, p. 20.

19. For about a year (March 1979 to February 1980), Zimbabwe was known as "Zimbabwe-Rhodesia," a frivolous compromise name agreed to between the RF government, which preferred the name Rhodesia, and the internally based nationalist leaders who preferred the name Zimbabwe.

20. It was at the Geneva Conference that Smith noticed the extent and magnitude of the factionalization in the nationalist movement and the forces behind them and decided to exploit the situation. He had this in mind when he finally decided to be arrogant and intransigent in his attitude to the talks. He, in fact, promptly left the talks for Rhodesia because "I have a country to run."

21. The "March 3rd Agreement" is the subject of a publication by Ndabaningi Sithole; *In Defense of the March 3rd Agreement* (Salisbury: Graham Publishing Co., 1979). It is articulate but unconvincing.

22. There were in all ten "observer groups" to the 1979 Zimbabwe-Rhodesia election. These were from: The United Kingdom, United States, West Germany, Canada, South Africa, Mauritius, France, Belgium, Australia, and the European Parliament. See *Report of the Australian Parliamentary Observer Group on the Zimbabwe-Rhodesia Common Roll Elections* (May 1979)

23. Ibbo Mandaza, *The Zimbabwe Public Service* (Paper presented at the United Nations Inter-Regional Seminar on Reforming Civil Service Systems for Development, Beijing: 14–24 August 1985), p. 24. (unpublished)

24. Every other party seemed to gang up against ZANU(PF). Some were even speculating on an arithmetic that would deprive ZANU (PF) of victory. See Martin Gregory, "Zimbabwe 1980: Politicization through Armed Struggle and Electoral Mobilization," in *Journal of Commonwealth and Comparative Politics*, 19, no. 1 (March 1981): p. 68, where he quotes some estimates of the Rhodesian Ministry of Home Affairs as "Muzorewa 43 seats, Mugabe 26, and Nkomo 20." Exact on Nkomo, totally off on the rest.

25. One of these incidents took place in the province of Masvingo when Mugabe was on a campaign tour of the area. See the *Herald*, 10 February 1980.

26. Eddison Zvobgo, Director of the 1980 ZANU (PF) campaign, was fond of making such comments at meetings with the Election Directorate where officials of other parties lodged complaints. The author attended the meetings.

27. For a detailed and candid account of the various procedures and problems encountered in administering this election, see the registrar-general's 1985 *General Election Report* (Harare), 13 September 1985.

28. In an interview following announcement of the results, Nkomo said that, "ZANU (PF) rule over the last five years has divided the country into tribal and racial groups. This is a tragedy that has never happened before," *Sunday Mail*, 7 July 1985. This, however, does not deny that the elections themselves were "free and fair." Moreover, "tribal and racial groups" predate ZANU (PF) rule.

29. Interview by author on 4 November 1985.

30. Registrar-general's *Report*, p. 22.

31. Bowman, *Politics in Rhodesia*, p. 18.

32. For an elaborate discussion of these factors, see Jeff Davidow, *A Peace in Southern Africa: The Lancaster House Conference on Rhodesia* (Boulder, Colo.: Westview Press, 1984).

33. At the 1964 First ZANU Congress held in the Midlands city of Gweru (only thirty miles from Ian Smith's farm), Robert Mugabe, then secretary-general of the party, warned that, if our freedom should depend on someone's lifetime, it may be necessary to eliminate that person so that we can be free soon. He was later convicted under the country's "Law and Order Maintenance Act" for making this statement. (I attended the 1964 ZANU congress and followed the subsequent trial).

34. Bowman, *Politics in Rhodesia*, p. 35.

35. Ibid., p. 43.

36. This is the suggestion made by David Martin and Phyllis Johnson in their "unconvincing" book, *The Chitepo Assassination* (Harare: Zimbabwe Publishing House, 1985). See my review of this book in *Journal of Modern African Studies* 24, no. 1 (1986).

37. For such neo-Marxist interpretations, see John Saul, "Zimbabwe: The Next Round," *Monthly Review* (September 1980): pp. 34–35. Also, Owen Tshabangu, *The March 11 Movement in ZAPU: Revolution Within the Revolution for Zimbabwe* (York: Tiger Paper Publications, 1979). Also, Giovanni Arrighi, "Black and White Populism in Rhodesia," unpublished but quoted in John Saul, ed., *The State and Revolution in East Africa* (London: Heinemann, 1979), p. 112.

38. See Masipula Sithole, "Focus On: Class and Factionalism in the Zimbabwe Nationalist Movement," *African Studies Review* 27, no. 1 (March 1984), for a critique of vulgar use of class analysis and romantic view of the proletariat.

39. See M. Sithole, *Zimbabwe Struggles*. Also his "Ethnicity and Factionalism in the Zimbabwe Nationalist Movement 1957–79," in *Ethnic and Racial Studies* 3, no. 1 (January 1980).

40. See the *Herald*, 21 June 1979.

41. A good discussion of the "goings-on" inside the liberation movement is in David Martin and Phyllis Johnson, *The Struggle for Zimbabwe* (Harare: Zimbabwe Publishing House, 1981). See, in particular, chaps. 11–14.

42. Nkomo, *The Story of My Life*, p. 200.

43. David Martin and Phyllis Johnson, *The Struggle for Zimbabwe*, pp. 328–329.

44. Ali Mazrui, speech at the *African Studies Association Annual Conference*, Chicago, Palmer House Hotel, 1974.

45. See his well-documented article, "In Search of Regime Security: Zimbabwe Since Independence," in the *Journal of Modern African Studies* 22, no. 4 (December 1984): pp. 529–558.

46. See "Amnesty International Report," 1985, pp. 115–119.

47. There are two jokes (but with serious implications) about the definition of a dissident in Zimbabwean political humor. The one says, "A dissident is a Ndebele," the other that "a dissident is a person who takes up arms against the state when he has lost an election." The one is tribalistic, while the other suggests strong disapproval.

48. The evidence is from a preelection survey conducted by the author in 1985.

49. However, satisfaction was more pronounced in rural than urban areas.

50. In this respect, both ZANU and ZAPU publish their own party publications, *ZANU News* and *Zimbabwe Review*, respectively. To date, there is no indexed political publication in Zimbabwe.

51. See the article, "Zimbabwe Newspapers: A Unique Experiment," by Colm Foy, in *Africasia* no. 32, 1986. Foy says that Zimbabwe's "new system of press ownership and operation distinguishes the country's newspapers from most others in the Third World."

52. See *Zimbabwe: Parliamentary Debates* (Harare: Government Printers), vol. 12, nos. 44 and 45, 9 and 10 April 1986, respectively.

53. In a brilliant analysis, "Farmer Organizations and Food Production in Zimbabwe," *World Development* 14, no. 3 (1986), pp. 367–384, Michael Bratton shows how small farmer groups improve access to household assets and argues that centralized statist policies often lead to conflict with local communities.

54. An election post-mortem in the ZANU (PF) journal, *Zimbabwe News* (September 1985), would suggest such awareness and preoccupation.

55. In this regard, it is commonly held that Joshua Nkomo, as a personality, has had phenomenal impact on the Ndebele and is almost irreplaceable as their leader.

56. Quoted in W. Walker, *The Bear at the Back Door: The Soviet Threat to the West's Lifeline in Africa* (London: Foreign Affairs Publishing Company, 1978), p. 38.

57. For an informed discussion of the status and role of the Zimbabwe Judiciary since independence, see Richard Sklar, "Reds and Rights: Zimbabwe's Experiment," *Issues: A Journal of Africanist Opinion* 14 (1985): pp. 29–31. In a conversation with the author on 14 November 1985, Zimbabwe's Chief Justice Enoc Dumbuchena categorically stated that government had never brought any undue pressure on him or the justice system as such. "No; never; not once," he said, and agreed to be quoted.

58. In 1986, Dr. Herbert Ushewokunze, ZANU (PF) secretary for the commissariat, member of the Politburo, and also minister of transport, was the object of severe scrutiny by the Public Accounts Committee. The prime minister did not interfere even when the whole affair appeared embarassing to both his government and party.

59. Mugabe has seven university degrees (not counting honorary) most of which he earned by private study during his ten years of detention. In 1985, he received the MSC in Economics from the University of London.

60. Raymond D. Gastil, *Freedom in the World: Rights and Civil Liberties, 1985–1986*, (New York: Greenwood Press, 1986), pp. 399–400.

61. For a discussion of the one-man tendency in Zimbabwe politics, see Masipula Sithole, "Unreal Opposition," in the *Herald* (Harare), 5 December 1983.

62. I once confronted a leader of one of Zimbabwe's opposition parties with the question: "You have never said anything good about Mugabe or the ruling party. Could it be that there is really nothing good in what they say or do? Are the millions who have voted for them that blind? His reply was quite interesting: "The problem with you academics," he said, "is that you see both sides. In politics there is only one side, your side." On reflection he was right. I have never heard leaders of the ruling party say anything complimentary about the opposition.

63. This insoucient attitude earned Bishop Muzorewa several months in detention.

64. Dunduza K. Chisiza, *Africa: What Lies Ahead* (New Delhi: Indiana Council for Africa), 1961, p. 2.

65. Ayi Kwei Armah's book is in fact titled, *The Beautiful Ones Are Not Yet Born* (Boston: Houghton Mifflin), 1968.

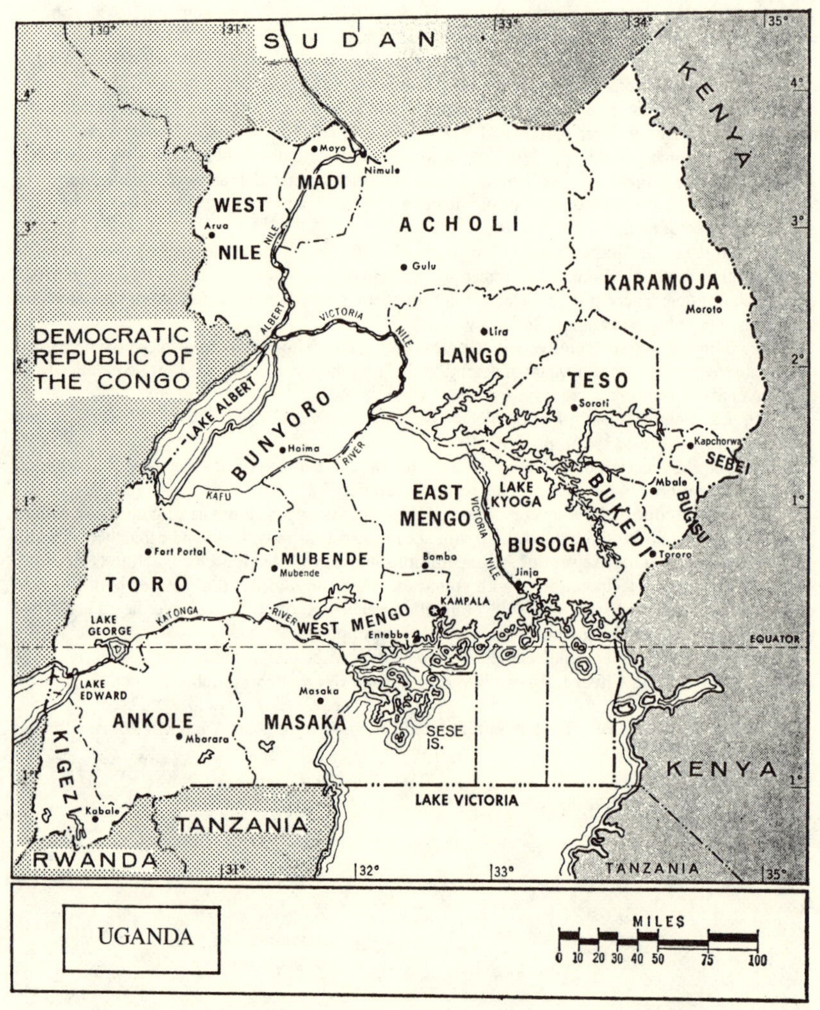

SUDAN
KENYA
DEMOCRATIC REPUBLIC OF THE CONGO
WEST NILE
Arua
MADI
Moyo
Nimule
ACHOLI
Gulu
KARAMOJA
Moroto
LANGO
Lira
TESO
Soroti
Kapchorwa
SEBEI
Mbale
BUGISU
BUKEDI
Tororo
LAKE ALBERT
ALBERT NILE
VICTORIA NILE
BUNYORO
Hoima
KAFU RIVER
LAKE KYOGA
EAST MENGO
Bombo
BUSOGA
Jinja
MUBENDE
Mubende
Fort Portal
TORO
LAKE GEORGE
KATONGA RIVER
WEST MENGO
KAMPALA
Entebbe
EQUATOR
LAKE EDWARD
ANKOLE
Mbarara
MASAKA
Masaka
SESE IS.
KIGEZI
Kabale
LAKE VICTORIA
TANZANIA
RWANDA
UGANDA
MILES
0 10 20 30 40 50 75 100

• CHAPTER SEVEN •

Uganda: The Dual Polity and the Plural Society

OMARI H. KOKOLE AND ALI A. MAZRUI

Ethnically, Uganda is a plural society and will remain so for the foreseeable future. However, since its independence from Britain on 9 October 1962, Uganda has also been a dual polity—divided between a Northern and a Southern power base. The struggle to evolve a democratic system in Uganda has been caught between the resilient forces of ethnic pluralism, on one side, and the more transient forces of functional dualism on the other.

• HISTORICAL REVIEW AND ANALYSIS •

The Plural Society

What does dual polity and functional dualism mean? There were two bases of state power on attainment of independence—economic and military. British colonial policies had resulted in a situation in which economic power and prosperity in Uganda were concentrated in the south of the country; while military power lay in northern hands. The bulk of the cash crops for export (coffee, cotton, tea, tobacco, and, for a while, sugar), and the bulk of the food of the country were grown in what were regarded as southern districts of Uganda, where rainfall is greatest (especially in the areas surrounding Lake Victoria and on the mountains). The first cash crop to be introduced was cotton, which remained concentrated in Buganda for a long time. In the case of coffee growth, it was in the hands of white farmers until the 1920s when the Baganda became the first group of Ugandans to get involved. The copper industry while it held sway was also part of the southern economy of the country.[1]

On the other hand, the army that British colonial rule had created was recruited overwhelmingly from northern ethnic groups—the Acholi, Langi, and Itesot, and the assorted tribes of the west Nile district in the northwest. A number of reasons were behind this northern bias in the British policy of military enlistment. Southern groups like the Baganda and Banyoro were already politically more threatening to the colonial order because of their larger size and superior organization. The British found it prudent to keep southerners demilitarized. Thus, the 1900 Uganda Agreement concluded between Buganda and Britain restricted the number and types of arms that the king of Buganda could keep or acquire. Paradoxically, the British found northerners better "warriors" and regarded their "tribes" as culturally "martial." The British tendency to recruit northerners into the army was reinforced by their belief that taller men made better soldiers.

The population of northern Uganda is only a fraction of the population of the Bantu "tribes" of the south. Table 7.1, presenting census figures by tribe for 1959, shows the Bantu districts to account for about two-thirds of Uganda's total population.[2] More recent figures indicate an even larger Bantu majority. According to the last official census taken in 1980, the population of Uganda was 12,636,179, with the population of the predominantly Bantu regions (East, West, and Central) between 3.2 million to 3.5 million each—roughly 80 percent of the total population. In other words, the south had in all approximately 10.2 million people. On the other hand, the north had a much smaller population of 2.4 million, or 18.6 percent of the national total, (see Table 7.1).[3]

Northern groups are preponderantly "Nilotic" and primarily belong to the Nilotic and Sudanic families of "tribes." Southern groups, by contrast, mainly belong to the Bantu family of ethnic groups. Northern groups speak different languages, have different cultures, and, to some extent, even look different. (Northerners tend to be not only taller, but also blacker in pigmentation than southerners.) These ethnic differences have, in the last two decades, reinforced the tensions of the functional divide between north and south.

After independence, this northern predominance in the Ugandan army was, for a while, deepened by two other factors. Ethnic nepotism in the armed forces led to discriminatory practices and further northern enlistment in the army. Northerners were naturally tempted to recruit fellow northerners as the post-colonial army expanded. In any case, more northerners than southerners wanted to join the army precisely because northern districts were poorer. Southern Ugandans generally enjoyed greater economic opportunities than northerners. British colonial policies had left northern Uganda, "very much to its own devices so far as economic and social development was concerned."[4] Likewise, in transportation and communications terms, northern Uganda generally remained unintegrated with the rest of the country for a rather long time. The military profession was far less prestigious among southerners partly because of these economic reasons—but also because of the simple fact that the army was already northern-dominated.

How did this functional dualism, this division of power between northerners and southerners, relate to the ethnic pluralism? To some extent, ethnicity reinforced the functional dualism. Two plural societies have faced each other within the borders of a dual polity—an ethnically plural north that, for twenty years, monopolized the "legitimate" use of physical force, and an ethnically plural south that economically is still the most productive part of the country.

Table 7.1 The Distribution of Tribes Among the Major Ethnic Groups of Uganda, 1959

Major Ethnic Groups of Uganda	Number	Percent of Total Ugandan Population
Bantu		
Baganda	1,004,878	16.60
Banyankole	519,283	8.30
Basoga	501,921	7.90
Bakiga	459,619	7.30
Banyarunda	378,656	6.00
Bagisu	329,257	5.20
Batoro	208,300	3.30
Banyoro	188,374	3.00
Barundi	138,749	2.20
Bagwere	111,681	1.80
Bakonjo	106,890	1.70
Banyole	92,642	1.50
Basamia	47,759	0.70
Bagwe	36,130	0.60
Baamba	34,506	0.50
Bakenyi	23,707	0.40
Batwa	2,592	0.04
	4,224,944	67.04
Nilotic		
Langi	363,807	5.80
Acholi	284,929	4.50
Alur	123,378	1.90
Badama	101,451	1.60
Jonam	27,422	0.40
	900,987	14.20
Sudanic		
Lugbara	236,270	3.80
Madi	80,355	1.30
Lendu	4,744	0.08
	321,369	5.18
Nilo-Hamitic		
Iteso	524,716	8.40
Karamojong	131,713	2.10
Kumam	61,459	1.00
Kakwa	37,628	0.60
Sebei	36,800	0.60
Pokot (suk)	21,850	0.40
Labwor	10,042	0.20
Tepeth	4,363	0.07
	828,571	13.37

Source: Adapted from A. G. Gingyere-Pinycwa, *Apolo Milton Obote and His Times* (New York and London: NOK Publishers, 1978), p. 18.

How have these divisions related to the tensions between democracy and stability in Uganda? There are two swords of Damocles hanging over prospects for democracy in Uganda—one is the pull toward anarchy in the plural society and the other is the pull toward tyranny as a result of the dual polity. In this chapter, anarchy refers to decentralized violence of neighbor against neighbor, unleashed by inadequate governmental control, and even a partial collapse of the moral order. Tyranny refers to centralized violence orchestrated by those in authority, partly in order to retain a monopoly of force in society. As a plural society, Uganda has had a strong tendency toward disintegration into anarchy. As a dual polity, Uganda has had a predilection for tyranny. Both tendencies have inevitably put enormous pressures on the third inclination in the country—the continuing quest for some degree of freedom for and popular participation by the people.

Cultural Traditions of the Plural Society

The cultural foundations of the democratic process in former colonies require either a preexisting indigenous democratic tradition, which possibly antedated the colonial order, or a deep level of Westernization that followed upon the colonial experience. India and Jamaica are examples of relative democratic stability, which has partly grown out of the deep Anglicization of the relevant elites. The period of colonial rule in Uganda was much shorter than that of either Jamaica or India. The level of the anglicization of the Ugandan elites cannot, therefore, be the same; nevertheless, some Westernization did, of course, occur in Uganda. First, concerning indigenous values, the north of the country has deeper democratic traditions than the south. On the other hand, strictly in terms of Westernization, the south is more deeply anglicized than the north. This raises the distinction between democratic instincts derived from ancestral values and democratic instincts introduced by Westernization and the colonial experience.

In what sense are northern ancestral traditions more compatible with democracy than southern ones? For one thing, southern societies before colonization were strong monarchies whereas northern ones were decentralized republics. The Baganda, for example, had evolved a highly complex monarchical system, operating on the basis of relatively centralized power. Other southern monarchies included Bunyoro, Ankole, and Toro. All four were not simply monarchies in dynastic terms, but imperial systems as well. Of these four, the Kingdom of Bunyoro is widely acknowledged to be the oldest and an ancestor to the other three.[5]

On the other hand, the Nilotic and Sudanic communities in the north were often virtually "tribes without rulers." Assuming, as classical U.S. liberalism asserts, "that government is best which governs least," the northern "tribes" of Uganda approximated that ideal the most closely. In their traditional systems, they had advisory elders rather than actual governors. Related to this quality is the traditional egalitarianism of the northern communities—as contrasted with the traditional hierarchy of Uganda's southern "tribes." The Baganda, Banyoro, Batoro, and Banyakole were almost feudal societies in their ancestral organization. Hierarchy was central to their sociopolitical systems.

Curiously enough, it was the monarchical tendency of the south that the British respected when they entered Uganda, rather than the decentralized republicanism of the north. For the British intruders, "tribes without rulers" were much harder to understand than the kings and emperors they encountered. Thus, the British enhanced the monarchical tradition in the south as a basis of sociopolitical cleavage in the new Uganda they created. Western anthropologists who divided African peoples and societies between "state" and "stateless" societies often betrayed their assumption that societies that had the elements for operating a state, especially monarchical institutions, approximate the "civilized" states of Europe. From this followed the conclusion that they had attained a higher level of social and cultural sophistication than others. One result in the case of Uganda was that people from the kingdoms considered themselves more civilized and superior to their other (nonmonarchical) compatriots. This tendency was reinforced by the special and privileged treatment the British extended to the kings and their kingdoms.

In short, the northern communities that produced the greatest violators of human rights and democratic principles in postcolonial Uganda—Milton Obote, Idi Amin, and Tito Okello—were ancestrally both more republican and more egalitarian than the southern groups. On the other hand, preeminent southern constitutional lawyers like Godfrey Binaisa, Uganda's president for a short term in 1979 and 1980, and outstanding southern defenders of human rights like George Kanyeihamba (briefly attorney-general in the same year) are descended from "tribes" that were traditionally monarchical, hierarchical, and sometimes even tyrannical. Both Binaisa and Kanyeihamba are highly Westernized voices in defense of liberal democracy in Uganda.

What factors in Uganda's colonial and postcolonial history resulted in the relative democratization of southern Ugandans, on one side, and the relative militarization of northerners on the other? What changes have occurred in Uganda in the 1980s in this configuration between the dual polity and the plural society? To these issues we now turn.

Toward Southern Democratization

Factors that have favored the liberal democratization of previously traditional monarchies in the south include higher levels of formal education, greater degree of urbanization, greater literacy in both English and indigenous languages, a larger southern bourgeoisie, higher per capita income, a relatively deeper level of cultural anglicization, and political consciousness of a numerical advantage over the north.

Precisely because Buganda was regarded as the most powerful traditional society in the area when Europeans first arrived, and because European penetration of Uganda made its entry through Buganda (where it paused to consolidate its dominance prior to extending farther), the kingdom received special attention from the new arrivals. Missionaries, as well as diplomats from Europe, paid homage at the court of the king of Buganda, the Kabaka. By 1900, the British had asserted political supremacy; the Uganda Agreement of that year established, to all intents and purposes, a British "protectorate" in Buganda—and, before long, the cultural anglicization of southern Uganda began.

In other parts of Africa, as well as elsewhere in sub-Saharan Africa, the missionaries—both Catholic and Protestant—were the vanguard of Western education in Uganda. Ugandans were taught to wear Western, read Western, speak Western, drill Western, and pray Western. But did they also teach them to *govern* Western? Initially, missionaries wanted to inculcate obedience to God and submission to colonial authority. Even missionaries from other parts of Europe rallied behind the British flag and promoted British education once the territory passed under "British jurisdiction." Did that education foster British constitutionalism?

Whatever the intentions of the colonial power, the Baganda especially quickly learned the techniques of using legal documents and procedures to enhance their interests. The Uganda Agreement, guaranteeing certain rights for Buganda in exchange for British "protection," created a kind of *treaty complex* in the political culture of Buganda. The identity of the region was supposed to have found legal expression and sanctity in that agreement. From this legal understanding with the British government emerged a tendency in Buganda whereby major tensions with the larger central government were somehow referred back to a preexisting fundamental law.

For as long as the British were there, the fundamental law invoked by Buganda was the "protectorate" agreement of 1900. But, in the first decade *after* independence, the fundamental law invoked by the Baganda shifted to the independence constitution of 1962 that launched the postcolonial era. Both these manifestations of the deep-seated treaty complex in Buganda's political maneuvers helped to give rise to, and later reinforced, the region's faith in litigation at large. As one commentator put it, the Baganda became "inveterately litigious."[6]

A related reinforcing agent in the colonial period was the whole ethos of British colonial administration and its commitment to formal procedures. Under the British, there was a kind of *administrative constitutionalism* that served and operated as the very foundation of colonial administration. Generally, the system had been increasingly characterized by a strong tendency toward formal accountability of the administrators. In Uganda, this had a strong legal bias, tending to justify actions by reference to the appropriate document. In previously nonliterate societies, the introduction of the written word by British created a whole new political culture. At the central administrative level, reference to ordinances was constant, at the provincial and district levels, reference was to formal rules and administrative procedures.

Clearly, such a procedural system was not unique to Uganda. The British used similar methods in most of colonial Africa. But, southern Uganda, the British colonial system interacted with other factors and, in later years, reinforced constitutionalist tendencies. The very existence in southern Uganda of British formal treaties with four Bantu kingdoms (Buganda, Bunyoro, Ankole, and Toro) created a predisposition to constrain the powers of the central government of the country as a whole.

Legalism is an important component of the liberal polity. Legalism was one of the factors that helped give Ugandan politics their strong constitutionalist tendency in the early years. In the south, the tendency was enhanced by a public that became increasingly politically sensitized. The Baganda especially have been among the most politically conscious of all Africans continentwide. Their politicization was also promoted by increasing literacy in the Luganda language, as well as in English; newspapers were started in southern Uganda both in English and in Luganda. There were no comparable trends in northern Uganda, nor was the level of literacy in the north in either English or the Nilo-Sudanic languages commensurate with that of the south.

Relevant, too, was the infinitely greater Bagandan participation in preindependence legislative politics. Thus, by 1956, when colonial authorities agreed to permit selective Black Ugandan participation in the Legislative Council, the governor announced that three indigenous Ugandan representatives would be chosen to represent Baganda, Western, and Eastern provinces. The Nilotic districts of the north were unrepresented.

Political consciousness in the south was also enhanced by the greater levels of urbanization. The presence of northerners in southern cities was itself a politicizing experience for the public in the south, as well as for those northern immigrants. Uganda's urban population percentage grew from 4.8 percent in 1969 to 8.7 percent in 1980.[7] Most of this growth was concentrated in southern cities, where northerners often came in search of jobs and other opportunities. The traffic in the reverse direction was virtually nonexistent. Kampala (the commercial, and also later political capital) together with Jinja (the industrial capital) were particularly strong magnets for northerners. Subsequent establishment of military units in those two cities—with soldiers recruited mainly from the North—deepened the processes of politicization among the masses of the south.

The expansion of the cash crop industries in the south and the expansion of trade and commerce resulted in a more rapid growth of the bourgeoisie in the southern parts of the country than in the north. To some extent, embourgeoisement expanded with the spread of a liberal ideology in southern circles. However, in the early years of Uganda's independence, southern liberalism was clearly selective. Southerners valued constitutional rights far more than individual rights. In Buganda especially, the social pressures for individual conformity were considerable. Opponents of the monarchical norm and other political heretics were often socially ostracized, even brutalized. And yet, paradoxically, Buganda remained a central element in the evolving constitutionalist style of politics. The whole tradition of readiness to challenge the central government when it appeared to act *ultra vires* owed its vigor to the militancy of Buganda. The Baganda became strong defenders of the doctrine of self-determination. But, they also fell short of championing the individual's right of dissent. The Baganda were eloquent defenders of the collective rights of the people—but were inadequately concerned about the individual's liberties. This was certainly true in the years before the death of their last king, Mutesa II, in 1969. The question now is whether Buganda, since Obote's abolition of monarchies in 1967 and the death of the last *kabaka* two years later, has become more consistently disposed toward the liberal preference.

There are signs—albeit still inconclusive—that the Baganda are beginning to restore the balance between the collective liberalism of self-determination and the liberalism of individual human rights. There are also tentative signs that similar liberalizing tendencies have been under way in the other former monarchies.

Toward the Militarization of the North

Some of the factors that contributed to the democratization of southern Uganda were precisely the same factors that had an impact on the north in the reverse direction. British infatuation with the monarchical societies in the south resulted in reduced resources for the development of the decentralized societies of the north. The rise of prestigious missionary and state schools in the south were sometimes at the expense of northern communities. The British argument that northern Uganda was not ready to utilize modern facilities and services compounded the general neglect and underdevelopment of the region. The majority of the infrastructure initiated by the colonial government and private Western organizations—including roads, factories, schools, and hospitals—were concentrated in Buganda.[8] All these factors together finally meant that northerners had fewer educational, economic, and professional opportunities than their southern compatriots. As indicated earlier, this tended to propel northerners into the Ugandan army and police because alternative opportunities were lacking.

In the colonial period, therefore, some of the northern societies naturally developed a special loyalty to the military profession; some even began to idealize it. British perceptions that northern "tribes" were "martial" were communicated to the northerners themselves, and helped to reinforce their self-perception as "brave warriors." The stage was set for a self-fulfilling prophecy—the militarization of the north.

While, traditionally, most northern societies had been relatively egalitarian and basically nonhierarchical, colonialism forced them to become part of a larger entity that encompassed monarchical and highly hierarchical societies to the south. Economic and educational changes during the colonial period awakened northerners to their own deepening marginalization in the new country called "Uganda." The very name of the country was southern-derived, taken from the Kingdom of Buganda, and the capital of the new country—Kampala—was in the heartland of the Baganda. Also, for a while, the British also used the Baganda as their own junior colonial administrators in other parts of the country.

Egalitarian northerners began to discover the indignities of being on the lower side of a new hierarchy. Particularly resented was the perceived "arrogance" of the Baganda. Evidently the Baganda and other southerners considered the northerners uncouth, unsophisticated, "naked," and more distant from Western civilization than the southerners.

The north acquired an inferiority complex that it had never had in the days before the creation of the new political entity of Uganda. This complex became the breeding ground of the inflated "machismo" of postcolonial northerners. Theirs was a level of cultural and gender assertiveness that was to attain exaggerated proportions under northerner Idi Amin, from 1971 to 1979.

Related to all these anomalies was the simple contradiction that the postcolonial state of Uganda was, for some time, ruled by people whose societies in the period before colonization were, in some cases, so decentralized as to be virtually stateless (like Obote's Langi, Amin's Kakwa, and Okello's Acholi). What happens when the legacy of statehood is under the control of the heritage of the stateless? Anarchy has competed with tyranny in the state of Uganda under the rule of both the stateless Langi (embodied in Obote) and the stateless Kakwa (embodied in Idi Amin).

Another contributory factor in the militarization and *authoritarianization* of the northern elite is their numerical insecurity. In a liberal democracy based on number of votes, northern ethnic votes (less than 20 percent of Uganda's total population) would be simply overwhelmed by southern ones. The only ways in which northern leadership could win against southern politicians has been *either* through popular ideology *or* outright military intimidation. Obote's "move to the left" in the First Republic of Uganda (1967–1971) was a northern attempt to create a *national* base through a popular ideology. On the other hand, Obote's style in his second political incarnation (1980–1985) resorted more to northern military intimidation of the south.

In his own quest for political support, Idi Amin (1971–1979) utilized the devices of both mass enthusiasm (like the expulsion of the Asians in 1972, and the recurrent humiliation of the whites who remained in the country) and sheer intimidation of political opponents and military dissidents. However, allegiance under Amin was divided between being pro- and anti-Amin rather than between north and south. In spite of being a northerner himself, Idi Amin when president, probably killed more fellow northerners than southerners. This was partly because the power rivalry within his administration was preponderantly among the contending factions of militarized northerners rather than between militarily powerful northerners and economically powerful southerners. At the same time, Idi Amin tried to redress the economic balance between north and south by expelling Asians—and giving northerners more economic opportunities to compete with indigenous southerners. Conceptually, the idea was a brilliant device for national integration. Unfortunately, Idi Amin lacked the sophistication to fulfill his own vision. On the contrary, his policies pushed Uganda even further toward the painful consequences of the two swords of anarchy and tyranny.

Also significant as a factor behind the militarization of northern Uganda were the neighbors across the colonial boundaries. Imperial policy had fragmented "tribes" and clans across two or more African countries. Southern Ugandan groups were divided by Uganda's boundaries with Kenya and Tanzania. Northern Ugandan groups were split by the frontiers with Sudan and Zaire. What is more, it was the borders in the north that were militarized. Tension and armed struggle in Sudan and Zaire sometimes spilled over into Uganda. The militarization of the Acholi and/or Langi in Uganda was not unrelated to the militarization of the Acholi and/or Langi in Sudan. Similarly, the militarization of the Kakwa of Uganda may not be unconnected with the military frustrations of the Kakwa of Zaire and Sudan.[9] Hence, northern Ugandans were harder to isolate from cross-border violence than southern Ugandans, who were not being militarized by their ethnic compatriots across the Kenyan and Tanzanian borders.

Postindependence Political Struggles

Although southern Uganda was not militarized before 1980, it had a past of *threatening* violence against the central government—a history stretching back to the colonial period. On the eve of independence, for example, the Baganda served notice on the British queen, providing a deadline for their secession from the rest of Uganda. Rather prudently, the British authorities simply ignored the ultimatum—and the deadline passed uneventfully.

On the other hand, the British did not have the political courage so late in the colonial period to force Buganda to return to Bunyoro two counties (Buyaga and Bugangazi) that Buganda had once annexed with British connivance. The threat of violence was recurrently made by Baganda spokesmen in an attempt to prevent the return of those counties to Bunyoro. At Uganda's constitutional conference of 1961, the two counties were temporarily transferred to the care of the central government, with the provision that a referendum be held no earlier than two years after independence.

Milton Obote decided to proceed with the referendum in November 1964 in spite of Baganda threats "to defend with their blood every inch of Buganda territory," including the counties in dispute. An overwhelming majority in the lost counties voted for their return to Bunyoro. The Baganda did not implement the threat of violent insubordination. Perhaps by *verbalizing* the society's latest violence, the Baganda postponed its real outbreak.

However, the question is whether Buganda's recurrent seditious statements and threats of violence, especially at a time when northerners controlled the central government, added to the sense of political insecurity among northerners. Was Buganda's volatile behavior itself a contributor to the increasing militarization of the north and deepening authoritarianism of northern rulers?

The ultimate crises in relations between Buganda and the northern rulers of Uganda occurred in 1966. Partly to save himself politically, Milton Obote first suspended the independence constitution of 1962 and then introduced a new constitution of his own. The 1966 crisis involved Idi Amin, then Obote's right-hand man in the Uganda. Amin had been involved in a scandal related to contraband in gold, ivory, and money across the border with Zaire. Amin's own integrity seemed to be intertwined with the political survival of Milton Obote, who was facing considerable opposition even within his own party early in 1966. Amin's apparent indiscretions (*golden* indiscretions) provided additional charges against the whole state machinery under Obote's leadership. The origins of tyranny in Uganda's postcolonial history have to be traced to that date.

Buganda's *treaty complex* was deeply outraged by Obote's trashing of the constitution. The Baganda regarded the independence constitution as a kind of social contract creating a new society (almost in the tradition of John Locke). Buganda's belief in self-determination—which had been temporarily abandoned over the lost counties—was now rekindled. In a social contract, the parties concerned surrendered some of their natural rights for the sake of joint agreement. That was what the independence constitution was all about. Among the "natural rights" of the Baganda was the very soil of their ancestors. On the basis of the national compact of 1962, Buganda had surrendered her rights to the city of Kampala to the new nation under the central government.

However, whenever a social contract of this kind is broken, all rights revert to their original holders. Given, then, that northerner Milton Obote had torn up the 1962 social contract and imposed a new constitution of his own, the soil of the ancestors of Buganda reverted to their descendants. The king of the Baganda, through the *lukiiko* (legislature), served notice on Obote's government to quit the premises—to leave "Buganda soil" by the end of May 1966.

Prime Minister Obote responded by declaring Buganda's ultimatum an act of high treason. On 24 May, 1966, the Battle of the Palace took place. Under Idi Amin's command, the Ugandan army attacked the *kabaka*'s residence. Following a sustained armed exchange with the *kabaka*'s defenders, the palace fell. The king (who had also been the nonexecutive president of Uganda), fled the country, but Buganda as a semiautonomous entity seemed, at last, to have come to an end.[10] The treaty complex of the Baganda, which had played such a central part in providing Uganda a constitutionalist style of politics since World War II had finally culminated in this 1966 armed confrontation between an army under northern command and the palace of the southern king. By helping to preserve strong indigenous institutions in Uganda, the British, through their imperial policy of indirect rule, had contributed to the military crisis between Buganda and the central government.

From 1966 onward, the whole political system of Uganda was increasingly influenced by armed forces. A kind of militarization of the polity ensued. Buganda itself was placed under a prolonged state of emergency for the remainder of the decade—with Baganda leaders going in and out of detention. The humiliation of Buganda gave considerable satisfaction to large numbers of northerners, especially those in the armed forces. The Baganda's perceived "arrogance" and their tradition of threatening "armed resistance" had contributed to this deepening crisis in north-south relations and to the further militarization of Uganda's political system. Obote became both head of state and head of government (president instead of prime minister), as well as commander-in-chief of the armed forces.

But the north itself was a plural society, a mixed bag of varied and diverse Nilotic and Sudanic ethnic groups. There never was complete northern political cohesion—except in their widely shared distrust of the Baganda and other southerners. From 1969 and after, severe tensions began to develop between Idi Amin and his supporters within the armed forces, on one side, and the more preponderant Acholi officers and men on the other. For a while, it looked as if Idi Amin was losing the battle and that President Obote was probably preparing to dismiss him as commander of the army and chief of general staff. Faced with the remarkable choice between taking power himself or risking being killed by his rivals in an impending struggle for power, Amin staged a successful military coup d'état on 25 January, 1971. The date marked a whole new stage both in the militarization of Uganda and in relations between north and south.

Clearly, the following years witnessed anarchic and tyrannical trends. And to be sure, these trends carried considerable implications for both national integration and prospects for democratic governance in Uganda.

Tyranny, Anarchy, and National Integration

At first sight, it would appear that the years under Idi Amin were basically a case of national *disintegration*.[11] Parliament and other representative institutions were abolished. Indeed, one proclamation "abolished politics." Before long, political decay began as judicial, administrative, diplomatic, and other political institutions became less effective, less subject to rules and procedure, and more corrupt.

In addition to decay in the sense of reduced capacity, there increasingly occurred the use of violence or its threat in political, economic, and social relationships. The moral order in Uganda partially collapsed, and ordinary citizens behaved illegally—a thing they would never have dreamt of doing a few years previously. Indeed, the law enforcement machinery became increasingly unreliable, and was constantly subject to intimidation by members of the armed forces. Anarchy quite often reigned supreme. By the second half of the Amin era, more people were killed as a result of decentralized violence or anarchy than in response to official orders.

However, the other trend of tyranny still remained devastating throughout the Amin years. Certainly, the murder of major political figures was on order from the dictator. The victims ranged from former Obote ministers in the First Republic to Chief Justice Benedicto Kiwanuka, from Vice-Chancellor Kalimuzo of Makerere University to Archbishop Janan Luwum of the Anglican Church in Uganda.

On balance, it ought to be affirmed that Idi Amin's impact on Uganda weighed heavily on the side of national *disintegration*. But there were trends in his administration that were potentially *integrative*. The first was the partial bridging, or narrowing, or the north-south gulf. Idi Amin's most dangerous enemies were fellow northerners. He certainly killed more northerners than southerners, especially within the armed forces. Under his administration, political allegiance crisscrossed ethnic, sectarian, and north-south fractures. He helped ameliorate the dangerous gulf between militarily powerful but economically underprivileged northerners and the economically prosperous but militarily handicapped southerners. Amin did this not by making the south militarily stronger, but by trying to make the north economically more prosperous.

Amin's explusion of British Asians from Uganda in 1972 was ostensibly designed to help black Ugandans become more successful in commerce and trade. But *which* black Ugandans? On the whole, black northerners benefited more from the expulsion of Asians than black southerners. Per head of the population there were more northern shopkeepers created than new southern shopkeepers, although many southerners also benefitted from the immediate aftermath of the Asian exodus.

Other economic favors bestowed by the Amin administration also went disproportionately to Nilotic and Sudanic Ugandans. If Idi Amin was using a calculus of "affirmative action" or "positive discrimination," he could have defended giving priority to particularly underprivileged fellow northern Ugandans. The effect of Amin's arbitrary discrimination in favor of his ethnic compatriots and other supportive northerners was in the direction of restoring the economic balance between north and south. To that extent, his actions were—however unintentionally—nationally *integrative*.

However, his policies were sometimes neutralized by the pressures of anarchy, on one side, and tyranny on the other. Lack of adequate national stability prevented some of Idi Amin's policies from becoming more functional and helpful to national integration than they might otherwise have been.

What should be borne in mind is that pluralism in Uganda was not only ethnic; it was also *sectarian*. The country's pendular swings between tyranny and anarchy were sometimes pulls and pushes of religious rivalries. It is to this domain of religion and politics that we must turn.

Religious Pluralism in Uganda

Protestantism, Roman Catholicism, and Islam are three imported religious traditions that have profoundly influenced politics in Uganda. In this sense, then, Uganda is *denominationally* what we said it was ethnically—a plural society. What is more, historically and to the present day, issues of religion have operated at the heart of Ugandan politics.[12]

A key question is whether denominational pluralism reinforces rather than moderates ethnic pluralism. If crisscrossing loyalties are integrative and reduce the danger of social polarization, Uganda is fortunate to be divided religiously, as well as ethnically. Acholi Catholics find a religious bond with Catholic Baganda in spite of the ethnic divide; Muslim southerners find solidarity with Muslim northerners across the ethnic-regional gulf. Comparative estimates of the sizes of the various religious communities in Uganda vary and are even sometimes contradictory, and partly depend on the methods and orientations of the different writers. But the following would appear to be reasonable: 33 percent of the total population are Roman Catholics, about 30 percent are Protestants, and between 10 percent and 13 percent are Muslims. The vast majority of the rest are believers in traditional African religions.[13] First, we present an exploration of the political history of the religious pluralism in independent Uganda before examining its implications for democracy and national integration.[14]

The Years of Protestant Supremacy (1962–1971)

Uganda came into independence in 1962 with a ruling political coalition of two Protestant-led parties—the Uganda People's Congress (UPC), led by Milton Obote, and Kabaka Yekka (KY), which is Luganda for "the king alone." From the time of the introduction of British rule in Uganda, Protestants have been at the center of political life in Uganda. The official opposition was the Democratic Party (DP), which was Catholic-led. The relatively powerless Muslim minority was scattered among the three parties. Partly because they were the least Westernized, Muslim Ugandans specialized as petty butchers and taxi drivers. Sometimes they were soldiers, policemen or prison guards.

In the last elections before independence, voting patterns between UPC and DP reflected a significant correlation with religious affiliation, although other variables were also at play. In the case of KY, support was more ethnic-specific than denominational. The great majority of the Baganda (Catholic, Protestant, and Muslim) voted KY, the party in support of the *kabaka*. The institution of the *kabaka* had enormous cultural and emotional importance for most Baganda. For its appeal to Bagandan cultural pride, the party was well assured of Ganda support in Buganda. But, although KY was an ethnic party rather than a sectarian one, the king of the Baganda was Anglican. Political power in the kingdom, too, was disproportionately in Protestant hands. The leadership of KY was also disproportionately Protestant.

Both the founding president of Uganda, Sir Edward Mutesa (the *kabaka*), and the founding prime minister, Milton Obote, were Protestants. The country aspired to be a secular state, though its motto was "For God and My Country." However, sectarian differences in Uganda were much more politicized than was average for the continent. In the 1960s, Uganda had already earned the name of "the Ireland of Africa"—long before it attracted, in the 1970s and 1980s, a more deadly notoriety as "the Lebanon of Africa."

The first decade of Uganda's independence witnessed the rapid political decline of the Catholics and the slow political rise of the Muslims. Also glaringly evident was the consolidation of an alliance between Protestant power and the new forces of secular radicalism in postcolonial Uganda.

The decline of the Catholics in the political arena was substantially connected with the decline of the DP. Although the marriage of convenience between Obote's UPC and the *kabaka*'s party lasted only a couple of years, the marginalization of the DP, in opposition, gradually worsened. Uganda had inherited the Westminster model of government, which allowed members of Parliament to "cross the floor" and join other parties. The system of political patronage in postcolonial Uganda saw the principle of "crossing the floor" stretched to the utmost. Between 1967 and 1970, a modest stampede resulted, with DP members crossing the floor to join the ruling UPC.

The political role of Catholicism in Uganda suffered other major blows as well. In 1966, the president-general of the DP, Benedicto Kiwanuka—who, for a while, was the most powerful political figure in the country—was detained along with other political opponents (in the UPC itself and in opposition parties) of Milton Obote. Kiwanuka's detention silenced the most eloquent Catholic voice in Ugandan politics. In that same year, Archbishop Joseph Kiwanuka died. In the postcolonial era, he had exercised enormous influence in the first few years of independence. The fourth and staggering blow was the decline of the Catholic church's control over its own denominational schools in Uganda. This was partly due to the consolidation of the state's role in education in postcolonial Uganda.

Nevertheless, since there were more Catholics than Protestants in Uganda, the state had to pay some attention to Catholic sensibilities. And the UPC was still trying to divert Catholic support from the DPC. Perhaps the most historic Protestant gesture to the Catholic church came when President Obote welcomed to Uganda in 1969 Pope Paul VI—the first reigning pope to have ever visited Black Africa.

As for Islamic influence in politics, the Trojan horse was the army. Uganda came into independence with four senior Ugandan officers in the armed forces. All four happened to be Muslim, including the army commander, Brigadier Shaban Opolot, and the deputy army commander, Colonel Idi Amin. Contrary to what many observers have tended to assume, the heavy Muslim presence in the Ugandan army was not due to Amin, but, rather, had begun in the colonial era. Partly because they were the most marginalized and the least Westernized, the military and other security forces in Uganda held special promise for the Muslims. History was to work out a special destiny for one of these Muslim top military officers—the then Colonel Idi Amin (later, ostentatiously, General Field Marshal, Al-Hajj, Dr. Idi Amin Dada, V.C., D.S.O., M.C., and C.B.E.) Whether he knew it or not, Amin's unambiguous partiality for titles was a personal way of compensating for his own social and intellectual marginality. In a sense, it was his way of "catching up" with his historically more privileged southern compatriots to the south.

With the help of the army under Amin's command, Obote subjugated Buganda, detained his major political opponents, suspended the constitution, and declared himself executive head of state. His most important pillar was Idi Amin—a Trojan horse for Kakwa and "Nubi" recruits in the Ugandan army, and for an increasing Islamic influence in Ugandan politics. Ultimately the genesis of tyranny in postcolonial Uganda has to be traced back to that political alliance in the 1960s between then Prime Minister Milton Obote and then Colonel Idi Amin.

In 1969, an attempt to assassinate Milton Obote was made. Amin was suspected of negligence, if not cowardice, during the crisis. The future of his second-in-command (an Acholi), Brigadier Pierino Okoya, who assumed military control when Amin mysteriously vanished, seemed to be brightening. Was Amin about to be replaced by Okoya?

On 21 January, 1970, Brigadier Okoya was murdered at his home in Acholi. Idi Amin vigorously denied complicity, but the government remained suspicious. Some of his responsibilities were taken away from him and given to two fellow Muslim and "fellow Nubi" officers.[15] Obote was cautious about dismissing or disciplining Amin because it was realized Amin had substantial support in the armed forces, especially among the ranks and noncommissioned officers. Obote wondered how to deal with Amin.

For Uganda, most of 1970 was a tense year, although it was camouflaged with radical rhetoric about a "move to the left." It was an open secret that Idi Amin was under a political cloud. Amin's own assertive self-confidence in public earned him popular admiration. He began to attend Muslim celebrations more ostentatiously to gain an additional constituency, and even declared at one point, "I fear no one but God," a remark widely assumed to be an open defiance of President Obote.[16]

When, in January 1971, Obote left Uganda to attend the Commonwealth conference in Singapore, Idi Amin faced a unique dilemma. He felt that his life was in danger and perceived his choice as between death and assuming the presidency himself. With the help of Israeli military advisers then within Uganda, and possibly the British from the outside, Idi Amin seized power on 25 January in a military coup. The era of Protestant supremacy seemed to have come to an end. A new era of a Muslim ascendancy had arrived.

Islam in the Ascendant (1971–1979)

One of the ironies of the 1970s for Uganda was that southern Sudan fostered Islamic expansion across the border but resisted Islamic expansion within southern Sudan itself. Many of the southern Sudanese who entered Uganda under Idi Amin were either already Muslims or chose to become Muslims in the Ugandan armed forces. While Islam under Arab leadership in Sudan was perceived as a threat to southern Sudanese cultural authenticity, Islam under black leadership south of the border in Uganda was perceived as an opportunity for power and influence.

In his first year in office, Amin wanted to turn Uganda into an ecumenical state—distinct from both a secular state and a state with an established church. A secular state, like Tanzania next door, separates church from state. A state with an established church (as in England) selects one of the denominations as the religious foundation of sovereignty. An ecumenical state, in contrast, neither distances itself from all churches nor embraces one to its bosom, but serves, rather, as a referee and mediator in interchurch relations.

Amin summoned interdenominational conferences to encourage a dialogue between Catholic, Protestant, and Muslim leaders. He established a Muslim Supreme Council to provide institutionalized leadership for the factionalized Muslim community. He encouraged greater discipline among the divided Protestants and made reassuring gestures toward the Catholic community. As part of this effort, Amin even claimed that two of his own sons were to be trained as Catholic priests (it never happened). The distinguished Catholic lawyer and politician, Benedicto Kiwanuka, was not only released from the detention imposed by Obote, but made chief justice. The Catholic community felt rehabilitated.

Idi Amin's decision to bring back the body of Sir Edward Mutesa (the *kabaka* who died in exile in London) for a state funeral in the ancestral royal burial grounds pleased Baganda of all denominations. The gesture was both ecumenical and transethnic as a basis for national solidarity. Although Idi Amin's initial efforts to transform Uganda into an ecumenical state seemed promising, the forces of sectarianism in Uganda were overwhelming. Before long, a gradual tilt by Amin toward the Muslims was discernible.

Was Idi Amin Muslim first and Kakwa second? Some of Amin's non-Muslim fellow Kakwa tended to believe and behave as if he was. Although the Kakwa as an ethnic group prospered under Amin, it was widely known that some of Amin's closest Kakwa but non-Muslim colleagues were not happy with the tyrant's excessive partiality toward Muslins, regardless of tribe. These tensions culminated in March 1974 in the abortive coup attempt by Amin's chief of staff, the late Brigadier Charles Arube (a Catholic), whose two coconspirators were fellow Christian Kakwa. As a humane and respected military officer personally known to one of these authors, Arube was probably more against tyranny and murder of political opponents than he was anti-Muslim, although Amin's unabashed pro-Islamism probably contributed an additional grievance. But, even after that abortive coup attempt, senior Kakwa officers (including even some Muslim Kakwa) were resentful of how the regime had become and was perceived more as a Muslim regime and less as simply a Kakwa oligarchy.

As a result of Amin's Muslim bias, Muslims from diverse tribes and backgrounds found solidarity and even prominence under Amin, and the non-Muslim Kakwa alienation remained limited, because of the need for collective self-preservation. By being transethnic, Islam helped Amin's Uganda from being ethnically too sharply fragmented. Hence, whereas his first cabinet included only two Muslims, by late 1975, the balance had shifted to probably over 60 percent Muslim. More significant, Amin himself remained the only Muslim Kakwa in his own cabinet.

A major opportunity for patronage arrived with the expulsion of Ugandan Asians in 1972. Although fewer than 100,000 in a population of over 11 million at the time, the Asians were a prosperous community that controlled much of the wholesale and retail trade in virtually all of Uganda's urban centers. Idi Amin's decision to expel them on a three-month notice stunned the world—and exhilarated many in East Africa. The shops and businesses they left behind became available as patronage material within Uganda. Ethnic and sectarian favoritism affected their distribution among black would-be entrepreneurs. Individual soldiers were among the major beneficiaries of the Asian exodus. An Islamic bias was also part of the design of redistribution.[17]

Amin's break with Israel in March 1972 resulted in a tilt toward the Arabs. This would remain the single most consistent aspect of his eight-year tenure. Amin also took Uganda into the Organization of Islamic Conferences (OIC), and the country still remains a full member, seven years after Amin's violent departure, despite the fact that Muslims are only a small minority (and now on the defensive).

Amin's tenure also coincided with the heyday of the predominantly Muslim- and Arab-led Organization of Petroleum Exporting Countries (OPEC). Amin's two most generous Arab benefactors were Saudi Arabia, whose King Feisal visited Uganda in late 1972, and Libya's Colonel Muammar Qaddafi, who visited the country in March 1974. Qaddafi also extended military aid in both the 1972 botched attempt to invade Uganda and overthrow Amin by Ugandan rebels from neighboring Tanzania and in the 1979 Ugandan-Tanzanian War, which culminated in Amin's decisive overthrow.

Even though it would be simplistic and reductionist to explain the eight-year survival of the Amin regime purely in terms of OPEC financial aid, it would be equally rash to underestimate the potency of this factor. Amin's capacity to reward his supporters (especially soldiers), and thus prolong his political survival, was due to earnings from Uganda's export crops (especially coffee in 1976 through 1978), the redistribution of the property of departed "Asians," and, last but not least, the flow of Arab petrodollars.

Toward a Militarized Democracy

Amin's violent overthrow in April 1979 was primarily done by Tanzanian troops, aided and supported by Ugandan dissidents. President Nyerere of Tanzania initially intended to play China to Uganda's Vietnam—attack, "punish," and then withdraw. But Nyerere soon decided, instead, to play Vietnam to Uganda's Kampuchea—by going all the way to the capital and overthrowing the regime. However, two issues remained unresolved: Would the anarchy initiated by Amin also come to an end? Would democracy, at long last, be restored?

The first democratic move was to try and get the different groups to choose an interim administration, pending elections. While the war against Amin was still going on, President Nyerere's government invited the different Ugandan factions to meet in Moshi, Tanzania. They were to choose an interim head of government. The factions chose the academic and former head of Makerere University College, Yusufu K. Lule, who assumed power when Idi Amin finally fled the country. Lule was a Muganda, that is, a member of the Baganda tribe.[18] For a while at least, it appeared as if power in post-Amin Uganda was being wielded primarily by southerners. But Uganda's anarchy had not ended with Idi Amin's departure. The anarchy affected the very factions that constituted the new interim administration. Y. K. Lule was eased out of power within sixty-eight days.

Julius Nyerere's role remains a matter of controversy. Did he connive in Lule's ousting? Was Nyerere part of a conspiracy to reinstate Milton Obote? The evidence suggests Nyerere's connivance in Lule's overthrow. Lule was succeeded by Godfrey Binaisa, an ardent supporter of Milton Obote in the 1960s, for eleven months. However, by 1979, Binaisa had his own designs on the presidency, hoping that the coming elections in 1980 would be conducted in a manner that would greatly strengthen his chances of winning it. But Binaisa (a Muganda himself) underestimated the fact that northern Ugandans, even after Idi Amin, still had an edge in military power over southern Ugandans. When he moved against the country's new chief of staff, Major General David Oyite-Ojok, a northerner and a Langi like Obote, the chief of staff rejected his transfer to a diplomatic position abroad—and Binaisa himself was soon out of power.

The third Muganda to take over after Idi Amin was Paulo Muwanga, who was cognizant of the military supremacy of northerners. Many people knew Muwanga was sympathetic to Obote's return to power; but the road to Obote's return was supposed to be through the impending general elections in 1980. Obote came back from exile in Tanzania to compete in those elections, and observers from the Commonwealth were present to ascertain their fairness. The observers affirmed that, all things considered, the elections were fair. Muwanga had managed the elections without alienating the Commonwealth observers—but without abandoning Milton Obote either. Obote assumed supreme executive power in Uganda as leader of the UPC—without having to stand in the general election himself. Most southern Ugandans regarded the elections as being rigged. The stage was set for a new phase in north-south relations in the country.

For the first time since the crisis of 1966 between Obote and Mutesa, southern Uganda seriously considered armed resistance against northern military power. It seemed as if southern Uganda's democratization since the colonial days had found a new point of outrage. A variety of southern groups began to consider going underground as guerrilla movements. Some were loyal to former President Lule, others to former Defense Minister Yoweri Museveni, and to others under separate southern banners. The best organized turned out to be Museveni's National Resistance Army (NRA). This movement's tactics in the field against the central government's army (Uganda National Liberation Army—UNLA) proved effective. Finding itself increasingly under pressure, the UNLA took its revenge on defenseless civilians. Whatever support Obote's new administration had enjoyed at election time in 1980 quickly evaporated.

What was different about the anti-Obote movements in Uganda—as compared with other armed movements elsewhere in Africa—was the fact that Ugandans seemed genuinely outraged by rigged elections. Africa has had movements against white minority rule, but seldom movements against *black* minority rule. Africa has had secessionist movements and externally supported movements against Marxist regimes, but the Ugandan phenomenon was essentially a protest against the abuse of the electoral process.

Why were Ugandans prepared to bear arms against Obote's second administration when they never rose against Idi Amin, a more brutal tyrant? A number of factors helped to strengthen the democratic sensibilities of Ugandans against Obote.

First, the very fact that Idi Amin had been overthrown by force of arms was a major *precedent*. Ugandans had fought against their own national army—and won. That the victory was mainly because of the Tanzanian army's superior firepower seemed less relevant to Ugandans in the post-Amin euphoria than their own participation in the struggle. If Amin could be overthrown, why couldn't Obote?

Second, many southerners felt that the end of their freedoms took place not in 1971 when Amin overthrew Obote, but in 1966 and 1967, when Obote scrapped the independence constitution and unilaterally inaugurated a constitution of his own. Indeed, the Baganda were, in addition, put under a state of emergency for five years, saw their monarchy destroyed, and their king hounded into exile and death in a foreign land. The great majority of the Baganda never forgave Obote for these "sins" in his first administration.

A third factor behind the militarization of southern Ugandan was Yoweri Museveni's capacity to transmit a credible sense of democratic purpose to his supporters in the anti-Obote struggle. Museveni seemed to be a genuine social and political reformer of the leftist persuasion. However, in the struggle against Obote, he emphasized more the liberal issues of human rights than leftist issues of class struggle and social justice. In southern Uganda, the clarion call of human rights was more unifying than that of socialism. The Museveni who triumphantly emerged as Uganda's first southern president with military muscle behind him was different from the one Ugandans and outside observers had known before. When he first appeared on Uganda's political scene, Museveni was widely perceived to be socialist or even communist. His party, the Uganda Patriotic Movement (UPM), stood on a leftist platform in the December 1980 elections pledging social justice and an eradication of corruption.[19] Although the elections were apparently rigged, the UPM fared far worse than the other political parties, which were themselves equally victimized by the rigging. Not even Museveni himself won a seat in Parliament. In fact, only one UPM candidate, nationwide, won a seat.

It would seem that one lesson Museveni drew from the 1980 general elections was that Uganda was not yet ready for a move to the left. His behavior since capturing power would seem to indicate a relative ideological shift from the left toward center.

A fourth factor aiding southern mobilization against Obote was that Uganda was then a significantly more open society than under Idi Amin. After all, there was under Obote's second administration an official opposition (the DP) that articulated its dissent openly and even catalogued atrocities committed by Obote's armed forces. There was still a Parliament where genuine debates took place in spite of threats to individual members of Parliament from time to time. There were opposition newspapers that continued to "expose atrocities" and to embarrass the government in spite of the periodic detention of editors and reporters. None of these values of dissent was even remotely open after the first year or two of Amin's rule.

Finally, one must include the sheer availability, after Amin, of arms and ammunition. Whereas Amin's regime had a monopoly or near-monopoly of the means of distribution, the whole process of overthrowing Amin involved raising a "rabble army" and the wide distribution of arms to its recruits, both by the invading Tanzanian army and the different dissident groups of Ugandans. With the war against Amin over, people who never would have handled guns suddenly had access to lots of them.

In short, although anarchy in Obote's Uganda got even worse than it was during the Amin years, tyranny under Obote was less brutal than it had been under Idi Amin. The relative political openness of Uganda in the 1980s helped recruitment for and mobilization of the armed resistance movements of the south.

There was some armed resistance to Obote in northern Uganda also, especially in West Nile, Amin's home district. Amin's ethnic compatriots were defending themselves against reprisals by Obote forces, rather than genuinely championing a new democratic order. But anti-Obote resistance in West Nile, with its peripheral location, was much less important nationally than resistance in the south. Amin's fellow "tribesmen" only became significant after Obote's second administration had finally collapsed—and the new Okello regime, in a desperate attempt at self-preservation, sought possible allies even if they had once served Idi Amin.

By the middle of 1985, the pressures that southern resistance had put on the national army were so great that tension began to occur within the Obote government between the Langi (Obote's "tribe") and the Acholi (the preponderant ethnic group in the national army). The tensions culminated in the fall of Obote's government in July 1985 and his own second flight into exile.

As previously indicated, other northerners took over under the leadership of General Tito Okello, as president, and Major General Basilio Okello, as armed forces chief of staff. Although not related, the two Okellos were both Acholi from the north, and their brief tenure was likewise Acholi-dominated. Four of the nine members of their military council were Acholi, although the Acholi are only a tiny fraction of Uganda's total population.[20] *Africa Confidential* characterized the new leadership as "far too preoccupied in asserting Acholi power."[21]

But the new northern government was confronted by Yoweri Museveni's NRA. The two armies seemed, at last, to be locked in a deadly stalemate. Then, finally, in January 1986, Museveni's NRA routed Okello's forces and captured Kampala, thus terminating northern dominance of Uganda's military and political power. It was a historic balancing of forces. Yoweri Museveni had restored the military balance between north and south—just as Idi Amin had once attempted to restore the economic balance. If democracy was to be reconstructed in Uganda on a more stable basis, it would need both kinds of balance. The north should share more equitably in the prosperity which the south had so far enjoyed. The south too should share more equitably in the power which the north had so far wielded.

Long-term equilibrium in the country as a whole needed much more than a peace conference (like the Nairobi peace talks of 1985) or even two. What was at stake was the prospect of a truly democratic and just society, defended by a genuinely *national* and *representative* army, and based on more vigorous standards of distributive justice than the country had so far attempted.

The Militarized South Triumphant

The NRA triumph marked at least the interruption, if not the termination, of over twenty years of northern political and military domination of Uganda. Partly because the NRA had waged its struggle against both Obote's second administration and against the short-lived Okello government, with the south as the theater of battle, it had naturally tended to recruit rather excessively from the south, although the National Resistance Movement (NRM—the parent organization of the NRA) did have some participants from other regions.

While the majority of Museveni's fighters were drawn from among the Baganda, especially the inhabitants of the notorious "Luwero Triangle," most of the NRA's military commanders tended to be Museveni's fellow Banyakole.

Museveni's first cabinet turned out to be more ideologically mixed than one would have anticipated. Monarchists rubbed shoulders with republicans, archcapitalists coexisted with socialists, riffraff ex-guerrillas intermingled with armchair intellectual sophisticates. President Museveni seemed to put national unity ahead of a socialist mission or ideological purity. In the interest of national cohesion, Museveni coopted as many different and disparate groups and individuals as possible. He even appointed a former Amin cohort (Moses Ali) to his cabinet as minister of tourism. Given the strong abhorrence among Ugandans for the Amin years, this was a rather risky decision to take. Yet, the move also illustrated the extent to which Museveni was prepared to go in pursuit of national cohesion. Before too long, the cracks in the "broad-based government" began to show. In September 1986, three cabinet ministers (all of them Baganda) were arrested in Kampala and charged with treason for attempting to overthrow Museveni's eight-month-old government.[22]

One apparent source of political tension between Museveni and a section of Ganda political opinion was the issue of restoring the *kabaka*ship.[23] It is unlikely that all Baganda in the mid-1980s are monarchists at heart. It is especially doubtful whether Museveni's very youthful Ganda-dominated army had ardent monarchists within it. Considering that most of Museveni's troops are below twenty years of age, they are unlikely to be passionate defenders of an institution abolished before their birth.

Yet monarchists in Buganda there are. Unlike the Amin regime, which summarily dismissed the issue and suppressed discussion of it, Museveni's response to the *kabaka* issue has been liberal and tolerant. Museveni asserted that, since its abolition by Obote in 1966 had been done undemocratically, it would be equally illiberal to recreate it unilaterally. Rather, he supported the idea of deciding the issue through a popular vote in 1989. Later on, he also indicated that he was not against reviving the *kabaka*ship as a cultural institution, implying a qualified approval of the institution, provided it did not generate undue political complications for the country.

Meanwhile, Museveni's ex-guerrillas turned out to be the most disciplined and responsible army in the history of independent Uganda. Certainly, reports about mistreatments, beatings, rapes, and looting of civilian property by soldiers were substantially reduced once Museveni's NRA was firmly in control. The regime also showed readiness to promptly arrest and demonstrably punish all erring soldiers—a radical departure from previous military regimes, which tended to behave as if soldiers were above the law.

Yet, one cannot be complacent about the future. For how long would the new army continue to be well-behaved amid relentless poverty, low productivity, a weak industrial and technological base, and a crippled, still-decaying infrastructure?[24] Unless the Ugandan economy picks up, and Museveni is able to provide for his troops and other Ugandans, it would be unrealistic to expect armed and hungry troops to indefinitely behave themselves. The future of democratic politics in Uganda would, therefore, depend upon (among other things) whether the economy improves and thrives. It would also depend on whether Museveni's broad-based, if ideologically disparate, government holds together for long; whether the northern rebel soldiers acquiesce in a new Bantu leadership and relinquish their struggle; and whether intrasouthern fractures (especially between the Baganda and Museveni's fellow westerners) do not become so strong as to paralyze and destroy the new Bantu leadership.

• THEORETICAL REVIEW •

Social Structure and Political Culture

What precise social variables determine the degree to which democratic institutions are viable in a given African country? More research into the social conditions of specific countries seems necessary before adequate answers can be provided for such probing questions. But, generally, we might begin by distinguishing between countries that are *structurally* hospitable to competitive institutions and countries that are *culturally* hospitable to those institutions.

Countries in Africa that are structurally hospitable to such institutions are those characterized by ethnic pluralism or other kinds of intergroup cleavage. A striking example in East Africa has, in fact, been Uganda. Until recently, Uganda showed a great capacity for vigorous pluralistic politics, arising out a a special kind of intergroup competitiveness.

Countries culturally hospitable to parliamentary institutions are those that have, either in their traditional or their acquired values, a distrust of excessive authority and a belief in relative individual autonomy.

Outside Uganda, traditional values favorable to liberal democracy are to be found in societies such as the Ibo of Nigeria and the Kikuyu of Kenya. The segmentary nature of these societies, and the greater degree of individualistic assertion, make them culturally receptive and germane to institutions that seek and strive to safeguard the autonomy of subunits of society. Neither the Ibo nor the Kikuyu constitute separate nations in which this particular cultural hospitality to parliamentary institutions could be allowed to flourish without the tensions of political interaction with other groups. Where the Ibo and the Kikuyu have to compete with groups altogether different in a wider society, their cultural hospitality for parliamentary institutions might be diluted at the national level. In other words, the Kikuyu have been known to become less inclined toward an open parliamentary system not because they would not have welcomed it had all of Kenya been Kikuyu, but because, when faced with other groups, their cultural liberalism sometimes stiffens into a kind of defensive intolerance.[25]

Before the first coup in 1966, the Ibo were, in many ways, the most natural liberal democrats of the three major ethnic groups in Nigeria. But, here, one needs to be cognizant of important differences between Uganda and Nigeria and their cultural and structural conditions for parliamentary institutions. Beyond the traditional values of the Ibo, there were important cultural factors in Nigeria favorable to the survival of parliamentary institutions, such as an intellectual tradition in southern Nigeria (influenced by the British political tradition). This was responsive to some liberal values. These cultural factors, however, were overwhelmed by some of the factors in the social situation.

Uganda, on the other hand, was structurally but not culturally congenial to parliamentary institutions. Certainly, in the case of the dominant Baganda, the belief in authority seemed to be a central part of its political culture. The Baganda contributed significantly to the survival of vigorous constitutionalism in Uganda until the collapse of liberal democracy in 1966. They repeatedly challenged the central government on issues affecting their rights as a group and as a region. They had great faith in law and the process of litigation on political matters. There was also tremendous vitality in the political organization for the defense of Baganda autonomy. But, as previously indicated, the desire was to safeguard the collective rights of a region rather than to promote respect for individual freedom. Indeed, much of Baganda society, and the pressures that operated in the political process, were hostile in effect, if not by intention, to the principle of individual choice. The Baganda objected to political authoritarianism from the central government but practiced it substantially in their own domestic local government.

The Baganda also imbibed important aspects of British traditions. They remain among the more anglicized of all East African groups and communities. Yet, what they acquired from the British was not so much British liberalism as British conservatism. That side of British culture is traditionalistic, refrains from too rapid a departure from ancestral ways, and respects institutions hallowed by time and experience. The Baganda responded to these British ways with impressive sophistication. However, the other side of the British tradition that respects individual liberties and personal idiosyncrasies was not readily embraced by the Baganda.

As previously indicated, the cultural values of the northern groups in Uganda seemed to be more hospitable to individualism and decentralization than Kiganda culture.[26] There was certainly more distrust of centralized authority among them than there was among the Baganda. However, the preexisting record of Ganda supremacy in the country may have influenced northern partiality for nonpluralistic politics at the national level. Traditional northern egalitarianism seems to have been shaken by the experience of the tense intergroup relations that culminated in a military confrontation in 1966.

Concerning the acquired values of the non-Ganda elite of Uganda, British conservatism is not entirely absent. But there has also evolved, partly in reaction to previous records and partly in competition with other African trends elsewhere, a partiality for centralized institutions and a strong executive.

The old dialectic between a party system and ethnic pluralism therefore needs reexamination. Does the nature of a multiparty system aggravate ethnic loyalties? Are there aspects of the Westminster model that peculiarly lend themselves to ethnic politics?

Electoral Schemes and Party Systems

It has been suggested that there is "a subtle bias built into the very way in which the single member constituencies" work in a country like Uganda to further the tendency to a strong "tribal voting bloc." Districts in much of former British Africa were drawn on the basis of ethnic lines. This is true of Ghana, Kenya and, even more strikingly perhaps, of Uganda. Sometimes changes have been made in the boundaries and, indeed, even in names of these districts, either in response to demographic considerations or tensions with minority groups in rebellion against the dominant group in a given district. Defining districts ethnically for territorial subdivision of the country could contribute to "tribal voting." Most constituencies are configurations of single-group dominance, but with some smaller "tribes" included. The fact that the constituency elects only one member converts the struggle into an ethnic contest.[27]

It could, therefore, be argued that what has tended to aggravate ethnic tendencies is less the party system than the electoral system. However, this reasoning, persuasive as far as it goes, overlooks the fact that the single-member constituency may often encourage multiple ethnic *alliances*, so that parties emerge not as representatives of single groups but as alignments of several ethnic groups. This might be a more desirable state of affairs than a situation in which the electoral system encourages not only the initial eruption of numerous small parties, but their survival through the campaign and election, thus fragmenting the national assembly into numerous, small ethnically based parties. The experience of Ghana, which began with its Second Republic in mid-1969 with a multiplicity of political parties, supports the theory that the single-member constituency system encourages coalescence into a two-party confrontation. There, the single-member constituency seems to have contributed to a kind of voting behavior that made groups otherwise distinct seeks bonds of alignment and alliance with one another.

Under the two Obote administrations, Uganda, too, revealed a tendency toward a two-party system based on multiethnic coalitions.[28] This helped the cause of national stability, but only modestly. From the point of view of ethnic pluralism, a *multi-party* system is less desirable than a *two-party* system. The Anglo-Saxon model of two major parties confronting each other at least encourages coalitions and alignments between groups that might have separate political organizations of their own. But the question persists whether, from the point of view of coping with ethnic cleavages, a *one-party* system would not be even better than a system of two-party dominance.

The answer depends upon the relationship between "tribes" and parties. A competitive party system would encourage ethnic affiliations and antagonisms where "tribes" and parties coincide too neatly. A competitive party system, on the other hand, would help to mitigate and even eliminate "tribalism" from politics if parties and tribes *crisscrossed*. As we mentioned earlier, Acholi Catholics in alliance with Baganda Catholics could moderate the tensions of both ethnicity and sectarianism.

• IMPLICATIONS FOR THE FUTURE OF DEMOCRACY IN UGANDA •

The central questions concerning the future of democracy in Uganda are, first, how to preserve and protect *civilian supremacy* in decisionmaking and, second, how to contain the forces of *ethnicity* in the arena of *competitive politics*. Failure to protect civilian supremacy is the most direct route to anarchy. The defense of civilian supremacy requires effective control of the military. The protection of representative institutions and national accountability demand restraining ethnic behavior.

Yoweri Museveni and Milton Obote have been cast by history as theoreticians of how to cope with those two threats to African democracy—militarism and "tribalism," respectively. Museveni has experimented with the task of giving his soldiers a sense of mission that transcends the use of the gun. A normative void has been precisely one of the difficulties of the average postcolonial army in Africa. Most African countries have no external military foes; in many cases, the soldiers are trained to fight external enemies. In reality, they end up fighting domestic political rivals. The soldiers are trained in the arts of killing and fighting, but should have been trained in the skills of law enforcement.

Because Museveni's army sprang from a revulsion against Obote's electoral rigging, his soldiers were not typical products of colonial militarization. Museveni and his cohorts trained their troops not only for combat, but also for administering "liberated" villages. They were also prepared for certain developmental and administrative functions in rural areas. Now that they have captured power, the question is whether that moral sense of purpose in the armed forces will be able to withstand the temptations of national power. Will Museveni be able to promote and protect the principle of *civilian supremacy* in government? He himself is now an ambiguous figure—half civilian and half liberation-warrior. More fundamentally, will his political reforms reduce the threat of military takeovers in the coming decades? In the postcolonial history of Uganda, Museveni has superceded all politicians in providing a credible alternative *paradigm of civil-military relations*.

Toward Military Checks and Civilian Balances

Democratic pluralist theory, at least since James Madison's theory of "*faction*," has often postulated a structure of checks and balances in the society—even before these checks became constitutional provisions and governmental institutions. A diversity of centers of power, and a plurality of intermediate groups have been deemed potential moderators of state power.

In an African country like Uganda, the issue is again linked to the crisis of civil-military relations. In Western liberal history, the problem has been how to balance the power of the executive with the power of the legislature, how to tame the privileges of the king with the leverage of the parliament. Later on the balance was between the executive, the legislative, and the judicial.

In Africa, the crisis, at its worst, has been within the executive branch itself—between the military and civilian decisionmakers. The most urgent of the needs for "checks and balances" concerns the armed forces. What kind of checks can be put on the military? And who indeed can bell the cat?

One approach is to civilianize some of the roles of the military. When soldiers fight a war, their role is military; when soldiers build houses for the poor, their particular role is civilian. The civilian roles of the military can be more easily checked than their combat roles. Yet, controlling the soldiers in one area of their functions could pave the way for a wider control of the armed forces by civilians.

Two safeguards against renewed military interventions in politics in the future are, therefore, particularly necessary in a situation like Uganda's—a diversification of the official functions of the military and the emergence of an effective countervailing force. Before Museveni's experiment, Ugandan soldiers were, at the most, trained in combat and physical self-defense. And yet, for much of the post-colonial period, Uganda had no obvious external enemies in the military sense. On the whole, Ugandan soldiers were far more likely to be dealing with fellow Ugandans at roadblocks at home than with "enemy troops" elsewhere. The soldiers' training in the arts of killing seemed wholly inappropriate for civic duties within their country's own borders.

In any case, only a minority of the soldiers had such civil duties as manning roadblocks. The bulk of the armed forces were functionally redundant—and suffering from a dangerous sense of purposelessness. Indeed, boredom in the barracks was one of the breeding grounds of conspiracies and military coups. That sense of purposelessness also contributed to the soldiers' roughness and callousness in their dealings with civilians.

Museveni's achievement in his struggle against Milton Obote was to instill in his troops a special sense of purpose, a striving for a more humane and more democratic Uganda. At least until he captured power at the center, the role of his troops involved more than combat: in the areas they occupied, they helped establish new structures of administration and development. The troops' success in overcoming professional anomie was a hopeful sign for the future of democracy in Uganda. The civilianization of their functions was one route toward "checking and balancing" the role of the army. Still, this sense of purpose in Uganda's military was bound to be fragile for as long as the army was too powerful.

A countervailing power to the military becomes necessary as a longer-term curb on ambition. One curb is through a strong political party in which the military is adequately represented. The nearest approximation to such an experiment in East Africa has been the ruling party in Tanzania (TANU and, later, CCM). In comparison, Uganda's political parties have been frail.

Another form of countervailing power is a special understanding with the former colonial power to serve as a disincentive against a local coup. This happens more openly in Francophone countries like the Ivory Coast and Togo than in East Africa. But Kenya's looser arrangement with Britain about periodic joint military exercises of British and Kenyan forces may have helped to delay, if not prevent, a successful coup. The 1982 attempted coup in Kenya may have been thwarted partly by British intelligence. Again, Uganda has not opted for such a solution to its problems of civil-military tensions—except for Obote's brief invitation to British troops in 1964 to come and disarm mutinous Uganda soldiers.

A third form of countervailing power is national service for the young in the country, partly to breach the military's monopoly of skills of force and organization. Tanzania has experimented with such a service. Obote's first administration was also planning to initiate a developmental national service, but Idi Amin's coup interrupted that symphony too.

Fourth, there is also the possibility of a special presidential guard as a countervailing force. Mobutu Sese Seko in Zaire, with Israeli help, has operated along those lines. In addition, it appears that so have Liberia's Doe, Togo's Eyadema, and Kenya's Arap Moi. Uganda's civilian presidents have hesitated to form a presidential guard lest such a unit precipitate a preemptive coup rather than prevent one. This route toward "checks and balances" in civil-military relations is particularly precarious.

Over and above all, however, the pluralization of centers of power requires a more balanced class structure in the society as a whole. At this stage of Uganda's history, the country needs a larger bourgeoisie. It is this *class challenge* in Uganda that we now examine.

Democracy and the Magendo Economy

In the first decade of Uganda's independence (1962–1972), the process of creating a national bourgeoisie was distorted by a racial factor—the disproportionate presence of Asians in the industrial and commercial sectors of the economy. The indigenous middle class was concentrated in the bureaucratic and liberal professions (the civil service, law, medicine, etc.) and in land and agriculture. The Asians—the majority *not* citizens of Uganda—controlled more than 60 percent of the import and export trade. They also dominated the distribution network with neighboring Kenya, eastern Zaire, Rwanda, and Burundi. The indigenous middle class, being disproportionately bureaucratic and "professional," was peripheral to the central sectors of the economy.

If democracy requires a plurality of power centers, the Chamber of Commerce in Uganda and other voices of the private sector were politically weakened by being overwhelmingly non-African, and mainly non-Ugandan, in composition. Prospects for democracy in Uganda did, in part, depend upon a more convincing Africanization and Ugandization of the commanding heights of the economy. Obote's nationalization measures, in 1969 and 1970, created state ownership but not an indigenous bourgeoisie.

Then in 1972, the tenth year of Uganda's independence, Idi Amin decided on what appeared to be an attempt to create an African bourgeoisie; he expelled all Asians who were not citizens. Most of the minority who were citizens also left. Although the methods used by Idi Amin were antithetical to the spirit of a humane political order, the departure of the Asians presented an opportunity to create more effective indigenous bourgeoisie and a more credible center of democratic power in the private sector.

However, the process of embourgeoisement was hampered by the anarchy and tyranny of the second decade of Uganda's independence (1972–1982). It was also complicated by the growth of a "parallel economy" locally known as *magendo* (Swahili for "smuggling"). The anarchy and tyranny created considerable uncertainty for long-term investment and much insecurity for the successful business person. Conspicuous prosperity under Idi Amin was often risky. In Uganda, "cut-throat competition" was meant literally. The emergence of a successful bourgeoisie was sabotaged by the omnipresent insecurity.

The relationship between democracy and *magendo* was more complex. The underground economy produced new forms of influence and centers of power. But when the private sector goes underground, it becomes doubly "private," even secret. How much "*secret* power" can an *open* society sustain? An economic class did emerge in Uganda, locally known as *mafuta mingi* (Swahili for "lots of fat"). In terms of liberal theory, it was one more center of power in one private sector to help create a democratic *plural* society. But, although these *mafuta mingi* plutocrats were not exactly Mafia tycoons, much of their wealth was from *magendo* and illicit trade. The process of embourgeoisement in Uganda had encountered yet another contradiction. What, then, are the limits of the privatization of power in an open society?

The problem was compounded by the fact that *magendo* was an avenue of social mobility for the disadvantaged. Many of the *mafuta mingi* plutocrats would not have prospered under the system that existed prior to the first decade of independence. If democracy requires fluid class distinctions and penetrable class barriers, the *magendo* economy in Uganda contributed significantly to that process. Many previously disadvantaged Ugandans scaled the social ladder via *magendo*. An illiterate millionaire was no longer a contradiction in terms.

Ironically, the *magendo* economy, still in existence, has been an equalizer. A wider range of Ugandans have participated in the commercial sector under *magendo* than was previously possible. If liberal democracy demands substantial economic participation in the private sector, *magendo* has helped in that process. Vastly more Ugandans now buy and sell a wide range of products.

The decline in the value of the Ugandan shilling has also encouraged this tendency. In the first decade of Uganda's independence, the U.S. dollar was equal to about seven Ugandan shillings. By 1987, the value of the U.S. dollar had "risen" to 10,000 Ugandan shillings.

Salaries and wages in Uganda lagged disastrously behind the national currency. One result was that nobody could live on his or her pay. All households now need extra income, thus, new skills of entrepreneurship emerged. Some families in cities were forced to strengthen their links with the countryside—

adding income from agriculture or horticulture to urban earnings. Many more Ugandans became middlemen in the traffic of goods and services—many of the links existed not only outside the formal economy, but also outside the law. Again, prospects for democracy seemed to be benefiting from the expansion of entrepreneurship and the expansion of economic participation in the populace.

However, in the final analysis, liberal democracy is predicated on the rule of law. While *magendo* has indeed been an alternative process of class formation, social mobility, and embourgeoisement, its illicit nature has militated against respect for the law. What democracy has gained from the wider economic participation of Ugandans, democracy has lost from cutting corners in illegal deals.

Reform: Between the Past and the Future

There is another political paradigm that needs to be created in Uganda if democratic institutions are to be recreated and preserved. This is *the paradigm of representative institutions* and how they are to be related to the forces of ethnicity, sectarianism, and the dual polity. At stake are, first, *party systems*—multiparty, two-party, or single-party approaches to politics. Second, there is the question of *electoral systems*—single-constituency or multiconstituency approaches to representation. If Museveni has been the most important theoretician of *civil-military relations* in Uganda, Milton Obote was the most important theoretician of representation in a plural society.

The new Museveni administration has postponed fundamental constitutional change until 1989. It would make sense if, in preparation for that important year, Ugandans reexamined the issues raised by their most extensive constitutional debate since independence—the debate on Milton Obote's *Document No. 5* in the last days of the First Republic.

On 17 July, 1970 President Obote announced new proposals concerning methods of electing members of Parliament and the president of the country. In many ways, the proposals were the most original political reform to be recommended in Uganda since independence. They were also the most innovative ideas to have emerged from the entire continent. The relevant proposals were known as *Document No. 5 On the Move to the Left Strategy.*[29]

Politics in Uganda had been confronted with two factors—one indigenous and the other imported. The indigenous factor was the pull of ethnic loyalties and commitment to individual regions in the country; the external factor was the electoral system as a whole. The interaction between these two could only have profound effects on Uganda. Did the single-member constituency, as inherited from the British, deepen some of the implications of ethnic loyalties in Uganda? Would a different system of constituencies engender different political behavior?

President Obote believed that a major innovation was needed if the pull of ethnic loyalties on a member of Parliament was to be diluted: hence, *Document*

No. 5. Some of the proposals addressed the major issue of how the president of the country was to be chosen—a critical factor in a country where the president wields such enormous and virtually unchecked powers. Yet, these proposals, although original in some respects, were in their totality less revolutionary than the proposals for electing members of Parliament. The latter proposals, we believe, were far more consequential for the future of "tribal" politics in Uganda.

The basic innovation by Obote was the substitution of the idea of four constituencies per member of Parliament for the existing system of one constituency per member. Under the proposed new arrangements, every potential candidate was required to indicate the constituency in which he wished to stand. That was to be his basic constituency. The candidate would register his candidature only in the *basic constituency*, and after that, he would then be required to stand as a candidate in three other *national constituencies* situated in the three other regions of the country. Each basic constituency had to have no fewer than two and no more than three candidates contesting for election as basic candidates. The National Council of the UPC later reviewed the proposals to make three candidates the minimum as well as the maximum number.

The term "electoral polygamy" has been used here in two senses—one metaphorical and the other literal. In the metaphorical sense, "electoral polygamy" would be the idea of marrying each member of Parliament to four constituencies, with the concomitant implications for loyalty and obligations that such an arrangement would have. However, the term has also been used in a literal sense, in suggesting that a future reform of a similar kind could encourage interregional political marriages as a way of consolidating political support. Life in Africa often makes matters of marriage and kinship touch issues of politics and social organization. And just as *Document No. 5* was, in rather important ways, likely to affect the political system as a whole, that same idea might in the future also affect those aspects of kinship and marriage that influence political behavior.

Political Confidence Versus Political Consent

Obote grasped the critical significance of the electoral system in relation to the party system. The case for the proposals contained in his reformist *Document No. 5* hinged on the concept of political trust. How could members of Parliament enjoy the trust and confidence of the whole nation, rather than merely that of their ethnic compatriots? The proposals grasped an important distinction between government with the *people's consent* and government with the *people's confidence*. There are occasions when government with the peoples' confidence is more important than government with the peoples' consent. (The electorate can become cynical and have little faith left in the integrity of their rulers.) As long as elections are held periodically, and choice is exercised by voting for one group of politicians instead of another, the principle of government with the peoples' consent is satisfied. But the country still has to develop a system that commands the people's confidence.

Document No. 5 argued that, if an assembly consisted of parliamentarians who were regarded as ambassadors of different "tribes," and if certain decisions did not favor certain "tribes," there would be a feeling of disappointment among those "tribes." The confidence of that part of the nation in the national legislature could be eroded. The entire exercise of legislation was viewed as one of competing ethnic interests, each seeking fulfillment through a national mechanism, but ultimately conscious primarily of its self-interest. Thus, paragraph 12 of *Document No. 5* argued:

> If the pull of the tribal force is allowed to develop, the unity of the country will be in danger. To reduce it to its crudest form, the pull of the tribal force does not accept Uganda as one country, does not accept the people of Uganda as belonging to one country, does not accept the National Assembly as a national institution but as an assembly of peace conference delegates and tribal diplomatic and legislative functionaries, and looks at the government of Uganda as a body of umpires or referees in some curious game of "Tribal Development Monopoly."

The document then singled out some of the absurdities of the ethnic pull. By being too concerned with tribal solidarity, a leader would tend to see any project outside his own ethnic area as having been based purely on ethnic grounds. The same person, however, would not admit that the projects in his own area, for which he happens to be responsible, were sited in that region regardless of ethnic considerations.

The document discussed the phenomena both of nepotism and counternepotism, with particular reference to the public service. It suggested that there were occasions when people thought that recruitment was facilitated by the support of "tribesmen" already within the system. There was, in addition, the phenomenon of counternepotism, involving the public officer so worried of being mistaken for a "tribalist" that he or she did not encourage even deserving members of his or her own group to join the public service. The document was profoundly disturbed about the operation of tribal and clan factors or family favoritism in affairs of state. At the same time, it was also concerned that citizens should not be discriminated against because of a misguided belief by public officers that helping people who happened to belong to their own tribes, even when such an action was merited, was somehow a disservice to the ethic of impartiality.

What *Document No. 5* sought to do was to attempt a *nationalization of confidence* in government. Government by consent could be achieved by having a free election in single-member constituencies. Government with the peoples' confidence might also be partly realized where each member of Parliament enjoyed the confidence of his own little sector of the society. However, *Document No. 5* sought to widen the boundaries of confidence and trust and challenged each parliamentarian to realize concrete political support in areas other than his or her own home base.

But was the document overzealous in its pursuit of the ambition to nationalize confidence? The stipulations allowed for the possibility of a candidate getting a minority of votes (even a small minority) in the basic constituency, and, nevertheless, winning the election through the majorities realized in the three national constituencies. Was there not a danger that the people of that basic constituency might somehow feel disenfranchised? They would have somebody in Parliament for whom only a minority of them had voted and brought into power by people far from the candidates's own home and the area chosen as the basic constituency.

Next, there is the nature of political trust in African societies. It is one of the realities of the human condition that trust is sometimes related to empathy. Empathy is, in turn, related to a sense of shared identity. In Africa, shared identity is often based primarily on "tribe," and voting behavior tends to correlate with tribal allegiance. *Document No. 5* sought to discourage this tendency. But, if the nature of political trust in African political behavior often lends itself to tribal empathy, was there not a danger that the implementation of *Document No. 5*, rather than increase and nationalize the confidence of the people in their representatives, might instead reduce it?

Another factor to be borne in mind in a system of multiple constituencies for candidates is the danger of favoring those who are better known. Figures already nationally conspicuous were more likely to be known in all four constituencies than people barely struggling to establish their political identities. It may be retorted that familiarity rather than admiration sometimes breeds contempt. A candidate who is nationally known is not necessarily nationally liked. Prominence in such an instance might be a liability, and detailed knowledge of the candidate in his or her own area might sometimes be a particular liability. On the other hand, to be well known generally is more likely to be an asset than a liability. The individual was perhaps a minister in a previous government. It might therefore be said that fame in districts other than the ex-minister's own home might well be a prior asset.

Imagine an election, where a minister loses in his basic constituency in his own "tribal" area. He or she wins massive votes of confidence in the national constituencies far from home. The votes of the national constituency, in this case, would be votes based on inadequate or superficial knowledge of the candidate. Is the majority of votes based on ignorance about the candidate a greater indication of confidence than the minister's rejection by his own basic constituency?

An additional factor that provides a margin of advantage to those who are already prominent is the high selectivity of news media in a country with a history of instability. Although not fully protected from the glare of a critical public opinion, those who hold public office in Uganda nevertheless enjoy substantial security. Criticisms of ministers and their ministries are indeed still heard in Uganda. But these are more rare than accounts of ministers' speeches, the applause they receive at public rallies, and the achievements of their departments. The selectivity is understandable given, thus far, the fragility of political institutions in Uganda. Sometimes the task of consolidating government with the people's confidence entails protecting the government from premature and ruthless scrutiny. However, given the prevalence of such selective coverage, it is preeminently in the basic constituencies of prominent personalities that their weaknesses are likely to be known. This, too, may argue for giving more weight to the preference of the basic constituency.

Some modifications of the proposals may go some way toward meeting these shortcomings. One possible modification is to retain the four constituencies, but require that a member of Parliament win a majority in his own basic constituency, as well as a majority of the total electoral votes of the four constituencies taken together. This carries the risk of having too many inconclusive elections. Other ways of giving additional weight to the basic constituency could be explored. What ought to remain vital is that the people have a sense of being represented by one of their own kind. And yet, under the modified arrangement, the candidate would still need to seek support from others.

Marriage and the Politics of Kinship

Let us now scrutinize the more literal meaning of electoral polygamy—the phenomenon of multiple marriages, interregional in nature, arising from the exigencies of political alignment. In order to understand the likely repercussions of *Document No. 5* on marriage patterns, we have to look at the wider meaning of marriage in African society against the background of modern politics on the continent.

Following extensive anthropological study of African systems of kinship and marriage, Radcliffe-Brown and Forde observed:

> In order to understand the African customs relating to marriage we have to bear in mind that a marriage is essentially a rearrangement of social structure. New social relations are created, not only between the husband and the wife, and between the husband and the wife's relatives on the one side and between the wife and the husband's relatives on the other, but also, in a great many societies, between the relatives of the husband and those of the wife, who, on the two sides, are interested in the marriage and in the children that are expected to result from it.[30]

Whether he intended it or not, the larger social and political implications of marriage were by no means absent in Obote's private life. A northerner from Lang'o, Obote married Miria Kalule from Buganda. Like Kwame Nkrumah of Ghana, who took an Egyptian bride, Obote was profoundly animated by a vision of greater Ugandan unity. Obote's vision was more immediate and domestically more desperate—forging "tribes" into a nation. Nkrumah's vision was more distant, even elusive—forging a nation out of a continent.

With Obote's *Document No. 5* and the idea of multiple constituencies for each member of Parliament, the question of marriage could well have become more explicit as a political dimension in Uganda than before. *Document No. 5* conceded that much of political trust in Africa has been connected with issues of kinship, lineage, and tribal links. The document chose to attack the idea of relating trust to kinship and tribe. And yet, can the habit of looking to kinship relationships for political allies and support be that easily eroded? Are there possibilities where politics of kinship ties would be expanded by marriage from the basic constituency of a candidate to at least one of his or her national constituencies? Were the vision of *Document No. 5* to be rediscovered and implemented, it is conceivable that, in the future, there would be more members of Parliament married to wives (or husbands, as the case may be) from regions other than their own than has so far been true. In fact, it would not be surprising if a large number of male parliamentarians were to have at least two wives, drawn from different regions.

Two factors would be particularly important in linking matrimony to constituencies in this manner: the parliamentarian's need for more than one home and more than one political base. An additional home may be needed to maintain contact with a constituency. The parliamentarian who hopes to attain the support of a national constituency in the next election has to "nurse" the constituency, and probably visit it from time to time. In a number of cases, this could mean needing—in a polity still essentially patriarchal and culturally congenial to polygamy—a second wife elsewhere, equipping her with a house and converting it into a political base. A cross-tribal marriage could also give a parliamentarian a second political base in a national constituency, making him at least a kinsman by marriage. The precise pattern of relationships would vary in different areas of Uganda and among different communities depending, for example, on whether descent was matrilineal or patrilineal. But in many instances new links established by a political marriage could promote a nucleus of political relatives.

The creation of interpenetrating linkages of this kind is by no means novel in Africa. Even in politics, as we have understood them so far, marriage has already played an important part. The 1962 elections in Uganda were not without instances of alliances between clans in support of candidates—alliances based ultimately on relations by marriage. The single-member constituencies permitted this at the cross-clan level. In the future, multiple constituencies could promote the phenomenon of transregional as well as transtribal matrimonial alignments in politics. However, alignments based on evolving kinship relationships may take decades or even generations.

The process of national integration requires substantial interaction between regions. This interaction could be economic, as exchange relationships are evolved and trade between different groups expands. The interaction would also include political dimensions. Obote's old dream of 1970 sought to promote precisely such a widening of political interaction. Candidates were to be encouraged to rely on areas other than their own and voters stimulated to think of politics in terms that transcended their immediate localities. Cultural interaction is the third area of nation-building, necessitating the gradual accumulation of shared norms and values and mutual perspectives on the universe, in spite of variations in emphases.

The meeting point between politics and personal intimacy, between elections and kinship ties, could provide one of the deeper areas of the integrative process. Parliamentarians who are provided with incentives to scatter their "maker's image" through the land could be politicians who are also nationalizing the concept of kinship itself.

• CONCLUSION •

We have traced the remarkable interplay of factors in Uganda's modern history that have had a bearing on the country's stability and prospects for democracy. Ethnically, Uganda is a plural society; historically, it has been a dual polity. The divide between northerners, who were militarily powerful but economically underprivileged, and southerners, who were militarily impotent but economically privileged, have, since the last years of colonial rule, consistently been the central theme of Ugandan politics.

Both the democratization of the south and the militarization of the north were the consequences of varied policies pursued by the British in colonial years. The British disproportionately recruited northerners into the colonial army, the King's African Rifles. The British also helped southerners build wealthier, better educated, more urbanized, and more Westernized societies than those then existing in the north.

The stage was set for postcolonial tensions between the forces of anarchy (arising from the ethnic diversity of the plural society) and the forces of tyranny (flowing from the north-south dual polity).

Two methods of redress were needed: helping the north to share more fully in southern prosperity and helping the south to share more equitably in northern power. Partly by allocating Asian businesses to fellow northerners, Idi Amin attempted to redress the economic imbalance between north and south; to some extent, he succeeded in that ambition. Yoweri Museveni has more successfully restored the military balance between north and south through the successes of his armed struggle against Milton Obote's second administration and, later, Tito Okello's.

By a strange twist of fate, northerners in Obote's first administration abolished the monarchies of the south in 1967, thus contributing to the democratization of southerners. It remains to be seen if southerners will repay the debt by helping northerners rediscover their own democratic and egalitarian past through the creation of a politically and economically more equitable modern Uganda.

However, two preconditions for democracy need to be fulfilled in Uganda—a new paradigm of civil-military relations that ensures civilian supremacy and a new paradigm of representation that disciplines ethnic rivalries. Museveni has pursued the former by encouraging among his soldiers a sense of mission beyond combat. Obote's idea of electoral polygamy envisaged a Uganda of multiple constituencies for each parliamentarian, thus cutting across ethnic lines. This contrasted with the European innovation of multiple legislative members from each single constituency. Africa needs decisive innovation in pursuit of greater discipline in ethnic behavior. The model in *Document No. 5* deserves another, if closer, look. It is a basis for possible experimentation. Being geographically compact, Uganda is conducive to the traveling between divergent constituencies demanded by the scheme.

Africa needs not only to control ethnic behavior, but also to soften ethnic divisions. Intermarriage between "tribes" is one biological approach to the creation of a "new breed of Ugandans." Since ethnicity is about kinship *writ large*, and marriage is kinship *extended*, electoral politics can literally be linked to the politics of matrimony. Transregional and transethnic marriages facilitate cultural intercourse and greater mutual awareness. To the extent that they also emphasize the bonds of kinship solidarity in politics, instances of electoral polygamy in the literal sense might turn out to be a major factor in the interregionalization of the ruling elite of the future.

Should the political elite become pacesetters in the cultural and political spheres, there might develop a significant demonstration effect in this field of transethnic matrimony. In fact, such matches have already begun to be promoted by the blind forces of urbanization and general economic rural-urban immigration. If politics also facilitated these mixed marriages, a new dimension could be added to the most fundamental of all levels of national integration—the level of mixing the blood of the nation.

Polygamy is often considered pre-modern. So is "tribalism." What the dream of *Document No. 5* could initiate is the mobilization of polygamy for the war against ethnicity. To mobilize polygamy for purposes of national integration is to utilize, once again, a primordial custom for the task of modernization.

Obote's *Document No. 5* was a new version of an older story in Uganda—the story of a society that has, in the past, often found areas of accommodation and interplay between tradition and innovation in the whole process of political development. National integration is one precondition of political stability. And stability itself is one of the foundations of a viable democratic order.

• NOTES •

1. Production of blister copper plummeted drastically from 17,000 tons in 1970 to 2,261 tons seven years later (1977). See Jane Carroll, "Uganda: Economy" in *Africa South of the Sahara 1986* (London: Europa, 1985) p. 994; and Jan Jelmert Jorgensen, *Uganda: A Modern History* (London: Croom Helm, 1981).

2. Although outdated (based on the 1959 census), and despite faulty arithmetic in totaling, these statistics are still useful in illustrating the demographic balance among the major ethnic groups in Uganda.

3. Colin Legum, "Uganda: Economic Recovery and Growing Political Stability," *Africa Contemporary Record: Annual Survey and Documents, 1983–1984*. vol. XVI (New York and London: Africana, 1985), p. B303. Two decades previously, about two-thirds of the population was Bantu. See B. W. Langlands, "Uganda: Physical and Social Geography," in *Africa South of the Sahara 1986*, op. cit., p. 985; and Commonwealth Team of Experts, *The Rehabilitation of Economy of Uganda*, 2 vols. (London: Commonwealth Secretariat, 1979).

4. Samwiri Rubaraza Karugire, *A Political History of Uganda* (London: Heinemann, 1980), p. 140; and A. G. G. Gingyera-Pinycwa, *Apolo Milton Obote and His Times* (New York and London: NOK Publishers, 1978).

5. See, for example, A. R. Dunbar, *A History of Bunyoro-Kitara* (Nairobi: Oxford University Press, 1965) p. 2; and Tarsis Kabwegyere, *The Politics of State Formation: The Nature and Effects of Colonialism in Uganda* (Nairobi: East African Literature Bureau, 1974).

6. J. M. Lee, "Buganda's Position in Federal Uganda," *Journal of Commonwealth Political Studies* 3, no. 3 (November 1965): pp. 175–176; and David E. Apter, *The Political Kingdom in Uganda*, 2nd ed. (Princeton: Princeton University Press, 1967).

7. Colin Legum, "Uganda: Economic Recovery and Growing Political Stability," op. cit., p. B303; and Mahmood Mamdani, *Politics and Class Formation in Uganda* (New York: Monthly Review, 1976).

8. A. G. G. Gingyera-Pinycwa, *Apolo Milton Obote and His Times*, p. 22; and Ali A. Mazrui, *Cultural Engineering and Nation-Building in East Africa* (Evanston, Ill.: Northwestern University Press, 1972).

9. Consult Dunstan M. Wai, *The African-Arab Conflict in the Sudan* (New York: The Africana Publishing Company, 1981), especially pp. 15–25; and Omari H. Kokole, "The 'Nubians' of East Africa: Muslim Club or African 'Tribe?' The View From Within," *Journal, Institute of Muslim Minority Affairs* 6, no. 2 (July 1985): pp. 420–448.

10. Sir Edward F. Mutesa, *The Desecration of My Kingdom* (London: Constable, 1967), and Mutesa, *Sir Edward's Appeal to the Secretary-General of the United Nations Organization: Uganda's Constitutional Crisis* (Kampala: Department of Information, Mengo, Buganda: 1966); and Grace S. K. Ibingira, *The Forging of an African Nation: The Political and Constitutional Evolution of Uganda from Colonial Rule to Independence, 1894–1962* (New York: The Viking Press, 1973).

11. See, for example, Aidan Southall, "Social Disorganization in Uganda: Before, During and After Amin," *The Journal of Modern African Studies* 18, no. 4 (1980): pp. 627–656; and Ali A. Mazrui, "Between Development and Decay: Anarchy, Tyranny and Progress Under Idi Amin," *Third World Quarterly* 11, no. 1 (January 1980).

12. Karugire, *A Political History of Uganda* op. cit., pp. 62–63. For a treatment of aspects of this theme in the early years, see Holger Brent Hansen, *Mission, Church and State in a Colonial Setting: Uganda 1890–1925* (New York: St. Martin's Press, 1984); and Semakula Kiwanuka, *Amin and the Tragedy of Uganda* (London and Munich: Weltforum Verlag, 1979).

13. Estimates of the total population of religious communities in Uganda are often contradictory and difficult to treat definitively. However, the general thrust of most figures available over the years suggest the largest religious community is that of the Catholics, followed by the Anglicans, with the Muslims being the smallest. A different source estimates the relevant numbers in the early 1980s as Catholics at 6,500,000 (or 49.2 percent), Anglicans 3,400,000 (or 25.76 percent), Muslims 870,000 (or 6.6 percent), with the Ugandan total population at 13,200,000. See David Barrett, ed., *World Christian Encyclopaedia* (New York and Oxford: Oxford University Press, 1982), p. 686.

14. For the earlier period, consult also Hansen's tables in *Mission, Church and State in a Colonial Setting: Uganda 1890–1925* (New York: St. Martin's Press, 1984).

15. Jorgensen, *A Modern History of Uganda*, op. cit., p. 256; and David Martin, *General Amin* (London: Faber and Faber, 1974).

16. See Akena Adoko, *From Obote to Obote* (New Delhi: Vikas Publishing House, 1983); and John B. Agami, *The Roots of Political Crisis in Uganda* (Kastrup, Denmark: H. P. Tryk, 1977).

17. Initially, Amin personally distributed approximately 500 businesses to individual friends and cronies. He later entrusted the distribution to the Business Allocation Committees of the Ministry of Industries and Commerce. Military officers played a central role in these committees, plus the subsequent Departed Asians' Abandoned Property Custodian Board. See, also, Henry Kyemba, *State of Blood: The Inside Story of Idi Amin* (London: Corgi Books, 1977); and Suleiman I. Kiggundu and Isa K. K. Lukwago, "The Status of the Muslim Community in Uganda," *Journal, Institute of Muslim Minority Affairs* 4, nos. 1 and 2 (1982): pp. 120–131.

18. Collectively, Lule's people call themselves the *Baganda*. An individual member of the community is a *Muganda*. Their language is *Luganda*. Their homeland is *Buganda*. They refer to their culture or way of life as *Kiganda*.

19. Jorgensen, *Uganda: A Modern History*, op. cit., p. 337; and Iain Grahame, *Amin and*

Uganda: A Personal Memoir (New York, Toronto, and London: Granada, 1980).

20. "Uganda: War of Nerves," *Africa Confidential*, 26, no. 16 (31 July 1985): pp. 1–2; and Colin Legum, annual articles on "Uganda," *Africa Contemporary Record: Annual Survey and Document* (from 1983–1986).

21. "Uganda: The Okello's Cauldron," *Africa Confidential* 26, no. 17 (14 August 1985): p. 3.

22. "18 Ugandans Charged with Plotting a Coup," *New York Times*, 8 October 1986, p. 5. Among the eighteen arrested were Commerce Minister Evaristo Nyanzi, Energy Minister Andrew Kayiira, and Environment Minister David Lwanga. See, also, "Uganda Detains Five on Subversion Charges," *New York Times*, 6 October 1986, p. 5.

23. See "Recovery First, Then a New Constitution," *Africa Report* 31, no. 3 (May–June 1986): p. 51; "Kabaka's Son Back Again in Uganda," *Times* (London), 16 August 1986; and "Monarchy Issue to be Studied," *Standard*, (Nairobi), 19 August 1986, p. 12; and Chege Mbituru, "Uganda: Monarchists' Coup Attempt Scotched," *Africa Now*, no. 65 (October 1986): pp. 14–15; Ed Hooper, "Bringing Back Life to the Luwero Triangle," ibid., pp. 22–23.

24. See "Uganda: A Black Economy" and "Uganda Battle for Acholi," *New African*, no. 229 (October 1986): pp. 19–20 and p. 34.

25. For a further discussion of some of these issues, consult Ali A. Mazrui, *Violence and Thought: Essays on Social Tensions in Africa* (London: Longmans Green, 1969) chaps. 5, 6, and 7; and F. B. Welbourne, *Religion and Politics in Uganda, 1952–1962* (Nairobi: East African Publishing House, 1965).

26. See Note 18.

27. Emily Card and Barbara Callaway, "Ghanaian Politics: the Elections and After," *Africa Report* 15, no. III, (March 1970): p. 11; consult also Swlwyn Douglas Ryan, "Ghana: The Transfer of Power," *Mawazo* (Makerere, Uganda) 2, no. 2 (December 1969); and Harry Eckstein and David E. Apter, eds., *Comparative Politics: A Reader* (London: Collier-Macmillan Ltd. 1963).

28. For a brilliant reevaluation of the polarization of single-member constituencies, consult Colin Leys, "Models, Theories, and the Theory of Political Parties," part IV, Harry Eckstein and David E. Apter, eds., *Comparative Politics: A Reader* (London: Collier-Macmillan Ltd., 1963) pp. 305–314. Consult also the remaining four chapters in that section of the book.

29. The official title of *Document No. 5* is *Proposals for New Methods of Election of Representatives of the People to Parliament* by A. Milton Obote. The previous documents concerning the "move to the left" strategy consisted of Document No. 1, *The Common Man's Charter*, a basic outline of Uganda's socialism; Document No. 2, *Proposals for the National Service*, to which many categories of citizens were to be eligible; Document No. 3, *The Communication from the Chair* or the president's speech opening Parliament in April 1979, specifying a new code for administrative leadership; Document No. 4, *The Nakivubo Pronouncements*, a speech by Obote at Nakivubo Stadium, Kampala, announcing nationalization of import and export trade and a 60 percent takeover by the state of all other major industries.

30. A. R. Radcliffe-Brown and Daryll Forde, *African Systems of Kinship and Marriage* (London: Oxford University Press, 1962 reprint) pp. 43–44.

• The Contributors •

LARRY DIAMOND is senior research fellow at the Hoover Institution, Stanford University. He is the author of *Class, Ethnicity and Democracy in Nigeria: The Failure of the First Republic,* as well as numerous articles on Nigerian politics and development and on ethnicity, class formation, and democracy in Africa. During 1982–1983 he was a Fulbright Visiting Lecturer in Nigeria at Bayero University, Kano.

JUAN J. LINZ is Pelatiah Perit Professor of Political and Social Science at Yale University. He has written dozens of articles and book chapters on authoritarianism and totalitarianism, fascism, political parties and elites, democratic breakdowns, and transitions to democracy both in Spain and in comparative perspective. His English-language publications include *Crisis, Breakdown and Reequilibration*—volume one of the four-volume work, *The Breakdown of Democratic Regimes,* which he edited with Alfred Stepan. From 1971 to 1979 he chaired the joint Committee on Political Sociology of the International Sociology and Political Science Associations. In 1987 he was awarded Spain's Premio Principe de Asturias in the social sciences.

SEYMOUR MARTIN LIPSET is senior fellow at the Hoover Institution and Caroline S.G. Munro Professor of Political Science and Sociology at Stanford University. He has published widely on various themes in comparative political sociology. His many books include *Political Man, The First New Nation, Revolution and Counterrevolution, The Confidence Gap* (with William Schneider), and *Consensus and Conflict*. He has served as president of a number of academic bodies, including the American Political Science Association, the Sociological Research Association, the International Society of Political Psychology, and the World Association for Public Opinion Research.

NAOMI CHAZAN is senior lecturer in political science and African studies at the Hebrew University of Jerusalem, where she also serves as senior research fellow and coordinator of the Africa Research Unit at the Harry S. Truman Institute. Her books include *An Anatomy of Ghanaian Politics: Managing Political Recession, 1969–82*, *Ghana: Coping with Uncertainty* (with Deborah Pellow), *The Precarious Balance: State and Society in Africa* (edited with Donald Rothchild), and *The Early State in Africa* (with S. N. Eisenstadt and M. Abitol). She has also written numerous articles on political behavior and change in Ghana and in Africa comparatively and on Israeli-African relations. During 1986–1987 she was visiting professor of government at Harvard University and Matina Souretis Horner Radcliffe Distinguished Visiting Professor at Radcliffe College.

CHRISTIAN COULON is codirector of the Center of Black African Studies at the University of Bordeaux. He is author of numerous articles and several books on politics and development in Francophone Africa, among them *The Marabout and the Prince: Islam and Power in Senegal*, *Local Autonomy and National Integration in Senegal,* and *Muslims and Power in Black Africa*. His current research interests include Islam and the situation of women in Senegal, Muslim minorities and power in East Africa, and popular modes of political action in West Africa.

JOHN HOLM is associate professor of political science at Cleveland State University. Author of two monographs and numerous articles on politics, development, and social change in Botswana, he has published analyses of U.S. political behavior, as well. Over the past ten years, he has done extensive field research in Botswana, and he served as a faculty fellow in social sciences at the University of Botswana during 1987–1988.

OMARI KOKOLE is a Ph.D. candidate in political science at Dalhousie University, Nova Scotia, Canada, and a research associate in the Afro-American and African Studies Center at the University of Michigan. His dissertation is entitled "Black Africa and the Nuclear Gap: From the Arab-Israeli Conflict to the Southern African Crisis." He has published articles on African economic relations with the European Economic Community, the Islamic factor in African-Arab relations, and ethnic politics in Uganda.

ALI MAZRUI is professor of political science at the University of Michigan and Andrew D. White Professor-at-Large at Cornell University. He is a past president of the African Studies Association. A native of Kenya, he was dean of the Faculty of Social Sciences at Makerere University in Uganda, where he taught for ten years. His many books on African politics, culture, social change, and foreign affairs include *Political Values and the Educated Class in Africa*, *Soldiers and Kinsmen in Uganda*, *The African Condition,* and *Nationalism and New States in Africa* (with Michael Tidy). His most recent book, *The Africans: A Triple Heritage,* accompanies a nine-part television series he wrote and narrated for the BBC and PBS during 1987.

MASIPULA SITHOLE is associate professor in the Department of Political Science and Administrative Studies at the University of Zimbabwe, where he served as dean of the Faculty of Social Studies in 1982–1985. During 1986 he was a visiting scholar at the Hoover Institution and visiting lecturer at Stanford University. His publications on ethnicity and factionalism in the Zimbabwean nationalist movement include *Struggles Within the Struggle*. He has also published articles on politics and elections in Zimbabwe, prospects for change in South Africa, and the impact of black Americans on U.S. African policy.

• Index •